Relational Knowledge Discovery

What is knowledge and how is it represented? This book focuses on the idea of formalising knowledge as relations, interpreting knowledge represented in databases or logic programs as relational data, and discovering new knowledge by identifying hidden and defining new relations. After a brief introduction to representational issues, the author develops a relational language for abstract machine learning problems. He then uses this language to discuss traditional methods such as clustering and decision tree induction, before moving onto two previously underestimated topics that are again coming to the fore: rough set data analysis and inductive logic programming.

Its clear and precise presentation is ideal for undergraduate computer science students. The book will also interest those who study artificial intelligence or machine learning at the graduate level. Exercises are provided and each concept is introduced using the same example domain, making it easier to compare the individual properties of different approaches.

M. E. MÜLLER is a Professor of Computer Science at the University of Applied Sciences, Bonn-Rhein-Sieg.

Relational Knowledge Discovery

M E Müller
University of Applied Sciences, Bonn-Rhein-Sieg

CAMBRIDGE
UNIVERSITY PRESS

CAMBRIDGE
UNIVERSITY PRESS

Shaftesbury Road, Cambridge CB2 8EA, United Kingdom

One Liberty Plaza, 20th Floor, New York, NY 10006, USA

477 Williamstown Road, Port Melbourne, VIC 3207, Australia

314–321, 3rd Floor, Plot 3, Splendor Forum, Jasola District Centre, New Delhi – 110025, India

103 Penang Road, #05–06/07, Visioncrest Commercial, Singapore 238467

Cambridge University Press is part of Cambridge University Press & Assessment, a department of the University of Cambridge.

We share the University's mission to contribute to society through the pursuit of education, learning and research at the highest international levels of excellence.

www.cambridge.org
Information on this title: www.cambridge.org/9780521190213

First published 2012

A catalogue record for this publication is available from the British Library

Library of Congress Cataloging-in-Publication data
Müller, M. E., (Martin E.), 1970–
Relational knowledge discovery / M.E. Müller.
p. cm. –
ISBN 978-0-521-19021-3 (hardback)
1. Computational learning theory. 2. Machine learning.
3. Relational databases. I. Title.
Q325.7.M85 2012
006.3′1–dc23

2011049968

ISBN 978-0-521-19021-3 Hardback
ISBN 978-0-521-12204-7 Paperback

Contents

About this book

If you want to make it right,
make it wrong first.

What it is about

This book is about *knowledge discovery*. There are many excellent books on machine learning and data mining. And there are many excellent books covering many particular aspects of these areas. Even though all the knowledge we are concerned with in computer science is *relational*, relational or logic machine learning or knowledge discovery is not that common. Accordingly, there are fewer textbooks on this issue.

This book strongly emphasises knowledge: what it is, how it can be represented, and, finally, how new knowledge can be discovered from what is already known plus a few new observations. Our interpretation of knowledge is based on the notion of "discernability"; all the methods discussed in this book are presented within the same paradigm: we take "learning" to mean acquiring the ability to discriminate between different things. Because things are different if they are not equal, we use a "natural" equivalence to group similar things together and distinguish them from differing things. Equivalence means to have something in common. According to the portion of commonness between things there are certain degrees of equality: things can be exactly the same, they can be the same in most cases or aspects, they can be roughly the same, not really the same, and they can be entirely different. Sometimes, they are even incomparable.

There are several well-known ways of describing similarities between sets of objects. If we arrange all our objects by their (measurable) properties, then their mutual distance to each other reflects their similarity. And if there are two different objects that have a zero distance, we have to find another property that will distinguish them. If all the objects are described by a set of features, then similarity means something like the number of features in which they agree. The utility of a feature for finding new knowledge is its information content. Because features induce equivalence relations, many features create many such relations. And by intersecting them, we gain a very fine-grained partitioning of the universe in many, many small classes of, well, equivalent or equal or similar things. Finally, we can describe objects and concepts by logic formulae or theories. Then, knowledge discovery means refining our set of formulae so that we are able to deduce something that we were not able to infer before.

Every paradigm is dedicated a chapter on its own.

How it is organised

This book tries to illustrate the common ideas behind several different approaches to machine learning or knowledge discovery. If you take a look at a set of books each of which specialises in any of these areas, you will find idiosyncratic notation in each of them. This does not really help in understanding the common processes and the parts in which they differ. And it is important to understand the differences between them to gain knowledge about them. It is also the differences that make one or another paradigm more suitable in a certain domain. Therefore it is important to be able to see them clearly. As a consequence this textbook has a leitmotif: we will always be speaking about simple geometric shapes like △, ●, or ■ – their differences, their common properties and how to construct different concepts like "grey boxes" or "things with at most n corners". If you consider this as a plus for reading this book, then I hope you consider the following a plus as well. To stress the common characteristics of the theories, we need a common language. As a result, I have tried to find a more or less consistent notation or notational principle (like "a $\cup$ is to a $\subseteq$ as $\sqcup$ is to $\sqsubseteq$; and $\longrightarrow$ is to $\Longrightarrow$ as $\vdash$ is to $\models$"). I think it is a nice idea to use the same notation throughout a book covering several topics that usually use different notations. But the downside is that the result is another nomenclature. I beg the reader's forgiveness for using Greek letters, upright and slanted function names, fraktur characters, and symbols you will never see elsewhere (unless you attend my classes).

The language used in this book is English with a German accent. In addition, I have tried to find a delicate balance between informal written text and a rather formal and exact notation. The text explains what all the formulae are about – and the formulae are there to have an indisputable and solid foundation for describing things. Additionally, there are many examples. As mentioned above, there is the running example of geometric shapes. But there are others from everyday life, some famous examples, and also some rather surprising ones that require very special knowledge in areas that not all readers will be familiar with.

However, if you are, I hope they are even more illustrative (did you ever notice that it takes three variables in Lambda-calculus to define exclusive disjunction?).

Then, there are exercises. They are for self-control only; solutions are not provided. You may understand the questions as just a few hints of directions for further thinking. I labelled the questions with marks from ◊ to ♦. The ◊ exercises should not require more than just a few minutes of thinking, some reading in other books, or performing simple calculations using the formulae from the text. ◊ exercises require a bit more thinking, for example, simple proofs or some questions that require a deeper understanding. Exercises with a ♦ mark are questions that go beyond the scope of the book. They might require longer proofs, some thinking about how to overcome hidden problems in the methods described in the text, or even writing a small program for solving longer calculations. All marks just represent the *suggested* effort that is worth spending on the question. It does not say anything about the actual hardness of the problem or the time you should spend on it.

Finally, there are "knowledge boxes." They are small grey boxes like this:

> **Box of knowledge**
> A box of knowledge summarises the relevant results of a section in a punchline, preferably in prose. By reading them alone, you ought to be able to tell someone else what this book is about and even explain the most important concepts in your own words.

Thanks to:

Helmar, who taught me to ask the right questions; Ivo, who was the first to introduce me to the beauty of formal thinking; and Bernhard, with whom I discovered the combination of both.

Alexander, Jonghwa, and Peter for friendship, help, and support.

All researchers I met during the past 15 years for their inspiration, discussion, clarification, and criticism.

All students who by their bravery and willingness to pass the exams contributed to all the previous versions.

David Tranah from CUP and Ali Jaoua, Simon Parsons, Andrzej Skowron, Harrie de Swart, George Tourlakis, and Michael Winter for inspiring discussion, useful comments, and proof reading.

Chapter 1
Introduction

Knowledge discovery, machine learning, data mining, pattern recognition, and rule invention are all about algorithms that are designed to extract knowledge from data and to describe patterns by rules.

One of the cornerstones of *(traditional) artificial intelligence* is the assumption that

> Intelligent behaviour requires rational, knowledge-based decisive and active processes.

These processes include the acquisition of new knowledge, which we call *machine learning* or *knowledge discovery*. However, when talking about *knowledge-based systems* we first need to explain what we mean by *knowledge*. If we try to define learning by intelligence, we need to explain intelligence, and if we want to explain intelligence, we need to explain knowledge. Bertrand Russell (1992, 1995) has given a very precise and in our case very helpful (and actually entirely sufficient) definition of *knowledge*:

> Knowledge is the ability to discriminate things from each other.

As a consequence, learning means acquiring the ability to recognise and differentiate between different things. Thus, the process of knowledge acquisition is a process that is initiated and (autonomously) run by a system whose purpose is to learn by itself. L. G. Valiant (1984) said that

> Learning means acquiring a program without a programmer.

To us, it means:

> **Learning as discovery of knowledge**
> *Learning* means acquiring the ability to discriminate different things from each other without being told about every single instance.

1.1 Motivation

Like any other computer science or artificial intelligence discipline, machine learning research evolves in many dimensions. This includes the interpretation of the learning process as a data processing technique, a rule discovery tool, or a model of cognitive processes. Machine learning (or an aspect of it) can also be described in terms of its successful application in the real world (whatever one might consider a successful result).

1.1.1 Different kinds of learning

Engineering and Theory: As an engineer or computer scientist who seeks patterns in data sets, one might ask how to extract knowledge from huge databases and how to make knowledge elicitation as efficient as possible. If, on the other hand, you are interested in the theory of computation, then it would be much more interesting to see if there are fundamental limitations of learning in terms of complexity or in terms of the problem classes.

Data-Driven Learning and Conceptual Learning: Data-driven learning means to take all data (or, rather, observations) without much further information about it and try to extract as much knowledge as possible. This means that data-driven learning focuses on what one can learn from the supplied data. However, quite often we already have a more or less precise image of what we think the world is like, i.e., an underlying model of the data. We then use a set of known concepts that a learning algorithm uses to describe unknown target concepts.

The difference is that in data-driven learning one tries to identify clusters of similar objects from a set of observations. On the other hand, *conceptual learning* supplies our algorithm with background knowledge about the world. As an example, data-driven learning may help in the discovery of classes like *mammals* and *birds*. Using knowledge about *habitats* and *domestication*, conceptual learning is able to describe penguins and polar bears by their habitat and it can tell a dog from a wolf by their domestication.

Clustering or Classification and Scientific Discovery: Engineers are often faced with huge sets of data, and the larger the sets are, the less is known about the (hidden) structures they may hold. In the course of developing growing data warehouses, some system operators are in need of handling petabytes of data. With too much data around and too little knowledge about them, one needs to devise algorithms that efficiently group similar cases into the same classes.

Classification means assigning a new unseen case one of the given class labels, but scientific discovery is rather concerned with finding new subclasses or relational dependencies between them. If such class hierarchies and dependencies are expressed in terms of rules, then the invention of a new concept and its description is what we call *scientific discovery*.

Algorithms and Cognitive Processes: Similar to the engineering–theory dichotomy, one can also consider the algorithmic issues in data mining or understand machine learning as a metaphor for human learning. For example, many data sets can be explained using decision trees – but using modules of artificial neural networks one can evaluate psychological models of human problem solving, too.

Data mining is a multi-stage (business) process leading to the automated detection of regularities in data that are useful in new situations. Particularly in the context of very large data sets, knowledge can be compared to a gem that is very well hidden under a huge mountain of rock-hard data. Knowledge discovery requires the extraction of

1. *implicit* (but hidden), previously *unknown*
2. and potentially *useful information* from
3. *data*

or even the search for relationships and global patterns that exist in databases.

1.1.2 Applications

Nowadays, knowledge discovery has become a very common technique in the (semantic) web. Its popularity in computational biology – especially in genetics or large-array marker scans – is still increasing. For example, sequencing of the genetic code allows us to understand the encoded protein – given that we can understand how tertiary structures of proteins develop during folding. Similarly, pattern recognition on marker arrays help in the identification of genomic defects and diseases, and the spatial properties of molecules can be expressed using a language of relations. It would be very interesting to explain – in terms of molecule structures – why some chemicals are carcinogenic while others are not (Muggleton et al. 1992, 1998).

Finding patterns and making up rules from them is a very popular research topic: nearly all observations consist of complex patterns from which we try to abstract by generalising. Sometimes, observations yield similarities that help us form class representatives (both a penguin and a sparrow are birds, but it is the sparrow that is a prototypical bird). Spam classifiers take emails as patterns of word occurrences and use rules defined by filters to keep your mailbox clean.

Recently, data mining has become one of the most important application areas of knowledge discovery. Just recall how it was a few years ago when you tried to find some information in data collections: the first problem was that we did not have enough data available – that is, we knew what kind of information we were looking for and the amount of available data could be easily surveyed. The result was that we could not find the information we needed simply because it was not there. The problem of second generation information retrieval systems was slightly different. With that, there was enough data available, but how could we effectively or efficiently find it? Early solutions required data items to be tagged with metadata until more powerful indexing and search methods were developed.

Example 1.1 Information retrieval in the World Wide Web is a very clear example. In the early 1990s, the Web was so small that personal link lists (and those of others) were sufficient for exhaustive searching. The next step introduced search engines like Yahoo (with manually tagged indices) and AltaVista and many other services competing for the largest search indices. Today, we simply "*Google*" the Web for information. ●

With an ever increasing amount of data available, the next question became how to integrate it all. The answer was data warehouses. In 2005, Yahoo was reported to maintain a 100-PetaByte data warehouse and AT&T was using two data warehouses with a total 1.2 ExaByte of data. The question that arose then was, what kind of information is hidden within all these data? And this is what *knowledge discovery* is all about. Commercially, it is referred to as *data mining* – because this is what we do to find some "gems", that is, important pieces of information, in the huge pile of data. There is a small difference, though: we use the term "knowledge discovery" to describe the process of extracting new knowledge from a set of data about that set of data. This means that the acquisition of new knowledge requires us to build a new model of the data. "Data mining" refers mostly to the extraction of parts of information with respect to a *given* model. One crucial problem is the interpretation of correlation: if two things correlate, it does not necessarily mean there exists some kind of causal dependency between them. This is where *relational* knowledge discovery enters the game: here, the primary interest is in the *relations between relations* and not the relations between *objects*.

Last, but not least, knowledge discovery, data mining, and machine learning are tools that can be used in any situation where the problem we are faced with is ill-posed. So if we are not able to devise an efficient deterministic algorithm that solves our problem within a predefined instance space, we simply give it a try and let the machine learn by itself.

In quite a few cases, the results are surprisingly good; in other cases, they are not. But then, we can at least blame the machine for being a bad learner rather than blame ourselves for being bad programmers.

1.2 Related disciplines

To us, knowledge discovery means learning how to discriminate between different objects. There are other disciplines that have slightly different understandings of the term "knowledge". But most of them also develop techniques that somehow correspond to what we call learning.

1.2.1 Codes and compression

The motivation behind coding is representing a *meaningful message* by a suitable sequence of symbols. The representation process is called *encoding* and maps *plain text (symbols)* or *(source) messages* onto *codes* that are other symbol strings. A one-to-one substitution of source symbols onto code symbols is called *enciphering*, and the result a *cipher*. The reverse processes of reconstructing the original message from a code (cipher) is called *decoding* (*deciphering*).

We assume the reader is familiar with the sequence of *Fibonacci numbers*. Yet, if asked, no one will ever reply by saying "Fibonacci numbers? Sure! 1, 1, 2, 3, 5, 8, ..." So, even if you are able to memorise the entire sequence of Fibonacci numbers, you have not *learned* anything about them because learning would require the ability of (intensionally) explaining a *concept*.[1] This also relates to *data compression*: The less compressible our data, the more information they contain and the harder it is to learn and compress them further. Any

[1] Note the difference between *intentional* and *intensional*. Explaining something intentionally means to explain it with a certain intention in mind. But explaining something intensionally (as opposed to extensionally) means to explain it by abstract concepts instead of concrete examples.

good learner needs to be able to *compress* data by giving a rule that can describe them.

Example 1.2 RLE compression. One of the simplest methods of encoding and compressing a stream of symbols is *run length encoding*. Consider the alphabet $\Sigma = \{\square, \bigcirc\}$. Then, strings will contain repetitive occurrences of each symbol. For example,

$$\square\square\bigcirc\square\bigcirc\bigcirc\bigcirc\bigcirc\bigcirc\square\square\square\square\bigcirc\bigcirc\square\bigcirc\bigcirc\bigcirc\square\square\square\bigcirc\cdots$$

A reasonable way of compressing such a sequence would be to precede each symbol by the number of times it occurs before another symbol appears. And if we assume that each sequence starts with a $\square$, we can even drop the symbol itself, because after every sequence of $\square$s there can only be a sequence of $\bigcirc$s, and vice versa. So, the above string can be compressed to

$$2.1.1.5.4.2.1.3.3.1.\cdots$$

which is certainly much shorter but requires a larger alphabet of symbols and a special delimiter symbol ".".

Finding (optimal, shortest) codes (that is, *encoding functions*) without the need for delimiters or any additional symbols is the topic of coding theory.

The notion of compression enters the game at two different points: first, a message that cannot be compressed further is free of any redundancies. Then, the message string itself must have maximum entropy and all the symbols occurring in the message are more or less of the same probability. However, they do *not* encode the same "amount of information": changing one symbol can result in just a small change after decoding, but it can also scramble the entire encoded message into a meaningless sequence of symbols. Second, a strong concept requires a complex representation language that basically is the same as finding a good *code*.

One example that we shall encounter is the encoding of messages (or hypotheses) into strings of symbols ("genomic codes"). The field of coding theory and compression has become a huge discipline of its own, which is why we refer to MacKay (2003). If you are more interested in coding and cryptography, consult Welsh (1988); and for the advanced reader we recommend Chaitin (1987), Kolmogorov (1965), and Li and Vitanyi (1993).

Example 1.3 There is a crucial difference between encoding the numbers $0, 1, 2, \ldots, 255$ using a three-digit decimal representation $x \cdot 10^2 + y \cdot 10^1 + z$ with $x, y, z \in \{0, 1, 2, \ldots, 9\}$ and by using a binary representation with eight bits $w \in \mathbf{2}^8$.

In both cases, changing one symbol creates an error of at least 1. The least dramatic change in the decimal representation is to replace z by $z + 1$ or $z - 1$, and in the binary representation one simply flips the least significant (that is, the last) bit. Things are different if we take a look at the maximum error possible in each representation formalism. For the binary representation, the maximum error corresponds to the value of the most significant bit – and that is 128. But for the decimal representation it is $9 \cdot 10^2 = 900$!

Imagine that the integer we want to encode has the value "three". Then, **10000011** – **00000011** is "one-hundred thirty-one minus three", which equals $2^8 = 128$. But the maximum error in the decimal representation is the result of maximising the difference on the most significant decimal place: 903 – 003 is "nine-hundred".

If you argue that 900 is not within the range of integers covered by our example, then imagine that $x \in \{0, 1, 2\}$ and $x + y + z \leq 255$. Then $203 - 003 = 200$ is still nearly twice as much as the maximum error of the binary representation.

It is clear that a sequence of symbols that can be compressed pretty well (e.g., by RLE) obviously contains some kind of redundancy. If we know that the next five symbols we receive are □s, then the sender's effort in transmitting □□□□□ is simply a waste of time (and, as we shall see, a waste of bandwidth).

Machine learning and coding

Learning means finding an optimal code to describe observations.

Coding and its role in cryptography are far beyond the scope of this book, but they are indispensable for *information theory* as well. The basic idea behind information theory is that the average randomness of a sequence (and thus its reverse redundancy) is a measure of the complexity of the system that emits the messages.

1.2.2 Information theory

There is much confusion about the term "information". Together with entropy, complexity, and probability, terminology often gets in the way of a proper understanding. To avoid misconceptions from the very beginning, we first and foremost need to make clear one crucial point:

Information

Information is not so much about *what* is being said, but rather what *could* be said.

As we will discover in detail later on, there exists a measure of the information content of a message expressed in terms of entropies:

$$H_{\max}(S) = \log_2 \omega \quad \text{and} \quad H(S) = -\sum_{i=1}^{\omega} p_i \log_2 p_i.$$

The first formula describes the "information content" of a system in terms of its complexity: it is determined by the number ω of possible states an element of the system can take (the log will be explained later). Since in communication theory not all possible messages are equally probable, Shannon and Weaver (1949) introduced the second formula. It measures the information that is hidden in the probabilities that an element of the system takes a *certain* value. This can easily be explained by a coin flipping game. Note that a coin can take only two states – heads (**1**) or tails (**0**). This means that $\omega = 2$. Therefore, $H_{\max}(coin) = \log_2 2 = \frac{\ln 2}{\ln 2} = 1$. In other words, any situation in which all possible outcomes are equally probable are situations of maximum entropy. The magnitude 1 of this measure of information is usually interpreted as the number of bits required to encode the information contained in one single element of the domain (here one single coin). After flipping two different coins 50 times, we find

$$\begin{aligned} &H(\texttt{01001111101000010010111110101010010011110101001000}) \\ &\quad = \; -0.5 \log_2 0.5 - 0.5 \log_2 0.5 = 1 \end{aligned}$$

and

$$\begin{aligned} &H(\texttt{00000000100000000000000000000000000000000000000000}) \\ &\quad = \; -0.02 \log_2 0.02 - 0.98 \log_2 0.98 = 0.14. \end{aligned}$$

Obviously, the first coin is rather fair, while the second is not. As one can see, the (expected) probability of the outcome of an experiment (or an *observation* or the probability of a message) crucially defines the information content and therefore describes the complexity of such a system (or the information content or the bandwidth required). Cheating means reducing the information content of a game: it reduces the uncertainty of the outcome. As we all know, we can cheat better when we know more (and conversely). As we shall see later on, knowledge about the domain can be expressed in terms of distributions on the domain.

From the viewpoint of information theory we conclude:

> **Machine learning and information theory**
>
> Machine learning means organising our concepts in a way that minimises the entropy of the system.

Shannon and Weaver (1949) were the first to introduce the formula; for a more recent and gentle introduction we recommend Ash (1965).

1.2.3 Minimum description length

The idea behind the minimum description length (MDL) principle is quite similar to the old law of parsimony – usually known as *Ockham's razor*:

> *Frustra fit per plura quod potest fieri per pauciora* (Ockham 1323);

that is, there is no point living with many explanations if just a few suffice. There are hundreds of (modern) interpretations of this principle, but only a few know that Aristotle already stated that

> *Nature does nothing in vain.*[2]

A modern explanation of the principle can be found in Barron et al. (1998). In machine learning, we can assume a hypothesis h to represent (a part of) a theory K that is to explain a set s of observations. The description length is a measure of the complexity of h with respect to s in terms of the costs for transmitting knowledge about s. As we shall see later, s is a set of entities together with a label that describes whether it belongs to the (unknown) target concept. The MDL principle seeks to find the shortest possible description of a set K of observations. For two competing descriptions h and h', one assumes the *shorter* one to be the better description. The MDL principle does *not* try to explain as many (unknown) objects of our domain as possible. Rather, it tries to *minimise* the amount of knowledge that is required to classify an object correctly. The problem here is to define what it means for a theory or hypothesis to be better (i.e., shorter) than another. Any theory aims to explain a set of observations; therefore, the quality of our hypothesis depends on at least two properties concerning our observations:

- Which subset s do we have to learn from?
- What is the nature of the set of objects that we want to describe?

As we shall see at the end of this book, one usually needs more examples to learn concepts from more complex domains. But even if we have sufficiently many and good examples to find a hypothesis that fits our data, the result crucially depends on the *randomness* of the sender, too.

> **Machine learning and MDL**
> Machine learning means finding the shortest description or the simplest explanation of our observations.

However, we still have to explain what it means for a theory to be *simpler* than another one.

[2] [Anima iii 12 434^{a}31-2]. Aristotle also used the attributes *random* and *superfluous* in similar contexts.

1.2.4 Kolmogorov complexity

Kolmogorov complexity is an *algorithmic* measure of expressiveness. It is one of the most important concepts in the theory of computation after the work of Turing and Gödel. The idea behind algorithmic complexity was independently developed by three scientists: Ray Solomonoff (1964), Andreji Kolmogorov (1965), and Gregory Chaitin (1966).

It aims to measure the expressiveness of a system by the length of a program that generates it. The simpler the system, the shorter the description. But if there are some parts of huge complexity in the system, it could be that the plan for this part only would require much more space than the object itself! In such a case it seems reasonable to transmit the object rather than a description of it. A special case arises when we divide a description that we *know* produces wrong results into several parts. Then the incorrect program together with information about *where* it produces wrong output and *what* the correct output would be could still be much shorter than the smallest correct program. In terms of the MDL principle we try to find the ideal trade-off between program complexity (length) and the length of a file of exceptions.[3]

Example 1.4 Consider the set $s = \{1, 2, 3, 4, 5, 6, 7, 8, 9\}$ and the target concept $c = \{x \in s : x \mod 3 = 0\} = \{3, 6, 9\}$. Let h describe the set of all odd numbers in s: $h = \{1, 3, 5, 7, 9\}$. Imagine that the program for h could be represented as $2n + 1$. Then, h is wrong on the set $\{1, 5, 6, 7\}$. The description length of h would be the length of h plus the encoding of this set. Imagine that it was $[2, n, +, 1, \#, 1, 5, 6, 7]$ (with the hash symbol being a delimiter). Then, h is a non-compressing description of $\chi(c)$ because the length of the description string equals the cardinality of c.

The *Kolmogorov complexity* $C(\vec{x})$ of a sequence $\vec{x}$ of symbols is the length of the *shortest* binary program π that generates $\vec{x}$ and then halts. Here, the "shortest binary program" means the shortest binary string that represents a program that can be interpreted by a universal Turing machine. This enables us to review the notion of compressibility: $\vec{x}$ is close to being incompressible if $C(\vec{x}) \approx |\vec{x}|$. It definitely cannot be compressed any further if $C(\vec{x}) > |\vec{x}|$ and the degree of compressibility (or information loss) increases with the term $f(\vec{x})$ in $C(\vec{x}) \approx |\vec{x}| - f(\vec{x})$.

Machine learning and complexity

Machine learning means finding a program π with the least $C(\pi|\vec{x})$ for any $\vec{x}$ in our problem class.

[3] The problem is to determine the length of the smallest program with a certain output (or, rather, to prove that it is the shortest program).

An excellent introduction to Kolmogorov complexity for the advanced reader is Li and Vitanyi (1993). For those interested in the theory of machine learning, we also recommend Valiant (1984), Anthony and Biggs (1997), Kearns (1990), and Kearns and Vazirani (1994).

1.2.5 Probability theory

Probability theory mostly deals with urns and marbles.

> **Machine learning and probabilities**
> Machine learning means approximating an unknown probability distribution on our set of objects by learning from statistical observations such that the error probability is minimised.

Let there be the following objects in our universe:

$$U = \{\blacktriangle, \square, \bullet, \blacksquare, \bigcirc, \triangle\}.$$

Each of these objects obviously has two properties: they each have a certain *shape* and *colour*. In probability theory, such features are represented by (not so) random variables S and C. The shapes and colours of objects are independent from each other, and so are the random variables S and C. If we now assume the probability of picking any of these objects from our urn to be uniformly distributed (also called an *independent identical distribution*, or *i.i.d.* for short), then

$$\begin{aligned}\mu(\{x \in U : S(x) = \mathit{triangle}\}) &= \mu(\{x \in U : S(x) = \mathit{square}\}) \\ &= \mu(\{x \in U : S(x) = \mathit{circle}\}) \\ &= \frac{2}{6} = \frac{1}{3}\end{aligned}$$

and

$$\begin{aligned}\mu(\{x \in U : C(x) = \mathit{black}\}) &= \mu(\{x \in U : C(x) = \mathit{white}\}) \\ &= \frac{3}{6} = \frac{1}{2}\end{aligned}$$

People quite often use a different notation and abbreviate $\Pr[S = c] := \mu(\{x \in U : S(x) = c\})$. Then, the probability of picking a black triangle from the urn is defined as

$$\Pr[S = \mathit{triangle}] \cdot \Pr[C = \mathit{black}] = \frac{1}{3} \cdot \frac{1}{2} = \frac{1}{6} = \frac{|\{\blacktriangle\}|}{|\{\blacktriangle, \square, \bullet, \blacksquare, \bigcirc, \triangle\}|}.$$

Things become more complicated the more they depend on each other. Accordingly, we usually assume most things to be independent even if they are not. This is a wise decision from a computational point of view – but in real life, most observations depend on something else. Consider the concept *form*, which describes whether an object is *angular* or *round*. Of course, the colour has no influence on the general geometric form, but the shape certainly has. This leads us to the notion of *conditional probabilities* and Bayes' rule. As an example consider the question, what is the probability of picking a triangle given the object is angular? With $U' = U \cup \{\bigstar\}$, we count:

$$\frac{|\{x \in U' : x \text{ is a triangle}\}|}{|\{x \in U' : x \text{ is angular}\}|} = \frac{|\{\blacktriangle, \triangle\}|}{|\{\blacktriangle, \square, \bigstar, \blacksquare, \triangle, \}|} = \frac{2}{5}.$$

Bayes' law offers much more to the Bayesian learner. Suppose that we have a sequence of observations described by a set of n attributes together with some information about the classes $c \in \mathfrak{c}$ to which they belong. Then we can easily estimate the probability of some element's properties given that it belongs to some class: we simply scan our case library for each of the classes c and store all information concerning

$$\Pr[X_1 = v_1 \wedge \cdots \wedge X_n = v_n | X_{\mathfrak{c}} = c].$$

Similarly, we can also estimate the prior probabilities

$$\Pr[X_1 = v_1 \wedge \cdots \wedge X_n = v_n] \quad \text{and} \quad \Pr[X_{\mathfrak{c}} = c].$$

Using both probability distributions together we can determine the value of

$$\Pr[X_{\mathfrak{c}} = c | X_1 = v_1' \wedge \cdots \wedge X_n = v_n']$$

for any new case $X_1 = v_1' \wedge \cdots \wedge X_n = v_n'$ and for each $c \in \mathfrak{c}$. By chosing the c for which the above term delivers the largest value we have built a so-called *maximum a posterior* classifier.

1.2.6 Approximation and searching

Learning from examples can also be interpreted as an *approximation* problem. Whether or not the world we live in is continuous, a classification is just the value a *classifier function* delivers when given an object of the domain. In many classification scenarios, the function is binary – it decides whether some x belongs to a concept c:

$$t : U \to \mathbf{2}$$

with $t(x) := \chi(c)(x)$. The inability to discern two different objects x and y where one belongs to c and the other does not requires *learning*. Our knowledge K is not precise enough to tell the objects from each other if $\chi K(c)(x) = \chi K(c)(y)$.

Imagine that $t : \mathbb{R} \to \mathbb{R}$ and that we are given a set of support points $\mathbf{s} = \{\langle x_i, t_c(x_i)\rangle : i \in \mathbf{m}\}$. We now need to find a function h that equals t on $\mathbf{s}$, or, more realistically, that comes as close as possible to each point. There are simple approximations like linear functions and there are more complex ones like polynomials of grade k. We can even combine sets of such functions. This book presents more and more sophisticated methods for approximating target concepts or their respective characteristic functions. But to *find* such a function, we need to *search* for it.

> **Machine learning as searching**
> Machine learning means searching for a function that approximates the target as close as possible.

Conclusion

Now that we have briefly described the terms of other (neighbouring) disciplines that are relevant to our notion of knowledge, we can try a first working definition of *machine learning* and *knowledge discovery* ourselves.

In most cases the data from which we want to extract knowledge are represented in *information systems*. Roughly speaking, an information system is just a table with all the rows representing entities and columns describing the objects' properties. The knowledge we want to acquire is a set of rules describing a model that we can then use to explain the data set and its structure.

> **Knowledge discovery by machine learning**
> In general, we will use the term *machine learning* to denote a method by which
>
> - a set of *data* is stored in an information system
> - is analysed and transformed
> - to *extract (new) knowledge* from it and to refine our *model* of the world in order to
> - increasingly *precisely discriminate more* concepts.
>
> While inference and analysis try to find out more about fewer things, learning is concerned with the task of finding out less specific information about more things.

Chapter 2
Relational knowledge

Talking about the discovery of knowledge requires us to understand "knowledge" first. In the last chapter we defined knowledge to be what it takes to discriminate different things from each other.

In this chapter we will develop a more formal framework of knowledge structures that enables us to describe the process of discovering new knowledge.

Information is something that may change knowledge, and knowledge is the ability to relate things by putting a structure on them. Knowledge is not made from the things we put into order, and information does not change the things themselves. It is, rather, that knowledge is a set of relations describing things and information helps us to describe a relation's utility for classifying things. But, then, why do we assume information to be describable by a set of entities each of which can take a certain number of different states – if they do not know whether there are entities they have never seen before nor how many states the entities can possibly take? Why do we explain causality by means of probabilistic dependence?

There are many definitions of what knowledge could be, and there are many approaches to knowledge representation formalisms. They all agree that there is knowledge of different qualities: factual knowledge, weak knowledge, procedural knowledge, hard knowledge, motor knowledge, world knowledge, and behavioural knowledge are just a few. A sloppy and weak definition of knowledge might well be what we want to acquire by learning. Even when talking about motory skills it is all about discriminating things from each other: *bad* moves and *good* moves. This is a very blunt and vague generalisation – but for our purpose the following definitions of knowledge will be sufficient.

2.1 Objects and their attributes

We now examine a few concepts from which we can build a *simple* theory of knowledge – without assuming too much about our world.

2.1.1 Collections of things: sets

A set is usually considered to be a collection of discernible objects. Because a and a seem to be indistinguishable, we all agree that $\{a, a\} = \{a\}$. There is a very special collection of things, that which is empty: $\emptyset = \{\}$. Sets can be defined by naming all their members or by giving a description that all members of this set have in common:

$$\{\mathrm{m, i, s, p}\} = \{x : x \text{ occurs in "mississippi"}\}.$$

The left side of the equation shows an *extensional* set definition while the right side is an equivalent *intensional* description. Just as we can put a number of bags with different collections of objects into a larger bag, sets can contain other sets. What happens if we put the same thing in a bag twice? Well, because it is the *same* thing, we must have taken it out of the bag before putting it back in again. Hence one and the same thing can be in a bag exactly once or not at all. Then, of course, putting the same bag into another one twice has the same result. Can we also put every bag into any other bag? At first glimpse it seems we can. But if x is a bag and every bag can be put into another and every bag can hold any bag, can we put bag x into bag x itself?

Example 2.1 Imagine the set r of those sets x that do not contain themselves:

$$r \quad := \quad \{x : x \notin x\}. \tag{2.1}$$

The set r seems to be quite an interesting collection of objects (some of which may contain other objects or collections thereof). This gives rise to the question of whether r belongs to it itself: is $r \in r$?

If it is, it cannot be because it violates the formula $x \notin x$. And if it is not, it must be because with $r = x$ we have $r \notin r$ and hence $r \in r$. Spooky.

This is known as Russell's paradox. It showed that Cantor's naïve set theory had a serious flaw – which cost many researchers sleepless nights. The smiles returned to many faces after the axiomatisation of set theory when Skolem finalised Zermelo and Fränkel's set theory. But those who remained sceptical could not but resent accepting Gödel's proof that axiomatic systems rich enough to describe integer arithmetic can describe problems that cannot be proven to be true or false within this system.

Let us assume that all the sets we deal with are well-behaving – that is, we presuppose that we never run into the dilemma of asking ourselves whether $x \in x$. Then we can now take a closer look at the inner structure of sets. People tend to collect things in an ordered way, which is why many sets have some structure, too. So, for example, the set {a, b, c, ..., z} together with a reflexive, transitive, and antisymmetric relation forms a *partially ordered set*. Such a relation is usually known as an *ordering* relation $\leq$ (here, lexicographic ordering). While collections appear to have no structure, others seem to have even more structure than just an ordering.

For the remainder of the chapter, we assume the reader to be acquainted with basic set operations such as $\cup$, $\cap$, and $-$. Consider the following recursive set definition starting with the empty set:

$$\begin{aligned}
\mathbf{0} &:= \emptyset = \{\} \\
\mathbf{1} &:= \mathbf{0} \cup \{\mathbf{0}\} = \emptyset \cup \{\emptyset\} = \{\emptyset\} \\
\mathbf{2} &:= \mathbf{1} \cup \{\mathbf{1}\} = \{\emptyset, \{\emptyset\}\} \\
&\vdots
\end{aligned}$$

Even though $\emptyset$ trivially has no structure at all, the subsequent sets (and the set of all these sets) do have a structure. More generally speaking, this method allows us to recursively define any set by its predecessor set:

$$\text{the set with } x+1 \text{ elements is defined as } \mathbf{x} \cup \{\mathbf{x}\}\,.$$

Exercise 2.2 (◊) Prove or disprove that

$$0 \leq x \Longleftrightarrow \mathbf{0} \subseteq \mathbf{x}, \qquad x < y \Longleftrightarrow \mathbf{x} \in \mathbf{y}, \quad \text{and} \quad x \leq y \Longleftrightarrow \mathbf{x} \subseteq \mathbf{y}.$$

So if the cardinality of some enumerable set s is $|s|$, then it can be mapped one-to-one onto the set **s**. In this way we have constructed the basis for integer arithmetics and, by the way, gained a set (usually referred to as $\mathbb{N}_0$) of index sets.

To continue our work on sets we need to be able to describe a set of sets made up from a fixed (finite) repertoire of objects. We call $\wp(x)$ the *powerset* of x, the set of all subsets of x:

$$\wp(x) \quad := \quad \{y : y \subseteq x\}. \tag{2.2}$$

It is clear that $|\wp(x)| = 2^x$, which equals the number of functions from x to $\mathbf{2}$. So, in general, there are y^x functions $f : \mathbf{x} \to \mathbf{y}$. Therefore, we sometimes write $\mathbf{2}^s := \wp(s)$.

But what is so special about integers and why do we insist on this topic in a textbook on knowledge discovery? The reason is quite simple: knowledge has been described as the ability to discriminate different things from each other. We now know how to speak about collections of entities: we can represent any (countable) set of such entities by a set with a certain structure. The structure comes for free, and the relation defined by this structure allows us to relate any pair of entities to each other. Furthermore, it even allows us to relate any pair of collections of entities to each other:

Collections of different things

Any (countable) collection of x things can be *represented* by a set $\mathbf{x}$ using a one-to-one mapping $f : x \to \mathbf{x}$. On $\mathbf{x}$ we have relations $\subseteq$ ($\leq$) and $\in$ that allow us to order (and, thus, discriminate) different objects. Furthermore we can even relate sets of entities ("classes") to each other.

Exercise 2.3 (◊) Prove that Peano's axiomatisation of integer arithmetic is satisfied by our definition of $\mathbb{N}_0$ in this section:

$$\exists 0 \in \mathbb{N}_0 \tag{2.3}$$

$$\forall n \in \mathbb{N}_0 : \exists succ(n) \in \mathbb{N}_0 \tag{2.4}$$

$$\forall n \in \mathbb{N}_0 : succ(n) \neq 0 \tag{2.5}$$

$$\forall m, n \in \mathbb{N}_0 : succ(m) = succ(n) \to m = n \tag{2.6}$$

$$\forall x \subseteq \mathbb{N}_0 : (0 \in x \land \forall n : n \in x \to succ(n) \in x) \to x = \mathbb{N}_0, \tag{2.7}$$

where $succ : \mathbb{N} \to \mathbb{N}$ denotes the successor function.

2.1.2 Properties of things: relations

In the previous section we spoke of "order relations" – but what is a *relation* anyway? To keep things simple, we will stick to *binary relations*. For two sets s_0 and s_1, the *cartesian* or *cross product* is defined as

$$s_0 \times s_1 \quad := \quad \{\langle x, y\rangle : x \in s_0 \land y \in s_1\}. \tag{2.8}$$

$\langle x, y\rangle$ is called an *ordered pair* or *tuple*. It is clear that in general $s_0 \times s_1 \neq s_1 \times s_0$.

Definition 2.4 — Binary relation. Binary relation

A *binary relation* R is an arbitrary subset of a cross product of two base sets $R \subseteq s_0 \times s_1$ and we write

$$xRy \quad :\Longleftrightarrow \quad \langle x, y\rangle \in R. \tag{2.9}$$

To indicate a left-to-right reading of the relation R we also write $R : s_0 \rightharpoondown s_1$. We call $s_0 = \mathrm{dom}(R)$ the *domain* and $s_1 = \mathrm{cod}(R)$ the *codomain*. ●

Tuples may be defined only for a subset of the domain and codomain. The corresponding subsets are called the *preimage* $\ulcorner R$ and *image* (or *range*) $R^{\urcorner}$:

$$\begin{aligned} \ulcorner Rs &= \{x : xRy, \text{ for all } y \in s \subseteq s_1\} \\ sR^{\urcorner} &= \{y : xRy, \text{ for all } x \in s \subseteq s_0\}. \end{aligned}$$

If $s = \{x\}$, we also write $\ulcorner Rx$ and $xR^{\urcorner}$ (called a *fibre*), and if $s_i = s$, we simply write $\ulcorner R$ and $R^{\urcorner}$. If $\ulcorner R = \mathrm{dom}(R)$, then R is called *left-total*; it is called *right-total* if $R^{\urcorner} = \mathrm{cod}(R)$. Finally, we define two further very important operations on relations:

Converse, complement

Definition 2.5 — Converse, complement.
For any R we call $R^{\smile}$ the *converse* (or *inverse*) relation if and only if (iff) $xR^{\smile}y :\Longleftrightarrow yRx$. The *complement* $\overline{R}$ of R is defined as $x\overline{R}y :\Longleftrightarrow \neg(xRy)$. ●

There are two important binary relations: the *empty* or *null* relation $\perp\!\!\!\perp := \emptyset = \{\} = \{\langle x, x\rangle : x \neq x\} \subseteq s_0 \times s_1$ and the *universal* or *all* relation $\top\!\!\!\top := \{\langle x, y\rangle : x \in s_0 \wedge y \in s_1\} = s_0 \times s_1$.

A natural way of visually representing two-dimensional data is a *map*. Binary relations are subsets of (binary) cross products and can be represented by matrices. For any binary relation $R \subseteq s_0 \times s_1$, we denote by $\mathbb{M}(R)$ a relation matrix (called a *coincidence matrix*) describing R:

$$\mathbb{M}(R) := \begin{bmatrix} c_{\langle 0,0\rangle} & c_{\langle 0,1\rangle} & \cdots & c_{\langle 0,s_1\rangle} \\ c_{\langle 1,0\rangle} & c_{\langle 1,1\rangle} & \cdots & c_{\langle 1,s_1\rangle} \\ \vdots & & & \vdots \\ c_{\langle s_0,0\rangle} & c_{\langle s_0,1\rangle} & \cdots & c_{\langle s_0,s_1\rangle} \end{bmatrix} \text{ with } c_{\langle x,y\rangle} = \begin{cases} \mathbf{1}, & \text{iff } xRy \\ \mathbf{0}, & \text{else.} \end{cases} \tag{2.10}$$

Exercise 2.6 (◇) Define $sR^{\urcorner}$ and $\ulcorner Rs$ in terms of coincidence matrices.

From the point of view of matrix representations, we can define subsets and elements by relations only. A subset $s' \subseteq s$ is defined by a total relation

$$S' : s \rightharpoondown \mathbf{2} \text{ such that } s' = \ulcorner S'\mathbf{1}.$$

We already know the relation under the name of characteristic functions $\chi(s')$:

$$\chi(s')(x) = 1 :\Longleftrightarrow xS'\mathbf{1}.$$

2.1.3 Special properties of relations

A very important class of binary relations is called *endorelations*. Such relations share the same set s as the domain and codomain, that is, $R \subseteq s \times s$.

Homogeneous relations

Definition 2.7 — Homogeneous relations.
A binary relation $R \subseteq s_0 \times s_1$ is called an *endorelation* or a *homogeneous binary relation* if and only if $s_0 = s_1$. ●

In addition to $\bot\!\!\!\bot$ and $\top\!\!\!\top$ there is a third very important relation that is defined for endorelations only: $I_s := \{\langle x, x\rangle : x \in s\}$. The *identity relation* relates all things to themselves (and only to themselves). Subsets of I_s are called *subidentities*. Relations can have several special properties:

Properties of relations

Definition 2.8 — Properties of relations.
We call a binary relation $R : s \rightharpoondown s$

reflexive	iff	xRx
symmetric	iff	$xRy \longrightarrow yRx$
antisymmetric	iff	$xRy \wedge yRx \longrightarrow x = y$
transitive	iff	$xRy \wedge yRz \longrightarrow xRz$
difunctional	iff	$xRy \wedge zRy \wedge zRw \longrightarrow xRw$

for all $w, x, y, z \in s$. ●

Reflexivity means being able to "reflect" an object onto itself; hence a relation R is reflexive if and only if $I \subseteq R$. Symmetry means that something is the same no matter from where we look at it. Accordingly, there is no difference between pre-images and images and the relation between objects in them. This means that $R \subseteq R^{\smile}$. Antisymmetry means that: if there are symmetric pairs in our relation, then the pairs must be reflexive, that is, $\langle x, x\rangle$. Transitivity means that we are able to append tuples from the relation whenever one image can be taken as a pre-image. The element "in between" is called a *witness*. Finally, difunctionality is a very important property in the way that it expresses correspondence between pre-images and images of subsets of the domain. Whenever two objects share one object in their image, the *entire* images of both objects are the same: $xRy \wedge zRy \Longrightarrow x\overline{R}^{\rceil} = z\overline{R}^{\rceil}$.

A binary relation is called a *partial ordering* relation if and only if it is reflexive, transitive, and antisymmetric.

Exercise 2.9 (◊) Prove that $\subseteq$ on $\wp(s)$ forms a poset.

Equivalently, $\subseteq$ is a partial order on index sets and $\leq$ is a partial order on $\mathbb{N}_0$. Another very important property of some endorelations is their power of being able to group objects into disjoint subsets of the base set.

Equivalence relation

Definition 2.10 — Equivalence relation.
An *equivalence relation* is a binary relation $R \subseteq s \times s$ that is symmetric, transitive, and reflexive: $xRy \rightarrow yRx$, $xRyRz \rightarrow xRz$, and xRx. ●

Why is an equivalence relation so-called? Reflexivity states that every object is related to itself. Symmetry means that if x *is-in-R-relation* to y, then y *is-in-R-relation* to x, too. For example, $\leq$ is *not* symmetric, because $2 \leq 3$, but not vice versa. In other words, to be equivalent, two objects need to be somehow "the same". Finally, transitivity requires that if x is *equivalent* to y and y is *equivalent* to z, then x is *equivalent* to z, too.

Example 2.11 Let

$$A = \{\mathrm{a}, \mathrm{b}, \ldots, \mathrm{z}\} \quad \text{and} \quad x = \{x_0 x_1 x_2 : x_i \in A, i \in \mathbf{3}\}. \tag{2.11}$$

Imagine three relations R_i with $x_0x_1x_2R_iy_0y_1y_2$ if and only if $x_i = y_i$. Then the R_i are equivalence relations that group all three letter strings by their i-th component: $\mathrm{abc}R_0\mathrm{abb}$ and $\mathrm{abc}R_1\mathrm{abb}$ but not $\mathrm{abc}R_2\mathrm{abb}$. ●

Note that for symmetric (and, thus, for every equivalence relation) R we have $\overleftarrow{Rx} = x\overrightarrow{R}$. For equivalence relations it is also that either $x\overrightarrow{R} = y\overrightarrow{R}$ or that $x\overrightarrow{R} \cap y\overrightarrow{R} = \emptyset$. In other words, $\overrightarrow{R}$ is a union of pairwise *disjoint* sets called *(R)-equivalence classes*.

For an equivalence class $x\overrightarrow{R}$ we call x a class *representative* and write $x\overrightarrow{R} = [x]_R := \{y : xRy\}$. This class can be identified by each of its elements, such that xRy implies $y \in [x]_R = [y]_R \ni x$.

Example 2.12 Let us consider a set of black and white geometric figures:

$$s = \{○, ◇, □, ●, ◆, ■\}.$$

We define two relations $C, S \subseteq s \times s$:

xCy iff x and y are of the same colour
xSy iff x and y are of the same shape.

Then, ●C■ and ◇C○ but not □C■. On the other hand, ■S□ and ◇S◆ but not ○S□. ●

The set $\{[x]_R : x \in s\}$ is called a *partition* of s; it is the set of all R-equivalence classes of objects that are *indiscernible* using the knowledge encoded in R. A partition induced by some relation R is also called a *quotient set*:

$$s/R = \{[x]_R : x \in s\}. \tag{2.12}$$

Example 2.13 The equivalence class $[●]_C$ is the set of all objects $x \in s$ that are C-related to ●. It is the set of all black objects:

$$[●]_C = \{●, ◆, ■\}.$$

The relation C creates the following quotient or partition on s:

$$\begin{aligned} s/C &= \{○, ◇, □, ●, ◆, ■\}/S \\ &= \{\{○, ◇, □\}, \{●, ◆, ■\}\} \end{aligned}$$

Similarly, $s/S = \{[x]_S : x \in s\} = \{\{□, ■\}, \{◇, ◆\}, \{○, ●\}\}$.

Exercise 2.14

◇ Is there a relation that is both a partial order relation and an equivalence relation?

◇ What does it take to make a difunctional relation an equivalence relation?

2.1.4 Information systems

Information systems basically are what we all know as *relational databases* or, even simpler, just tables or *feature-value maps*:

Information system

Definition 2.15 — Information system.
An information system $\mathfrak{I} = \langle s, \mathbf{F}, V_{\mathbf{n}} \rangle$ consists of a *base set* of objects s, a set $\mathbf{F} = \{f_i : s \to V_i : i \in \mathbf{n}\}$ of n *features* that assign a value of the feature's codomain V_i to each object in s. An information function I delivers for some object $x \in s$ and feature $f \in \mathbf{F}$ the value $f(x)$:

$$I : s \times \mathbf{n} \to V_{\mathbf{n}} \quad \text{with} \quad I(x, i) = f_i(x). \tag{2.13}$$

All $f \in \mathbf{F}$ are (partial) *functions*. ●

Features create partitions in a rather natural way: the set $\{x \in s : f(x) = y\}$ is the set of all objects in s that share the same value $y \in V_f$. If f is a total function (i.e., $\overleftarrow{f} = \mathrm{dom}(f) = s$), then all classes together form the quotient

$$s/f \quad := \quad \{[x]_f : x \in s\}. \tag{2.14}$$

Therefore, a total function f induces an equivalence relation R_f as follows:

$$x_0 R_f x_1 \quad :\Longleftrightarrow \quad f(x_0) = f(x_1) = y. \tag{2.15}$$

Equivalence relations R_f that are induced by functions f are also known as *kernel relations*.

Example 2.16 The information system

	s	*colour*	*shape*
0	●	*black*	*circular*
1	□	*white*	*square*
2	◇	*white*	*rhombus*
3	◆	*black*	*rhombus*
4	■	*black*	*square*
5	○	*white*	*circular*

represents the knowledge shown in Example 2.12.

The kernel relations can be represented in *kernel matrices* where all 1-entries in $\mathbb{M}(R_f)$ are replaced by $f(x)$:

$$\mathbb{K}(R_f) = \left[o_{\langle x,y \rangle}\right] := \begin{cases} f(x) = f(y) & \text{iff } xR_f y \\ \bot & \text{otherwise.} \end{cases} \tag{2.16}$$

Example 2.17 We drop the brackets and write the matrices in table form for better readability. Then, for S, $\mathbb{K}(S)$ is

s	●	□	◇	◆	■	○
●	*circular*					*circular*
□	*square*				*square*	
◇			*rhombus*	*rhombus*		
◆			*rhombus*	*rhombus*		
■		*square*			*square*	
○	*circular*					*circular*

(2.17)

We have seen that the features in an information system induce equivalence relations on the base set. We also know that all objects of some class $[x]_{R_f}$ are indiscernible using information about f. Therefore, the class $[x]_{R_f}$ is often called the concept of all $f(x)$-ish things. Given a set $\mathbf{F}$ of features we build a set $\mathbf{R} = \{R_f : f \in \mathbf{F}\}$ of equivalence relations on s. We then define a *discernability matrix* $\mathbb{D}(\mathbf{R})$ as

$$\mathbb{D}(\mathbf{R}) = \left[d_{\langle x,y \rangle}\right] = \{R \in \mathbf{R} : y \notin [x]_R\}. \tag{2.18}$$

The entries $d_{\langle x,y \rangle}$ of the matrix $\mathbb{D}(\mathbf{F})$ consist of the names of all relations by which x can be discriminated from y. Clearly $d_{\langle x,x \rangle} = \emptyset$ because

$$d_{\langle x,x \rangle} = \{R \in \mathbf{R} : x \notin [x]_R\} = \emptyset.$$

In terms of commonsense reasoning, any object x is indiscernible from itself; hence there are no equivalence relations or features that deliver varying information about x.

Example 2.18 The discernability matrix for Example 2.12 has the following form:

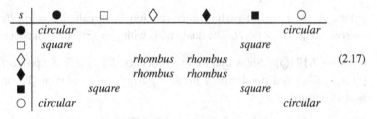

$$
\mathbb{D}(\mathbf{F}) \;=\; \begin{array}{c|cccccc}
s & \bullet & \square & \lozenge & \blacklozenge & \blacksquare & \circ \\
\hline
\bullet & \emptyset & & & & & \\
\square & C,S & \emptyset & & & & \\
\lozenge & C,S & S & \emptyset & & & \\
\blacklozenge & S & C,S & C & \emptyset & & \\
\blacksquare & S & C & C,S & S & \emptyset & \\
\circ & C & S & S & C,S & C,S & \emptyset
\end{array} \qquad (2.19)
$$

The concept of discernability will become of great importance when discussing the issue of a varying granularity of knowledge: if there are different objects that cannot be distinguished from each other (i.e., their corresponding entry in a discernability matrix is $\emptyset$), then we need to *learn* by acquiring knowledge in the form of new relations.

2.1.5 Structured sets

Posets. A set s with a partial order relation $\sqsubseteq$ is called a *partially ordered* set $\langle s, \sqsubseteq \rangle$ or *poset*. The dual $\langle s, \sqsupseteq \rangle$ with $\sqsupseteq = \sqsubseteq^{\smile}$ is also a poset.

Exercise 2.19 ($\lozenge$) Show that for two posets $\langle s_i, \sqsubseteq_i \rangle$, $i \in \mathbf{2}$, the product $\langle s_0 \times s_1, \sqsubseteq_\times \rangle$ is a poset with a *product partial order relation* $\sqsubseteq_\times$ on $s_0 \times s_1$ defined as

$$\langle x_0, x_1 \rangle \sqsubseteq_\times \langle y_0, y_1 \rangle \text{ if } x_i \sqsubseteq_i y_i.$$

For any two elements x and y of a set s we call x and y *incomparable* if neither $x \sqsubseteq y$ nor $y \sqsubseteq x$. If all x and y are comparable, then $\langle s, \sqsubseteq \rangle$ is a *total order*. Let there be two posets $\langle s_i, \sqsubseteq_i \rangle$, $i \in \mathbf{2}$. Suppose there is an isomorphism $f : s_0 \to s_1$ that preserves the ordering relation such that

$$x \sqsubseteq_0 y \Longleftrightarrow f(x) \sqsubseteq_1 f(y).$$

Then, if x and y are incomparable in s_0, it follows that $f(x)$ and $f(y)$ are also incomparable in s_1.

An element $\top$ of a poset s is called a *maximal element* of s if there is no $y \in s$ such that $\top \sqsubset y$; conversely $\bot$ is called a *minimal element* of s if there is no $y \in s$ such that $y \sqsubset \bot$. If there is exactly one maximal (minimal) element x of a set s, then x is called the *greatest* (*least*) element. If there is a greatest element, it is often called a *unit* element and denoted by $\mathbb{T}$ (or $\mathbf{1}$ to avoid confusion with a maximal element); a least element is also called a *zero* element and denoted by $\perp\!\!\!\perp$ (or $\mathbf{0}$).

For a subset $s' \subseteq s$, an element $x \in s$ is called an *upper* (*lower*) *bound* of s' if for all $x' \in s'$, $x' \sqsubseteq x$ ($x' \sqsupseteq x$). We call $x \in s$ a *least upper* (*greatest lower*) bound of $s' \sqsubseteq s$ if x is an upper (lower) bound of s' and if for any other upper (lower) bound y of s' it holds that $x \sqsubseteq y$ ($x \sqsupseteq y$). The dual concepts of upper and lower bounds carry over to dual posets.

Lattices. A poset $\langle s, \sqsubseteq \rangle$ is called a *lattice* if every subset $\{x_0, x_1\} \subseteq s$ has a greatest lower and a least upper bound in s. The least upper bound of x_0 and x_1 is denoted $x_0 \sqcup x_1$ and is called the *join* of x_0 and x_1. The greatest lower bound of x_0 and x_1 is denoted $x_0 \sqcap x_1$ and is called the *meet* of x_0 and x_1.

Example 2.20 For any finite set s, $\mathbf{2}^s$ is a lattice with $\subseteq$ as the order relation and $\cup$ and $\cap$ as the join and meet.

The following equivalences show how order relations are connected to meet and join operators:

$$x \sqcup y = y \iff x \sqsubseteq y \quad \text{and} \quad x \sqcap y = x \iff x \sqsubseteq y. \tag{2.20}$$

Meet and join are idempotent, commutative, associative, and absorbing. As we have seen in the axiomatisation of integer arithmetic through set theory, the correspondence to sets and integers is trivial. We conclude this section on set-theoretic structures with a small but very important example:

Example 2.21 We consider the set $\mathbf{z}$ of the first z natural numbers (including 0). There exists a natural bounded lattice that has the form

$$\mathbf{0} \subseteq \mathbf{1} \subseteq \mathbf{2} \subseteq \cdots \subseteq \mathbf{z},$$

where $x \sqsubseteq y :\iff \mathbf{x} \subseteq \mathbf{y}$. We define $x \sqcup y := \mathbf{x} \cup \mathbf{y}$. Then,

$$x \sqcup y = y \iff x \sqsubseteq y.$$

Similarly, we define $x \sqcap y := \mathbf{x} \cap \mathbf{y}$. If we read the set names x, y as natural numbers (including 0), then $\sqcap$ corresponds to the max operator and $\sqcup$ to the min operator. From this we can conclude that $\langle \mathbf{z}, \sqcup, \sqcap \rangle$ is a distributive lattice with least element 0 and largest element z.

Next we define a *complement* operation $\mathbf{x} \cup \overline{\mathbf{x}} = \mathbf{z} \iff x + \overline{x} = z$. So $\overline{\mathbf{x}}$ is the set of elements needed to make $\mathbf{x}$ equal to $\mathbf{z}$. In other words, y complements x with respect to z. One can easily verify that $\overline{x} \sqcap x = 0$.[1]

This example motivates the definition of a *Boolean algebra*:

Boolean algebra

Definition 2.22 — Boolean algebra.
The structure $\langle s, \sqcap, \sqcup, \overline{} \rangle$ is called a *Boolean algebra* if $\langle s, \sqcap, \sqcup \rangle$ is a lattice that satisfies

$$x \sqcap (y \sqcup z) = (x \sqcap y) \sqcup (x \sqcap z) \quad \text{and} \quad x \sqcup (y \sqcap z) = (x \sqcup y) \sqcap (x \sqcup z)$$

[1] Note that this is true in Boolean algebras only. For any other algebra our definition of complementary satisfies the definition of a relative pseudo-complement.

and if there exist a least element $\perp\!\!\perp \in s$ and a greatest element $\top\!\!\top \in s$ such that for every $x \in s$ there exists $\bar{x}$ with

$$x \sqcap \bar{x} = \perp\!\!\perp \quad \text{and} \quad x \sqcup \bar{x} = \top\!\!\top.$$

A Boolean algebra is a distributive lattice with a complement. Its greatest and least elements $\top\!\!\top$ and $\perp\!\!\perp$ are also known as **1** ("true") and **0** ("false"). ●

Exercise 2.23 (◊) Give a fourth interpretation of this algebra along the lines of the definitions of $\sqsubseteq$, $\subseteq$, and $\leq$ from the previous example! Hint: think logic.

Exercise 2.24 (◊) Look up "Heyting algebra" in the literature and relate the definition of relative pseudo-complements to Example 2.21. Focus on the sentence that "$\bar{\mathbf{x}}$ is the set of elements in **z** that are needed to make **x** equal to **z**"!

2.1.6 Probabilities

Another kind of structure is *probability*. To us, probability is a *measure* for describing how often some *event* occurs.

A measure μ is a mapping that assigns to any finite subset $s \subseteq U$ some value that describes its *magnitude*. So the bigger a set, the larger its measure. We refrain from giving a more detailed definition here and settle for the following example.

Example 2.25 Let there be a set U. We assign to each finite subset $s \in U$ its cardinality. Then, $|\cdot| : \wp(U) \to \mathbb{N}_0$ is a measure. The powerset $\wp(U)$ contains the empty set and $|\emptyset| = 0$. For all $s \in \wp(U)$, we also have $\bar{s} \in \wp(U)$. And, finally, for a countable subset $S \subseteq \wp(U)$, it holds that $\bigcup S \in \wp(U)$ (the same holds for intersections). ●

If s and s' are disjoint and their measures add up to the measure of their union set,

$$\mu(s \dot{\cup} s') = \mu(s) + \mu(s'),$$

and $\mu(U) = 1$, then μ is called a *probability distribution*. In this case, we write ϕ for μ.

If we regard every element of U as an observation (or "outcome"), every subset $s \subseteq U$ is an *event* – something that happens. Intensional set definitions often have the form

$$s_y = \{x \in U : f(x) = y\}$$

for some $y \in \text{cod}(f)$. Therefore, the event of x having the value y under f is represented by the set s_y. A mapping $F : \text{cod}(f) \to \wp(U)$ is called a *random variable* and one usually writes

$$\Pr[F = y] := \Pr(F \in s_y) := \phi\{x \in U : f(x) = y\}.$$

Because the kind of knowledge we are talking about is defined in terms of sets and the ability to sort different objects into different classes, we will stick to the measure-like notation using ϕ. Probability and measure theory are far beyond the scope of this book; however, the interested reader might want to learn about probability theory from Jaynes (2003), Kolmogorov (1965), and Li and Vitanyi (1993).

2.1.7 Relation algebra

Without notifying the reader we implicitly introduced some ideas from relation algebra. An abstract algebra of relations is a structure of relations on a base set and operators on these relations satisfying certain properties. So, for the sake of completeness, we now define what we already presumed earlier:

Relation algebra

Definition 2.26 — Relation algebra.
An algebra of relations is a structure

$$\mathfrak{R} = \left\langle \mathbf{R}, \cup, \circ, ^{-}, ^{\smile}, \perp\!\!\!\perp, \top\!\!\!\top, \mathit{1} \right\rangle \tag{2.21}$$

with a *base set* $\mathbf{R}$; binary operators $\cup$, and $\circ$; unary operators $^{-}$ and $^{\smile}$; and special elements $\perp\!\!\!\perp$, $\top\!\!\!\top$, and $\mathit{1}$ for which the following hold:

1. $\mathbf{R}$ together with $\cup$ and $^{-}$ form a Boolean algebra.
2. $\mathbf{R}$ together with $\circ$ and $\mathit{1}$ form a monoid.
3. It holds that $(R^{\smile})^{\smile} = R$, $(R \circ S)^{\smile} = S^{\smile} \circ R^{\smile}$.
4. $^{\smile}$ and $\circ$ distribute over $\sqcup$.
5. deMorgan's laws are satisfied.

Using deMorgan's law, we can define $R \cap S := \overline{\overline{R} \cup \overline{S}}$. The zero- and one-elements in an algebra of relations are, of course, the *empty* relation $\perp\!\!\!\perp$ and the *universal* relation $\top\!\!\!\top$. $\mathit{1}$ denotes the identity relation on s. ●

In relation calculus, the operators are often written as ";" for concatenation, "+" for join, and "·" for the meet.

It is very important to be able to speak about objects and sets of objects. For example, $5 \in \mathbb{N}$ and $\mathbb{N} \subset \mathbb{R}$. But because we are interested in *relations*, we want to talk about the properties of different relations. So if $R \subseteq \mathbb{N} \times \mathbb{N}$ and $S \subseteq \mathbb{N} \times \mathbb{N}$, what is the difference between R and S? Or, in simple terms, it is nice to know that Clarabelle is a cow and that Pluto is a dog. It is even nicer to know that dogs are descendants of wolves and that cows are tame bovinae. But the nicest thing is to know that dogs are to wolves as cows are to bisons: they are the domesticated versions.

Example 2.27 Let $R, S \in \mathbb{N}^2$ and $xRy :\Longleftrightarrow x < y$ and $xSy :\Longleftrightarrow x \leq y$. In other words, $R =<$ and $S =\leq$ (it may look a bit odd the first time you read this). But whenever $x < y$, we also know that $x \leq y$. Therefore – and this might look even odder – we can state that $<\subset\leq$.

Let us take a look at a two-valued propositional logic again:

Example 2.28 Imagine a finite set $\mathrm{Var_{PL}} = \{\mathrm{a}, \mathrm{b}, \mathrm{c}, \ldots\}$, which we call the set of propositional variables. Suppose there is total function $\alpha : \mathrm{Var_{PL}} \to \mathbf{2}$. Because $\mathbf{0} \subseteq \mathbf{1}$ we know that for any $x, y \in \mathrm{Var_{PL}}$

$$\alpha(x) = \mathbf{0} \Longrightarrow \alpha(x) \subseteq \alpha(y). \tag{2.22}$$

Similarly, we know that if $\alpha(x) \neq \alpha(y)$, then

$$\alpha(x) \cup \alpha(y) = \mathbf{1} \quad \text{and} \quad \alpha(x) \cap \alpha(y) = \mathbf{0}. \tag{2.23}$$

We then define operators $\vee, \wedge, \longrightarrow$, and $\neg$ with the following properties:

$$\begin{aligned} \alpha(x \wedge y) &:= \alpha(x) \cap \alpha(y) \\ \alpha(x \vee y) &:= \alpha(x) \cup \alpha(y) \\ \{\alpha(\neg x)\} &:= \mathbf{2} - \{\alpha(x)\} \\ \alpha(x \longrightarrow y) &:= \alpha(\neg x) \cup \alpha(y). \end{aligned}$$

In this way we have defined the syntax *and* semantics of propositional logic in only four lines. We call **2** the set of Boolean truth-values, written $\mathbf{2} := \{\mathbf{0}, \mathbf{1}\}$.

Exercise 2.29 (◊) Define a three-valued propositional logic.

What is the benefit of relation algebra? Take a look at the definition (2.8) of properties of relations. All the properties were defined *element-* or *pointwise*. For example, to show that R is reflexive we have to show that xRx for all $x \in \mathrm{dom}(R)$. This might become a rather cumbersome task with large or even unknown domains. Instead of examining a relation elementwise, we can simply express its properties by equations in relational calculus. So if R is reflexive, then it follows that $I \subseteq R \Longleftrightarrow I \cup R = R$. Symmetry means that $R = R^{\smile}$, and transitivity, that $R \circ R \subseteq R$.

So whenever we can prove that for some relation R the three equations are true we know it is an equivalence relation – without taking a closer look at a single object of our domain. As an example, consider the following proposition:

A reflexive, difunctional relation is an equivalence relation.

Exercise 2.30 (◊) Prove the proposition using the standard set-theoretic properties. Note that a standard "pointwise" proof requires us to show that

$$\forall a,b,c,d,x : \left(xRx \wedge \left(\left(aRb \wedge bR^\smile c \wedge cRd\right) \Longrightarrow aRd\right)\right)$$
$$\Longleftrightarrow$$
$$\forall a,b,c,d,x : (xRx \wedge ((aRb \wedge bRc) \Longrightarrow aRc)).$$

Using the laws of relation algebra, the proof is very simple. First we reformulate the equivalence from the previous excercise in relation algebra (in-)equations:

$$(\underset{(1)}{\mathit{1} \subseteq R} \wedge \underset{(2)}{RR^\smile R \subseteq R}) \Longleftrightarrow (\underset{(1')}{\mathit{1} \subseteq R} \wedge \underset{(2')}{RR \subseteq R} \wedge \underset{(3')}{R^\smile \subseteq R})$$

We then show that equivalence relations are reflexive and difunctional. Equivalence relations are reflexive by definition (1′), and therefore (1) is true. Then

$$R \overset{(2')}{\supseteq} RR \overset{(2')}{\supseteq} RRR \overset{(3')}{\supseteq} RR^\smile R$$

proves that (2) holds.

To show that every reflexive difunctional relation is an equivalence relation, we need to prove that (1) and (2) imply (1′–3′). Again, (1′) trivially implies (1). To show that reflexivity follows, we need to know that (3): $\mathit{1} = \mathit{1}^\smile$, which is clear by the definition of $\mathit{1}$. Then,

$$R \overset{(2)}{\supseteq} RR^\smile R \overset{(1)}{\supseteq} R\mathit{1}^\smile R \overset{(3)}{=} R\mathit{1}R \overset{\mathit{1}}{\supseteq} RR.$$

This means that $RR \subseteq R$, and hence (2′) is true. Finally, symmetry can be derived as

$$R \overset{(2)}{\supseteq} RR^\smile R \overset{(1)}{\supseteq} \mathit{1}R^\smile R \overset{(1)}{\supseteq} \mathit{1}R^\smile \mathit{1} \overset{\mathit{1}}{\supseteq} R^\smile$$

which proves that (3′): $R^\smile \subseteq R$ holds.[2]

[2] As you can see, this proof is very, very simple. It is, in terms of notational and logic effort, much simpler than the proof required for Exercise 2.30, though in order to find such a simple and short proof, it takes a human a few years of experience. The biggest advantage of all is that this proof can be carried out mechanically using an automated theorem proving system. Because such a system lacks all the intuition and experience, the proof takes about 75 steps there – but it is carried out in less than a quarter of a second.

Once we understand the general laws of relation algebra, we are not only able to talk about *things* but also about the *relations* between them. Then, the set of all relations again is a set with relations of objects – so we can examine relations between relations, and so on. This achievement is not just art for art's sake, but it is a *fundamental* requirement for knowledge discovery:

> **Relations and knowledge**
> If knowledge is defined by relations, then learning is about reasoning with relations on relations.

A relational view of knowledge is one that delivers a vocabulary for speaking about it for free.[3]

For a deeper understanding of the underlying relational mathematics and reasoning, the reader should consult Schmidt (2011) or Maddux (2006). More in-depth knowledge that is useful but not mandatory for understanding the semantics part of Chapter 7 is presented in Goldblatt (2006).

2.2 Knowledge structures

We now examine the families $\mathbf{P}, \mathbf{Q}, \mathbf{R}$ of equivalence relations over a base set s.

2.2.1 Concepts, equivalence relations, and knowledge

Consider a set s and relations C, S as in Example 2.12. The knowledge represented by these relations can be used to answer several questions:

1. What colour is a □?
   Hence, we examine $\mathbb{K}(C)$ and find $f_C(\square)$'s value: □ is *white*!
2. What shape is a □?
   We examine the kernel matrix for S and find that $f_S(\square) = square$.
3. But the interesting thing is that a □ is a *white square*:

$$\square \in [\square]_C \cap [\square]_S.$$

We answered the question for white *and* squarish objects by intersecting the respective equivalence classes. How can we use our knowledge of the corresponding equivalence relations? One approach is to create an overlay of the respective matrices.

[3] With all of its implications. While Boolean algebras are still decidable, relation algebras are *un*decidable.

Consider the following kernel matrices for the relations C and S:

C	◇	●	■	□	○	◆
◇	w			w	w	
●		b	b			b
■		b	b			b
□	w			w	w	
○	w			w	w	
◆		b	b			b

and

S	◇	●	■	□	○	◆
◇	r					r
●		c			c	
■			s	s		
□			s	s		
○		c			c	
◆	r					r .

The overlay of the kernel matrices $\mathbb{K}(C)$ and $\mathbb{K}(S)$ then is

$C \oplus S$	◇	●	■	□	○	◆
◇	wr			w	w	r
●		bc	b		c	b
■		b	bs	s		b
□	w		s	ws	w	
○	w	c		w	wc	
◆	r	b	b			br .

Finally, we consider the relation $R := C \cap S$, which discriminates objects by colour *and* shape, and draw the corresponding equivalence classes as $\mathbb{M}(C \cap S)$ (left matrix). We then identify colour and shape information by selecting only the entry in $\mathbb{K}(C) \oplus \mathbb{K}(S)$ for which the left matrix carries **1**:

$\mathbb{M}(C \cap S)$	◇	●	■	□	○	◆
◇	**1**					
●		**1**				
■			**1**			
□				**1**		
○					**1**	
◆						**1**

$\otimes$

$C \oplus S$	◇	●	■	□	○	◆
◇	wr			w	w	r
●		bc	b		c	b
■		b	bs	s		b
□	w		s	ws	w	
○	w	c		w	wc	
◆	r	b	b			br.

In this case, $C \cap S$ happens to be the same as 1_s. Then, $\square(1_s \circ (C \cap S))^{\urcorner} = \{\square\}$, and reading $C \oplus S$ as a relation $(s \times s) \rightharpoonup \wp(\mathrm{cod}(\mathit{colour}) \cup \mathrm{cod}(\mathit{shape}))$, we find $\langle \square, \square \rangle\, (C \oplus S)^{\urcorner}\, \{\{w, s\}\}$. This means that □ is a *white square*.

2.2.2 Operations on equivalence relations

A corollary from the observation that every equivalence relation induces a partition (the quotient), and vice versa, is that two equivalence relations are equal if and only if their quotients are equal. Let $R, S \in \mathbf{R}$ be two equivalence relations. Then,

$$
\begin{aligned}
R = S &\iff xRy \longleftrightarrow xSy \\
&\iff \{\langle x, y\rangle : xRy\} = \{\langle x, y\rangle : xSy\} \\
&\iff \{[x]_R : x \in s\} = \{[x]_S : x \in s\} \\
&\iff s/R = s/S.
\end{aligned}
$$

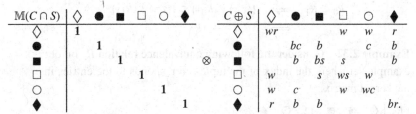

Therefore, the intersection of equivalence relations can be defined in terms of the intersections of the equivalence classes:

Intersection of equivalence relations

Definition 2.31 — Intersection of equivalence relations.
For n equivalence relations $R_i \in \mathbf{R}$, their intersection $\bigcap_{i \in \mathbf{n}} R_i$ is also an equivalence relation:

$$\begin{aligned}
\bigcap_{i \in \mathbf{n}} R_i &= R_0 \cap R_1 \cap \cdots R_{n-1} \\
&= \{\langle x, y\rangle : xR_0y\} \cap \{\langle x, y\rangle : xR_1y\} \cap \cdots \cap \{\langle x, y\rangle : xR_{n-1}y\} \\
&= \{\langle x, y\rangle : xR_0y \wedge xR_1y \wedge \cdots \wedge xR_{n-1}y\}.
\end{aligned}$$

Equivalently, it holds that

$$\begin{aligned}
[x]_{R_0 \cap \cdots \cap R_n} &= \{y : x(R_0 \cap \cdots \cap R_{n-1})y\} \\
&= \{y : xR_0y\} \cap \cdots \cap \{y : xR_ny\} \\
&= [x]_{R_0} \cap \cdots \cap [x]_{R_n}.
\end{aligned}$$

●

By intersecting equivalence relations we obtain further, *smaller* equivalence relations with *finer* classes. This is worth a second thought: what does it mean for a certain equivalence relation to be a subset of another? Let us take a closer look:

$$\begin{aligned}
R_0 \subseteq R_1 &\iff \{\langle x, y\rangle : xR_0y\} \subseteq \{\langle x, y\rangle : xR_1y\} \\
&\iff xR_0y \longrightarrow xR_1y.
\end{aligned}$$

Example 2.32 Consider the following equivalence relation R_3 on our example set where the index of the tuples corresponds to the entries in the kernel matrix:

R_3	◇	●	■	□	○	◆
◇	□			□		
●		△				△
■			◇			
□	□			□		
○					○	
◆		△				△

$$= \left\{ \begin{array}{lll} \langle 0,0\rangle_{\square}, & \langle 0,3\rangle_{\square}, & \langle 3,0\rangle_{\square}, \\ \langle 3,3\rangle_{\square}, & \langle 1,1\rangle_{\triangle}, & \langle 1,5\rangle_{\triangle}, \\ \langle 5,1\rangle_{\triangle}, & \langle 5,5\rangle_{\triangle}, & \langle 2,2\rangle_{\diamond}, \\ & \langle 4,4\rangle_{\bigcirc} & \end{array} \right\}.$$

If we recall the definition of C we can easily verify that $R_3 \subset C$:

C	◇	●	■	□	○	◆
◇	w			w	w	
●		b	b			b
■		b	b			b
□	w			w	w	
○	w			w	w	
◆		b	b			b

$$C = R_3 \cup \left\{ \begin{array}{lll} \langle 1,2\rangle, & \langle 2,1\rangle, & \langle 1,4\rangle, \\ \langle 4,1\rangle, & \langle 2,5\rangle, & \langle 5,2\rangle, \\ & \langle 3,4\rangle, \langle 4,3\rangle & \end{array} \right\}.$$

In other words, R_3 is *finer* than C, and C is *coarser* than R_3, or, more formally, $R_3 \subseteq C \iff xR_3y \longrightarrow xCy$.

There are, of course, more operations on (equivalence) relations than just intersections (i.e., conjunctions). For equivalence relations $P, R : s \rightarrow s$:

1. $\overline{R}$ is not an equivalence relation, but $\overline{R} \cup I_s$ is;
2. $R^{\smile}$ is an equivalence relation;
3. $P \cup R$ is not an equivalence relation;
4. $P \circ R = \{\langle x, z \rangle : \exists y : xPyRz\}$ is not an equivalence relation.

Exercise 2.33 (◈) Prove the above.

So far we have talked about *objects*, sets, and classes of objects and their relations to each other. But knowledge is made of *relations*, not of collections of things. Therefore, we call $\langle s, \mathbf{R} \rangle$ a *knowledge base*. To conclude this chapter on knowledge structures, we finally discuss the relations *between* different knowledge bases.

2.2.3 Indiscernability and knowledge

Two objects x and y are *indiscernible* with respect to an equivalence relation R if xRy. As a special case, if $x = y$, then they are indiscernible from each other. With a set $\mathbf{R}$ of equivalence relations, $\bigcap \mathbf{R}$ is also an equivalence relation. We find that if $\bigcap \mathbf{R} \in \mathbf{R}$, it is a minimal element: $\forall R \in \mathbf{R} : \bigcap \mathbf{R} \subseteq R$. It creates the finest partition on the base set s. If xRy for all $R \in \mathbf{R}$, then x and y are indiscernible with respect to $\mathbf{R}$ and it also holds that $x(\bigcap \mathbf{R})y$. The higher the resolution of our knowledge $\mathbf{R}$ on the objects of our domain, the fewer indiscernible objects there are – and the coarser our knowledge, the more indiscernible objects we have.

Indiscernability relation

Definition 2.34 — Indiscernability relation.
Let there be a set of equivalence relations $\mathbf{R}$. Then we call

$$\bar{\bar{\mathbf{R}}} = \bigcap_{R \in \mathbf{R}} R = \bigcap \mathbf{R}$$

the *indiscernability relation* over $\mathbf{R}$. ●

Elements of s/R for any $R \in \mathbf{R}$ are called *elementary categories*. They correspond to R-equivalence classes and can be identified by appropriate kernels. Elements of $s/\bar{\bar{\mathbf{R}}}$ are called *basic categories*. Elementary categories (R-equivalence classes) are unions of basic categories ($\bar{\bar{\mathbf{R}}}$-equivalence classes), and a basic category is always a subset of an R-equivalence class.

Exercise 2.35 (◇) Compute $\bar{\bar{\mathbf{R}}}$ for $\mathbf{R} = \{R_i : i \in \mathbf{3}\}$ as defined in Example 2.11!

In other words, elementary categories are equivalence classes generated by some equivalence relation $R \in \mathbf{R}$. Given an information system $\langle s, \mathbf{F}, V_{\mathbf{F}} \rangle$ we have a knowledge base $\mathbf{R}$ with $\mathbf{R} = \{R_f : f \in \mathbf{F}\}$. Every elementary category $[x]_{R_f}$ then has a "name" that is x's value under f or, in simple terms, the entry in R_f's kernel matrix, $f(x)$. Basic classes are sets of objects that are not discernible by any of the $R_f \in \mathbf{R}$. So if x and y are elements of the same basic class, then $f(x) = f(y)$ for all $f \in \mathbf{F}$.

Example 2.36 Let $\mathbf{R} = \{C, S\}$ as in Example 2.16. Then $\overline{\overline{\mathbf{R}}} = \bigcap\{C, S\} = C \cap S$ is

$$C \cap S = \left\{\begin{matrix} \langle 0,0\rangle_b, & \langle 3,3\rangle_b, & \langle 0,3\rangle_b, \\ \langle 3,0\rangle_b, & \langle 3,4\rangle_b, & \langle 4,3\rangle_b, \\ \langle 0,4\rangle_b, & \langle 4,0\rangle_b, & \langle 4,4\rangle_b, \\ \langle 1,1\rangle_w, & \langle 2,2\rangle_w, & \langle 5,5\rangle_w, \\ \langle 1,2\rangle_w, & \langle 2,1\rangle_w, & \langle 2,5\rangle_w, \\ \langle 5,2\rangle_w, & \langle 1,5\rangle_w, & \langle 5,1\rangle_w \end{matrix}\right\}_{R_0} \cap \left\{\begin{matrix} \langle 0,0\rangle_c, & \langle 5,5\rangle_c, \\ \langle 0,5\rangle_c, & \langle 5,0\rangle_c, \\ \langle 1,1\rangle_s, & \langle 4,4\rangle_s, \\ \langle 1,4\rangle_s, & \langle 4,1\rangle_s, \\ \langle 2,2\rangle_l, & \langle 3,3\rangle_l, \\ \langle 2,3\rangle_l, & \langle 3,2\rangle_l \end{matrix}\right\}_{R_1}$$

$$= \left\{\begin{matrix} \langle 0,0\rangle_{bc}, & \langle 5,5\rangle_{wc}, & \langle 1,1\rangle_{ws}, \\ \langle 4,4\rangle_{bs}, & \langle 2,2\rangle_{wl}, & \langle 3,3\rangle_{bl} \end{matrix}\right\}_{C \cap S} = I_s.$$

Equivalently, we can take a look at the partitions instead:

$$\begin{aligned} s/R_0 &= \{\{0,3,4\},\{1,2,5\}\} \\ s/R_1 &= \{\{0,5\},\{1,4\},\{2,3\}\} \\ s/(R_0 \cap R_1) &= \{\{0\},\{1\},\{2\},\{3\},\{4\},\{5\}\}. \end{aligned}$$

Neither R_0 nor R_1 is capable of discriminating all objects from each other, whereas their intersection is.

Whenever the indiscernability relation equals the identity, $s/\overline{\overline{\mathbf{R}}} = \{\{x\} : x \in s\}$, then knowledge $\mathbf{R}$ is maximal in the sense that we cannot have any more knowledge. Then we can discriminate any two different objects from each other. But what happens if we choose *different* sets $\mathbf{P}$ and $\mathbf{R}$ of equivalence relations? It could well be that $s/\overline{\overline{\mathbf{P}}} = s/\overline{\overline{\mathbf{R}}}$. Then the information content of $\mathbf{P}$ and $\mathbf{R}$ seems to be the same because they create the same quotients. It could also be that one knowledge base is finer than the other: if there is some $x \in s$ for which

$$[x]_{\overline{\overline{\mathbf{P}}}} \subset [x]_{\overline{\overline{\mathbf{R}}}},$$

then $\mathbf{P}$ creates a smaller basic category including x than $\mathbf{R}$ does. Therefore, there are fewer objects that are $\mathbf{P}$-indiscernible from x than there are $\mathbf{R}$-indiscernible objects of x.

Definition 2.37 — Equivalent knowledge. Equivalent knowledge

Let there be two knowledge bases with a base set s and families of equivalence relations $\mathbf{P}$ and $\mathbf{R}$. We say $\mathbf{P}$ and $\mathbf{R}$ are *equivalent* if

$$\mathbf{P} \cong \mathbf{R} \quad :\Longleftrightarrow \quad \bar{\bar{\mathbf{P}}} = \bar{\bar{\mathbf{R}}} \Longleftrightarrow s/\mathbf{P} = s/\mathbf{R}. \tag{2.24}$$

We call **R** *coarser* (*more general*) than **P** if

$$\mathbf{P} \preceq \mathbf{R} \quad :\Longleftrightarrow \quad \bar{\bar{\mathbf{P}}} \subseteq \bar{\bar{\mathbf{R}}} \Longleftrightarrow [x]_{\bar{\bar{\mathbf{P}}}} \subseteq [x]_{\bar{\bar{\mathbf{R}}}}. \tag{2.25}$$

If **R** is more general than **P**, then **P** is *finer* than **R**. ●

Knowledge representation is a research discipline in its own right, and so it is relational concept analysis.

Yet, there is still much more to knowledge. Human knowledge and human skills are not just entities but rather processes that are massively parallel and unsynchronised. Accordingly, we have biologically inspired artificial neural networks as mathematical simulations of reasoning and we have, for example, back-propagation as an algorithm for learning. Our knowledge of the world is not very crisp, either. Concepts are vague, and rules are fuzzy, too. And many observations and conclusions drawn from them are probabilistic. This has led to a multitude of different knowledge representation and inferencing methods. And, accordingly, to many different learning methods as well.

We now have a proper understanding of the required concepts and we have acquired the necessary skills to study *knowledge* and *representations* thereof in a more detailed way.

Chapter 3
From data to hypotheses

No software without a program, no program without an algorithm. No algorithm without a theory, and no theory without a clear syntax and semantics. In this chapter we define the fundamental concepts that we need to speak about knowledge discovery in a clear language without too much confusion.

If we try to put all the important information about machine learning in just a small box, it would look like this:

> **Machine learning**
> *Machine learning* is concerned with the problem of inducing a *concept* from a *sample* of instances of our *domain*. Given a classification, the task is to define a mapping that approximates an unknown *target function* that assigns to each object a target class label.
>
> The outcome is a hypothesis h of a certain *quality*, and the process of inducing such a hypothesis crucially depends on the *representation* of our domain.

This rather rough picture is described in detail in the following sections.

First we need to specify what we will be talking about and the terms we will be using.

3.1 Representation

Machine learning and knowledge discovery are concerned with:

- grouping *objects* (like entities, processes, atoms, complex structures, etc.)
- from a *domain* (i.e., a set of such objects)

- into *target concepts*
- with respect to their *properties* and/or the *classes* they belong to.

First we need to ask ourselves how to *represent* our knowledge of the world. The part of the world that we live in and that we shall reason about is called the *domain*. To be able to talk about objects of the domain we need to have representations thereof.[1]

Domain, universe, representation

Definition 3.1 — Domain, universe, representation.
Let $\mathfrak{D}$ denote our *domain*, which is the part of the world that we are interested in. A *representation* is a morphism from the domain into a structure of objects called a *representation space* or *universe* $\mathfrak{U}$:

$$\rho : \mathfrak{D} \to \mathfrak{U}. \tag{3.1}$$

The base set of $\mathfrak{U}$ is denoted by U. ●

Note that for $x, y \in \mathfrak{D}$, $x =_{\mathfrak{D}} y$ does not imply that $\rho(x) =_{\mathfrak{U}} \rho(y)$.

Example 3.2 Let $\mathfrak{D} = \mathbb{Q}$ and $\mathfrak{U} = \mathbb{N}$. One possible representation of rational numbers as natural numbers is defined by $\rho(x) = \lceil |x| \rceil$. Then, for example, $\rho(-6.81) = \rho(\frac{20}{3}) = \rho(\sqrt{47\frac{1}{3}})$. ●

Exercise 3.3 (◊) (a) Define two more (reasonable) representation functions. (b) Define a reasonable $\rho : \mathbb{R} \to \mathbb{N}$. (c) Find a reasonable representation for the complex numbers $\mathbb{C}$ by more simple structures.

Exercise 3.4 (◆) Discuss the properties of the representations you defined in the previous exercise. Are order relations preserved? What about operations?

Of course, our world $\mathfrak{D}$ has much more structure than just a set and, of course, so has $\mathfrak{U}$. For example, a truck has *more* wheels than a motorcycle. A suitable representation mapping a truck on, say, 18 and a motorcycle on 2 also preserves the relationship between them: a truck is to some extent "more" than a motorcycle and, similarly, 18 is somehow "more" than 2.

Concept, class

Definition 3.5 — Concept, class.
A *concept* is a meaningful subset $C \subseteq \mathfrak{D}$ of objects in our domain. A *(representation) class* is a subset $c \subseteq U$. ●

It is very important to understand that we defined a representation class independently from concepts. If we had defined a representation class c to be C's image under ρ, we would have to have knowledge about $\mathfrak{D}$

[1] Actually, we never ever talk about domains but always about our model of parts of the world that we assume to be "true".

and ρ. It might seem a bit odd to the reader, but we do not know what $\mathfrak{D}$ looks like:

> **Representation gap**
> Any representation or any model is an image of the domain, and the way the image is drawn is always a lossy process, as we shall see later. More importantly, knowledge discovery means to discover rules by *looking at the data* we are provided with. It means that all we have is $\mathfrak{U}$; we do not even know anything about ρ. Knowledge discovery takes place when we interpret the result (a description of a class c) back in $\mathfrak{D}$.

Accordingly, $C \neq D$ does not imply that $\rho(C) \neq_{\mathfrak{U}} \rho(D)$.

Example 3.6 Imagine $\mathfrak{D} = \mathbb{R}$ and $\mathfrak{U} = \mathbb{N}$. Let there be two concepts in $\mathbb{R}$: the set of non-natural rational numbers $Q = \mathbb{Q} - \mathbb{N} \subset \mathbb{R}$ and the set of non-natural real numbers $R = \mathbb{R} - \mathbb{N} \subset \mathbb{R}$. We now define a partial representation $\rho : \mathbb{R} \to \mathbb{N}$ by

$$\rho(x) = \begin{cases} x, & \text{if } x \in \mathbb{N} \\ ?, & \text{else.} \end{cases}$$

Then, $Q \subset R$ but $\rho(Q) = \rho(R) = \emptyset$.

We already stated that concepts usually have a meaning. This is why we are able not only to collect all blue things and call the set of all blue things *blue*; we can also *explain* or *describe* the abstract property of something *being blue*. This is similar to having a general idea of "blueishness" and the ability to communicate this idea to someone else. This idea does not refer to all instances of the set of things that share the property of being blue, but to the intentional meaning of the concept "blueishness" itself. This is why we need to discriminate concepts from representation classes and intensional meaning from extensional enumeration.

Example 3.7 In his *Tractatus Logico-philosophicus*, the philosopher Ludwig Wittgenstein tried to establish a logically sound theory of meaning. In this case, human language was the representation space he examined. First he defined the "world" to be everything "that is the case". His "world" corresponds to what we call a domain. He also stated that models ("logical pictures") are based on elementary propositions about things (which correspond to characteristic functions of classes). Of course, he also came to the conclusion that there are things in the world that cannot be expressed in terms of our language. This left him speechless for a long time. Then, after several years more he finally concluded that the *meaning of a word is its use*.

Linguists and especially those who deal with lexical semantics (i.e., the meaning of the words or the units of language) face a similar problem. They eventually agreed that the meaning of the word "scooter" is *scooter'* (pronounced "scooter-prime").

But still, there is more to concepts than just sets. Concepts obviously contain *more* information than sets of objects that are represented by representation classes. Therefore, we define *concept representations*:

Representation of a concept

Definition 3.8 — Representation of a concept.
A concept $C \in \mathfrak{D}$ is represented by classes of objects:

$$\rho : C \mapsto c \quad \text{where} \quad c = \bigcup_i \bigcap_j c_{i,j} \tag{3.2}$$

with $c_{i,j} \subseteq U$. ●

The idea behind joins of class intersections has already been discussed in the previous chapter on knowledge representation; now we use it to demonstrate the difference between the *structure* of representation space $\mathfrak{U}$ and the mere set of representable objects U. While all the classes $c_{i,j} \subseteq U$ are simply representation classes, the complex expression $\bigcup \bigcap c_{i,j} \in \mathfrak{U}$ requires a structure that allows us to operate on classes to yield a description of a concept representation.[2] Of course, when evaluating the complex expression c, its value also becomes a simple subset of U. Nevertheless, the difference between $\mathfrak{U}$ and U is important even though all the important processes of knowledge discovery take place in representation space. In representation space, concepts from $\mathfrak{D}$ are unknown and do not matter, and expressions are inherently evaluated. Hence, we also use the words "concept representation," "representation class," and "class," interchangeably when clear from context.

Example 3.9 The concept C = "white square" subsumes many different objects, some of which can be represented as □,⬜,◇. The representation class {□,⬜,◇} can be described by the concept {□,○,◊,⬜,◯,◇}∩({▪,■,□,⬜}∪{◆,◇,◆,◇}), that is, all squares or diamonds that are white. With $U = s$ as in Example 2.12, we have ρ("white square") = {□}. ●

At this point, a third property of suitable representation functions becomes clear. The first one was that we map different (or rather distinguishable) objects on different representations. The second feature of a good representation is that it preserves relationships between objects. And in the preceeding example we saw that classes of similar objects were defined by their common *properties*. As we shall see later,

[2] Of course, c is a class too – but readers familiar with logic will have noticed that the definition of a concept representation simply corresponds to the conjunctive normal form of a propositional logic formula with the propositional variables defined by the elementary categories.

there is no big difference in the latter two characteristics of a good representation – they are more or less interchangeable: We could also represent the truck by a symbol T and the motorcycle by a symbol M and then also represent the number of each object's wheels by a function that is defined by $w : \mathtt{T} \mapsto 18$ and $w : \mathtt{M} \mapsto 2$. Then, the fact that a truck has more wheels than a motorcycle is expressed by $w(\mathtt{T}) > w(\mathtt{M})$.

Now that we have different classes and we can define *sets of classes*. For example, the set $\{r, g, b\}$ with r, g, and b being classes of red, blue, and green objects, respectively, would be a classification of objects with respect to their colour.

Definition 3.10 — Classification. Classification

A *classification* $\mathfrak{c}$ of objects from a set $s \subseteq U$ is a family of k classes $c_i \subseteq s$:

$$\mathfrak{c} = \{c_0, c_1, \ldots, c_{k-1}\} \tag{3.3}$$

with $c_i \subseteq s$ and $\bigcup c_i = s$, $i \in \mathbf{k}$. ●

For each c_i, we can define $\chi(c_i) : s \to \mathbf{2}$, which, for each x, delivers $\mathbf{1}$ if and only if $x \in c_i$ (note that $\chi(c_i)$ is not total on U). Usually it is implicitly assumed that

$$s = U = \bigcup_{1 \le i \le k} c_i \quad \text{and} \quad c_i \cap c_j \neq \emptyset \longrightarrow c_i = c_j, \tag{3.4}$$

which makes all classes of a classification mutually exclusive and their respective characteristic functions total on U. Of course, concepts are not disjoint; quite often they overlap. Even if they did not overlap, disjointness would be hard to determine because concepts usually have rather vague boundaries (recall that concepts have meanings).

The disjointness assumption is very popular because a *classifier* then becomes a function:

Definition 3.11 — Classifier. Classifier

A *classifier* is a function $f_\mathfrak{c} : s \to \mathbf{k}$ such that

$$f_\mathfrak{c}(x) = i \in \mathbf{k} :\Longleftrightarrow x \in c_i \Longleftrightarrow \chi(c_i)(x) = 1. \tag{3.5}$$

In many cases we will consider binary classification problems with $\mathbf{k} = \mathbf{2}$. Then,

$$\mathfrak{c} = \{c, \overline{c}\}$$

and we abbreviate

$$f_c(x) \quad := \quad \chi(c)(x). \tag{3.6}$$

Simply speaking, a binary classifier is a function that implements a characteristic function of a representation class. ●

The problem is that we want to find a (*total*) function definition in representation space approximating an unknown classifier – but all we have are just a *few* object representations and their corresponding values under $\chi(c)(x)$.

Now that we have a rather clear language to talk about our domain and its elements and relations between them, we can reformulate our first working definition of machine learning into:

> **Concepts and learning classifiers**
>
> Concept learning means answering the questions
>
> What is the common property of a set of objects? What makes them different from all other objects? Which yet unknown concepts do the objects belong to?
>
> Learning a classifier means answering the questions
>
> Given several classification examples, what are the underlying rules that we need in order to correctly classify new and yet unseen cases? How can we find a function that approximates a perfect classifier?

To answer these questions and find a classifier, we

1. Represent the problem domain $\mathfrak{D}$ in representation space $\mathfrak{U}$ with the least possible loss through a representation function ρ
2. Try to describe all object representations $\rho(x_i)$ in terms of representation classes $c \subseteq U$
3. Hope we can find some representation concepts that have some proper meaning when interpreted with respect to $\mathfrak{D}$.

To satisfy the requirement of a "proper" meaning, our learning process should deliver a hypothesis for the classifier such that the following are true:

1. All *known* and most *unknown* objects $x_1, x_2, \ldots, x_m \in U$, to which we would attribute the property C, are represented by members of the concept representation.
2. For all non-C-ish objects y_i, their respective representations $\rho(y_i)$ do not fall into c.

Then, with some luck, the description of concept representations c in $\mathfrak{U}$ has a reasonable concept C' as a pre-image in $\mathfrak{D}$. Let us briefly summarise what we have learned so far:

> **The data mining process**
>
> Take a look at Figure 3.1. We build a model $\mathfrak{U}$ with a base set U for describing entities and relations of our domain $\mathfrak{D}$. Representation classes c_i are used to define concepts. Using characteristic functions χ_i on a subset of objects (s), we learn a hypothesis h that shall approximate some concept c (or, rather, its characteristic function). The big question is whether h actually is reasonable at all when interpreted as some concept C in $\mathfrak{D}$.

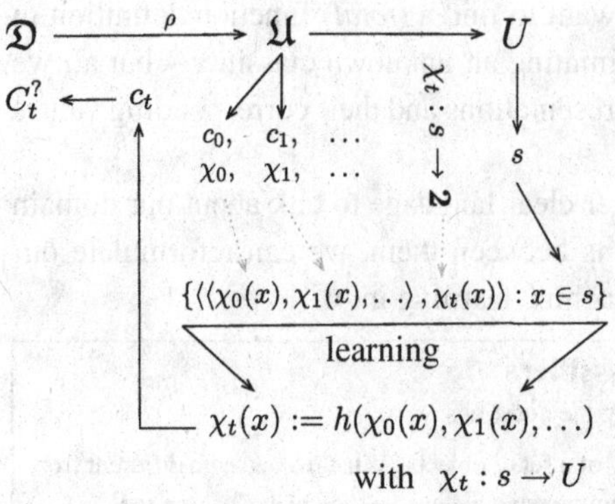

Fig. 3.1 Domain, universe, representation

Example 3.12 Let the domain be the world of our solar system and the concepts and names that we have for all the objects and phenomena that occur there. There are domain objects like Mars, Jupiter, Io and Pluto, Venus, Halley, and so on. There are concepts, too: *Planet*, *Morningstar*, *Moon*, and *Asteroid*.[3]

We now represent every single object of our solar system by the name of the object it is orbiting, the mean orbit radius (in astronomical units, the mean distance between the Sun and Earth), the time it takes for one rotation around the centre of the orbit (in days), and the mass of the object (in Earth masses). For the Sun, ρ delivers a representation as follows:

$$\langle \text{sun}, 0, 25, 333 \cdot 10^3 \rangle,$$

which means that it only rotates around itself in 25 days and it is 333,000 times heavier than the Earth. The Earth itself would be represented as $\langle \text{sun}, 1, 365, 1\rangle$. There are two concepts in $\mathfrak{D}$ that usually map onto the same representation:

$$\begin{aligned} \rho(\textit{Morningstar}) = \rho(\textit{Eveningstar}) &= \rho(\text{Venus}) \\ &= \langle \text{sun}, 0.7, 225, 0.8\rangle. \end{aligned}$$

So once we talk about Venus, we cannot determine whether we speak about the concept *Morningstar* or the *Eveningstar* (except we had extra knowledge about the current time of the day). To make things even more complicated, there is also another planet,

$$\rho(\text{Mercury}) = \langle \text{sun}, 0.05, 88, 0.8\rangle,$$

[3] Please note: The "Sun" is a domain object. It is represented as an object in our universe by the symbol "sun". Concepts are meaningful sets of domain objects, e.g., *Planet* and *Morningstar*. Such concepts are represented as classes of objects, i.e., c.

that can be seen both at dusk and dawn. So if we invent a new representation concept

$$\begin{aligned} c &:= \{\langle \text{sun}, 0.7, 225, 0.8\rangle, \langle \text{sun}, 0.05, 88, 0.8\rangle\} \\ &= \{\rho(\text{Mercury})\} \cup \{\rho(\text{Venus})\} \\ &\subseteq U, \end{aligned}$$

then we can interpret c as the domain concept C of all the *Planets OneCanSeeAtDuskOrDawn*.

Exercise 3.13 (◇) . The unknown concept *Planet* could be learned if we compare all the object representations of Mars, Jupiter, Pluto, and Earth and try to find a feature that discriminates this set from the set of Moon, Io, or Triton. How?

Exercise 3.14 (◆) Modify ρ such that each object's representation also includes some knowledge about its mean surface temperature. Then develop two different classifiers f_h and f_h' for the binary representation concept *MostlyHarmless* where the Earth is the only instance.

Usually, several representation processes are concatenated or intertwined without being noticed. But as we are used to explaining new observations in terms of our already existing model of the world, we sometimes fail to recognise something new as being new (and sometimes we do not even recognise it at all). Our tendency to put things into relation already makes us represent things in a way that makes them comparable (even if they are not). Very popular formal analogies to such processes are the application of discretisation and quantisation in measuring or interpreting data. The problem with forgetting about such *biases* is that they may lead to a situation in which a theoretical result is carelessly transferred back into the domain (this is called confirmation bias). Doing so is very tempting as we are seemingly able to say even more about more things.

But the need for learning often arises from the need for *abstraction* and *compression*, which is why a certain *loss* of detail is desirable. We will discover that deliberate suboptimality is *necessary* to also guarantee a certain degree of accuracy. Therefore, *learning* could be interpreted as *pruning* away as much irrelevant knowledge as possible to get to the essence of something.[4]

[4] In fact, the human being also first needs to learn how to ignore before he can learn more.

3.2 Changing the representation

It is very important to understand that the world we live in, our domain $\mathfrak{D}$, can be represented in many different ways:

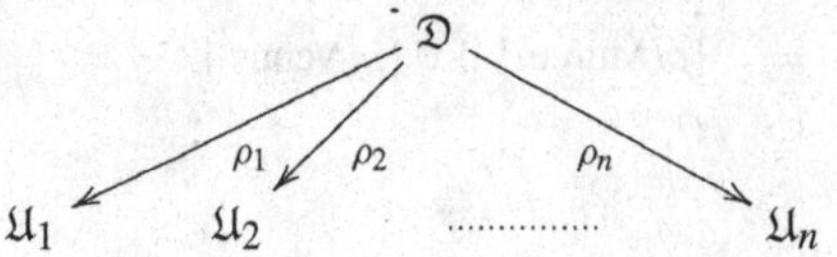

When working with information systems, the representation space $\mathfrak{U}$ is structured by a set **F** of features. Then ρ maps $\mathfrak{D}$ on a feature space on the base set U:

$$\rho : \mathfrak{D} \to \mathfrak{I} \quad \text{with} \quad \rho(x) = \langle f_0(x), f_1(x), \ldots, f_{n-1}(x) \rangle, \tag{3.7}$$

where $\mathfrak{I} = \langle U, \mathbf{F}, V_{\mathbf{F}} \rangle$. This is quite easy – but it is not easy to find a "good" representation. Whether a representation is good or not depends on its expressive power (are we able to formulate sufficiently precise hypotheses at all?), its computational complexity, and, last but not least, on its readability. Due to one or another problem with these requirements, it sometimes is necessary to change a representation system into a more suitable one.

Example 3.15 Some things appear to be indistinguishable, for example, sequences of numbers: Are the following two numbers equal?

646942834178564068362
175483462854068362649

Of course they are not. But are they equal in a sense that the numbers of occurrences of all the digits are the same? Without a lot of counting, the question cannot be answered easily. But if we change our point of view, the representation may change into

1223344445**6**6666788890
1223344445**5**6666788890

and it is easy to see that in the second sequence one 6 has changed into a 5.

Exercise 3.16 (◇) Compare the two representations from the previous example (random digit distribution versus sorted appearance) with respect to the computational complexity of tests for equality!

So what we need to do is to find an *appropriate* representation ρ' or a transform (shift) $\tau : \rho \mapsto \rho'$:[5]

5 Caution! Each arrow in this diagram may produce information loss.

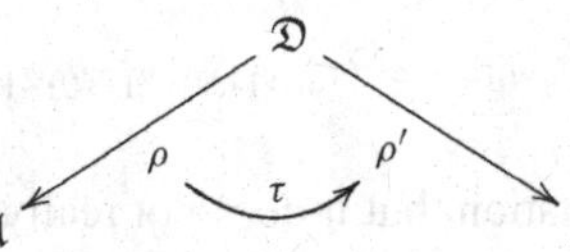

In Example 3.15, τ was simply the sorting function.

Representation transform

Definition 3.17 — Representation transform.
We call a mapping τ a *representation transform* (shift, change):

$$\vec{x} = \langle x_0, x_1, \ldots x_{n-1} \rangle \longmapsto \vec{\tau}(\vec{x}) = \langle \tau_0(\vec{x}), \tau_1(\vec{x}), \ldots, \tau_{N-1}(\vec{x}) \rangle. \tag{3.8}$$

If $N < n$, then τ is an operation that reduces dimensionality. A simple example could be *feature selection*, where $\tau(\mathbf{F}) \subset \mathbf{F}$. ●

Exercise 3.18 (◇) Find examples where $n < N$. Find examples where $N > n$ is appropriate. Where do $f_n, f_{n+1}, \ldots, f_{N-1}$ come from?

Exercise 3.19 (◈) Compare the random digit distribution (ρ) versus sorting and comparison ($\rho \circ \tau$) with respect to the computational complexity of tests for equality in Example 3.15.

> **Representation change**
> A change of representation is a mapping from one representation system into another to make the representation or the learning problem less complex.

Example 3.20 Suppose we want to learn the concept c of multiples of π, that is, $c = \{n\pi : n \in \mathbb{N}\} \subseteq \mathbb{R}$. It is not easy to describe the concept of π on the ray of real numbers if you try to mark every $n\pi$ without any other tool (such as dividers). But if we transform the representation on the ray $\mathbb{R}$ into $\tau : \mathbb{R} \to (\mathbb{R} \times \mathbb{R})$, things become easier if we find a suitable definition of τ. We choose

$$\tau : x \mapsto \langle x, \sin x \rangle.$$

Then, $x \in c \iff \sin x = 0 \iff \tau(\rho(x)) = \langle x, 0 \rangle$; that is, we found a rather simple characteristic function for the target concept: it is the set of all points where the curve intersects with the x-axis or the set of all tuples whose second argument is 0. ●

Another concrete example is the following description of Newton's law of gravity:

Example 3.21 Given two bodies of mass m_0 and m_1, Newton's law describes the gravitational force $f : \mathbb{R}^3 \to \mathbb{R}$ between them as

$$f(m_0, m_1, r) = c \frac{m_0 m_1}{r^2},$$

where r is the distance between two objects. If we were to represent objects in space, we would usually do so by defining their x, y, z-coordinates. Together with their masses m, we need eight real numbers to represent an object:

$$\rho : \mathfrak{D} \rightarrow \mathbb{R}^8 \text{ with } \vec{x} = \langle x_0, x_1, y_0, y_1, z_0, z_1, m_0, m_1 \rangle.$$

This is a nice representation, but it does not really help in applying the function f as we need to know the distance r between m_0 and m_1 rather than the objects' positions. Therefore, we change the representation by mapping the position data of m_0 and m_1 onto their Euclidean distance, that is, $\tau : \mathbb{R}^8 \rightarrow \mathbb{R}^3$ with

$$\tau(\vec{x}) = \left\langle \sqrt{\sum_{p \in \{x,y,z\}} (p_0 - p_1)^2}, m_0, m_1 \right\rangle \in \mathbb{R}^3.$$

If f were interpreted in the first representation (using the 8-tuples), we would have to evaluate the expression

$$f(x_0, x_1, y_0, y_1, z_0, z_1, m_0, m_1) = c \frac{m_0 m_1}{\sum_{p \in \{x,y,z\}} (p_0 - p_1)^2}.$$

By using τ (and the inverse) we can now shift the definition of f into the representation or outwards (leaving the work to the one who has to interpret the data).[6]

Exercise 3.22 (◊) Give a second transform $\tau' : \tau(\rho) \rightarrow \rho''$ where all the arithmetic operations we need are $+$ and $-$.

We now go into a bit of detail using an example that has become famous for two reasons: it was used as an argument against the omnipotence of perceptrons and it introduced the notion of *linear separability* into machine learning.

3.2.1 Linear separability

Consider the following linear equation $and : \mathbf{2} \times \mathbf{2} \rightarrow \{\mathbf{1}, \mathbf{-1}\}$, which describes the logical "and":

$$and(x, y) \quad = \quad \begin{cases} \mathbf{1}, & vx + wy + b > 0 \\ \mathbf{-1}, & vx + wy + b < 0. \end{cases} \tag{3.9}$$

Then we need to find b, v, and w such that $and(x, y) = \text{sgn}\,(vx + wy + b)$ satisfies Equation (3.9). The hypothesis space can be illustrated by truth tables:[7]

6 Another representation of Newton's law is given in Watterson (1996): "*Yakka foob mog. Grug pubbawup zink wattoom gazork. Chumble Špuzz.*"

7 The tables are mirrored so we can easily define linear functions.

y		
1	**0**	**1**
0	**0**	**0**
$\wedge$	**0**	**1** x

This problem can be described by three different representations: first as the problem of defining a separating plane, second by defining exclusive conjunction in terms of other operators, and, finally, by a quick look at Church's encoding of Boolean operators.

The logic of exclusive disjunction

To define *and* we choose as parameters $\langle v_{and}, w_{and}\rangle := \left\langle \frac{1}{2}, \frac{1}{2} \right\rangle$ and $b_{and} = -\frac{3}{4}$, which gives

$$and(x, y) \;=\; \operatorname{sgn}\left(\frac{1}{2}x + \frac{1}{2}y - \frac{3}{4}\right). \tag{3.10}$$

Using the same method, we define disjunction (OR) and negated conjunction (NAND):

$$or \;:\; \langle v_{or}, w_{or}\rangle := \left\langle \frac{1}{2}, \frac{1}{2} \right\rangle \text{ and } b_{or} = -\frac{1}{4} \tag{3.11}$$

$$nand \;:\; \langle v_{nand}, w_{nand}\rangle := \left\langle -\frac{1}{2}, -\frac{1}{2} \right\rangle \text{ and } b_{nand} = \frac{3}{4}. \tag{3.12}$$

But the exclusive disjunction $\dot\vee$ (XOR) cannot be expressed in terms of a linear function, because we need at least two cuts through the plane to separate all **0**s from all **1**s:

y		
1	**1**	**0**
0	**0**	**1**
$\dot\vee$	**0**	**1** x

To solve this problem logically, one transforms $\dot\vee$ as follows:

$$\begin{aligned} x \dot\vee y \;&\Longleftrightarrow\; (x \bar\wedge y) \wedge (x \vee y) \\ &\Longleftrightarrow\; \neg(x \wedge y) \wedge (x \vee y) \\ &\Longleftrightarrow\; (x \wedge \neg y) \vee (\neg x \wedge y). \end{aligned}$$

Logically, this is a simple trick – but if we understand logical operators as a special kind of function, it becomes clear why $\dot\vee$ poses a tricky problem: we model conjunction by the function *and* but we do not have a function-wise definition of negation $\neg$. Instead, we have to make do with *and*, *or*, and *nand* only. This requires a definition like

$$xor(x, y) \;:=\; and(nand(x, y), or(x, y)),$$

which shows that we then run into a problem with nested operators: we first evaluate the $\bar\wedge$-expression, then the $\vee$-expression, and then pass their results to the outermost $\wedge$-expression. This procedure requires some extra memory for storing the intermediate result.

A brief digression on λ-calculus

The Church encoding of Boolean operators in λ-calculus explains the problem in a beautifully concise way: λ-calculus requires us to reformulate such a definition with "inline" definitions of anonymous unary functions. For example, $f_\wedge(x, y)$ becomes a function that, upon receiving x, delivers a *new* function with a parameter y. Any variable is a λ-expression and a variable itself evaluates to its own value. We represent a Boolean variable by a pair $x = (t, f)$, where the first argument represents **1** and the second one **0**. The function $\mathbf{1} :\rightarrow \{t, f\}$ then can be defined as

$$\mathbf{1} \quad := \quad \lambda t.\, \lambda f.\, t = t; \tag{3.13}$$

that is, **1** is a function that always returns t (the first argument of the Boolean value tuple). Similarly, $\mathbf{0} := \lambda t.\, \lambda f. f = f$. We now define $\wedge$ and $\vee$ for two Boolean variables x and y by

$$\begin{aligned} \mathit{and} \quad &:= \quad \lambda x.\, \lambda y.\, xyx && (3.14)\\ \mathit{or} \quad &:= \quad \lambda x.\, \lambda y.\, xxy. && (3.15) \end{aligned}$$

Example 3.23 Let $x = \mathbf{1}$ and $y = \mathbf{0}$. Then

$$\begin{aligned} \mathit{and}(x, y) \quad &= \quad \lambda t.\, \lambda f.\, tft = \lambda t.\, \lambda f.\, (\lambda t.\, \lambda f.\, t)(\lambda t.\, \lambda f. f)(\lambda t.\, \lambda f.\, t)\\ &\quad \{\!\!\mid \text{Evaluate first } (\lambda t.\, \lambda f.\, t)\text{; resolve by Def. of } \mathbf{0} \mid\!\!\}\\ &= \quad \lambda t.\, \lambda f.\, (\lambda t.\, \lambda f. f) = \lambda t.\, \lambda f. f\\ &\quad \{\!\!\mid \text{Again, by Def. of } \mathbf{0} \mid\!\!\}\\ &= \quad f = \mathbf{0}. \end{aligned}$$

Exercise 3.24 (◇) For $x = \mathbf{1}$ and $y = \mathbf{0}$, compute $x \vee y$.

Now fun the begins. Let us consider negation. Negation means that if x, $\neg x$ is false; but if x is false, $\neg x$ is true. The simplest method for defining negation is

$$\mathit{not} \quad := \quad \lambda x.\, \lambda t.\, \lambda f.\, xft. \tag{3.16}$$

Example 3.25 Let $x = \mathbf{0}$. Then

$$\begin{aligned} \neg \quad &= \quad \lambda x.\, \lambda t.\, \lambda f.\, xft = \lambda t.\, \lambda f.\, \mathbf{0}ft\\ &\quad \{\!\!\mid \text{Defn. } \mathbf{0} \text{ and Evaluation} \mid\!\!\}\\ &= \quad \lambda t.\, \lambda f.\, (\lambda t.\, \lambda f. f)ft = \lambda t.\, \lambda f.\, t\\ &\quad \{\!\!\mid \text{Defn. } \mathbf{1} \mid\!\!\}\\ &= \quad t = \mathbf{1}. \end{aligned}$$

Exercise 3.26 (◇) Compute $\mathit{not}(\mathbf{1})$!

Exercise 3.27 (◊) Define a function *nand* that models $\bar{\wedge}$!

Now the trouble begins. The attentive reader will have noticed that we needed *three* variables to model the unary negation operator, while the binary operators $\wedge$ and $\vee$ needed only two. So what does it look like with $\dot{\vee}$?

$$\begin{aligned}
x \dot{\vee} y &\iff ((\neg(x \wedge y)) \wedge (x \vee y)), \text{ hence:}\\
xor &:= and((not(and(xy)))(or(xy)))\\
&= and((not \lambda x.\lambda y.xyx)(\lambda x.\lambda y.xxy))\\
&= and((\lambda n.\lambda x.\lambda y.(xyx)ft)(\lambda x.\lambda y.xxy))\\
&= \lambda e.(\lambda n.\lambda x.\lambda y.(xyx)ft)(xxy)(\lambda n.\lambda x.\lambda y.(xyx)ft)\\
&= \lambda e.\lambda n.\lambda x.\lambda y.((xyx)ft)(xxy)((xyx)ft).
\end{aligned}$$

Obviously, $\dot{\vee}$ requires *more* variables to be evaluated than $\wedge$ or $\vee$. In general, the number of variables required to express a rule, a function, or a procedure is a very good and reliable estimate of complexity.

Exercise 3.28 (◊) Compute the truth table for $\dot{\vee}$ using the definition above.

Computing a separating hyperplane

With this result in mind, we return to our functional view in representation space $\mathbf{2}^2$. Using the definitions from Equations (3.10) and (3.11) we derive

$$\begin{aligned}
xor(x, y) := \operatorname{sgn}\Bigg(&\frac{1}{2}\operatorname{sgn}\left(-\frac{1}{2}x - \frac{1}{2}y + \frac{3}{4}\right)\\
&+\frac{1}{2}\operatorname{sgn}\left(\frac{1}{2}x + \frac{1}{2}y - \frac{1}{4}\right) - \frac{3}{4}\Bigg).
\end{aligned} \tag{3.17}$$

We now shift our representation space $\mathfrak{U}$ by a transform $\tau : \mathbf{2}^2 \to \mathbf{2}^3$ with $\tau(f(x, y)) = f'(x, y, x\bar{\wedge}y))$ for all binary logical operators f. Then we can define

$$\begin{aligned}
and'(x, y, z) &:= nand(nand(x, y), nand(x, y))\\
or'(x, y, z) &:= nand(nand(x, x), nand(y, y))\\
xor'(x, y, z) &:= nand(nand(x, z), nand(y, z)).
\end{aligned}$$

To define conjunction and disjunction, we need two (x and y) variables, but for exclusive disjunction we need all three variables – once we represent our logic operators in $\mathbf{2}^3$, we do not need any additional variables to compute the result of $\dot{\vee}$, but we could not do it with only two variables in $\mathbf{2}^2$. Thus we have found a simple solution by shifting the problem into a more complex space. The idea behind a transform into higher dimensional spaces is nearly trivial: Figure 3.2 shows that the XOR problem cannot be solved with a single cut through a plane. If you want to realise

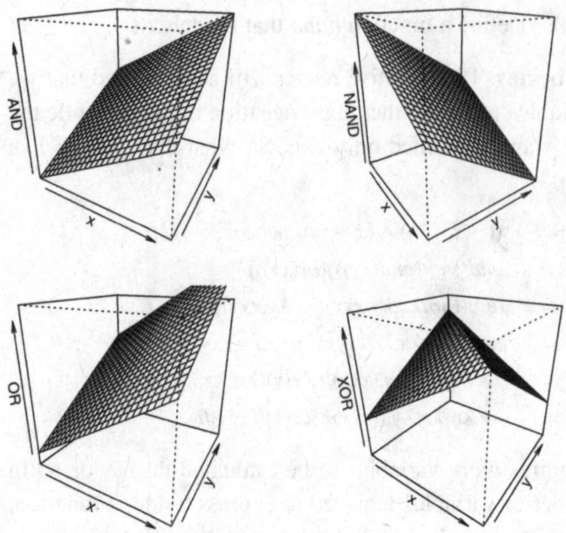

Fig. 3.2 Linear separability

two cuts by one slice, then you have to fold the paper sheet. But folding requires a third dimension.

Example 3.30 Another representation change is that of rule extraction from decision trees, which we will discuss in detail in Section 5.5. Imagine that a tree represents a conjunction of literals along each path leading to a conclusion in the leaf. Representing this tree as a set of implications allows us to weaken each single rule by dropping individual literals. Translating them back into trees, some edges could be missing, resulting in syntactically incorrect hypotheses.

Simplifying the framework (Figure 3.1)

In knowledge discovery we cannot try to derive new knowledge about objects from observations in the real world. All we can do is ground our enterprise on *representations of objects*. Because this is the case in *every* setting, we simply *identify* objects by their representations:

$$\langle \chi(c_0)(x), \chi(c_1)(x), \ldots \rangle \equiv_\rho x.$$

The set of objects (or rather their representation) we work on is a subset s of all the objects U we can talk about; that is, U is the base set of our representation space $\mathfrak{U}$. The examples we have are representations of observations and the information whether an object x belongs to an unknown concept is provided by a teacher signal:

$$\chi(c_t) =_\rho t.$$

The hypothesis h is a function extrapolating t on U.

From now on we will speak of objects $x \in s$, target functions $t : s \rightarrow \mathbf{2}$, and hypotheses $h : U \rightarrow \mathbf{2}$. Nevertheless, the reader should always keep in mind that one of our fundamental assumptions is that ρ is *appropriate*.

3.3 Samples

In general, we learn from a *sequence of observations of examples*.

Samples

A sample **s** is a set or sequence of observations or instances from which we shall learn. Usually, each example in a sample is *labelled*. If we understand this label as a target function t's value, then a sample is a set of support points. Hence, machine learning is about approximating t through these points.

A sequence can be transformed into a simple set when we assume an implicit assignment of the position of an object to the object itself (i.e., $[a, a] = \{\langle a, 1\rangle, \langle a, 2\rangle\}$). Additionally, all objects in **s** are examples *for* something. This means that every example is labelled with a so-called *teacher signal* that explains what this object is a proper example for:

Sample, **s**, t

Definition 3.31 — Sample, s, t.
A *(labelled) sample* **s** is a set of m objects of the universe together with one out of k different *labels* defined by a *teacher* t:

$$\mathbf{s} \subseteq U \times \mathbf{k} \tag{3.18}$$

$$\mathbf{s} := \{\langle x_0, t(x_0)\rangle, \langle x_1, t(x_1)\rangle, \ldots, \langle x_{m-1}, t(x_{m-1})\rangle\} \tag{3.19}$$

with $x_i \in U$, $i \in \mathbf{m}$ and $t : U \rightarrow \mathbf{k}$. We also refer to t as a *target function* and all elements of a sample as *examples*. ●

If $\mathrm{cod}(t) = \mathbf{2}$, we sometimes speak of the *positive* and *negative* samples (examples), written $\mathbf{s}^y := \{\langle x, y\rangle : \langle x, y\rangle \in \mathbf{s}\}$ for $y \in \mathbf{2}$.

But where do **s** and t come from? We consider t first. The aim in machine learning is to induce new concepts c. Therefore, we need a set of examples that belong to this yet unknown example. The target function t can be seen as the characteristic function of the unknown concept; but because it is unknown, we cannot define it as such. Actually, t is as unknown as c, but we will try to learn a hypothesis h that approximates t.

The sample itself is, as suggested by the name, *sampled* from the universe. It contains a subset of all objects and the choice is subject to a sampling function. But there is even more to it: it seems reasonable to assume an (unknown) distribution μ over $\mathfrak{D}$ that is preserved by ρ:[8]

[8] Note that "which is preserved by ρ" is a fundamental assumption.

Example 3.32 We are much more likely to observe birds that can fly than birds that cannot, especially if the sample is drawn from the rainforest. In Antarctica, things are quite different. ●

Therefore, we define a sample to be the result of a sampling function that picks elements from our domain with respect to their "probabilities".

Definition 3.33 — Sampling function. Sampling function

A *sampling function* S generates a sample as a set $\mathbf{s}$ of m elements $x \in U$ with a target label $t(x)$:

$$\mathbf{s} = S_\mu(m, t) = \{\langle x_0, t(x_0)\rangle, \langle x_1, t(x_1)\rangle, \ldots, \langle x_{m-1}, t(x_{m-1})\rangle\}. \quad (3.20)$$

Due to the nature of μ, $S_\mu(m, t)$ is not a function but rather a *procedure*: it draws an x m times from U with respect to μ with replacement. ●

Accordingly, for two samples delivered by the same sampling method we have

$$\mathbf{s}_1 \neq \mathbf{s}_2.$$

Now we can reformulate the assumption that up to now we only mentioned in footnote 8:

Definition 3.34 — Sampling assumption. Sampling assumption

Let there be n samples $\mathbf{s}_0, \ldots, \mathbf{s}_{n-1}$ generated by repeated and independent executions of $S_\mu(m, t)$. Then, for $i \in \mathbf{n}$,

$$\lim_{n \to \infty} \frac{|\{\mathbf{s}_i : \langle x, t(x)\rangle \in \mathbf{s}_i\}|}{n} = \phi(x),$$

where $\phi(x)$ denotes a normalised version of $\mu(\{x\})$ such that $\sum_{x \in U} \phi(x) = 1$. ●

The sampling assumption can be verbalised as follows:

> **Sampling assumption**
> When drawing samples of objects from a base set with respect to an underlying distribution, the probability that an object occurs in a sample is proportional to the "mass" of the object.

Accordingly, if we have enough (say at least m) observations, then the probability of making a certain observation about x corresponds to the frequency of occurrences of x in the samples.[9]

But if we do not have a teacher around who could give us a teaching signal t, we need to learn all by ourselves.

[9] Therefore, if m is big enough, then the approximate value for the probabilities does not change significantly for increasing k.

Learning

Definition 3.35 — Learning.
(Un-)supervised learning is about learning from a (un-)labelled sample. An unlabelled sample is a sample where $t(x) = ?$ (which is a constant symbol denoting that t is not defined for x). ●

Supervised learning means that we have some evidence for and against an unknown concept c in $\mathfrak{U}$ given by $t : U \to \mathbf{2}$ but we have no *intensional* description of t. Unsupervised learning means that we do not even have information about possible targets. Because there is no knowledge about t, the target function remains undefined. It is not even clear how we can choose a proper codomain for t because we do not have any information about the target concept either. In such a case we need to learn how to group objects together such that they form "meaningful" groups that might correspond to some concepts.

But even if we *have* a teacher, the teacher might give us incorrect information.

Example 3.36 Imagine a binary classification problem on $\mathfrak{D} = \{a, e, b, c\}$ and $\mathfrak{U} = \mathbf{2}$. Let the target concept be $vowel = \{a, e\}$. Now we apply ρ with $\rho(a) = \rho(b) = \mathbf{0}$ and $\rho(e) = \rho(c) = \mathbf{1}$. Let $t = \mathit{1}$. Then we have the representation of e and c labelled as vowels and the representation of a and b as consonants. ●

The problem behind (lossy) representation functions is that they generate two kinds of *noise* on our example sets.

Noise

Definition 3.37 — Noise.
A sample is called *noisy* if the teacher's label does not agree with the actual characteristic function of the sought-for concept. There are two possible reasons:

- *Representation noise* means that $x \in C \not\Longleftrightarrow \rho(x) \in c$.
- *Sample noise* means that there exist $\mathbf{s}, \mathbf{s}' := S_\mu(m, t)$ such that $\langle x, y \rangle \in \mathbf{s} \wedge \langle x, z \rangle \in \mathbf{s}' \wedge y \neq z$.[10]

●

Now that we have seen that there is a huge difference between the domain and our representation, we need to make a large simplification: from now on, we forget about the domain and target concepts. *All we have is the data* we are given. The data we have are just a *representation* of the domain, and so there might be a lot of information loss involved.

[10] The reasons for this are manifold. One possible source of noise is that t is not a function as assumed but rather a relation. An example are classifications whose classes are not pairwise disjoint.

We need to rely on the fact that $\mathfrak{U}$ is a sufficiently precise representation of $\mathfrak{D}$ and that $t : \mathfrak{U} \rightarrow \mathbf{2}$ is a sufficiently precise representation of t. Any results we achieve will be results modulo the underlying ρ. And any such result may be pretty "accurate" on $\mathfrak{U}$, but whether it is a reasonable hypothesis only (and entirely) depends on our interpretation of the result back into $\mathfrak{D}$.

Essential stipulations for learning

1. The concept we want to learn is representable.
2. The data we have appropriately represent the domain.
3. If a concept representation is meaningful on a sufficiently large subset of the data, it is true on all objects.

The last stipulation is commonly known as the *inductive assumption*. Finally, we assume that we can evaluate the quality of a hypothesis within $\mathfrak{U}$.

So far we have derived the notion of t from the characteristic function of a set of objects. Therefore, t was always a binary function $t : \mathfrak{U} \rightarrow \mathbf{2}$. There are many more paradigms for describing concepts, for example, fuzzy sets or complex concepts with more than just two possible values. In such cases, the codomain of t is a more complex set or even a structure. For binary learning tasks, $\text{cod}(t) = \mathbf{2}$; if the target concept discriminates k different values, then $\text{cod}(t) = \mathbf{k}$. A target function with fuzzy descriptions over $\mathbf{k}$ linguistic variables requires $\mathbb{R}^{\mathbf{k}}$ as a codomain. Since most learning problems are binary, or can be reduced to such problems, we usually assume $\text{cod}(t) = \mathbf{2}$ unless noted otherwise.

Now that we have defined what we are talking about and what the examples we are given look like, we can again reformulate our working definition of machine learning into a first description that we can safely call a "definition":

Definition 3.38 — Learning algorithm. Learning algorithm

A machine learning algorithm `Alg` receives a *sample* $\mathbf{s}$ of representations of objects of our domain and computes a *hypothesis* h. The goal is to approximate the unknown target function $t : U \rightarrow \text{cod}(t)$ by $h : U \rightarrow \text{cod}(t)$ using the teaching signal $\chi(c) : s \rightarrow \text{cod}(t)$:

$$\texttt{Alg}(\mathbf{s}) = h \approx t, \tag{3.21}$$

where $\mathbf{s} = S_{\mu}(m, t)$ and c is the unknown concept we want to learn. Note that $\chi(c)$ is a partial, extensionally defined function whereas h is a total function that approximates t on the entire base set of the representation space. ●

Machine learning is a search procedure for an approximation h of the representation of a target concept in a (possibly very large) hypothesis space. This space cannot be searched exhaustively, which is why the search requires heuristic guidance. Hence the solutions of the search process can be more or less accurate with respect to our representation of the target concept.

With `Alg` generating some h on $\mathfrak{U}$, we have gained a hypothesis on our representation space. What needs to be done is to *interpret* h on $\mathfrak{D}$. Since ρ is not necessarily injective, there might not be a clear definition of an interpretation function $\breve{\rho}$, and so it is not always clear how to interpret a hypothesis in the real world $\mathfrak{D}$.

Evaluation of h

Definition 3.39 — Evaluation of *h*.
Usually the interpretation step $\breve{\rho}$ is omitted. The hypothesis h is learned from data from U and it is evaluated within $\mathfrak{U}$. ●

This is a quite strong assumption, because it presupposes that our representation space suffices to describe everything we want to be able to describe. We shall come back to this when discussing *biases* in section 3.6.

3.4 Evaluation of hypotheses

Whatever we learn will be "correct" or "wrong". Similarly, a hypothesis $h = \texttt{Alg}(\mathbf{s})$ may or may not agree with t on the sample or any other subset of U. However, we can define some kind of relative correctness of h as follows.

Correctness of h

Definition 3.40 — Correctness of *h*.
We call h *$\langle s, f\rangle$-correct* if h agrees with f on s:

$$\forall x \in s : h(x) = f(x), \tag{3.22}$$

where s is an arbitrary subset of U. ●

Therefore, if `Alg` has learned h from $\mathbf{s}$, then h is $\langle \mathbf{s}, t\rangle$-correct if and only if h agrees with t on the sample. Because we can discriminate agreement from disagreement, we can determine *sets* of instances on which h agrees with t or not. The set of examples on which we find an agreement is the set of objects that are learned correctly; the set of objects on which t and h disagree is the *error set* of h.

> **Evaluation of hypotheses (I)**
> The *error set* of a hypothesis h is the subset of instances on which a test of h disagrees with t. The relative size of such an error set (together with a probability distribution) can be used to describe the magnitude of the error of h on a set.
>
> Because we usually do not know the exact probability distribution, and because we have only a subset of the entire domain for testing, we approximate the error by *precision* and *recall*, and their respective generalisations *accuracy* and *coverage*.

3.4.1 Error sets and error measures

Error set

Definition 3.41 — Error set.
The *error set* of h on s is the set of all objects in s for which h delivers a wrong prediction:

$$\text{errset}_s(h, t) \quad := \quad \{x \in s : h(x) \neq t(x)\}. \tag{3.23}$$

The size of the error set on s in relation to the size of s is a numerical measure of the error of h on s.

Error rate

Definition 3.42 — Error rate.
The *error rate* of h on s is defined as

$$\text{err}_s(h, t) \quad := \quad \frac{|\text{errset}(h, s)|}{|s|}. \tag{3.24}$$

So far we only have considered binary decisions: an object x can be classified correctly or incorrectly. But for more complex domains, misclassification may have a quantitative measure, too: for example, ■ is not so different from ■ than it is from ○. Orange is less different from red than blue. To define the quantitative measures of errors, we require a distance measure (which in the example of colour classification could be satisfied by different spatial representations of colours like the RGB or YUV models). A very simple idea is to use the numerical difference between possible values of t as such an error:

Example 3.43 Learning intervals on rays: imagine $t : \mathbb{R} \to \mathbf{3}$, where the target classes represent the intervals $C_0 = [\ldots, -5)$, $C_1 = [-5, 5]$, and $C_2 = (5, \ldots]$. It is clear that the observation 6 is a positive example for class **2**; that is, $t(6) = \mathbf{2}$. We compare two hypotheses: $h(6) = \mathbf{1}$ and $h'(6) = \mathbf{0}$. Because $t(6) = \mathbf{2}$ is closer to class **1**, the error of h should not be as large as the error of h'.

More formally, we define:

Weighted error

Definition 3.44 — Weighted error.
Let $s \subseteq U$ and $\text{dist}(x, y)$ be a distance function on $\text{cod}(t)$. Then, the *weighted error* of h on s with respect to t is

$$\text{error}_s(h,t) = \sum_{x \in s} \text{dist}(h(x), t(x)). \tag{3.25}$$

The definition of the metric dist depends on the structure of cod(t). Usually one defines

- For a continuous, numeric cod(t):
$$\text{dist}(h(x), t(x)) := (h(x) - t(x))^2. \tag{3.26}$$
- For cod(t) = $\mathbf{2}$,
$$\text{dist}(h(x), t(x)) := \begin{cases} \mathbf{0}, & h(x) = t(x) \\ \mathbf{1}, & \text{otherwise.} \end{cases} \tag{3.27}$$
- For nominal cod(t) = $\mathbf{k}$, one usually also chooses a simple binary distance measure.

The function $\text{error}_s(h,t)$ can be normalised by a factor $\frac{1}{|s|}$ assuming an independent identical distribution. ●

Exercise 3.45 (◇) Determine $\text{errset}_s(h, \chi(c))$, $\text{err}_s(h, \chi(c))$, and $\text{error}_t(h, \chi(c))$ for the example in Figure 3.3. Determine $\text{errset}_s(h,t)$, $\text{err}_s(h,t)$, and $\text{error}_s(h,t)$ for the example in Figure 3.3. What are the differences?

Exercise 3.46 (◇) Take a look at Figure 3.4 and compare it to Figure 3.3. Explain errors and noise.

Now the error measure has been parametrised in some way by the magnitude of the error – some misclassifications are worse than others. But there is a second issue in error measures: a single "large" error that happens only once in a million times is not as disturbing as a nearly constant small misclassification error. Accordingly, one should take into account the probability of the event that causes an error: since for the occurrence for $x \in s$ it usually holds that $\mu(\{x\}) \neq \frac{1}{|s|}$, we can define the *true error* as the dist-error with respect to μ:

Fig. 3.3 A hypothesis

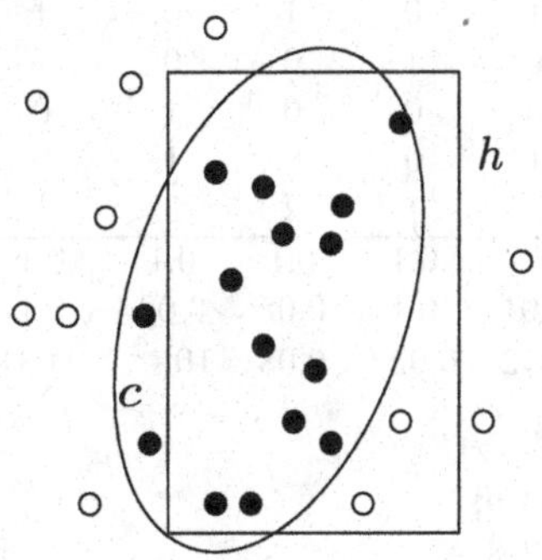

The elliptical area is the target concept c for which $\chi(c)x = \mathbf{1}$; the rectangle represents the hypothesis h.

The set of positive examples is the set of all black dots; the white dots denote an example in **s** with $t(x) = \mathbf{0}$.

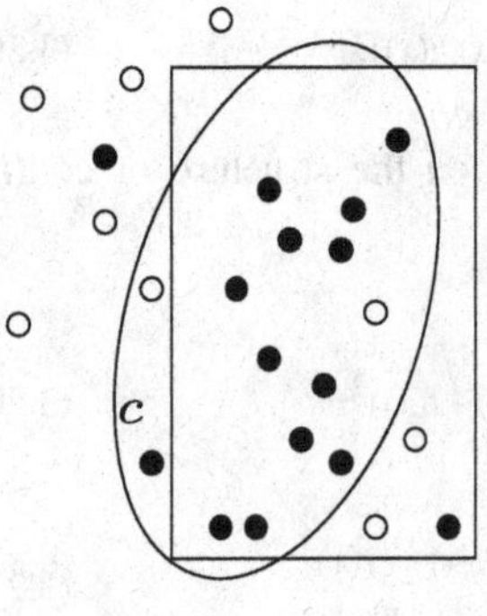

The elliptical area is the target concept c for which $\chi(c)x = \mathbf{1}$; the rectangle represents the hypothesis h.

The set of positive examples is the set of all black dots; the white dots denote an example in **s** with $t(x) = \mathbf{0}$.

Fig. 3.4 A hypothesis for a noisy sample

True error

Definition 3.47 — True error.
The *true error* of h on s with respect to t is

$$\begin{aligned} \mathrm{error}_s^{\mu}(h,t) &:= E_{\mu}\,(\mathrm{error}_s(h,t)) && (3.28)\\ &= \sum_{x\in s} (\mu(\{x\}) \cdot \mathrm{dist}(h(x), t(x)))\,, && (3.29)\end{aligned}$$

where E_{μ} denotes the expected value. With our inductive assumption we can approximate μ by ϕ. This results in

$$\mathrm{error}_s^{\mu}(h,t) \;:\approx\; \sum_{x\in s} (\phi(x) \cdot \mathrm{dist}(h(x), t(x)))\,. \qquad (3.30)$$

Because μ is unknown by definition, we usually use the error measure as defined in Equation (3.30). ●

Let us examine the differences between all those error measures by an example. Consider the set $s = \{0, 1, \ldots, 10\}$ and functions denoting prime numbers, even and odd numbers, multiples of 3 and 4 and the Fibonacci numbers:

$x \in s$	1	2	3	4	5	6	7	8	9	10
$prm(x)$	0	1	1	0	1	0	1	0	0	0
$evn(x)$	0	1	0	1	0	1	0	1	0	1
$odd(x)$	1	0	1	0	1	0	1	0	1	0
$f_3(x)$	0	0	1	0	0	1	0	0	1	0
$f_4(x)$	0	0	0	1	0	0	0	1	0	0
$fib(x)$	1	1	1	0	1	0	0	1	0	0
$g(x)$	3	2	1	2	2	1	2	2	1	2
$\mu_1(\{x\})$	0.1	0.1	0.1	0.1	0.1	0.1	0.1	0.1	0.1	0.1
$\mu_2(\{x\})$	0.1	0.2	0.25	0.1	0.01	0.1	0.05	0.08	0.1	0.01
$\mu_3(\{x\})$	0.015	0.05	0.1	0.07	0.12	0.028	0.08	10^{-9}	0.031	0.01

Then, for example,

$$\begin{aligned} \mathrm{errset}_s(odd, prm) &= \{1,2,9\}\\ \mathrm{errset}_s(odd, fib) &= \{2,7,8,9\}\\ \mathrm{errset}_s(prm, g) &= \{1,2,4,5,6,7,8,9,10\}.\end{aligned}$$

The corresponding error rates are

$$\mathrm{err}_s(odd, prm) = 0.3, \qquad \mathrm{err}_s(odd, fib) = 0.4, \qquad \mathrm{err}_s(prm, g) = 0.9,$$

which is quite easy to see because $m = 10$. The value of $\mathrm{error}_s(h,t)$ depends on dist, of course. We define dist_1 as in Equation (3.27) and dist_2 as in Equation (3.26). Then, the corresponding results are

dist_1			dist_2		
$\mathrm{error}_s(odd, prm))$	=	0.3	$\mathrm{error}_s(odd, prm))$	=	3.0
$\mathrm{error}_s(odd, fib))$	=	0.4	$\mathrm{error}_s(odd, fib))$	=	4.0
$\mathrm{error}_s(prm, g))$	=	0.9	$\mathrm{error}_s(prm, g))$	=	26

It is clear that with dist_1, the weighted error equals the error rate. It is also clear that by using dist_2 we obtain values proportional to dist_1 on binary learning problems: the term $(h(x) - t(x))^2$ delivers 0 if and only if $h(x) = t(x)$ and 1 if and only if $h(x) \neq t(x)$. Therefore, $\mathrm{error}_s(h,t)$ with dist_1 simply delivers $|\mathrm{errset}_s(h,t)|$. But what if we take into account different distributions on U? In that case,

dist	h	t	μ_2 $\mathrm{error}_s^{\mu}(h,t)$	μ_3 $\mathrm{error}_s^{\mu}(h,t)$
1	*odd*	*prm*	0.40	0.096
2	*odd*	*prm*	0.40	0.096
1	*odd*	*fib*	0.43	0.161
2	*odd*	*fib*	0.43	0.161
1	*prm*	*g*	0.75	0.404
2	*prm*	*g*	2.12	0.764

Exercise 3.48 (◇) When computing $\mathrm{err}_{\mu_1,\mathrm{dist}_2}(prm, s)$ with $t = g$, the result is 2.6, but all the other values remain unchanged. Explain!

Exercise 3.49 (◆) Write a program that computes all the error measures with arbitrary definitions of dist and μ and run it on the example data above.

> **Error measures**
> Given $\mathrm{s} = S_\mu(m,t)$ and `Alg`, the true error of h = `Alg(s)` can only be estimated. The reasons for this are that $s \subseteq U$, μ is unknown, t may be noisy, dist can be chosen arbitrarily, and ϕ is just an estimate of μ.

In knowledge discovery, it is *representation* and the definition of *error measures* that are no less important than the induction process itself.

3.4.2 Precision, accuracy, and others

Because μ is unknown, we need to *estimate* the error that h will produce on the data we shall feed into the system later on. But once we derive a hypothesis the following questions can help to draw a clearer picture of its error behaviour:

1. How many $x \in s$ that h predicts to be $h(x)$ actually have the same value $h(x)$ according to t? Simply speaking, it is the same as the number of predictions that are correct.
2. And how many $x \in s$ that are $t(x)$ according to t are also predicted to be $t(x)$ by h? This question addresses the coverage of our hypothesis; that is, it describes the number of objects that the hypothesis is able to classify.

These values are usually defined in terms of so-called *confusion matrices*. If the target function is a binary classifier, the corresponding confusion matrix is a 2 × 2-matrix. For the sake of readability, the rows and columns in this matrix are labelled which results in the following table:

	$t(x)$	
$h(x)$	0	1
0	h and t agree that $x \in c_0$	h and t disagree
1	h and t disagree	h and t agree that $x \in c_1$

If $|\text{cod}(t)| \geq 2$, we need to count the cases for each pair of predicted and actual target values. Then we obtain a $k \times k$-matrix.

Confusion matrix

Definition 3.50 — Confusion matrix.
A *confusion matrix* for a learning problem with k classes is defined as

	$t(x) =$				
$h(x) =$	0	1	$\cdots$	$k-1$	$\sum$
0	v_{00}	v_{10}	$\cdots$	$v_{(k-1)0}$	s_1
1	v_{01}	v_{11}	$\cdots$	$v_{(k-1)1}$	s_2
$\vdots$			$\ddots$		$\vdots$
$k-1$	$v_{0(k-1)}$	$v_{1(k-1)}$	$\cdots$	$v_{(k-1)(k-1)}$	s_{k-1}
$\sum$	t_0	t_1	$\cdots$	t_{k-1}	$m = \|s\|$

where

- v_{ij} is the number of objects for which t predicts class i and h predicts class j: $v_{ij} = |\{x \in \mathbf{s} : t(x) = c_i \wedge h(x) = c_j\}|$.
- s_j is the number of objects that h classifies as c_j: $s_j = |\{x \in \mathbf{s} : h(x) = c_j\}| = \sum_{l \in \mathbf{k}} v_{lj}$.
- t_i is the number of objects that t classifies as c_i: $t_i = |\{x \in \mathbf{s} : t(x) = c_i\}| = \sum_{l \in \mathbf{k}} v_{il}$.

We use the index i to denote the columns of the matrix (fixed target) and j to denote the rows (fixed hypotheses). ●

Exercise 3.51 (◊) Write the confusion matrices for the graphical example in Figure 3.3.

We introduced confusion matrices as a means of counting the cases in which our hypothesis agrees or disagrees with the teacher signal. The first measure one is usually interested in is "preciseness". Preciseness means not making a wrong prediction in the first place.[11]

- How many $x \in s$ that h predicts to be $h(x)$ actually are also $h(x)$ according to t?

This leads us to the definitions of *precision* and *accuracy*:

Precision

Definition 3.52 — Precision.
The *precision* of h is the fraction of the *correct* $h(x)$-predictions in relation to all $h(x)$-predictions on s. It is a "local" measure as it is defined in terms of a feature's value $j \in \operatorname{cod}(f)$:

$$\begin{aligned} \operatorname{prc}_s(h = j) &:= \frac{|\{x \in s : h(x) = t(x) = j\}|}{|\{x \in s : h(x) = j\}|} \\ &= \frac{v_{jj}}{\sum_{i \in \mathbf{k}} v_{ij}} = \frac{v_{jj}}{s_j}. \end{aligned} \tag{3.31}$$

●

The first line of the definition is based on error sets, whereas the last one uses the entries from a confusion matrix. The definition of precision can be visualised by confusion matrices: it is, for a given row j, the number in the j-th column (i.e., the entry on the diagonal) divided by the sum of all entries in the j-th row.

Accuracy

Definition 3.53 — Accuracy.
The *accuracy* of h is a generalisation of the precision measure. There exist several slightly different versions. However, they all share the property that *accuracy* shall describe the whole feature's precision. We define

$$\operatorname{accuracy}_s(h, t) := \frac{|\{x \in s : h(x) = t(x)\}|}{|s|} = \frac{\sum_{i \in \mathbf{k}} v_{ii}}{m}. \tag{3.32}$$

This value is simply the sum of the diagonal entries in the confusion matrix divided by the sum af all entries, m.

●

Because most classifier learning problems are binary (or are reduced to binary problems), we give a final example with much less notational effort: any 2×2–confusion matrix of a binary classification problem ($\mathfrak{c} = \{c, \overline{c}\}$) has the form

[11] Being overly precise often results in making too few predictions so as not to risk a wrong prediction.

$h(x)$	$t(x)$: c	$\overline{c}$
c	A	B
$\overline{c}$	C	D

Then

- $\text{prc}(h(x) = c) = \frac{A}{A+B}$ and $\text{prc}(h(x) = -c) = \frac{D}{C+D}$.
- $\text{accuracy}_s(h,t) = \frac{A+D}{A+B+C+D} = \frac{A+D}{m}$.

In relation to the concept c, A is the number of *true positive* answers of h, D is the number of *true negative* answers, and B and C are the *false positive* and *false negative* answers of h.

Example 3.54 Imagine the following confusion matrix:

$h(x)$	$t(x)$: c_0	c_1	c_2
c_0	5	1	2
c_1	2	4	2
c_2	0	1	7

The accuracy of h is $\text{accuracy}_s(h,t) = (5+4+7)/24 = \frac{2}{3}$. The hypothesis h delivers the most precise predictions on c_2, while c_1 is worst ($\frac{1}{2}$ precision).

Our second question was

- How many $x \in s$ that are $t(x)$ according to t are also predicted to be $t(x)$ by h?

The answer is given by measures called *recall* and *coverage*.

Definition 3.55 — Recall. Recall
The *recall* of h is the fraction of the correct $t(x)$-predictions of h in relation to all $t(x)$-predictions on s:

$$\begin{aligned} \text{rcl}_s(h=j) &:= \frac{|\{x \in s : h(x) = t(x) = j\}|}{|\{x \in s : t(x) = j\}|} \qquad (3.33) \\ &= \frac{v_{jj}}{\sum_{j \in \mathbf{k}} v_{ji}} = \frac{v_{jj}}{t_j}. \end{aligned}$$

It is the dual concept of precision. Therefore, it is simply the number in the j-th row of the j-th column divided by the sum of entries in the j-th column. One might say that coverage is to recall what accuracy is to precision. However, because accuracy is the "mass" of the diagonal line to the entire matrix weight, there is no rotation or translation that is sensible and/or delivers a meaningful result. Therefore, we define *coverage* as the average recall.

Coverage

Definition 3.56 — Coverage.
The *coverage* of h is defined as the average recall:

$$\begin{aligned}\mathrm{coverage}_s(h,t) &:= \frac{1}{k}\sum_{j\in\mathbf{k}} \mathrm{rcl}_s(h=j)\\ &= \frac{1}{k}\sum_{j\in\mathbf{k}} \frac{v_{jj}}{t_j}\\ &= \frac{1}{k}\sum_{j\in\mathbf{k}} \frac{|\{x\in s : t(x)=h(x)=j\}|}{|\{x\in s : t(x)=j\}|}. \end{aligned} \tag{3.34}$$

Exercise 3.57 (◇) Why don't we define

$$\mathrm{coverage}_s(h,t) := \frac{1}{m}\sum_{i\in\mathbf{k}} t_i \cdot \mathrm{rcl}_s(h(x)=c_i)\ ?$$

Again, we consider a 2 × 2–confusion matrix to illustrate a simplified notation:

	$t(x)$	
$h(x)$	c_0	c_1
c_0	A	B
c_1	C	D

Then we can define $\mathrm{rcl}_s(h=c_0) := \frac{A}{A+C}$ and $\mathrm{rcl}_s(h=c_1) := \frac{D}{B+D}$. $\mathrm{coverage}_s(h,t)$ is $\frac{1}{2}(\frac{A}{A+C}+\frac{B}{B+D})$.

Example 3.58 Imagine the following confusion matrix:

	$t(x)$		
$h(x)$	c_0	c_1	c_2
c_0	5	1	2
c_1	2	4	2
c_2	0	1	7

The recall values are $\frac{5}{7}\approx 0.71$, $\frac{4}{6}\approx 0.67$, and $\frac{7}{11}\approx 0.64$. Recall is best for class c_0 and worst for c_2. Therefore, $\mathrm{cov}_s(h) = \frac{1}{3}(\frac{5}{7}+\frac{4}{6}+\frac{7}{11})$, which is approximately 0.67.

As one can see from the last example, there is a loose relation between precision and recall on the one hand and between accuracy and coverage on the other: the more detailed our information, the greater the chance of being wrong on more general cases. As a rule of thumb, the higher the precision, the lower the recall, and vice versa. The same holds for accuracy and coverage. Accordingly, a more detailed evaluation takes into account *both* of them or a combination of them (known as

f-measure in information retrieval). There are many, many other methods of defining a reasonable measure of quality. A very conservative measure of quality based on prc could be

$$\text{accuracy}_s(h,t) = \min_{i \in \mathbf{k}} \text{prc}(h(x) = c_i), \tag{3.35}$$

such that the overall hypothesis quality is determined by the weakest local predictive preciseness (coverage can be defined analogously). Accordingly, using the maximum precision is a rather hypocritical estimate.

Furthermore, it is quite common to test the quality of h on a set s that is *disjoint* from the sample $\mathbf{s}$ that we used to learn h. Only then we can evaluate h's quality in terms of generalisation: is h's predictive competence on new evidence as good as it is on the cases `Alg` has already used to build h? Therefore, one usually splits a provided sample $\mathbf{s}$ into two disjoint subsets for learning and evaluating h.

Definition 3.59 — Sample splitting.

Sample splitting

We split $\mathbf{s}$ into two disjoint samples $\mathbf{s}_{\text{train}}$ and $\mathbf{s}_{\text{val}}$. Only the *training set* $\mathbf{s}_{\text{train}}$ is used for learning. We then evaluate `Alg`($\mathbf{s}_{\text{train}}$) against its predictions on objects from the *evaluation set* $\mathbf{s}_{\text{val}}$. Sometimes, `Alg` internally cuts off a *test sample* $\mathbf{s}_{\text{test}}$ from $\mathbf{s}_{\text{train}}$. ●

The difference between $\mathbf{s}_{\text{test}}$ and $\mathbf{s}_{\text{val}}$ is that the one is used for learning, in the sense that `Alg` itself uses it to refine h, whereas examples from $\mathbf{s}_{\text{val}}$ are never fed into `Alg`. Examples from $\mathbf{s}_{\text{val}}$ are exclusively used for estimating the quality of h on U. Accordingly, a proper forecast would be

$$\text{accuracy}_{\mathbf{s}_{\text{val}}}(\texttt{Alg}(\mathbf{s}_{\text{train}}), t) \quad \text{and} \quad \text{coverage}_{\mathbf{s}_{\text{val}}}(\texttt{Alg}(\mathbf{s}_{\text{train}}), t). \tag{3.36}$$

As we shall see later, $\text{accuracy}_{\mathbf{s}_{\text{train}}}(h,t) \geq \text{accuracy}_{\mathbf{s}_{\text{val}}}(h,t)$. But this is *good* news because we want h to perform well on U rather than on the already seen cases $s \subseteq u$ only.

At this point, a student usually claims he has understood accuracy and coverage measures. However, there are hundreds of different quality measures around – some have small "corrective" parameters, others are computed on specially chosen subsets of the training or validation set and so on. Therefore, one *always* has to be very, very careful when comparing the results of different evaluations – accuracy may not always be the same.

A detailed analysis of the predictive power of h always requires a decent amount of statistical evaluation including κ-analysis or ROC/AUC analysis. However, this is beyond the scope of this book. For the interested reader we recommend Venables and Ripley (2002).

Evaluation of hypotheses (II)
Learning takes place in representation space. Therefore, evaluation of h must be carried out in $\mathfrak{U}$ as well. It is impossible to determine the true error of some h, which is why we have to make do with error estimates and functions thereof (like accuracy, coverage, etc.). To increase the accuracy of these estimates one divides the given sample into two disjoint subsets: one for training and one for evaluation.

3.5 Learning

In the previous section we introduced many methods and measures for evaluating hypotheses delivered by a machine learning algorithm given a set of examples. But aren't the properties of hypotheses delivered by `Alg`, given **s**, properties of `Alg` itself (if we assume `Alg` to be deterministic)? The general idea leads to computational learning theory that is concerned with the question of learnability.

For now, we simply need to understand that from the input/output behaviour of an algorithm one can infer several properties. Therefore, we ask:

- Given some data (sample), what kind of hypotheses are generated?

The definitions of a hypothesis' correctness can be carried over to `Alg` as follows:

- `Alg` is called *s-correct* if it generates a $\langle t, s\rangle$-correct h:
$$h(x) = t(x), \forall \langle x, t(x)\rangle \in s \text{ and } \mathtt{Alg}(\mathbf{s}) = h.$$
- `Alg` is called *correct* if it is a $\langle t, U\rangle$-correct h.

But the big question is, are there correct `Alg` at all? Are there "nearly" correct `Alg`? In practical terms, this depends on the learning problem.[12] Nevertheless, without going into too much detail here, we *always assume that, given some example, we can gather at least a rough picture*. This is the fundamental *inductive hypothesis*, which is the only bias that is inseparably connected to any approach to machine learning:

Inductive hypothesis

Definition 3.60 — Inductive hypothesis.
If h approximates t sufficiently well on a sufficiently large sample **s**, it also will approximate t on U. ●

Based on the inductive hypothesis, machine learning algorithms try to deliver "good" hypotheses. In practice, this creates the problem of *how* one can find a good approximation h of target concept t. From the viewpoint of theory, it is the easy part: all one has to do is

[12] In general, answers to these questions or answers that include even an estimate of the degree of correctness are topics of learning theory again.

1. Collect all possible (representable) hypotheses.
2. Arrange (order) them in a nice way.
3. And then ... *search for the best*![13]

To get it done efficiently, some systematics might be helpful. But systematic searching requires a guided search, which in turn needs a guide. Then machine learning becomes a classical search problem: we need to find a good

1. Representation space that can be navigated.
2. Distance measure that helps us to compare alternatives and choose the most promising ones using suitable.
3. Heuristics.

This not overly impressive insight makes a nice working definition of machine learning but does not suffice to replace Definition 3.38. Therefore, we simply conclude:

> **Machine Learning as Search**
> Machine learning means searching for a suitable hypothesis in a hypothesis space.

3.6 Bias

When concerned with searching, one has to deal with two fundamental problems. First, if there are solutions, one ought be able to find at least one. Second, if there are solutions, one should be able to find the "best" one as quickly as possible. To do so, it is a good plan not to search in places where we know we cannot find a solution. It is also a good idea to look for solutions in places where we expect them to be. In other words:

- One would like to *restrict the search space*.
- One would like to define a *threshold*.
- One would like to determine *bounds* in a lattice.
- One needs a suitable *bias* in the search process.

By ordering the set of hypotheses, by restricting the search space or heuristically guiding the search thorough the space, we also predetermine whether we find a certain hypothesis at all and, if so, when we will find it. By ruling out impossible cases we *deliberately* introduce bias as *additional knowledge* for better control. But at the same time we restrict ourselves in representation, abstraction, and the degrees of freedom in the search for a solution. The more we reduce the expressiveness of the representation language (the complexity of the representation

[13] In real life, such a procedure would also require us to *hope* for the best.

space), the smaller the language becomes and, accordingly, the smaller the hypothesis space.

Example 3.61 Imagine we choose full predicate logic as the hypothesis space. By restricting ourselves to Horn logic we consider only a subset. A further language bias could be to restrict the number of different variables that may occur within a formula.

This kind of *language bias* is very effective, but it is very likely that by simplifying $\mathfrak{L}$ we can no longer represent a hypothesis that explains our learning target in $\mathfrak{D}$.

Exercise 3.62 (◊) Explain the danger of losing too much expressiveness by language bias. Build your arguments on the definitions of $\mathfrak{D}$, $\mathfrak{L}$, ρ, and τ.

Exercise 3.63 (◆) If you are familiar with Prolog, consider the following definition of the membership predicate:

$$member(X,[Y|Z]) \quad :- \quad X = Y$$
$$member(X,[Y|Z]) \quad :- \quad not(X = Y), member(X,Z).$$

Redefine the predicate with a minimal number of variable names. Why is such a definition more desirable?

Now that we have chosen an (already biased) representation space, we need to think about how to navigate through space to find a good solution as quickly as possible. By guiding the search we apply *search bias*: first of all, the general principle of searching determines the behaviour of `Alg` finding a solution. Imagine how a breadth-first search or a depth-first search would deliver different solutions on the same graph in hypothesis space. However, because the hypothesis space usually is very large, one needs to utilise some kind of intelligent, heuristic search rather than an exhaustive search. But then the accuracy of the heuristic measure also determines the search result.

Example 3.64 Consider the case where we want to learn intervals of real numbers on a ray. Then, choosing the step size by which we change the interval boundaries can be used as the search bias. The longer we try to adjust our interval boundaries it seems reasonable to reduce the step width to avoid some oscillation behaviour, which would be another good idea for search bias.

Example 3.65 In the domain of logic expressions, consider the following two observations: $p =$ *I have seen lots of black crows* and $q =$ *I have never seen a white crow*. Now, which of the following inductive generalisations appears most suitable to you: $h =$ *There are no white* *crows* or $h' \;\hat{=}$ *All crows are black*. The problem is that $p \mathrel{|\!\!\approx} q$ but $q \mathrel{|\!\!\not\approx} p$. And because entailment is not always easy to prove, one would opt for an easier measure (heuristic) to determine which hypothesis to choose.

Finally, a very important kind of bias is *validation* bias. In simple terms, validation bias defines the tolerance threshold that tells us when to stop searching and return the current best hypothesis as the solution. There are many such possible biases. A simple example is that h has to reach a certain degree of accuracy or coverage on a validation set. One could also define a validation bias in conjunction with search bias as follows.

Example 3.66 Consider a search routine that delivers as a solution the first local maximum of accuracy using a gradient descent search. Then it would be a reasonable idea to decrease the step size with decreasing gradient and, once the gradient has fallen below a predefined threshold, simply abort and return the current hypothesis.

Exercise 3.67 (◊) Explain search and validation biases using $\mathbf{s} = \{\langle x, t(x)\rangle : x = 1, 2, \ldots, n\}$, where t is the characteristic function of the subset of all prime numbers in $s = \{1, 2, \ldots, n\}$. Assume that $\mu(\{x\}) = \frac{1}{n}$ for all $x \in s$. (Hint: choose several and some very large n!)

Figure 3.5 shows an abstract learning algorithm that utilises all three different kinds of biases: in lines 3 and 6 validation bias is applied. Non-deterministic choice in line 5 usually is biased by search, and filtering and refinement, as in lines 7 and 9, require search and language biases.

```
01  H = init();
02  C = {};
03  WHILE (!(stop_crit(C, t, s_test))) DO;
04  {
05      h := choose(H); H := H − {h};
06      IF (good(h)) THEN
07        C := filter(C ∪ {h});
08      ELSE
09        H := H ∪ refine(h);
10      ENDIF
11  }
12  return(C)
```

Fig. 3.5 A biased learning algorithm

Bias

Bias is a crucial concept in machine learning. On the one hand, bias makes learning feasible. But on the other hand, any kind of bias (be it deliberate bias or unwanted bias such as noise) may cause accidental pruning of better results from the hypothesis space.

Talking about *deliberate* bias, we also need to discuss *unwanted* biases. The most important ones are *sampling* bias and *selection* bias.

Any subset of entities that is drawn from a larger set is a *biased sample* if the probability of the entities being drawn is not independently identically distributed. In other words, *any* sample is biased by μ. But then it would be good to have a *similar*, not independent identical, distribution in the sample. The only problem is that, because μ is unknown, we just can't prove whether our sample is biased in a way that corresponds to μ or whether ϕ is otherwise created.

Biased samples

Definition 3.68 — Biased samples.
A sample is biased if some members of the domain are more likely to be chosen in the sample than others. The larger the sample, the more the distribution ϕ on $\mathbf{s}$ approximates the distribution μ on $\mathfrak{D}$. It is clear that any $\mathbf{s} = S_{\mu}(m, t)$ is biased to a certain degree because we can only draw finitely many finite samples. ●

Selection bias is used to control sampling bias. If we know of a subset that preserves μ, then we choose just this subset as a sample. One famous example for "representative samples" is a small town in northern Germany that was a nearly *un*biased estimator for nationwide elections in Germany. Another important application of deliberate selection bias is learning by *boosting*.

Confirmation bias is more a cognitive bias than a phenomenon that is observed in learning machines. Therefore, it plays a central role during the representation process: knowledge engineers usually represent data in a way that is already structured with respect to an intended meaning or a supposed model. Since a knowledge engineer does not realise that his understanding of the data already determines what kind of unknown information can be extracted, confirmation bias is a very important, hidden unwanted bias. Also, learning algorithms are susceptible to confirmation bias in a very interesting way. If we consider a learning algorithm as in Figure 3.5, then it becomes obvious that the choice of some h in line 5 determines the behaviour of the algorithm in the next `WHILE`-loop. As a consequence, the sequence of examples and the sequence of hypotheses as generated play an important role in the selection of the next example and the choice of a next hypothesis.[14]

So far we have seen that there is always hidden noise and hidden bias – and the hypothesis space is still too big to be searched efficiently without any further deliberate bias. In fact, we shall discover that results can always be optimised or fine-tuned to a certain degree. But cutting-edge optimisation always tends to become optimisation with respect to a fixed set of observations, which will lead to *overfitting*. The reason for this is beautifully explained by the *no-free-lunch theorem*.

The no-free-lunch theorem

There Ain't No Such Thing As A Free Lunch, "TANSTAAFL"

[common idiom attributed to many different authors]

This means that in any system (society) no one can get anything for the price of nothing. Even if there is a happy hour, you (or somebody else) always pays for the loss (usually through higher regular prices). More formally, we define:

Theorem 3.69 *(No-Free-Lunch Theorem (NFLT)): All algorithms from a set of search algorithms looking for an optimal solution using a (local) cost function perform exactly equally well when averaged over all possible cost functions (i.e., problems) (Wolpert and Macready 1997).*

If we assume the average to be constant, a higher peak performance means a lower average performance, as shown in Figure 3.6. The solid-line graph is a hypothesis with very high accuracy in just a small region and a less-than-average accuracy everywhere else. The dotted line represents a simple hypothesis that on average performs equally well, but without areas of excellent expertise or complete failure. This puts us in a quite embarrassing position somewhere between pride and prejudice: when being biased, one seeks to optimise a concept that is based on prejudice. Once we have found such an "optimal" concept, it is announced with quite inappropriate pride. But one consequence of the NFLT is that *the better your peak performance on known cases, the worse your performance on unknown cases.*

14 There are many interesting results for so-called *online-learning* algorithms, which, for every single example they receive, deliver a hypothesis that then becomes refined with every additional example. For example, some artificial neural network architectures and learning algorithms are very error prone in such cases, which is why sample sequences are shuffled.

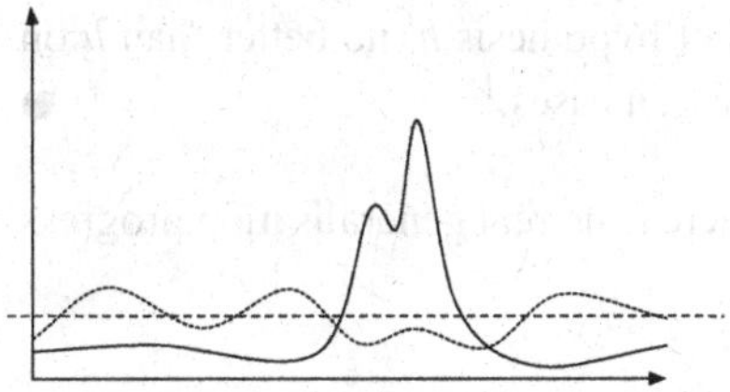

Fig. 3.6 The no-free-lunch theorem

Biases
There are numerous biases involved in learning. Many of them are wanted, and others are unwanted. The most important bias in learning is inductive bias. If we want to learn by examples, we *must* assume that from a small set of observations we can inductively conclude to all observable cases.

3.7 Overfitting

In terms of the no-free-lunch theorem, *overfitting* refers to the phenomenon of peak performance on training data $\mathbf{s}_{\text{train}}$ but a dramatic loss of accuracy on the remaining data in $\mathbf{s}_{\text{test}}$ or $\mathbf{s}_{\text{val}}$.

How do we come to find ourselves in such a situation? Usually we try to learn by adapting as precisely as possible. But learning to solve a specific task as accurately as possible does not necessarily help us improve our ability to solve a similar task. So again with the no-free-lunch theorem in mind, it appears more suitable to solve a few tasks somewhat better than solving one perfectly and being an utter failure on the remaining cases. Therefore:

Overfitting
To be able to learn, one should risk to perform locally suboptimally.

It is very nice if h agrees with t on s, but if h disagrees with t on all remaining $x \in U - s$, then h is *useless*. First, U usually is much larger than s, and, second, the reason we want to learn is to achieve knowledge from s that explains an entire concept we can then use to describe arbitrary sets of new objects! The phenomenon of generating some h that precisely explains $\mathbf{s}$ and is useless otherwise is known as *overfitting*. Since t is known on $\mathbf{s}$ only, it is hard to determine whether h is overfitted. Therefore, $\mathbf{s}$ is split into disjoint $\mathbf{s}_{\text{train}}$ and $\mathbf{s}_{\text{val}}$. Then:

Overfitting

Definition 3.70 — Overfitting.
A hypothesis h *overfits* t on s if there is another hypothesis h' such that

$$\begin{aligned} \text{error}^{\mu}_{\mathbf{s}_{\text{train}}}(h,t) &\leq \text{error}^{\mu}_{\mathbf{s}_{\text{train}}}(h',t) \\ \text{error}^{\mu}_{\mathbf{s}_{\text{val}}}(h,t) &> \text{error}^{\mu}_{\mathbf{s}_{\text{val}}}(h',t). \end{aligned}$$

We say h is overfit if there is another hypothesis h' no better than h on the training sample but better on unseen cases.[15] ●

In other words, if h is overfit, there is no real generalisation progress and hence no learning.

3.8 Summary

If you got this far, the rest of the book is a piece of cake.

This chapter gave an introductory overview into the scenario where knowledge discovery takes place. We are simply concerned with a set of data that is represented in an information system. Our task is to understand and formulate a general concept that is supported by a set of examples that may be labelled with some additional information from a teacher.

We have seen that machine learning can be related to compression, to function approximation, or to information theory. We have learned that there is a fundamental source of noise and information loss in the process of representation – but we also have seen that the change of representation may result in much easier learning problems and that some further deliberate bias may help us find better hypotheses even faster.

In the later chapters we will discover the exciting research discipline of machine learning with many different algorithms from different approaches. The differences between all those approaches can be described by the primary motivation behind machine learning:

- Scientific discovery vs. data mining

  Are we interested in the discovery of knowledge that has not yet been discovered? Then we will need a lot of background knowledge for describing our data in an appropriate representation space and we need to interpret the resulting hypothesis in our domain.

  Data mining is more focused on the facts: what kinds of patterns are there in the data and what can be inferred from these patterns?
- Symbolic vs. subsymbolic

  Most people believe we think rationally, and most people assume that rational thinking means logical thinking. Neither is true. However, we *like* to think that we think logically. And, undoubtedly, terminological representations have been proven to be a means for communicating knowledge. The implementation of learning algorithms takes place in a space of symbols with a certain semantics. On the other hand, the human brain, which we can safely

[15] The choice of the actual error measure is subject to our own deliberate validation bias.

assume to be the place where learning takes place, is neither a discrete nor a logical apparatus. Instead, if there is information at all, it is distributed.

- Engineering vs. cognition
  One can be interested in machine learning simply out of the need for handling, describing, or explaining huge sets of data. Then one takes the data and applies appropriate algorithms until the results appear reasonable. That would be an engineer's approach. A psychologist might be interested in a human's learning behaviour and, to test his theses he might want to simulate his model of human learning using a machine. If a machine then shows similar learning progress to a human, this might support the thesis that human learning works in a way similar to the method implemented.

But whatever the objectives are when concerned with machine learning, one always has to keep in mind that:

Knowledge discovery and machine learning

Knowledge discovery has nothing to do with knowledge – and machine learning has nothing to do with learning. All we can do is identify patterns and give them names or analyse their correlations. The process of knowledge discovery or machine learning has nothing to do with intelligence, either: knowledge is represented by symbols, and reasoning about knowledge is simulated by simple rules for symbol manipulation. Machine learning aims to find such rules for symbol manipulation, and therefore

Knowledge Discovery and Machine Learning are simple calculus.

If there is any intelligence or knowledge involved in these processes at all, then it is only in our representation of the problem and our interpretation of the outcome.

Chapter 4
Clustering

If we are given 5 pebbles, 3 marbles, 4 dice, and 2 keys, then we have 14 little objects of 4 different kinds. We also have 8 objects made of stone, 4 made of wood, and 2 made of metal. And we have 7 toy objects, 2 office tools, and 5 things we have collected during our last walk at the beach.

In the previous chapters, we saw that relations can be used to represent knowledge about sets of things. We also discovered that learning means to find a suitable set of relations with which we can describe or define concepts (see Definition 2.37). Now we describe a first approach to efficiently discover relational concept descriptions. Our starting point is an information system with a feature-based representation of the objects in our domain.

4.1 Concepts as sets of objects

Our working hypothesis is that knowledge is the ability to discriminate things and learning is knowledge acquisition. Therefore,

> Learning means to acquire the ability to discriminate different objects from each other.

There are, in general, two different methods to group similar objects together and distinguish them from other groups of entities:

- Building sets or classes of objects that we assume to share certain properties by grouping them into the same *cluster*
- Inducing a concept that serves as a description of a representation class in terms of properties of objects.

The problem is that the latter requires more knowledge about the world and the entities, whereas the former just requires some kind of "distance" measure that reflects the similarity of objects.

Exercise 4.1 (◇) Find several classifications of the set

{▲, ◇, △, ●, ◇, ◇, ○, □, ●, ■, ◆, ◇}

by clustering the elements. Do the same using intentional descriptions of the objects.

To form groups of similar objects or to classify a certain (new or unknown) object as a member of one of the classes, we must be able to

1. Tell which group of objects a new object belongs to
2. Form cluster sets based on some information concerning their similarities
3. Form clusters based on a teacher's information and conceptual descriptions.

The first action means to *classify* objects with respect to their similarities to other objects. It is assumed that there already exists a classification and that it can be expressed in terms of the similarity measure. The latter two actions are processes by which we learn to group objects to form elements of a classification, that is, classes. The first is done by unsupervised learning and the second by supervised learning. To illustrate the idea behind similarities and feature-based indiscernability, consider the following example.

Example 4.2 Imagine we have four objects {◇, ◆, ○, ●}. They are described by the features *shape* and *colour*, which yield an information system as follows:

	shape	*colour*
○	round	white
●	round	black
◇	polygon	white
◆	polygon	black

So ● is similar to ○, because they are both round, and ◇ is similar to ○, because they are both white. But ○ and ◆ have a maximum dissimilarity because they do not share any feature values. Geometrically, this yields the following diagram:

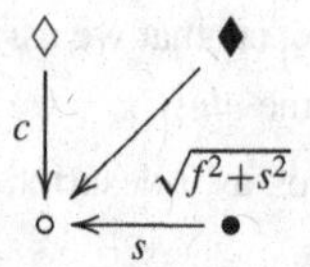

where the diagonal entries represent maximum dissimilarity if we assume the two features to create a Euclidean two-dimensional space (with *colour* creating the horizontal and *shape* defining the vertical dimension).

Exercise 4.3 (♦) You might be surprised that this simple question earns a black ◊: In the last example a fundamental assumption was not mentioned. Which one?

4.2 *k*-nearest neighbours

Nearest neighbour classification is a very simple and human thing to do: Imagine 90% of the people from a city block anywhere in the world speak, say, French. Someone else living in this neighbourhood will speak French with a very high probability, too. Conversely, if most of your neighbours live, for example, in Paris, then the probability that you live in Paris, too, is very high.

> ***k*-nearest neighbours**
> *k*-NN is simply a majority voting method for classification: Assign to an unknown entity the same label that most of the *k* most similar entities have.

Assume we arrange all objects of our domain in a space that is defined by the features we use to describe our entities. There can be two, three, or many more such dimensions and they can be discrete or continuous. Then, we add knowledge concerning the target class of each object by assigning it a corresponding label. As a result, we will receive a more or less coherent distribution of target labels in this space. If we now encounter a new instance, we simply put it on its proper place in this space and assign it the most common target class label among the *k*-nearest instances.

To classify an object using information from its neighbourhood, we simply assign to it the class label most of the *k*-nearest neighbours share. Let $U = \mathbb{R}^n$, that is, $|\mathbf{F}| = n$. Then, every $\vec{x} \in U$ has the form

$$\vec{x} = \langle f_0(x), f_1(x), \ldots, f_{n-1}(x) \rangle.$$

The Euclidean distance between two objects $\vec{x}$ and $\vec{y}$ is

$$\mathrm{dist}(\vec{x}, \vec{y}) = \sqrt{\sum_{i \in \mathbf{n}} (f_i(x) - f_i(y))^2}. \tag{4.1}$$

Given an information system $\mathfrak{I} = \langle s, \mathbf{F} \cup \{t\}, V_{\mathbf{F}} \cup \{\mathbf{k}\} \rangle$, the classification for an unknown object $x \in U \supset s$ works as follows. First, using $\mathbf{F}$, x is represented as $\vec{x} \in U$. The target function $t : s \to \mathbf{k}$ is a classifier for a target classification $\mathfrak{c}$. But because $x \notin s$, $t(x) = ?$. To answer the question, we construct a hypothesis as follows. First we collect a set of $\vec{y} \in s$:

$$NN_l(\vec{x}) := \{\vec{y} \in s : \text{dist}(\vec{x}, \vec{y}) \leq r\}\,, \tag{4.2}$$

where r is the smallest value such that NN_l contains exactly l elements.[1] The k-nearest neighbour classifier then predicts that x belongs to the same class that most of the l neighbours belong to. In other words, x has the "most common value" among its closest l neighbours. This concept is important enough to deserve a definition on its own.

Most common value

Definition 4.4 — Most common value.
Let s be a set and f a total function. We define the *most common value* of f on a set s as the value $c \in \overrightarrow{f}$ with the largest preimage $\overleftarrow{f}c$:

$$\text{mcv}_f(s) \quad := \quad \arg_{f(x)} \max \left\{ |[x]_f| : x \in s \right\}. \tag{4.3}$$

●

The most common value can be defined in terms of relational calculus as well: $\text{mvc}_f(s)$ is the most frequent entry in the kernel matrix for the equivalence relation induced by f: $\mathbb{K}(R_f)$. Formally,

$$[x]_{R_f}\overrightarrow{f} = f(y) \quad \text{for} \quad |[x]_{R_f}| \geq |[x]_{R_f}|.$$

Now that we have a proper definition of most common values (or "majority votes"), we can happily carry on with a satisfying definition of a k-nearest neighbour hypothesis.

Nearest neighbour classification

Definition 4.5 — Nearest neighbour classification.
Using the most common value, we define

$$h_{\mathfrak{c}}^{NN_k}(x) \quad := \quad \text{mcv}_t(NN_k(x))). \tag{4.4}$$

●

As already mentioned, this is a simple voting approach: x is assigned the value that most eligible voters have where eligibility is determined by a voter's distance to x. Figure 4.1 shows a $k = 12$ case where the radius around the unknown object in the centre is just the right size for the sphere to cover 12 cases in space. In this sphere, most objects are white (7), which is why we would assign *white* as the class label to $\vec{x}$ as well. Accordingly, the k-nearest neighbour algorithm can be defined as follows:

[1] We assume that k from k-NN has the value l to avoid confusion with the number $k = |\mathbf{k}|$ of classes in $\mathfrak{c}$.

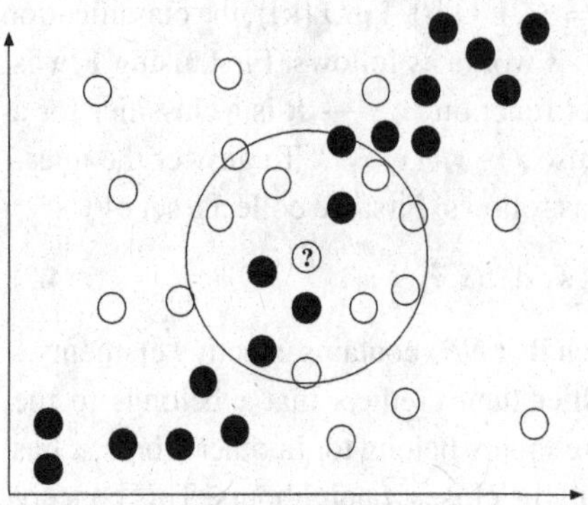

Fig. 4.1 *k*-nearest neighbours

Nearest neighbour algorithm

Definition 4.6 — Nearest neighbour algorithm.
The following procedure predicts $t(\vec{x}) \in \mathbf{k}$ for some $\vec{x} \in U$:

$kNN := \emptyset;\ r = 0;\ t_0 = t_1 = \cdots = t_{k-1} = 0;$
`WHILE` $(|kNN| < k)$ `DO`
{
  $r := r + \varepsilon;$
  $kNN := \{\vec{y} : \text{dist}(\vec{x}, \vec{y}) \leq r\}$
};
`return` $(\text{mcv}_t(kNN))$

where ε is the step width with which we increase the radius of the sphere. ●

It is important to understand that this classification is simply due to the number of black and white dots in the sphere, but not to the location of $\vec{x}$ in relation to all other dots – it is a pure coincidence that $\vec{x}$ appears to belong to a diagonal "milky way" of black dot entities in Figure 4.1.

Taking into account the spatial distribution of objects in each class, we will find a centre of gravity for each class that also represents the "average" or prototype representative of this cluster. This is depicted in Figure 4.2. The diamonds represent the centre of the classes of dots according to colour. Note that these points do not have to exist as actual data points but only represent the clusters that are formed by the objects. For an unclassified object $\vec{x}$ (labelled with a question mark) we then predict its class by the class of the nearest centroid – in this case the class of light grey objects.

Exercise 4.7 (◇) Determine $h_{\mathfrak{c}}^{NN_{17}}$(?).

Once we have a spatial representation of objects described by an information system, there are many different ways to model different metrics

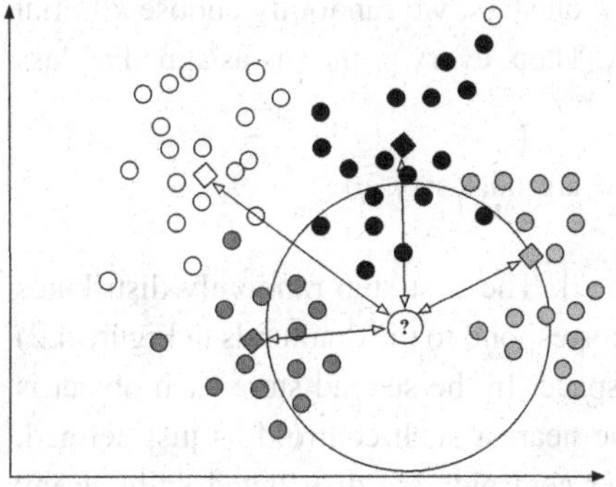

Fig. 4.2 Clusters and cluster centres

or to define different methods for classifiers, all of which focus on different aspects in classification. While *k*-nearest neighbours is rather a majority voting approach, a distance measure refers to prototypes of clusters. Classifying an unknown object by computing its distance from or degree of membership to certain clusters or cluster centroids requires us to have

1. an extensional cluster description and/or
2. an intensional cluster description with boundaries and/or centre and radius information.

Classification itself is not the main issue in machine learning; machine learning is rather concerned with the problem of *finding* the classes.

4.3 *k*-means clustering

Trying to learn clusters in an extensional distance-measure setting again offers several general methods. The two most important ones are to generate clusters on a set of data where we are given the number of clusters we want to obtain. The second clustering method divides the data set into clusters until the objects grouped together have a minimum mean distance but a maximum mean distance to all other groups.

We first discuss clustering with a fixed number of target clusters.

> ***k*-means clustering**
> The idea behind *k*-means clustering is to randomly define *k* cluster centroids. Then, every object in our domain is assigned the cluster id of the closest cluster centroid. The actual dynamic means clustering now repeatedly recomputes the centre of each cluster. Since the centre "moves", it is quite likely the cluster itself moves, too. The bigger the step, the more likely some entities will be assigned different cluster ids in the next step – most likely those from boundary regions. If the centroids do not move any further, we are done.

If we want to discriminate k clusters, we randomly choose k initial cluster centroids $\vec{c}_i \in \mathbb{R}^n$, $i \in \mathbf{k}$. Then, every point $\vec{x}$ is assigned a class label i where

$$h(\vec{x}) = i := \arg\min_{i \in \mathbf{k}} \text{dist}\,(\vec{x}, \vec{c}_i)$$

such that $c_i := \{x \in U : h(\vec{x}) = i\}$. The first step randomly distributes some cluster centroids (which correspond to the diamonds in Figure 4.2) over the entire representation space. In the second step, each object is assigned the target value of the nearest such centroid as just defined. In most cases, the initial cluster centroids are distributed without any correspondence to actual clouds in the data distribution of the representation space. To make the cluster centroids move to where the actual data clouds are, we repeatedly redefine class centroids by

$$\vec{c}_i := \frac{1}{|c_i|} \sum_{x \in c_i} \vec{x}$$

until the classification is "good enough." Every redefinition step causes all the centroids to move towards the centre of the sets of points that were classified as objects of the corresponding class in the previous step. But because the set of objects that belong to this centre is redefined in each iteration too, the centre can move across the whole set. This yields an algorithm called *k-means clustering*.

k-means clustering

Definition 4.8 — k-means clustering.
The following procedure generates k clusters on a set of multidimensional data $U \subseteq \mathbb{R}^n$:

```
FOREACH (i ∈ k) DO { c⃗_i := randomelement(ℝ^n); c_i := ∅; }
WHILE (1) DO
{  FOREACH (x⃗ ∈ U) DO h(x⃗) := arg min_{i∈k} dist(x⃗, c⃗_i);
   FOREACH i ∈ k DO
   {  c_i := {x⃗ ∈ U : h(x⃗) = i};
      c⃗_i := 1/n · Σ_{x⃗∈c_i} x⃗;
   }
}
```

with scalar multiplication · and componentwise addition. ●

A closer look reveals that this method depends on the initial distribution of centroids.

Exercise 4.9 (◊) Discuss the k-means clustering algorithm on the following example:

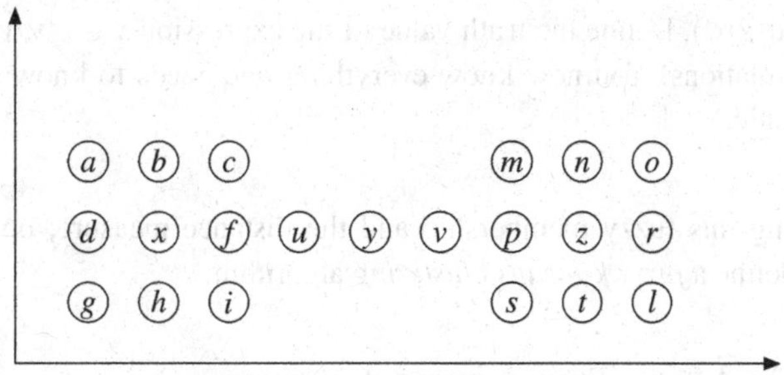

Consider $k = 2$ with u and v or x and u being initial centroids. Consider $k = 3$ with x, y, and z or u, y, and v being initial centroids. Consider $k = 2$ and $k = 3$ with initial centroids u, v, and u, v, z, where point y is absent.

Exercise 4.10 (♦) Write a program that performs *k*-means clustering on *n*-dimensional data.

The problem with membership is that regions are not always defined by crisp boundaries. Just as we consider distances in space here and a centroid as a prototype of concept, some things more or less belong to a class or a concept. Similarly, an object that is close to the centre of a cluster appears to be more like the prototypical element of the cluster than one object in the boundary region. As soon as boundaries are blurred, there is some kind of *fuzzification* involved. The idea is simple. Let $\tilde{f}(x) = \langle \mathrm{dist}(x, c_0), \mathrm{dist}(x, c_1), \ldots, \mathrm{dist}(x, c_{m-1}) \rangle$. So, instead of assigning x a single value $f(x)$, it is assigned a vector of distances to each of the values' representative centroids. If all the vectors are normalised such that the sum of their arguments becomes 1, then each argument expresses the probability that x takes value v_i.

Probabilistic (fuzzy) classification

Definition 4.11 — Probabilistic (fuzzy) classification.
Let $\mathfrak{c} = \{c_0, c_1, \ldots, c_{k-1}\}$ be a classification. We define a *fuzzy classification* by assigning to each object a vector of k probability values each of which describes x's degree of membership to the according class:

$$\begin{aligned} \tilde{\chi}(c_i) &: U \to [0,1] \\ \tilde{\chi}(c_i)(x) &:= \phi(\{x\} \cap c_i) := n \cdot \mathrm{dist}(\vec{x}, \vec{c}_i), \end{aligned} \tag{4.5}$$

where n is a normalisation factor such that $\sum_{i \in \mathbf{k}} \mathrm{dist}(\vec{x}, \vec{c}_i) = 1$. ●

Exercise 4.12 (◇) Let there be a fuzzy classification $\mathfrak{c}$ with a fuzzy membership function $\tilde{\chi}(\mathfrak{c})$. Define a method for *defuzzification* that takes $\tilde{\chi}(\mathfrak{c})$ and returns k characteristic functions for each class in $\mathfrak{c}$.

Exercise 4.13 (◈) Let there be two binary fuzzy classifications $\mathfrak{c} = \{c, \overline{c}\}$ and $\mathfrak{c}' = \{c', \overline{c}'\}$. Give a definition for $\chi(c \cap c')(x)$ in terms of

$\tilde{\chi}(c)$ and $\tilde{\chi}(c')$. Define the truth value of the expression $x \in c \vee x \in \overline{c}'$. Congratulations! You now know everything one needs to know about fuzzy logic.

Using this fuzzy membership and the distance measure, one can easily define a *fuzzy k-means clustering* algorithm:

Fuzzy *k*-means clustering

Definition 4.14 — Fuzzy *k*-means clustering.
The following procedure generates k fuzzy clusters on a set $U = \mathbb{R}^n$ of data:

$\texttt{FOREACH}\ (i \in \mathbf{k})\ \texttt{DO}\ \{\ \vec{c}_i := \texttt{randomelement}(\mathbb{R}^n); c_i := \emptyset\ \}$
$\texttt{WHILE}\ (\mathbf{1})\ \texttt{DO}$
$\{\quad \texttt{FOREACH}\ (\vec{x} \in U)\ \texttt{DO}$
$\quad\quad \{\ \vec{c}(\vec{x}) := \langle \mathrm{dist}(\vec{x}, \vec{c}_0), \mathrm{dist}(\vec{x}, \vec{c}_1), \ldots, \mathrm{dist}(\vec{x}, \vec{c}_{k-1}) \rangle;$
$\quad\quad\quad h(\vec{x}) := \arg\min_{i \in \mathbf{k}} \mathrm{dist}(\vec{x}, \vec{c}_i);$
$\quad\quad \};$
$\quad\quad \texttt{FOREACH}\ i \in \mathbf{k}\ \texttt{DO}$
$\quad\quad \{\ c_i := \{\vec{x} \in \mathbb{R}^n : c(\vec{x}) = i\};$
$\quad\quad\quad \vec{c}_i := (\sum_{\vec{x} \in c_i} (\mathrm{dist}(\vec{x}, \vec{c}_i) \cdot \vec{x})) / (\sum_{\vec{x} \in c_i} \mathrm{dist}(\vec{x}, \vec{c}_i));$
$\quad\quad \}$
$\}$

The only difference between fuzzy and non-fuzzy clustering is that with fuzzy clustering the centroids do not move towards the centre of all objects but towards the average of all distance vectors. ●

There are hundreds of different improvements on these base algorithms. First, the validation bias (i.e., the stopping criterion; in our case **1**) can be defined in relation to other (dynamic) parameters, that is, maximum intra-cluster distances. One can also introduce different distance measures like quadratic functions and other non-Euclidean measures. It is also possible to have different dimensions of the vectors weighted differently. MacKay (2003) discusses several more advances in clustering and many other probabilistic approaches; Hastie et al. (2001) deal with advanced issues. But with increasing demands of machine learning towards the induction of conceptual or "semantic" hypotheses, one wants to go a step beyond, say, to "descriptive" clustering. For example, it appears that if a human begins to cluster observations, he does so by grouping similar objects into a few clusters and then recursively clusters each group with respect to an increased amount of detail in (dis-)similarity. At a certain (rather early) level, dogs and cats belong to the same cluster of pets. Only with more detailed knowledge can one discriminate cats from dogs – and generalise cats and dogs to carnivore pets (as opposed to hamsters).

4.4 Incremental concept formation

In the last section we learned how to classify a new object into a given classification of clusters in space by using a Euclidean distance measure as a measure of similarity. In the next step we discussed two algorithms to *discover* a classification based on unsupervised clustering of multidimensional data. If we now understand multidimensional data points as entries in an information system, the task ahead is *unsupervised learning* of *concepts* from examples that are described by an information system. Just to recall the difference between classes and concepts, concepts in U are *sets*. Therefore they are classes as well. But the classes originate from classifications, which in turn correspond to *elementary categories*. They are sets of things that share a certain property. A *concept* is a *description* of properties in terms of elementary categories (building *basic categories*): being a "white square" means to be an element of the set of white things *and* of the set of squares.

Again, our goal is to group *similar* projects into one class, but this time by generating hierarchies of concepts. Rhomboids are a special kind of tetragon, but squares are even more special. And they are all different than triangles, but even more different than circles. The relationships between geometric figures is shown in Figure 4.3.

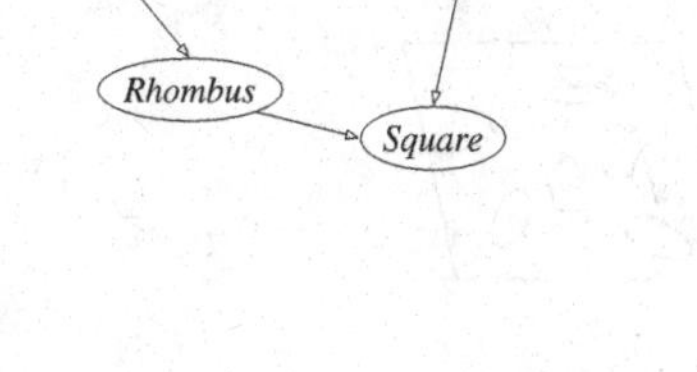

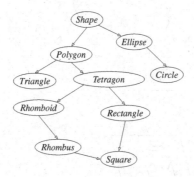

Fig. 4.3 A concept hierarchy of geometric shapes

Incremental concept formation

In contrast to classification with given classes or clustering given a fixed number of target classes, concept formation seeks to build hierarchies of concepts that reflect partitions of objects at different levels of granularity. We can clearly discriminate parrots from robins and dogs from cats – but together they form the concepts of birds and mammals.

Incremental concept formation seeks to find a hierarchy of such concepts such that (1) the similarity of all objects in a class is maximised, (2) the dissimilarity of all concepts is maximised, and (3) the conceptual structure is as simple as can be.

The process of incremental (top-down refinement) clustering is depicted in Figure 4.4: the basic classes correspond to the smallest clusters on the first level of abstraction. Here different objects of the same kind are grouped together: *Triangles*, *Rhombuses*, *Rectangles*, and *Circles*. On the second level, the cluster of *Tetragons* is made up of *Rhomboids* and *Rectangles*, while *Circles* are generalised to *Ellipses*. On third level, *Triangles* and *Tetragons* form *Polygons*, and all together they finally form the concept of *Shapes*.

But the human cognitive apparatus does not really work in one direction only. When learning concepts, we simultaneously learn by

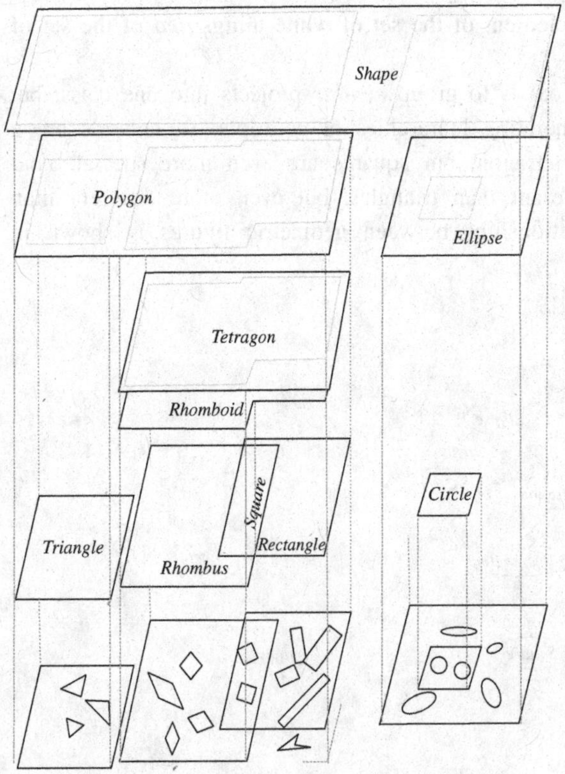

Fig. 4.4 Hierarchical incremental clustering

abstraction (bottom-up, generalisation, unifying) but also by differentiation (top-down, specialising, discriminating). So, for example, the concept *Squares* can be defined as the intersection of *Rectangles* and *Rhombuses*. The point to start with in hierarchical clustering actually is "somewhere in the middle".

Example 4.15 The concept *bird* (or *hammer*, or *car*) can be learned faster than the concept *animal* (or, similarly, *tool* or *mobile*) and *robin* (*sledge hammer*, *van*). This is because the more general concepts (e.g., *insect*) subsume subconcepts that may differ significantly (like *flies* and *beetles*) and because the rather detailed concepts are quite homogeneous (*ants*) but not always clearly distinguishable from brother concepts (*bees* and *wasps*).[2]

The key to the right level of abstraction is *homogeneity*. Homogeneity within a class and separation between classes is expressed in terms of *intra-* and *inter-class similarities*, respectively. Because we need probabilities to express the similarity measures, we shall agree on the following.

Let $g : U \to \mathbf{k}$ such that $g(x) = i :\Longleftrightarrow x \in c_i$, where $c_i \in \mathfrak{c} = U/g$. Let $\mathbf{F} = \{f_0, f_1, \ldots, f_{n-1}\}$ and $\vec{x} = \langle f_0(x), f_1(x), \ldots, f_{n-1}(x)\rangle$. Then, every $f \in \mathbf{F}$ is a random variable that assigns a value $v \in \mathrm{cod}(f)$ to x. We write

$$\Pr[F = v] := \phi(\{x \in U : f(x) = v\}) = \frac{|\{x \in U : f(x) = v\}|}{|U|}. \tag{4.6}$$

Then, the probability that an object has a certain property given it belongs to a certain class is

$$\Pr[F = v \mid C_i] = \Pr[F = v \wedge G = i]/\Pr[G = i] = \frac{\phi(\{x \in U : f(x) = v\} \cap \{x \in U : g(x) = i\})}{|c|/|U|} \tag{4.7}$$

$$= \frac{|\{x \in U : f(x) = v\} \cap c_i|}{|c_i|} \tag{4.8}$$

for $f \in \mathbf{F}$, $c \in \mathfrak{c}$ and $v \in \mathrm{cod}(f_i)$. This again clarifies the fact that random variables are in fact *functions*.

Exercise 4.16 (◇) Determine the probability that x belongs to a class c given that for some $f \in \mathbf{F}, f(x) = v$.

[2] They *are* clearly distinguishable for experts but many people cannot tell the difference between a wasp, a bee, a bumble bee, or harmless hover flies. In fact, wasps are more closely related to ants than to bees.

Intra-/inter-class similarity

Definition 4.17 — Intra-/inter-class similarity.
The *intra-class similarity* of a class $c \in \mathfrak{c}$ is the probability that object representations are similar given the information that they belong to the same class:

$$sim(c) := \frac{1}{|\mathbf{F}|}\sum_{f\in\mathbf{F}}\left(\frac{1}{|\mathrm{cod}(f)|}\sum_{v\in\mathrm{cod}(f)}\Pr[f(x)=v|C]\right). \quad (4.9)$$

The *inter-class dissimilarity* is the reverse: it is the probability that an object belongs to a certain class given that it has a certain probability:

$$disim(c) := \frac{1}{|\mathbf{F}|}\sum_{f\in\mathbf{F}}\left(\frac{1}{|\mathrm{cod}(f)|}\sum_{v\in\mathrm{cod}(f)}\Pr[C|f(x)=v]\right). \quad (4.10)$$

●

Exercise 4.18 (◊) Explain why $\Pr[C|F=v]$ expresses dissimilarity rather than $\Pr[\neg C|F \neq v]$!

So, the more homogeneous a class, the higher its intra-class similarities. Given that they belong to the same class, they have many similar properties. The more a class can be discriminated from another one, the higher the probability a property determines the class membership. There are many different ways to define cluster homogeneity and heterogeneity, and we presented just one based on our metaphor of distances in representation space. The general idea behind these two measures is illustrated in Figure 4.5. The double-headed arrows (cluster radii) illustrate an intra-cluster similarity, while the lines connecting all the centroids represent the inter-class dissimilarities. A clustering appears to be more adequate, the higher the intra-class similarity and inter-class dissimilarities, which means we have to find an ideal trade-off between both class similarities: the clusters will be as homogeneous as possible and yet discriminating enough.

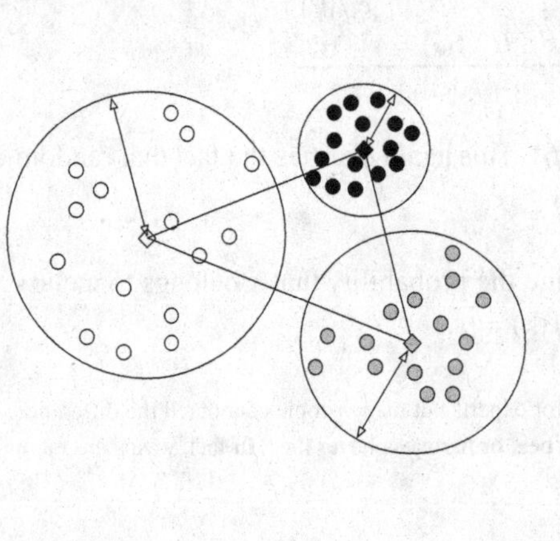

Fig. 4.5 Intra- and inter-class similarities

Therefore, our task is to find $f \in \mathbf{F}$ that induces a partition that has maximal intra-class similarities and inter-class dissimilarities. To find such a good partition, we need a measure to describe the utility of such a partition, that is, the utility of feature f to cluster the data.

A straightforward way to define such a measure is to multiply the product of similarity and dissimilarities as induced by f with the prior probability of the corresponding feature-value combinations:

Partition utility

Definition 4.19 — Partition utility.
The *utility* of a partition is described by

$$utility(\mathfrak{c}) := \sum_{c \in \mathfrak{c}} \frac{|c|}{|U|} \sum_{f \in \mathbf{F}} \sum_{v \in \mathrm{cod}(f)} \Pr[F = v|C] \cdot \Pr[C|F = v]. \quad (4.11)$$

This is equivalent to evaluating a feature (hypothesis) h's utility in partitioning the universe ($U/h = \mathfrak{c}$). ●

To conclude this chapter on clustering methods, we examine an approach to incremental hierarchical clustering:

- *Incrementally* means that we successively develop and refine a partition over a set of data.
- *Hierarchically* means that we do not create flat clusters but that we want to merge or split clusters if the data encountered suggest such operations of generalisation or specialisation.

To define an appropriate procedure, four different operators are required. These are *cluster refinement*, *cluster introduction*, *cluster join*, and *cluster split*. A refinement is required each time we encounter an object that belongs to an already existing cluster. This can change the cluster form (just recall the k-means principle). If an object does not belong to any of the already existing clusters, it is taken to form a new cluster. It is easy to imagine that such an action would be chosen if the resulting intra-class similarities decrease once the object is forced into one of the old clusters. Sometimes, objects bridge a gap between two disjoint clusters. This means that the point belongs to both clusters to the same degree – and the result is that the point is pretty well located in the centre of the joined clusters. Therefore it seems reasonable to induce a new cluster that subsumes this object and all the clusters that are similar to this object for more or less the same degree. Finally, whenever a cluster grows too large (in terms of the number of members or a poor intra-class similarity in relation to other clusters), it would be a good idea to divide the cluster into more special subclasses. Another criterion is that whenever an object "disturbs" the balance of a cluster with already pretty low intra-class similarity, there must exist several subgroups. Putting these operations together, one yields an abstract description of a hierarchical clustering algorithm that is both *agglomerative* and *divisive*, which means it builds a cluster hierarchy bottom-up and top-down for generalisation and specialisation, respectively.

Example 4.20 Consider our domain of geometric shapes as shown in Figure 4.3. Recall at this point that in the picture "similarity" corresponds to "distance" – even though the vector representation of the objects can be much more complex: For the set of all these objects x that have at most four corners, we define

$$\vec{x} \ := \ \langle x_0, y_0, \ldots, x_3, y_3, x_{c_1}, y_{c_1}, x_{c_2}, y_{c_2}, r_1, r_2 \rangle .$$

Two arguments x_i, y_i define the x- and y-coordinates of the i-th corner, and the two last pairs define the centre and r_1, r_2 the radiuses. Then a triangle is defined by a vector with only the first six arguments instantiated and the rest filled with zeros.

Suppose we begin an incremental bi-directional hierarchical search with known classes *Triangles*, *Tetragons*, and *Ellipses*. Note that each of these classes appears on a different level in our target concept hierarchy. A closer look at each of the three sets shows that the cluster of *Tetragons* divides into two subclusters. At the same time, all the *Tetragons* are closer to the *Triangles* than to *Ellipses*. Therefore, we would join the clusters to form a new one. The resulting clusters are *Rhomboids*, *Rectangles*, and *Polygons*.

A further analysis of *Ellipses* shows that there are two kinds: one for which the two centre coordinates and radii are the same and one for which they are different. We therefore identify a subcluster *Circles*. Similarly, we find a subclass of *Rhomboids*, those whose four sides have the same length: *Rhombuses*.

Finally, there is a huge difference between the three different clusters we have so far. *Ellipses* have six zero entries at the beginning, and *Triangles* and *Tetragons* have four zeroes at the end. Accordingly, we join the latter two and obtain *Polygons*.

We do not need to define an algorithm that implements this behaviour here: top-down construction (i.e., divisive clustering) will be discussed in the next chapter – and agglomerative methods fall into the category of generalisation operators, which will also be discussed in a later chapter.

4.5 Relational clustering

This chapter was concerned with a lot of distance measures, similarities, and vectors in high-dimensional spaces. One might ask what this kind of clustering actually has to do with relational knowledge discovery. The answer is very simple.

Every object in space is represented by a vector. This vector comprises of arguments each of which corresponds to a function. Recall that *sim* and *disim* were defined by way of random variables. And random variables are functions – and each object representation can be formulated as the same vector where each component holds the corresponding value of a random variable.

Either way, representation space is a feature space. And this again means that all the objects in this approach can be described by an information system. Now recall that every single feature of an information system induces an equivalence relation – and any clustering of a set of objects is a classification. This means that hierarchical clustering is simply repeated classifier learning. In other words, hierarchical clustering means finding a family of equivalence relations

$$R_0 \subseteq R_1 \subseteq \cdots \subseteq R_{k-1} \tag{4.12}$$

such that $\bigcap_{i \in \mathbf{k}} R_i$ induces a partition with classes whose elements are most similar. The fewer relations we choose and the coarser they are, the fewer clusters we can describe – and the more general our classification.

Clustering is nothing more than unsupervised classification – it is just that we assume (or define) some distance measure to describe similarity and to help ourselves get over the missing teacher signal.

COBWEB (Fisher 1987) and UNIMEM (Lebowitz 1987) were the first systems for clustering objects without a teaching signal.

CN2 (Clark and Niblett 1989) finally made use of a teaching signal to allow for supervised concept formation and was one of the first systems to describe clusters by rules. It is based on Michalski's AQ algorithm, whose underlying star search covering algorithm was first published in Michalski (1969).

The next chapter deals with supervised, hierarchical clustering – known as the top-down induction of decision trees.

Chapter 5
Information gain

Describing objects by features is a very common thing to do. For example, many decision support systems use a tree-like representation of cases, where every branch in the tree corresponds to a feature and its observed value. But which features can be used to model a certain concept? What is the shortest and most meaningful rule with which we can describe a distinct set of objects using our knowledge?

In the previous chapter we saw how similarity measures can be used to group objects into (hopefully) meaningful clusters. Given an information system $\mathfrak{I}$, we now want to describe a feature's utility with respect to a given object's classification. Relationally speaking, we need to recursively apply those features $f_i \in \mathbf{F}$ that generate a partition on U that is similar to U/R_t to learn a compressing classifier this way. It appears to be a good idea to start with a feature that appears to be the most "similar" to t. A feature being quite similar to the target function can be assumed to carry relevant information with respect to t. And this leads us to the information-theoretic notion of entropy.

Information gain driven classifier learning

While clustering tries to find hierarchies of groups of objects, so-called decision trees represent a hierarchy of feature-induced partitions. Unlike (unsupervised) similarity measures in clustering, one uses a target-specific information measure called *entropy*.

People often try to explain Shannon and Weaver's (1949) information-theoretic measure of entropy by the laws of entropy in thermodynamics. In fact, this approach is much more demonstrative than the original works of Shannon and Weaver. However, both measures were developed independently from each other and with completely different motivation and background.

5.1 Entropy

In 1865, Rudolf Clausius introduced the notion of entropy into physics by describing a closed system of constant temperature T and the result of applying energy (i.e., heat) onto it (ΔQ). A commonsense picture of this situation is that all particles in the system now move more vigorously; that is, it becomes harder to tell "where" they are. Then, in 1877, Boltzmann stated that the entropy S of a system can be described by the number Ω of possible states consistent with its thermodynamic properties:

$$S = k \cdot \ln \Omega,$$

where k is known as the famous Boltzmann constant.

Entropy and information

The entropy $H(s)$ of a set s is a measure of the complexity of a system. Given all possible states of the system and their respective probabilities, the entropy describes the average length of the shortest description specifying an arbitrary system state.

In the 1940s Shannon and Weaver were working on the question of how much channel capacity one needs to securely transmit a message with a certain amount of noise involved. This gave rise to two questions:

1. How does one measure the *amount of information*?
2. How does one measure the *capacity* of a communication channel?

First, it is very important not to confuse the two different terms *information* and *meaning*: *meaning* usually denotes the semantic content of a message, whereas *information* is rather a measure of the complexity of the message source:

> [I]*nformation* must not be confused with meaning. ... Information ... relates not so much to what you *do* say, as to what you *could* say. That is, information is a measure of one's freedom of choice when one selects a message.
>
> Shannon and Weaver (1949)

Even a meaningful message loses information when repeated over and over again. Now that information is compared to degrees of freedom, it is clear why information-theoretic entropy can be related to the definition of entropy as it is known in thermodynamics: The number of

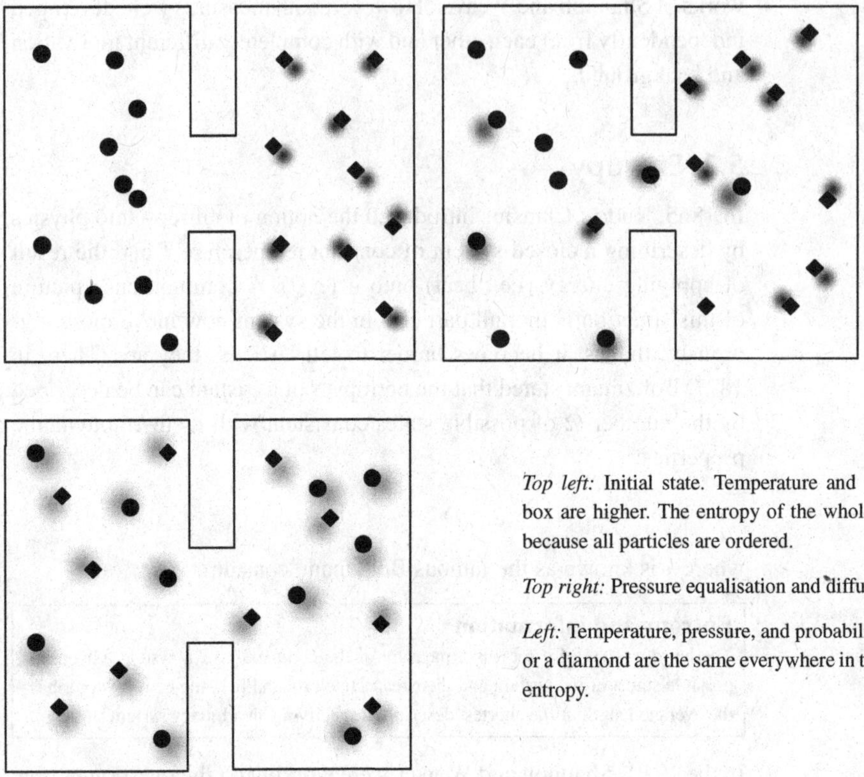

Top left: Initial state. Temperature and pressure in the right box are higher. The entropy of the whole system is minimal, because all particles are ordered.

Top right: Pressure equalisation and diffusion.

Left: Temperature, pressure, and probability of picking a circle or a diamond are the same everywhere in the system: maximum entropy.

Fig. 5.1 Entropy change of a closed system

possible system states increases with the degree of freedom of each particle in it. For a very brief but demonstrative example, see Figure 5.1.

But before we start defining a measure of information, it is a good idea to understand which properties we will require from this measure. These are

- The more "usual" an event or message, the less is its information content. Or, conversely: the less the probability we observe some event, the higher its information.
- The information of a joint observation of two independent messages should be the sum of the information of the individual messages.

Let us reconsider our example from the introduction:

Example 5.1 When flipping a fair coin, the probability for heads is the same as for tails: it is 50% in both cases. We have a maximum degree of freedom, a maximum degree of uncertainty, and a maximum of information. A biased coin predestines the outcome of a throw: it decreases the degree of freedom, and it introduces certainty and loses information.

Cheating makes the game more predictable: the probability of throwing heads is much lower than tails. Accordingly, we already *expect* tails, and the number of throws where our expectation is not met and we make an erroneous prediction is rather small. Playing a fair game increases the amount of information in a throw: because all throws are conditionally independent, it is clear that for each throw we have a fifty-fifty chance of either outcome. So the information in a message string generated by a source that is playing a fair game is much higher than that of a biased sender (a simple but true observation we make in our everyday lives as well).

In the last example we saw how the probability of a signal in a message determines the information content; we also saw that information about several events is summed up. We now examine how the likeliness of a sequence of events in relation to the number of possible events changes. This time, it is easier to examine the issue in the light of thermodynamics: Let there be a system with ω entities each of which can take n states. Then, the system can take one out of $\Omega = n^\omega$ different states.

Example 5.2 Consider

Number of: Entities ω	States n	System states n^ω
7	2	$2^7 = 128$
2	10	$10^2 = 100$

By adding *one* entity we can increase the number of possible system states by the factor n:

Entities ω	States n	System states n^ω
7+1 = 8	2	$2^{7+1} = 2^8 = 256$
2+1 = 3	10	$10^{2+1} = 10^3 = 1000$

and adding m entities results in

Entities ω	States n	System states n^ω
$7 + m$	2	$2^{7+m} = 2^7 \cdot 2^m = 128 \cdot 2^m$
$2 + m$	10	$10^{2+m} = 10^2 \cdot 10^m = 100 \cdot 10^m$

So the number of system states increases exponentially with the number of entities.

Exercise 5.3 (◇) Relate the growth rates of adding different numbers of entities and states.

If we increase the number ω of entities (atoms, symbols) by the *factor* of a, then the possible number of system states (or messages) increases exponentially in a. Because $\Omega = n^{\omega}$, we have

$$\Omega' = n^{a \cdot \omega} = n^{(\omega)^a} = \Omega^a. \tag{5.1}$$

Let us interpret the number of entities as the length of a message and the number of states as the number of different symbols. Then, Ω is the number of possible messages. If we then add the length of the message, we have a factor in the number of possible messages. This number, Ω, describes what we could say and therefore describes the information content of the system.

Now that we have gained a pretty detailed idea of how entropy as a property of physical entities works, it is time to consider information systems again. Here we do not deal with particles, but with events that are described by variables or with objects that are described in information systems. First we consider events that are described by several discrete random variables. Let there be a set $\mathcal{F} = \{F_0, \ldots, F_{n-1}\}$ of random variables where F_i corresponds to elementary events represented by $f_i \in \mathbf{F}$. Then, all F_i can take values from $V_i = \mathrm{cod}(f_i)$. For every elementary event there is a measure μ_i describing the probabilities that for some $x \in U, f_i(x) = v$.[1] Events are described by sets of elementary events, which in our case is a vector of all values F_i. We can use this measure to define a probability distribution:

$$\Pr[F_0 = v_0 \wedge F_1 = v_1 \wedge \cdots \wedge F_{n-1} = v_{n-1}] \tag{5.2}$$
$$:= \mu^n(\{x \in U : f_i(x) = v_i\}). \tag{5.3}$$

By some abuse of language this probability is often denoted p_x. Usually, the probability of the co-occurence of two mutually independent events with two different probabilities results in the product of the probabilities. It is *very* important to understand that the assumption of mutual independence is a fundamental bias. Even worse, the sequential ordering of symbols as they appear in the sequence of a message is *not* independent! Information-theoretic entropy makes an assumption that is true only in the context of thermodynamics, but *not* in the context of meaningful sequences.[2] Nevertheless, we need to live with certain biases if we want our algorithms to perform sufficiently efficiently.

[1] We omit indices here to avoid overly extensive subscripting (v_{j_i}). It is assumed that for $f_i(x) = v_j$ it always holds that $v_j \in \mathrm{cod}(f)_i$.

[2] This has been shown by an impressive counterproof given by the work of Bletchley Park in breaking the enigma of the German Shark code during the Second World War. By analysis of the sequences of codes only, the codebreakers were able to reduce the number of possible encoding functions to a degree that enabled the "bombes" to decrypt German messages.

To make the probabilities behave additively when occurring together we now apply a simple trick: instead of multiplying probabilities, we *add* the logarithms, and so get exactly what we were looking for:

Entropy

Definition 5.4 — Entropy.
Shannon and Weaver's (1949) measure of information content describes the information content of some observation that $f_i(x) = v$:

$$\text{entropy}(f_i(x) = v) := \log_2 \frac{1}{\Pr[F_i = v]}. \tag{5.4}$$

It is the negative logarithm of the probability that this observation is made. We also write $\text{entropy}(v) = \log_2 \frac{1}{p_v}$ when it is clear from the context. ●

But what about *sets*? Whenever we talk about several messages we should always weight each one by its own probability of occurrence. This leads to a preliminary definition of information-theoretic entropy as a probability weighted sum of information content. The entropy of a source ("sender") is the expected information content of a message being sent by this system:

$$\text{entropy}(s) \quad = \quad -\sum_{i=1}^{\omega} p_i \log_2 p_i. \tag{5.5}$$

So the entropy of a set s of possible messages is the probability weighted sum (i.e., expected or average value) over the information content of each symbol. The base 2 of the logarithm originates from the assumption that we are dealing with "particles" that can take only *two* different states. It can be easily computed using the following transformation:

$$\text{entropy}(s) = -\sum_{i=1}^{\omega} p_i \log_2 p_i = -\sum_{i=1}^{\omega} p_i \frac{\ln p_i}{\ln 2} = -\sum_{i=1}^{\omega} p_i \ln p_i \cdot \frac{1}{\ln 2}.$$

In other words, *information* is a dimensionless measure just as entropy, but we agree to write "x bit" instead of "$x\frac{1}{\ln 2}$".

Exercise 5.5 (◇) Explain why the three actions described in Figure 5.2 increase the entropy of a system.

Exercise 5.6 (◈) Describe three actions on information systems that are equivalent to those shown in Figure 5.2 and explain the increase of entropy using Shannon and Weaver's (1949) measure of information.

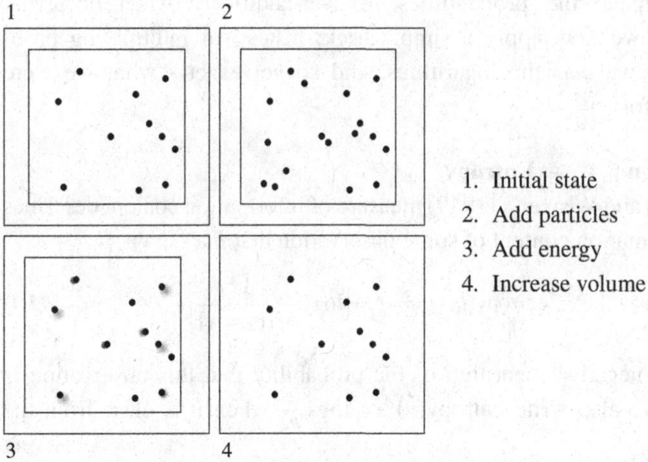

Fig. 5.2 Three ways to increase a system's entropy

5.2 Information and information gain

Relational knowledge discovery is the same all the time: we want to create a method with which we can construct sets of relations that we can use to describe a concept. The problem is just to guide the search to speed up the learning process:

Entropy and information gain

When learning classifiers, we will usually refer to entropies in relation to a target classification. Given a set of observations with different target labels assigned, the entropy with respect to the target label describes the complexity of the learning problem. If we manage to partition the set into disjoint subsets that have a lower entropy, then we have *gained* some information. The cuts performed during partitioning are correlated to the boundaries of the target classes. The idea behind information gain methods is to recursively partition the set using features that produce maximal information gain.

5.2.1 Entropy

We start right off with a definition:

Definition 5.7 — Entropy of a set s.

Entropy of a set s

We define the *(f-relative) entropy* of a set to be

$$\text{entropy}_f(s) := -\sum_{v \in \text{cod}(f)} \Pr[F = v] \log_2 \Pr[F = v], \quad (5.6)$$

$$\text{where } \Pr[F = v] = \frac{|\{x \in s : f(x) = v\}|}{|s|}.$$

When $f = t$, we may drop the index and write $\text{entropy}(s) := \text{entropy}_t(s)$. ●

Because the true distribution is unknown, we use the relative frequency of observations to approximate the probabilities of symbols.[3] Furthermore, information content is always determined in relation to a certain property f of objects (which are, again, equivalence classes).

Example 5.8 Imagine the following set of six different symbols each in a white or black version:

$$\{\bigcirc, \square, \Diamond, \triangleright, \triangleleft, \triangle, \bullet, \blacksquare, \blacklozenge, \blacktriangleright, \blacktriangleleft, \blacktriangle\}.$$

Then the information content of message that reads $\Diamond\bullet\Diamond\square\Diamond\bullet$ is determined as follows:[4]

1. The set of symbols used is $\{\Diamond, \bullet, \square\}$.
2. The message length is 6, so the approximate probabilities of the three symbols are $p_{\Diamond} = \frac{3}{6} = \frac{1}{2}$, $p_{\bullet} = \frac{2}{6} = \frac{1}{3}$, and $p_{\square} = \frac{1}{6}$.
3. We assume this approximation of probabilities to be sufficiently precise and compute the information content as follows:

$$\begin{aligned} \text{entropy}(\{\Diamond, \bullet, \Diamond, \square, \Diamond, \bullet\}) &= -\sum_{x \in \{\Diamond, \bullet, \square\}} p_x \log_2 p_x \\ &= -\frac{1}{2}\log_2\frac{1}{2} - \frac{1}{3}\log_2\frac{1}{3} - \frac{1}{6}\log_2\frac{1}{6} \\ &\approx 1.46. \end{aligned}$$

More specifically, we can also determine the information of this message with respect to the colour or shape of each symbol:

Example 5.9 We now want to determine the entropy of the message set with respect to each object's colour which we assume to be described by a feature $colour \in \mathbf{F}$:

$$\begin{aligned} &\text{entropy}_{colour}(\{\Diamond, \bullet, \Diamond, \square, \Diamond, \bullet\}) \\ &= -\sum_{colour(x) \in \{\text{white}, \text{black}\}} p_{colour(x)} \log_2 p_{colour(x)} \\ &= -\frac{|\{\Diamond, \Diamond, \square, \Diamond\}|}{6} \log_2 \frac{2}{3} - \frac{|\{\bullet, \bullet\}|}{6} \log_2 \frac{1}{3} \\ &\approx 0.92 \end{aligned}$$

[3] Knowing μ means having knowledge about what the sender is going to say. Such knowledge is used in source-coding compression methods.

[4] We assume all the symbols to be subscripted by a running index, i.e., $\{\Diamond_0, \bullet_1, \Diamond_2, \square_3, \Diamond_4, \bullet_5\}$. Multiple occurrences of a symbol in a set actually means multiple observations of the symbol.

Just to be absolutely sure that the information-theoretic entropy of a set s is always a measure *with respect* to some property of objects, we give a last example:

Example 5.10 Let us consider the entire set s and determine its entropy with respect to the number of vertices an object has:

$$
\begin{aligned}
& \text{entropy}_{vertices}(\{○, □, ◇, ▷, ◁, △, ●, ■, ◆, ▶, ◀, ▲\}) \\
= \; & \text{entropy}_{vertices}(\{0,4,4,3,3,3,0,4,4,3,3,3\}) \\
= \; & -\sum_{vertices(x)\in\{0,3,4\}} p_{vertices(x)} \log_2 p_{vertices(x)} \\
= \; & -\frac{1}{6}\log_2\frac{1}{6} - \frac{1}{3}\log_2\frac{1}{3} - \frac{1}{2}\log_2\frac{1}{2} \\
\approx \; & 1.46
\end{aligned}
$$

Because an entropy value greater than 1 appears a bit odd, we can norm $\text{entropy}_f(s)$ by changing the base of the log to $|\text{cod}(f)|$. Then, the entropy of the set above with respect to *vert* is 0.92.

Exercise 5.11 Here are a few exercises to get a feel for entropies:

- ◇ Give an example of an arbitrary set of symbols with maximum entropy with respect to colour.
- ◇ It appears a bit odd that the entropy in Example 5.8 takes a value larger than 1. Which part of the definition of $\text{entropy}_f(s)$ in Equation (5.6) has to be changed to normalise the entropy value to $[0, 1] \subseteq \mathbb{R}$?
- ◇ Determine $\text{entropy}_f(\{◀, ♡, ◁, ▷, ◆, ◁, ▶, ◀, ◁, ◇, △, ▲\})$ for three different f.
- ◇ Determine $\text{entropy}_f(s)$ for all features $f \in \mathbf{F}$ in Figure 5.3(left).
- ◇ Determine $\text{entropy}_f(s)$ for all features $f \in \mathbf{F}$ in Figure 5.3(right).

5.2.2 Information

Recall that our idea was to select some $f \in \mathbf{F}$ that is *most informative* with respect to t. The set of our objects or observations has a certain

s	t	f	g	t'	id	c
1	1	1	1	1	1	1
2	1	1	1	1	2	1
3	1	2	1	1	3	1
4	0	2	1	2	4	1
5	0	3	2	2	5	1
6	0	3	2	2	6	1

s	f_0	f_1	f_2	f_3	t
0	1	■	♡	c	0
1	0	■	♠	b	/
2	2	■	♣	b	1
3	1	■	♣	c	/
4	1	■	♡	a	1
5	2	■	♣	b	1
6	2	■	♠	b	/
7	0	■	♠	a	1

Fig. 5.3 Two information systems

entropy (measured with respect to an arbitrary property). Usually we define entropy with respect to the target classification t. This is why we agreed to drop the index in this case: $\text{entropy}_t(s) = \text{entropy}(s)$.

But the big question is, what is the *information in a feature*? It is, so to say, a measure of its entropy in relation to the entropy of s with respect to some property. In other words, there are two features involved here. And this leads us to the definition of *feature entropy* or *feature information*:

Entropy of a feature f

Definition 5.12 — Entropy of a feature f.
The information of a feature $g \in \mathbf{F}$ on a set s with respect to a feature $f \in \mathbf{F}$ is

$$\text{entropy}_f(g, s) = \sum_{v \in \text{cod}(g)} \Pr[G = v]\, \text{entropy}_f(\{x \in s : g(x) = v\}) \quad (5.7)$$

$$\text{with } \Pr[G = v] = \frac{|\{x \in s : g(x) = v\}|}{|s|},$$

which is the (relative class size weighted) entropy of g on the quotient s/R_f. As usual, we drop the index if $f = t$ and write $\text{entropy}(g, s) := \text{entropy}_t(g, s)$. ●

Exercise 5.13 (◊) Determine the value of $\text{entropy}_f(f, s)$.

Exercise 5.14 (◊) Determine the information of all features relative to t in Figure 5.3.

To approximate t it appears to be a good idea to partition s into classes induced by a feature with the most information. This would reduce each class entropy and, therefore, create a partition that is closer to t than the partition induced by any other feature.

Reducing the entropy of a set means losing predictive uncertainty – that is, a loss of indeterminacy, a reduced number of degrees of freedom, or, simply, *information gain*. Accordingly, we define:

Information gain

Definition 5.15 — Information gain.
We define the information gain obtained by a feature g on s with respect to f as

$$\text{gain}_f(g, s) := \text{entropy}_f(s) - \text{entropy}_f(g, s). \quad (5.8)$$

The gain is the difference of the current entropy on s minus the information we gain by applying knowledge g. Again we may drop the index for $f = t$; that is, we abbreviate $\text{gain}(g, s) := \text{gain}_t(g, s)$. ●

The larger $\text{gain}_f(g, s)$, the more entropy is lost, the greater is the information content of g, and the larger is the information gain by using g to partition s.

Exercise 5.16 Let's practise some gain computations.

◊ Compute $\text{gain}_t(f, s)$, $\text{gain}_t(g, s)$, and $\text{gain}_t(id, s)$ from the left part of Figure 5.3.

◊ Compute $\text{gain}_t(f_i, s)$ with $i \in \mathbf{3}$ from the right information system in Figure 5.3.

◊ Compute $\text{gain}_{f_i}(f_{i+1}, s)$ for $i \in \mathbf{2}$ from the right information system in Figure 5.3.

Exercise 5.17 (◊) Prove or disprove $\text{gain}_g(f, s) = \text{gain}_f(g, s)$.

Exercise 5.18 (♦) Write a short program that determines $H(s)$ for an input string s.

5.3 Induction of decision trees

> **Decision trees**
> A decision tree is a classifier representation that allows one to classify an object with increasing accuracy by asking a sequence of questions about the values that the object takes under a certain feature.
>
> Learning such a classifier means building a tree in a way that its leaf nodes represent sets of objects that are more or less contained in equivalence classes induced by the target feature. We can stop building a tree if at a current node all the objects covered fall into the same target class – which means that its entropy is zero. If we cannot reduce the entropy any further, or if we run out of features, then we have to stop growing the tree.

As we have already mentioned and as we shall see in detail later, any feature f induces an equivalence relation R_f on s. Also, the binary target function $t(x) = \chi(c)(x)$ induces an equivalence relation R_t such that $s/R_t = \{s^1, s^0\}$. The entropies in s^1 and s^0 are 0. To approximate t we can also try to approximate s/R_t. We do so by hierarchically partitioning s using $R_{f_0}, R_{f_1}, \ldots$ until t-entropies in the resulting classes are 0. This is equivalent to building a tree with s as the root node and all elements of a quotient induced by f as the successor nodes of the node f until the leaves are subsets of either s^1 or s^0. Such a tree is called a *decision tree*. But how can one build such a tree efficiently, and how can one keep a tree as small as possible so as to guarantee a maximum compression? Not surprisingly, we will use the information-theoretic entropy measure to guide our search.

5.3.1 Hunt's classifier trees and Quinlan's ID3

Decision trees are a widely accepted method for classifying objects. Most decision support systems make use of flowcharts to quickly identify a certain class (e.g., in medicine where a structured sequence of tests for symptoms quickly leads to a diagnosis).

Fig. 5.4 Hunt's algorithm for finding classifier trees

```
01 proc class (s)
02 {
03     IF (∀x, y ∈ s : t(x) = t(y)) THEN
04     {  return (s) }
05     ELSE
06     {
07         IF (F = ∅) THEN return (⊥)
08         ELSE
09         { f := choose(F); F := F − {f};
10             return ({ class({x ∈ s : f(x) = v_0}),
                   ...,
                   class({x ∈ s : f(x) = v_|cod(f)|});
11         }
12     }
13 }
```

Accordingly, the induction of such trees is still one of the most popular techniques in knowledge discovery. Because of their relative high efficiency and wide acceptance, they are a standard method provided by nearly every data mining tool.

The rise of decision tree induction started with Quinlan's (1986a) *iterative dichotomiser*. The idea of hierarchical clustering was not new – it was the entropy measure of information that turned out to be the real knack. The idea dates back to 1966, when Hunt, Marin, and Stone introduced *classifier trees* and developed the system CLS. The pseudo-code of CLS is shown in Figure 5.4. The idea behind this algorithm is to *divide and conquer* until all examples can be classified (see the recursive call on all induced classes in line 10). But the problem with it is that it involves a non-deterministic choice in line 9. Different features usually differ in their feature entropy relative to t, so it seems a good idea to choose the feature with maximum information gain. Therefore, the idea behind top-down induction of decision trees (TDIDT) is simply to take CLS and add an information gain heuristic:

1. The root of the decision tree subsumes all entities $x \in s$.
   We choose the $f \in \mathbf{F}$ from which we expect a maximum information gain and create successor nodes for each $f(x) \in \vec{f}$.
2. Now check the nodes left to right:
   (a) If all entities subsumed by the current node belong to either $s^{\mathbf{1}}$ or $s^{\mathbf{0}}$, label the node **1** or **0**, respectively.
   (b) Otherwise, recursively choose the next $f \in \mathbf{F}$ that does not occur on the path from the current node back to the root and create successor nodes for each $f(x) \in \vec{f}$. If there is no attribute left, stop and report "Unsuccessful attempt".

Exercise 5.19 (◊) In the algorithm above, only features that have not been used yet are taken into account in step 2(b). This sure makes the algorithm more efficient, but will the result change if we consider all features? Why?

Figure 5.5 shows a famous decision tree: a decision tree that is built to describe a large set of observations about whether one should go for playing tennis depending on the current weather conditions. The data used for inducing this tree are weather reports for the past two weeks:

Day	Forecast	Temperature	Humidity	Wind	t
1	sunny	high	high	no	**0**
2	sunny	high	high	yes	**0**
3	overcast	high	high	no	**1**
4	rainy	med	high	no	**1**
5	rainy	low	high	no	**1**
6	rainy	low	low	yes	**0**
7	overcast	low	low	yes	**1**
8	sunny	med	high	no	**0**
9	sunny	low	low	no	**1**
10	rainy	med	high	no	**1**
11	sunny	med	low	yes	**1**
12	overcast	med	high	yes	**1**
13	overcast	high	high	no	**1**
14	rainy	med	high	yes	**0**

As one can easily see, $s^1 = \{3, 4, 5, 7, 9, 10, 12, 12, 13\}$ and $s^0 = \{1, 2, 6, 8, 14\}$, which makes nine instances for $t(x) = \mathbf{1}$ and five instances for $t(x) = \mathbf{0}$. In Figure 5.5, every node is labelled with a tuple $\binom{p}{n}$, with p being the number of positive and n being the number of negative instances in this node.

The sums of all positive numbers and all negative numbers in successor nodes equal the numbers in their parent node. In leaf nodes, either $p = 0$ or $n = 0$, and the sum of all numbers in all leaf nodes is 14. So every node N in a decision tree subsumes a certain subset of elements and every layer of a tree is a partition.

Let us now take a more formal look at decision trees. We define:

Definition 5.20 — Decision tree. Decision tree

A *decision tree* consists of *decision nodes* and *leaf nodes* (*class node*). A *decision node* N_f carries a feature value of a parent node, a feature name f, and edges to a set of successor nodes, one for each possible value of f:

$$N_f := \langle v_i, f, \{N_i : i \in |\mathrm{cod}(f)|\}\rangle \quad (5.9)$$

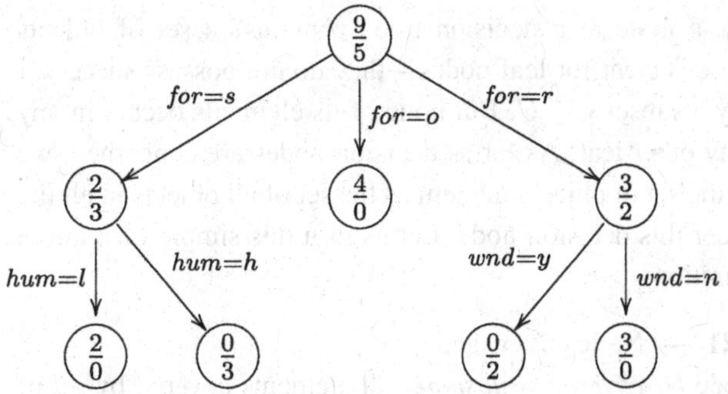

Fig. 5.5 The famous tennis player's example

for is the *forecast* (sunny, rainy or overcast), *hum* is the *humidity* (low or high), and *wnd* is the *wind* (yes or no).

We call a node N a *leaf node*, if it has no successors. It represents the set of all objects that take a value y as defined by the edge from its parent node under the feature defined by its parent node:

$$N_{\perp} \quad := \quad \langle v_i, \perp, s\rangle \,. \tag{5.10}$$

Similarly, the root node has no predecessor:

$$N_{\top} \quad := \quad \langle \top, f, \{N_i : i \in |\mathrm{cod}(f)|\}\rangle \tag{5.11}$$

Note that this definition is entirely *descriptive* and that it does not give a recipe to build a decision tree. ●

For a better reading, we denote leaf nodes by simple capital letters like N and decision nodes N_f with indices denoting the feature f that determines its sucessor nodes. For a decision node N_f we refer to its successor nodes by N_i, where $i \in |\mathrm{cod}(f)|$ or N_y with $y \in \mathrm{cod}(f)$.

So whenever a decision tree has more than just one leaf node, it must have at least one decision node. Then, the topmost decision node is the decision tree's root node. The tree for the tennis player's example in Figure 5.5 is formally represented as

$$\left\langle \top, \mathit{for}, \left\{ \begin{array}{l} \left\langle s, \mathit{hum}, \left\{ \begin{array}{l} \left\langle c^{\mathbf{1}}, \{x \in U : \mathit{for}(c) = s \wedge \mathit{hum}(x) = l\}\right\rangle \\ \left\langle c^{\mathbf{0}}, \{x \in U : \mathit{for}(c) = s \wedge \mathit{hum}(x) = h\}\right\rangle \end{array} \right\} \right\rangle, \\ \langle o, \perp, \{x \in U : \mathit{for}(x) = o\}\rangle\,, \\ \left\langle r, \mathit{wnd}, \left\{ \begin{array}{l} \left\langle c^{\mathbf{0}}, \{x \in U : \mathit{for}(c) = r \wedge \mathit{wnd}(x) = y\}\right\rangle \\ \left\langle c^{\mathbf{1}}, \{x \in U : \mathit{for}(c) = r \wedge \mathit{wnd}(x) = n\}\right\rangle \end{array} \right\} \right\rangle \end{array} \right\} \right\rangle.$$

The tuple $\langle \mathit{for}, \{\ldots\}\rangle$ represents the root node that subsumes two decision nodes (*hum* and *wnd*) and one leaf node (c_o^1). Both decision nodes subsume two leaf nodes each.

Obviously, a node in a decision tree "contains" a set of objects $x \in U$. The case is clear for leaf nodes – they do not possess successor nodes but only a subset $s \subseteq U$. But none of its elements occurs in any other set of any other leaf. As far as decision nodes are concerned, we simply define the set of objects in them as the set of all objects in all the leaf nodes under this decision node. Let us turn this simple idea into a satisfying definition:

Node coverage

Definition 5.21 — Node coverage.
A decision node N_f *covers* or *subsumes* all elements covered by *all* of its successor nodes. Let $N_\bot$ be a leaf node. Then,

$$\mathrm{cvr}(N_\bot) = \mathrm{cvr}(\langle v, \bot, s \rangle) := s. \tag{5.12}$$

Let N_f be a decision node. Then,

$$\mathrm{cvr}(N_f) \quad := \quad \bigcup_{y \in \mathrm{cod}(f)} \mathrm{cvr}(N_y). \tag{5.13}$$

We use cvr to determine the (sub)set of elements that satisfy the conditions formulated along the edges of the tree. ●

Note that the coverage sets of all leaf nodes (and all nodes on the same layer of the tree) are pairwise disjoint and that their union always equals U. As we will discover later, a decision tree is simply a layered representation of partitions of increasing granularity.

Example 5.22 The decision tree in Figure 5.5 has five leaf nodes and three decision nodes. The root node is N_{for}, with $\mathrm{cvr}(N_{for}) = s$ and three successor nodes N_s, N_o, and N_r. N_o happens to be one of the leaf nodes with $\mathrm{cvr}(N_o) = \{3, 7, 12, 13\}$. $N_s = N_{hum}$ and $N_r = N_{wnd}$ are decision nodes with $\mathrm{cvr}(N_{hum}) = \{1, 2, 8, 9, 11\}$ and $\mathrm{cvr}(N_{wnd}) = \{4, 5, 6, 10, 14\}$. N_{hum} is further divided into the two leaf nodes N_l and N_h with coverages $\{9, 11\}$ and $\{1, 2, 8\}$; the remaining leaf nodes are subsumed by N_{wnd} with $\mathrm{cvr}(N_y) = \{6, 14\}$ and $\mathrm{cvr}(N_n) = \{4, 5, 10\}$. ●

There is an extended graphical notation that adds information about the number of subsumed objects with respect to their classification: the set of objects covered by a node N can be ordered according to their target classification. In Figure 5.5, for example, each node is labelled $\left(\frac{p}{n}\right)$, where p is the number of elements subsumed by N and for which $t(x) = \mathbf{1}$. Similarly, n is $|\mathrm{cvr}(N_f) \cap \{x \in U : t(x) = \mathbf{0}\}$. This comes in quite handy in binary classification tasks; for larger $\mathrm{cod}(t)$ one has to specify the labelling carefully (see Example 5.34). In the best case, each leaf node contains elements of only one target class. But what is the meaning of a node covering elements of different target classes? We

Fig. 5.6 Top-down induction of decision trees (TDIDT)

```
proc tdidt(s, F)
{
    IF (entropy_t(s) = 0) THEN   % c.f. Defn. (5.6)
    { return (s) };
    ELSE
    {
        f = arg max{gain_t(f, s) : f ∈ F}   % c.f. Defn. (5.15)
        s'' := {}
        FORALL (v ∈ cod(f)) DO
        {
            s' := tdidt({x ∈ s : f(x) = v}, F − {f});
            s'' := s'' ∪ {⟨f, v, s'⟩};
        }
    }
    return (s'')
}
```

now define the semantics of a decision tree by explaining the hypothesis defined by a node.

Decision tree hypothesis

Definition 5.23 — Decision tree hypothesis.
Every node N in a decision tree represents a hypothesis h_N:

$$h_f(x) \quad = \quad \mathrm{mcv}_t(\mathrm{cvr}(N)). \tag{5.14}$$

This means that every node is labelled with the majority of target classifications (see Figure 5.6) and every decision node inherits the majority vote from the sum of its successors. ●

Example 5.24 The leaf node hypotheses of the tree in Figure 5.5 are from left to right $h_{N_l} = \mathbf{1}$, $h_{N_h} = \mathbf{0}$, $h_{N_o} = \mathbf{1}$, $h_{N_y} = \mathbf{0}$, and $h_{N_n} = \mathbf{1}$.

Exercise 5.25 (◇) Determine the hypotheses represented by the decision nodes.

Top-down decision tree induction
Inducing a decision tree means recursively partitioning the set of all objects by equivalence relations represented by the features of the underlying information system. In each step, the feature chosen for partitioning is the one with the maximum information gain.

From Section 5.1 we know that the best feature to choose in each step is the one with the maximum information gain. Accordingly, we can now formulate an algorithm for decision tree induction as shown in Figure 5.6. Starting with the root node (i.e., a top decision node) N that covers all objects described by our sample, we recursively choose the feature with the maximum information gain to split the current node into successor nodes where each one represents an equivalence class of objects with respect to this feature. We continue from left to right until we have classified all objects (i.e., all leaf nodes have zero t-entropy or until we run out of features). Finally, we can define the hypothesis represented by a tree N_f. For known elements x of our universe, the case is simple: we take all the leaf trees and determine the one that contains x. There is exactly one such leaf node N, and we then apply a majority voting to assign a target label to x. If all the leaves N_c contain only subsets of target classes (formally spoken: if for all N_c it holds that $N_c \subseteq c \in \mathfrak{c}$), then the majority is always 100%. Things are a bit more complicated if we want to determine $h(x)$ for some $x \notin \mathrm{cvr}(N_f)$. Then, we simply determine x's value under f and stuff it into the cover set of the according successor node. We repeat this until x arrives in a leaf node – and then we again return the majority vote of this leaf.

This algorithm already motivates an idea towards decision tree pruning: if the error of a majority vote does not dramatically increase when pruning away all successors of a decision node, then why keep the successors at all?

Exercise 5.26 (◇) In Definition 5.23, the hypothesis is defined by the sum of the majorities of the successors. The set of subsumed nodes is defined via set union. Why can we safely define the hypothesis equationally whereas $|s \cup s'| \leq |s| + |s'|$?

Exercise 5.27 (◇) Reproduce the decision tree in Figure 5.5 by computing all the necessary entropies and gains for all the given features.

Exercise 5.28 (◇) Build a decision tree from the following information system:

s	f	g	h	t	s	f	g	h	t
○	h	0	0	1	◆	s	4	0	1
□	h	4	45	0	△	h	3	0	0
►	s	3	90	1	▷	h	3	90	1
◁	h	3	270	1	◀	s	3	270	0
●	s	0	0	1	■	s	4	315	0
◇	h	4	180	0	▲	s	3	0	0

However, there remain a few open questions. We will not always be able to create leaves that are subsets of either s^1 or s^0. What shall we do then? And, even if we do have enough different features, is it always a good idea to fully grow the tree? After all, a tree with 100% accuracy is likely to be overfit and a tree with leaves that cover only one element each is nonsense. But before considering only growing smaller trees or cutting down large trees, we consider a few improvements of the gain function.

5.4 Gain again

The problem with *keys* is that they are unique. It certainly is not a problem for your door key, and it is not a problem for keys as they are used in database systems. Keys help to quickly get access to a unique item.

A feature $f \in \mathbf{F}$ is called a key feature if it is injective: $f(x) = f(y) \Longrightarrow x = y$. In such a case, s/R_f is a set of singletons, and a singleton set is trivially a set with no entropy in it. As a consequence, applying a key feature f always results in maximum information gain. Key features are more identifiers than properties that carry *information*: passport numbers do not correlate to the actual name of a person or the place where the person lives; and course numbers at the university are not always (or at most loosely) correlated to the course's content. However, both id's are unique descriptors by which we can unambiguously identify single objects. Objects can be *identified* by keys, but they are not *described* by them. In other words, they have no *meaning*. So if the gain function delivers a maximal value for key features, it simply overestimates the amount of information in them. In fact, the more values a feature has, the more the gain function as defined in Equation (5.8) tends to overestimate its information. It seems a good idea to penalise features with "too many" values. This leads to the following definition:

Normalised gain

Definition 5.29 — Normalised gain.
Normalised gain is defined as the gain function gain weighted with the expected amount of information f as estimated by the number of its values:

$$\mathrm{gain}_t^{\mathrm{norm}}(f, s) = \frac{\mathrm{gain}_t(f, s)}{\log_2 |\mathrm{cod}(f)|}. \tag{5.15}$$

So $\mathrm{gain}_t^{\mathrm{norm}}(f, s)$ can be understood as a normalised version of $\mathrm{gain}_t(f, s)$ with respect to f's expressiveness. ●

It is only very rarely the case that f actually takes all the values with equal probabilities: even if there are many values, f will most likely have a non-uniform distribution, otherwise it would be a not very informative feature.

Example 5.30 Let $s = \{x \in \mathbb{N} : 1 \leq x \leq 100\}$ be the set of the first 100 natural numbers and $t(x) = \mathbf{1}$ if and only if x is odd. The identity relation I_s is a relation induced by a key feature, and s/I_s is $\{\{x\} : x \in s\}$. Let *prime*(x) be $\mathbf{1}$ if and only if x is a prime. Then, $\mathrm{cod}(prime) = \mathbf{2} = \{\mathbf{1}, \mathbf{0}\}$ and

$$s/R_{prime} = \{\ \{2,3,5,7,11,\ldots,89,97\}, \{1,4,6,8,9,\ldots,98,99\}\ \}.$$

Because there are 25 primes in the first 100 natural numbers, we calculate

$$\text{entropy}_{id}(s) = 0 < \text{entropy}_{prime}(s) < 1 = \text{entropy}_t(s).$$

Next,

$$\text{entropy}_t(\mathit{1}, s) = 0 < \text{entropy}_t(\mathit{prime}, s) \approx 0.76 < 1 = \text{entropy}_t(s).$$

The gain functions then deliver

$$\begin{aligned} \text{gain}_t(\mathit{1}, s) &= \text{entropy}_t(s) - \text{entropy}_t(\mathit{1}, s) = 1 - 0 = 1 \\ \text{gain}_t(\mathit{prime}, s) &= \text{entropy}_t(s) - \text{entropy}_t(\mathit{prime}, s) \approx 0.24. \end{aligned}$$

Clearly, the gain by *1* is 1, because *1* induces a partition of singletons. The gain by *prime*, however, is much less. The set of primes contains 1 even number and 24 odd numbers and the other class 49 even and 26 odd numbers. We now compute the normalised gain:

$$\begin{aligned} \text{gain}_t^{\text{norm}}(\mathit{1}, s) &= \frac{\text{gain}_t(\mathit{1}, s)}{\log_2 |s/R_{id}|} = \frac{1}{\log_2 100} \approx 0.15 \\ \text{gain}_t^{\text{norm}}(\mathit{prime}, s) &= \frac{\text{gain}_t(\mathit{prime}, s)}{\log_2 |s/R_{prime}|} = \frac{1 - \text{entropy}_t(\mathit{prime}, s)}{1} \approx 0.24. \end{aligned}$$

Now the primes appear to be a much better predictor for odd numbers.

There is a huge problem with codomain size weighted information gain: if a feature f has a very large codomain but takes only very few different values, then $\text{gain}_t^{\text{norm}}(f, s)$ underestimates. Supposing that $|\text{cod}(f)| \geq |\overline{f}|$ it holds that

$$\frac{\text{gain}_t(f, s)}{|\text{cod}(f)|} \leq \frac{\text{gain}_t(f, s)}{|\overline{f}|}.$$

Thinking a bit further we can find an even better normalisation. It seems much more reasonable to use the cardinality of the *range* of f as a normalising factor. Consider $\overline{f} = \{x, y\}$ and suppose $|\overline{f}x| = 1$ and $|\overline{f}y| = |s| - 1$. In such a case f helps to discriminate only one single object from all the others: its information content is poor. So instead of statically penalising a feature f by the size of its codomain or range, it appears much more reasonable to take into account the *distribution* of the feature values – and this is again measured in terms of entropy:

Gain ratio

Definition 5.31 — Gain ratio.
We define the *gain ratio* of a feature $f \in \mathbf{F}$ as its gain in relation to its splitting information. The gain ratio is the quotient of the actual gain $\text{gain}_t(f, s)$ (with respect to t) and the information of f:

$$\text{gain}_t^{\text{ratio}}(f, s) = \frac{\text{gain}_t(f, s)}{\text{entropy}_f(s)}. \tag{5.16}$$

●

One can, of course, define many different gain functions, one for every problem domain. But one must always be aware of the bias introduced by the definition. For example, $\text{gain}_t^{\text{ratio}}(f, s)$ is just the same as $\text{gain}_t(f, s)$ if we assume the entropies of all features to be 1. Also, if we assume all features to have the same number of possible values, then $\text{gain}_t^{\text{norm}}(f, s)$ is the same as $\text{gain}_t(f, s)$. If we *know* that a certain assumption is true on our data, then we can speed up the learning process considerably. If our knowledge of the domain is rather limited, every bias also limits the knowledge we can discover.

Exercise 5.32 (♦) Solve Exercises 5.16, 5.17, 5.27, and 5.28 using all the different gain functions we have defined. You might want to try to solve Exercise 5.18 first.

But even the most sophisticated gain measure will not help to overcome the biggest problem: the "better" a tree for classification, the bigger the chance for overfitting. We pick up again the idea from the end of the previous section: with a highly accurate or simply huge tree we want to know whether we should prune the tree – and, if so, how should we prune it?

5.5 Pruning

Quinlan (1992) describes an observation he made during a test run:

> [Given] an artificial [random] data set with 10 [binary] attributes ... with equal probability. The [target] class was also binary, **1** with probability 1/4, **0** with probability 3/4. One thousand randomly generated test cases were split into a training set of 500 and a test set of 500. From this data, C4.5's initial tree building routine produces a nonsensical tree of 119 nodes that has an error rate of more than 35% on the test cases.

It is clear that learning from random noise is impossible. Yet, the most interesting fact is that the resulting tree consists of 119 nodes and only reaches an accuracy of 65%. Because learning also requires some compression, it could be that a much smaller tree will not produce significantly worse results. As we already know, it is reasonable to return a suboptimal hypothesis rather than an overfit one.

Pruning

Exhaustive decision trees tend to be (1) too big in relation to their accuracy, or (2) they overfit (i.e., perform worse on test data). Accordingly, one would like to restrict tree growth or prune a fully grown tree afterwards. This way, the predictive accuracy/tree complexity can be increased and overfitting decisions can be cut off.
Pre-pruning uses error/complexity measures to stop the recursive deepening of a tree while post-pruning allows one to transform a tree into rules and prune individual rules or even only parts of rules.

An overly specific tree can be pruned by two different methods: first, during tree growth (i.e., we stop the inductive tree building process prematurely), and, second, after exhaustive tree construction. These two methods are called *pre-* and *post-pruning*, respectively:

- *Pre-pruning* means to abort the tree induction process as soon as some criterion is fulfilled (it is a bit like growing Bonsai).
- *Post-pruning* requires exhaustive growth and post-mortem pruning (which is a bit like clearing the rainforest).

In both cases the pruning methods can fail to produce a proper tree-cut. When pre-pruning, one can stop growing the tree if an added branch will not result in some information gain that is beyond a certain threshold (which again can be chosen statically or dynamically). Other simple heuristics are based on maximum number of nodes or leaves, branches per (sub)tree, or simply leaf the size. Quinlan (1986b) proposes a χ^2-test for significance of further branching a node. A completely different method of pre-pruning is some kind of a validation bias that tells us when a growing tree is considered to be good enough. Either way, pre-pruning is always *myopic*: because information gain decreases with tree depth, we can be sure not to lose more information than is gained in the last step, but we could just stop a few steps too early.

Post-pruning means to first grow a tree and then prune it. It can be regarded as a generate-and-test method with all its advantages and disadvantages:

> [B]ut this cost [of post-pruning] is offset against benefits due to a more thorough exploration of possible partitions. *Growing and pruning trees is slower but more reliable.* Quinlan (1992)

In the following sections we present two kinds of post-pruning: *reduced error pruning* defines an error estimate on decision trees (or rather their nodes). Then it prunes away leaves until an error threshold is reached. A completely different approach first disassembles the tree into an unordered set of rules. Then, *rule post-pruning* tries to drop the irrelevant rules or rule antecedents to generalise the rule set.

5.5.1 Reduced error pruning

Reduced error pruning cuts off subtrees (leaves or entire subtrees for internal nodes) to reduce the error of the hypothesis represented by that tree. To evaluate a node's error, one uses the following error estimate:

Node error rate

Definition 5.33 — Node error rate.
Let N be a node in a decision tree. If N is a leaf node, then

$$\operatorname{err}(N,t) := \frac{|\operatorname{errset}(N,t)|}{|\operatorname{cvr}(N)|}, \tag{5.17}$$

where $\operatorname{errset}(N,t) := \{x \in \operatorname{cvr}(N) : h_N(x) \neq t(x)\}$. If N is a decision node, then it has a set of successor nodes $\{N_i : 0 \leq i < |\operatorname{cod}(f)|\}$ and we define

$$\operatorname{err}(N,t) = \gamma(N)\frac{\sum_{i \in \operatorname{cod}(f)} |\operatorname{errset}(N_i,t)|}{\operatorname{cvr}(N_f)}. \tag{5.18}$$

$\gamma(N)$ is a weight function with which the error estimate can be adjusted to the branching factor (i.e., the cardinality of $\operatorname{cod}(f)$), the depth of N_f, or any other additional costs or benefits. ●

For now it suffices to take $\operatorname{err}(N,t)$ as an error measure that increases from root to leaves (we will come back to this later). This is somehow counterintuitive, but the reason for it is in the pruning algorithm we describe now. From the monotonicity it follows that if we prune away a subtree, the error measure overestimates the error in the remaining leaf by at least the depth of the pruned tree. But by overestimating the error we are at least on the safe side. A top-down pruning algorithm is shown in Figure 5.7.

Example 5.34 Recall our example domain as shown in Figure 4.3. Now let there be a set s with $|s| = 50$ different geometric objects. We want to classify them into four different classes: diamonds, triangles, rhomboids, and ellipses; that is, $\operatorname{cod}(t) = 4$. Let there be three features

```
01 proc prune(N, ϑ)
02 { IF (err_s(N,t)) ≤ ϑ) THEN
03     { return(N) };
04   ELSE
05     { FOREACH N_i ∈ sucessors(N) DO
06         { N_i := prune(N_i, ϑ) };
07       return (N);
08     }
09 }
```

Note that when returning N in line 7, its value has changed since the procedure call because of the reassignment of N_i in line 6. Simple improvements include a dynamic change of ϑ in line 6 or an adaptation of γ used in $\operatorname{err}_s(N,t)$.

Fig. 5.7 Top-down reduced error pruning

$\mathbf{F} = \{f_0, f_1, f_2\}$ with codomains $\{1, 2, 3\}$, $\{a, b, c\}$, and $\{\bullet, \circledcirc, \circ\}$, respectively. Now imagine that $tdidt(s, \{f_0, f_1, f_2\})$ delivers a tree N as follows:

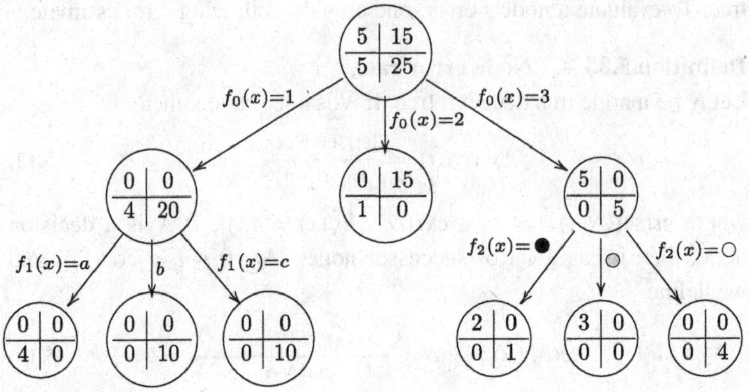

The four quadrants in each node represent the number of objects for which

$$t(x) = \begin{array}{c|c} 0 & 1 \\ \hline 2 & 3 \end{array}$$

We assume $\gamma(N) = 1$. Then, all leaves except two nodes have zero error:

$$\mathrm{err}_s\left(\begin{array}{c|c} 2 & 0 \\ \hline 0 & 1 \end{array}, t\right) = \frac{1}{3} \qquad \mathrm{err}_s\left(\begin{array}{c|c} 0 & 15 \\ \hline 1 & 0 \end{array}, t\right) = \frac{1}{16}.$$

The error estimates for the second layer of the tree are

$$\mathrm{err}_s\left(\begin{array}{c|c} 0 & 0 \\ \hline 4 & 20 \end{array}, t\right) = \frac{4}{24} = \frac{1}{6} \qquad \mathrm{err}_s\left(\begin{array}{c|c} 5 & 0 \\ \hline 0 & 5 \end{array}, t\right) = \frac{5}{10} = \frac{1}{2}.$$

For the root node we obtain $\frac{5+15+5}{50} = \frac{25}{50} = \frac{1}{2}$. ●

Exercise 5.35 (◇) Determine the node errors for the tree in Figure 5.5.

We apply the pruning algorithm from Figure 5.7 on the tree from Example 5.34 and call *prune*(N) with N being the root node and $\vartheta = 0.2$. Because $\frac{1}{2} > \vartheta$, we call *prune* recursively on all of the root node's successor nodes. For $f_0(x) = 1$, the error is $\frac{1}{6} \leq 0.2$. Therefore, its successor nodes are pruned away. For $f_0(x) = 2$, it is $\frac{1}{16}$. But because it is a leaf node, there is nothing left to be pruned away. For $f_0(x) = 3$, it is still $\frac{1}{2} > 0.2$, which is why we need to call *prune* recursively on all of its successor nodes. The resulting tree after reduced error pruning is

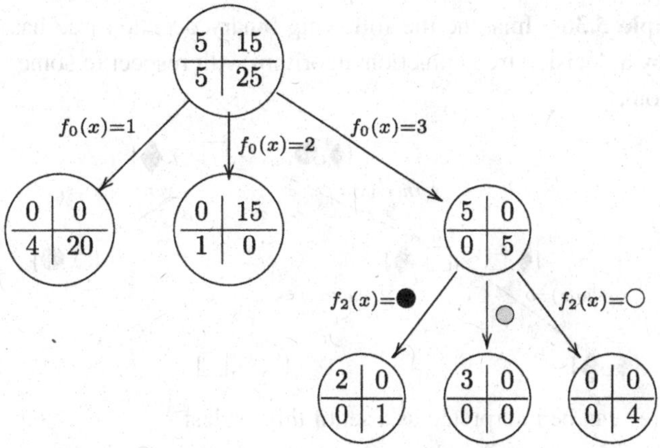

Another method for reduced error pruning is to start at the leaf nodes and prune a node and all of its brothers if the error in the parent node does not increase by more than a certain threshold. The advantage of this algorithm is that we do not recompute error measures as in the algorithm shown in Figure 5.7.

There are many related error measures and according algorithms; the error complexity measure presented here was first used in CART (Breiman et al. 1984).

Niblett and Bratko (1986) and Cestnik et al. (1987) describe a minimal error pruning method and Mingers (1989) gives an empirical comparison of different pruning methods. As a successor to ID3, Quinlan's (1992) C4.5 also allows for reduced error post-pruning.

5.5.2 Rule-based post-pruning

A completely different idea is to translate a tree into a set of rules and then prune the rule set. This method has a huge advantage: one can delete entire rules from a set of rules and rules can be weakened by pruning away parts of their antecedents.

Rule representations of decision trees
A decision tree can be expressed by a set of rules where each rule represents a path in the tree. The premise of each rule is a conjunction of all the feature-value restrictions along the edges and the conclusions consist of the hypotheses represented by the leaf nodes.

Decision trees can be translated into a set of rules very easily. As a tree is a hierarchical partitioning with respect to increasingly fine grained equivalence relations, tree traversal from root to leaf is simply a conjunction of predicates derived from the intersections of the equivalence relations induced by the respective features.

Example 5.36 Imagine the following binary decision tree has been built by a decision tree induction algorithm with respect to some target function t:

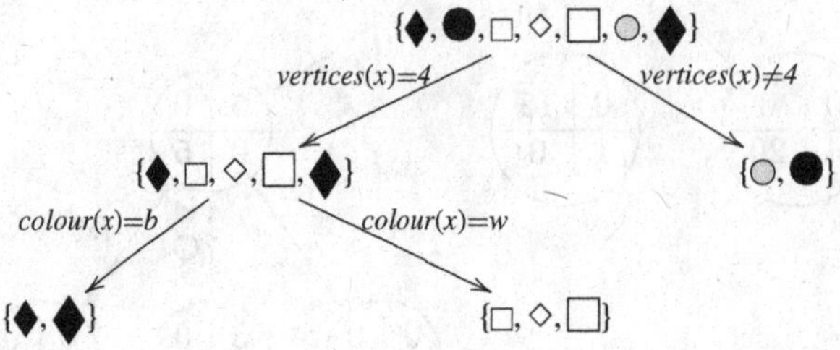

This tree can be interpreted as a set of three rules:

$(vertices(x) = 4) \quad \wedge \quad (colour(x) = black) \quad \longrightarrow \quad x \in \{$◆, ◆$\}$
$(vertices(x) = 4) \quad \wedge \quad (colour(x) = white) \quad \longrightarrow \quad x \in \{$□, ◇, □$\}$
$(vertices(x) \neq 4) \quad \longrightarrow \quad x \in \{$○, ●$\}$.

Depending on cod(t), this rule set can be further interpreted: the first rule defines the predicate *rhombus*(x), the second one *square*(x), and the third one *circle*(x). If we were not restricted to decision trees, we could even formulate the following rules:

$$\begin{array}{lcl} (vertices(x) = 4) & \longrightarrow & rhombus(x) \vee square(x) \\ (colour(x) \neq white) & \longrightarrow & rhombus(x) \vee circle(x) \\ (colour(x) = white) & \longrightarrow & square(x). \end{array}$$

Perhaps we could even generalise further and guess that *rhombus*(x) implies *colour*(x) = *black*.

Exercise 5.37 (◇) Explain why ($colour(x) = black) \longrightarrow rhombus(x)$ is wrong.

Formally, every leaf in a decision is connected to the root along a path through several decision nodes along edges that define an object's value for the decision node's feature.

Definition 5.38 — Rule representations of decision trees.

Rule representations of decision trees

Let N_f be the root node of a decision tree. As a hypothesis it always returns the most common class value. We define

$$\varphi(N_f) := \left\{ (h(x) = h_{N_f}(x)) \right\}. \tag{5.19}$$

This set, when read as a set of literals, is a Horn clause with an empty premise (that is, it is true: **1**):

$$\mathbf{1} \longrightarrow h(x) = h_{N_f}(x).$$

Every non-root node has all the feature-value restrictions along its path as premises. Let M be a successor of a node N_f such that M subsumes all the objects covered by N_f for which $f(x) = v$. Then,

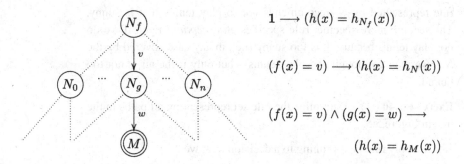

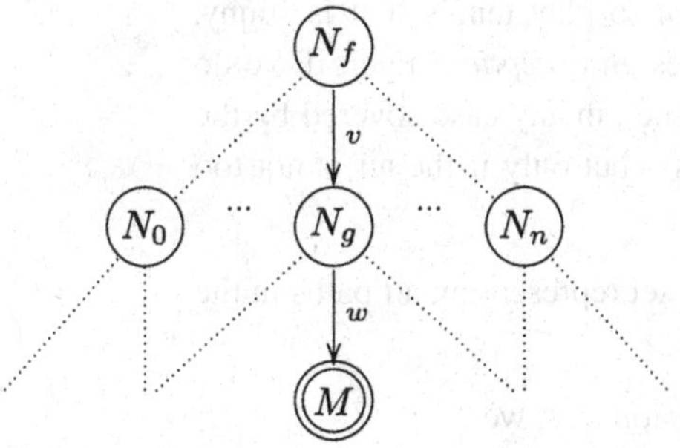

$$\mathbf{1} \longrightarrow (h(x) = h_{N_f}(x))$$

$$(f(x) = v) \longrightarrow (h(x) = h_N(x))$$

$$(f(x) = v) \wedge (g(x) = w) \longrightarrow (h(x) = h_M(x))$$

Fig. 5.8 Converting a decision tree into a set of decision rules

$$\begin{aligned} \varphi(M) \quad := \quad & \varphi(N_f) \\ & - \left\{(h(x) = h_{N_f}(x))\right\} \\ & \cup \{\neg(f(x) = v), (h(x) = h_M(x))\}\,. \end{aligned} \tag{5.20}$$

This expression adds the literal $f(x) = v$ to the set of premises and changes the tree hypothesis to the hypothesis represented by M. An example is shown in Figure 5.8. ●

Let us consider the tree from Figure 5.5 again.

Example 5.39 We build the tree beginning at the root node and proceed all the way down to the leaves:

$$\varphi(N_t) \quad = \quad \left\{(h(x) = h_{N_t}(x))\right\}.$$

The root node is divided by *forecast* into three successor nodes. The first one is N_s with

$$\begin{aligned} \varphi(N_s) \quad &= \quad \varphi(N_t) - \left\{(h(x) = h_{N_t}(x))\right\} \cup \left\{\neg(\mathit{forecast}(x) = s), \right. \\ & \qquad\qquad \left. (h(x) = h_{N_s}(x))\right\} \\ &= \quad (\mathit{forecast}(x) = s) \longrightarrow (h(x) = \mathrm{mcv}_t(\mathrm{cvr}(N_s))) \\ &= \quad (\mathit{forecast}(x) = s) \longrightarrow (h(x) = \mathbf{0}). \end{aligned}$$

The next step is to partition N_s by *humidity*:

$$\begin{aligned} \varphi(N_l) \quad &= \quad \varphi(N_s) - \left\{(h(x) = h_{N_s}(x))\right\} \cup \left\{\neg(\mathit{humidity}(x) = l), \right. \\ & \qquad\qquad \left. (h(x) = h_{N_l}(x))\right\} \\ &= \quad (\mathit{forecast}(x) = s) \wedge (\mathit{humidity}(x) = l) \longrightarrow (h(x) = \\ & \qquad\qquad \mathrm{mcv}_t(\mathrm{cvr}(N_l))) \\ &= \quad (\mathit{forecast}(x) = s) \wedge (\mathit{humidity}(x) = l) \longrightarrow (h(x) = \mathbf{1}). \end{aligned}$$

Now the rule set $\{\varphi(N_s), \varphi(N_l)\}$ obviously is inconsistent. But as long as we cannot prove that the weather is sunny with low humidity, we could still try and prove a sunny forecast only. The first, more general, rule represented by N_s recommends *not* to play tennis if it is sunny. The second, more specific, rule specifies an *exception*: Even if we do not play tennis because it is too sunny (i.e., in any case covered by the N_s), we may go though and play tennis – but only if the air is not too humid.

Exercise 5.40 (◇) Determine the rule set representing all paths in the tree in Figure 5.5.

To apply rule post-pruning to a decision tree, we

1. Induce a full tree (unbiased).
2. Translate the tree into rules.
3. Prune the rules instead of the tree.
4. Sort and/or translate rules back into a tree.

With rule-based post-pruning we are able to prune away subtrees just as we did in pre-pruning. In addition, we can also delete *parts* of paths, which, graphically, does not result in a tree any more but rather in a forest. To give you an idea, we examine the geometric shape domain again.

Example 5.41 Recall the decision tree from Example 5.36. Obviously, the feature *colour* is sufficient to discriminate squares from non-squares, but it is not sufficient to tell circles from tetragons in general (and, specifically, rhombuses). All the squares are white (◇, □, □) and none of the other shapes are white. On the other hand, ● and ◆ or ◆ are black, but only the former one is a circle whilst the latter two shapes are rhombuses. So whenever discriminating squares from non-squares we can safely drop the restriction to tetragons ($vertices(x) = 4$). Let us take at the leaf nodes. From

$$\begin{array}{lclcl} (vertices(x) = 4) & \wedge & (colour(x) = black) & \longrightarrow & rhombus(x) \\ (vertices(x) = 4) & \wedge & (colour(x) = white) & \longrightarrow & square(x) \\ (vertices(x) \neq 4) & & & \longrightarrow & circle(x) \end{array}$$

we delete the first premise of the second rule and obtain

$$\begin{array}{lclcl} (vertices(x) = 4) & \wedge & (colour(x) = black) & \longrightarrow & rhombus(x) \\ & & (colour(x) = white) & \longrightarrow & square(x) \\ (vertices(x) \neq 4) & & & \longrightarrow & circle(x). \end{array}$$

The result is a tree that is no longer a proper decision tree. And if $x \in \{□, ◇, □\} \Longrightarrow t(x) = \mathbf{1}$, then we can drop the entire root node:

$$\begin{array}{lcl} white(x) & \longrightarrow & square(x) \\ \neg white(x) & \longrightarrow & \neg square(x). \end{array}$$

This example shows that rule-based post-pruning – despite its increased computational effort due to full tree expansion – has at least three important advantages over ordinary (pruned) decision trees:

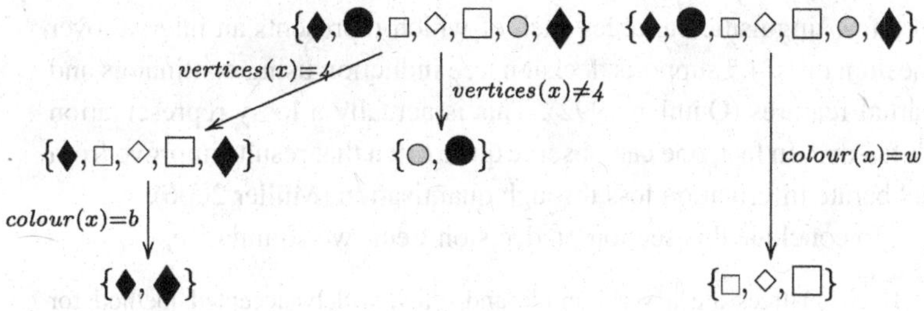

Fig. 5.9 Rule pruning results in a forest of trees

- Even though the trees are a very simple and scrutable representations of hypotheses, small rule sets are better suited for conceptual descriptions.
- Based on rule sets and appropriate operators (rule and literal dropping) we can formulate both more specific and generic hypotheses with less error.
- With rule sets we can express things that are not representable by a single decision tree at all

The "forest" of trees corresponding to the rule sets from the previous example is shown in Figure 5.9. After the second pruning step, the forest in Figure 5.9 finally implodes to

$$\{\blacklozenge, \square, \diamond, \square, \blacklozenge\}$$
$$colour(x)=w \downarrow$$
$$\{\square, \diamond, \square\} .$$

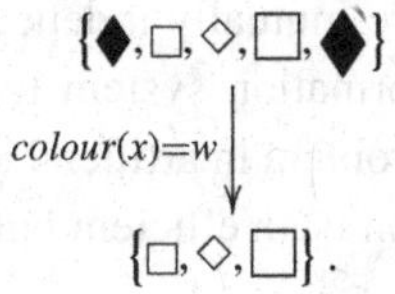

5.6 Conclusion

This chapter presented a purely relational view on a popular machine learning method, namely, decision tree induction. The various algorithms are nothing more than a heuristically driven search for a partitioning of the base set with respect to a decision attribute (i.e., the target function). The relational view makes it much easier to understand several interesting properties of decision trees.

There remain a few open questions.

First, we have not explained how to deal with (quasi-)continuous feature values. If, for example, the humidity in Figure 5.5 is not described by three qualitative linguistic variables but by an integer from the interval [0, 99], then we would have to split a node in up to 100 successor nodes, which is not really informative. Instead, one applies a quantisation algorithm like *binning* first. This yields a "discretised" set of a few linguisitic variables each of which represents an interval over the domain. C4.5 supports decision tree induction using continuous and partial features (Quinlan 1992). This is actually a lossy representation shift – and, in fact, one can observe quite often that results improve from deliberate information loss through quantisation (Müller 2006).

To conclude this section on decision trees, we summarise:

1. Decision trees are a very simple and, thus, widely accepted method for representing classifiers
2. Objects of the domain are described by attribute–value pairs
3. All features have discrete codomains. This can be forced by quantisation.
4. TDIDT can cope with noisy training data due to its entropy-based measure of information
5. An exhaustive search for the smallest, **s**-consistent tree is NP-complete as shown by Hyafil and Rivest in 1976, but an information gain guided search is a very quick greedy approach.

Finally, we again stress the fact that entropy usually assumes a uniform distribution over all possible system states. This is taken into account by a probability weighted sum as introduced with the measure of information-theoretic entropy by Shannon and Weaver in 1949. In thermodynamics we operate with mutually independent states of closed systems. In a domain of information processing, it is hardly the case that messages in a sequence are mutually independent – and it is not clear what it means for an information system to be closed (an issue that might point to the frame problem in artificial intelligence again). Therefore, decision tree induction is an efficient but biased tool for relational knowledge discovery.

Chapter 6
Rough set theory

All of the algorithms we have come across so far make several (severe) assumptions on the domain. Together with the knowledge we feed into our learning systems, the representation itself and the implementation of algorithms may result in heavy biases. But what if we just look at the objects we are given and their relational properties? Why should we try to discriminate indistinguishable objects instead of interpreting indiscernability as "being-of-the-same-breed" – whatever our current knowledge of different existing breeds is?

At the beginning of the last chapter we discovered that features induce equivalence relations and that equivalence relations create blocks of indiscernible objects, that is, "small groups of similar, equal, or equivalent things". Any two objects in an equivalence class cannot be distinguished from each other, but two objects from different classes can be well discriminated. For our information systems that usually provide a large number of features, we also have many equivalence relations. Furthermore, any intersection of any subset of such equivalence relations also forms a new equivalence relation. And because equivalence relations are relations, and because relations are sets, it appears to be an interesting idea to consider the *intersection* of equivalence relations as a much finer and more detailed partitioning of our base set.

6.1 Knowledge and discernability

For an arbitrary set of equivalence relations $\mathbf{R} = \{R_i : i \in \mathbf{n}\}$, the intersection

$$\bigcap_{i \in \mathbf{n}} R_i \tag{6.1}$$

is also an equivalence relation.

Exercise 6.1 Is it that time already? Yes, it is that time! Prove that the intersection of two equivalence relations is an equivalence relation. Because you have read the first chapter, this exercise is not even worth a single ◇.

Now that the intersection of two equivalence relations somehow corresponds to a logical conjunction, it is clear that the blocks get smaller because the premises become more special (we already discovered this fact at the end of Chapter 5). Accordingly, the most detailed knowledge we can get from **R** is $\bigcap \mathbf{R}$.

Definition 6.2 — Indiscernability relation.

Indiscernability relation

For a set **R** of equivalence relations over s we call

$$\bar{\bar{\mathbf{R}}} = \bigcap_{R \in \mathbf{R}} R = \bigcap \mathbf{R} \tag{6.2}$$

the *indiscernability relation over* **R**. Of course, $\bar{\bar{\mathbf{R}}}$ is an equivalence relation. Sometimes we write $x \overset{\mathbf{R}}{=} y :\Longleftrightarrow x\bar{\bar{\mathbf{R}}}y$. ●

With given knowledge **R** we can examine s in terms of different partitions, blocks, and blocks of different partitions:

- Elements of s/R for any $R \in \mathbf{R}$ are called *elementary categories*. They correspond to R-equivalence classes and determine the sets of objects that share the same value under the feature that induced R.
- Elements of $s/\bar{\bar{\mathbf{R}}}$ are called (**R**-) *basic categories*. Any element of the quotient $s/\bar{\bar{\mathbf{R}}}$ is a set of objects that are indiscernible using *all* the relations in **R**.

Because basic categories include the knowledge of several relations, they usually are *finer* than elementary categories, while elementary categories are *coarser*.

Exercise 6.3 (◇) Prove that elementary categories are unions of basic categories, and that every basic category is a subset of an elementary category.

The finest partition of s, which is induced by $\bar{\bar{\mathbf{R}}}$, is what we call the *(indiscernability) knowledge* about s. More technically speaking, it forms a *knowledge base*.

Knowledge base

Definition 6.4 — Knowledge base.
For an information system $\mathfrak{I} = \langle s, \mathbf{F}, V_{\mathbf{F}} \rangle$, we use $\mathbf{R}$ to denote the set of equivalence relations induced by $\mathbf{F}$:

$$R_i \in \mathbf{R} \Longleftrightarrow f_i \in \mathbf{F} \text{ and } xR_iy \Longleftrightarrow \forall x \in s : f_i(x) = f(y).$$

Then we call

$$\mathfrak{K} = \left\langle s, \mathbf{R} \cup \left\{ \bar{\bar{\mathbf{P}}} : \mathbf{P} \subseteq \mathbf{R} \right\} \right\rangle \tag{6.3}$$

the *knowledge base* (of $\mathbf{R}$ on s). ●

Exercise 6.5 (◇) Show that $\bar{\bar{\mathbf{R}}} = \bigcap \left\{ \bar{\bar{\mathbf{P}}} : \mathbf{P} \subseteq \mathbf{R} \right\}$.

A knowledge base does not contain any more information than the information system from which it is derived – the only thing that makes knowledge from information is that we are able to express the information in several ways. We now shall see why.

Example 6.6 Figure 6.1 shows a set of objects and two equivalence relations on it. Each equivalence class of the colour or shape relation forms an elementary category. The left part shows the equivalence classes with respect to colour and the right one shows the shape-elementary classes. ●

Indiscernability

An indiscernability relation describes all objects of the universe by means of *all* the relational knowledge we have. Different objects that belong to the same equivalence class of such an indiscernability relation are not distinguishable by any piece or the entirety of our knowledge.

If we are able to describe all the objects well enough, then we are interested in minimal sets of knowledge that still suffice to distinguish different things from each other.

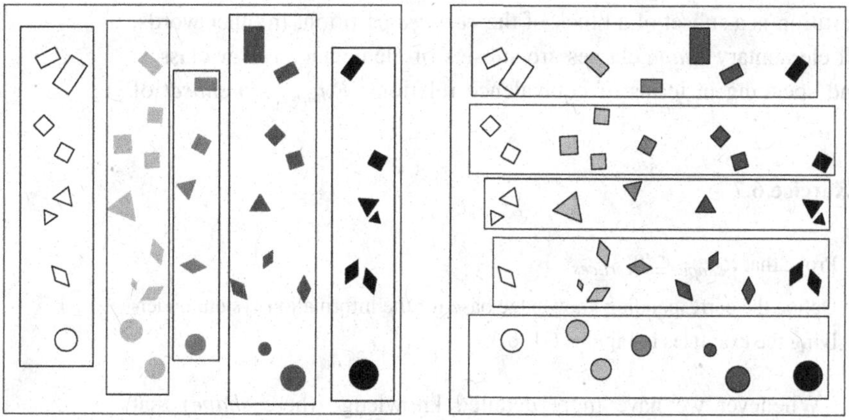

Fig. 6.1 A universe and two equivalence relations on it

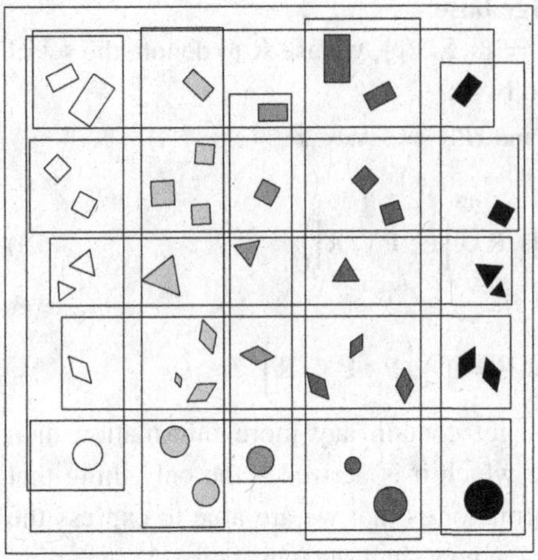

Fig. 6.2 An indiscernability relation

By intersecting the shape and colour relations from Figure 6.1 we obtain a much finer partition of the set: we can, for example, discriminate dark squares from white squares (which we could not do without the knowledge of colours) and grey circles from grey diamonds (which we could not do without the knowledge of shapes). This is shown in Figure 6.2. Let us take a look at a further equivalence relation. Imagine a feature *vertices* : $U \to \mathbb{N}$ that describes the number of corners of an object. The induced equivalence relation would then partition our base set into three blocks: one containing all the circles ($vertices(x) = 0$); one containing all the rectangles, squares, and rhombuses ($vertices(x) = 4$); and one containing all the triangles ($vertices(x) = 3$). This is shown in the left part of Figure 6.3. As one can see, every block of the *shape* partition is a subset of a block of the *vertices* partition. In other words, all elementary *shape* classes are subsets of elementary *vertex* classes, and speaking in terms of equivalence relations, R_{shape} is a *subset* of $R_{vertices}$.

Exercise 6.7

- Prove that $R_{shape} \subseteq R_{vertices}$.
- Define the corresponding knowledge base for the information system underlying the examples in Figures 6.1–6.3.

Whenever we have more detailed knowledge (here *shape*) that allows us to formulate more accurate concepts, we usually say that the additional information contributes to our knowledge by *refining*

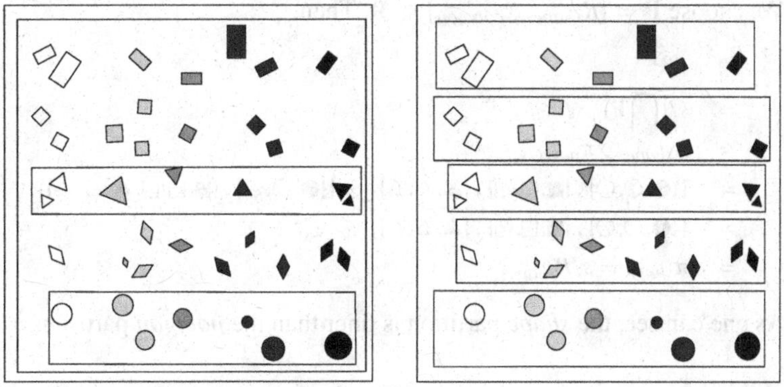

Fig. 6.3 Another equivalence relation

our previously rather rough conceptualisations.[1] This leads us to the following definition.

Refinement

Definition 6.8 — Refinement.
For two sets $\mathbf{P}, \mathbf{R}$ of equivalence relations we say that $\mathbf{R}$ is *finer* (*less general*) than $\mathbf{P}$:

$$\mathbf{R} \preceq \mathbf{P} \quad \text{if and only if} \quad \bar{\bar{\mathbf{R}}} \subseteq \bar{\bar{\mathbf{P}}}. \tag{6.4}$$

If $\bar{\bar{\mathbf{R}}}$ *refines* $\bar{\bar{\mathbf{P}}}$, then $\mathbf{P}$ is *coarser* than $\mathbf{R}$. ●

The choice of $\preceq$ as a symbol for refinement is, as one can see in the definition, motivated by the fact that the refined induced equivalence relation, when viewed as sets of tuples, in fact is a *subset* of the coarser relation. This becomes clear when representing the relations graphically in coincidence $\mathbb{M}(\bar{\bar{\mathbf{R}}})$ or kernel matrices $\mathbb{K}(\bar{\bar{\mathbf{R}}})$ (see Section 2.2.1). To familiarise the reader with the formal aspects (rather than just painting Venn diagrams), we now apply our definitions to a subproblem of our graphical example.

Example 6.9 Let $\mathfrak{K} = \langle s, \mathbf{R} \rangle$ be an information system as follows:

$$\begin{aligned} s &= \{●, ■, ▲, ◍, ▩, ◬, ○, □, △\} \\ \mathbf{R} &= \{R_{colour}, R_{shape}, R_{polygon}\}. \end{aligned}$$

[1] An extreme case is where $s/\bar{\bar{\mathbf{P}}} = \{\{x\} : x \in s\}$. Then, $\bar{\bar{\mathbf{P}}}$ creates a set of singleton equivalence classes and *all* objects $x \in s$ are pairwise discernible using knowledge $\mathbf{P}$.

We choose $\mathbf{P} = \{R_{shape}, R_{polygon}\} \subset \mathbf{R}$. Then,

$$
\begin{aligned}
& s/\bar{\bar{\mathbf{P}}} \\
= \; & s/(\bigcap \mathbf{P}) \\
= \; & \pi_{shape} \odot \pi_{polygon} \\
= \; & \{\{●,◍,○\},\{■,▨,□\},\{▲,◬,△\}\} \odot \{\{●,◍,○\},\{■,▨,□,▲,◬,△\}\} \\
= \; & \{\{●,◍,○\},\{■,▨,□\},\{▲,◬,△\}\} \\
= \; & \pi_{shape} = s/R_{shape}.
\end{aligned}
$$

As one can see, the *shape* partition is finer than the *polygon* partition.[2]

●

So what if two sets of equivalence relations of a knowledge base have exactly the same degree of coarseness in the sense that one refines the other, and vice versa? From $x \leq y$ and $y \leq x$ we usually infer that $x = y$. Similarly, mutual refinement defines the *equivalence* of knowledge:

Equivalence of knowledge

Definition 6.10 — Equivalence of knowledge.
R and **P** are called *equivalent* if

$$\mathbf{R} \equiv \mathbf{P} \;:\Longleftrightarrow\; \bar{\bar{\mathbf{R}}} \preceq \bar{\bar{\mathbf{P}}} \wedge \bar{\bar{\mathbf{P}}} \preceq \bar{\bar{\mathbf{R}}} \Longleftrightarrow \bar{\bar{\mathbf{R}}} = \bar{\bar{\mathbf{P}}}. \tag{6.5}$$

Then, $s/\mathbf{R} = s/\mathbf{P}$. ●

Note that $\mathbf{P} = \mathbf{R}$ implies $\mathbf{P} \equiv \mathbf{R}$, but *not* vice versa. This is a very important observation. It expresses the fact that the same knowledge can be expressed in different terms!

Keep in mind that $\bar{\bar{\mathbf{R}}}$ is a relation.
Note that whenever we speak of a set **R** of equivalence relations, $\bar{\bar{\mathbf{R}}}$ is also an equivalence relation. Therefore, if we consent to denote by R an arbitrary equivalence relation, there is no difference between $\mathbf{P} \equiv \mathbf{R}$ or $P = R$, because $P = \bar{\bar{\mathbf{P}}} = \bar{\bar{\mathbf{R}}} = R$.

Nevertheless, we will carefully distinguish between sets **R** of relations and relations R. Therefore, $\bar{\bar{\mathbf{R}}}$ is a single relation (e.g., $R := \bar{\bar{\mathbf{R}}}$), but for a single relation R, $\bar{\bar{R}}$ is not defined (whereas $\overline{\overline{\{R\}}} = R$ is well defined).

Example 6.11 Recall Example 6.9. As one can see, $R_{shape} \preceq R_{polygon}$ such that $\pi_{shape} \odot \pi_{polygon} = \pi_{shape}$. We choose $\mathbf{P} = \{R_{shape}, R_{colour}\} \subset \mathbf{R}$. Then,

$$
\begin{aligned}
& s/\bar{\bar{\mathbf{P}}} \\
& = \pi_{shape} \odot \pi_{colour} \\
& = \{\{●,◍,○\},\{■,▨,□\},\{▲,◬,△\}\} \odot \{\{●,■,▲\},\{◍,▨,◬\},\{○,□,△\}\} \\
& = \{\{●\},\{■\},\{▲\},\{◍\},\{▨\},\{◬\},\{○\},\{□\},\{△\}\}.
\end{aligned}
$$

[2] "$\odot$" denotes pairwise intersection: $s_0 \odot s_1 := \{s'_0 \cap s'_1 : s'_0 \in s_0, s'_1 \in s_1\} - \emptyset$.

Similarly,

$$
\begin{aligned}
& \{\blacksquare, {\color{gray}\blacksquare}, \square\} \cup \{{\color{gray}\bullet}, {\color{gray}\blacksquare}, {\color{gray}\blacktriangle}\} \\
= & \{\blacksquare\} \cup \{{\color{gray}\blacksquare}\} \cup \{\square\} \cup \{{\color{gray}\bullet}\} \cup \{{\color{gray}\blacktriangle}\} \\
= & \{\blacksquare, {\color{gray}\blacksquare}, \square, {\color{gray}\bullet}, {\color{gray}\blacktriangle}\}
\end{aligned}
$$

is the $\mathbf{P} = \{R_{shape}, R_{colour}\}$–category of squarish or dark objects.

We end this introductory section with a small remark. In most books on rough set theory there are Venn diagram-like examples for the concepts presented in this chapter. They all differ slightly from Figures 6.1–6.4 in this book. Take Figure 6.1: the boundaries of the different equivalence relations do *not* coincide, not even in cases where they create the same line of distinction between discernible objects. The reason for this is that relations carry *intensional knowledge* while discernability on object level carries information about memberships, that is, *extensional knowledge*. So if two collections of things (called a set) are equal, then an object belongs to one of these collections if and only if it belongs to the other collection as well. This is called (*elementwise* or *pointwise*) equality of sets. But if we understand sets as collections that are *defined* in terms of relations, the sets are defined by their meanings, which is not the same as their content. Accordingly, a set can be a subset of another when looking at it elementwise – but it may also have an "empty" region outside the superset (see Figure 6.4 in the next section).

6.2 Rough knowledge

Let us briefly recall the definition of a knowledge base. A knowledge base contains all intersections of all subsets of our set of relations $\mathbf{R}$. Accordingly, $R \in \mathbf{R} \Longrightarrow \bar{\bar{\mathbf{R}}} \subseteq R$ and all pairwise intersections of relations are elements of $\mathfrak{K} = \langle s, \mathbf{R} \rangle$, and so are the elements of the closure under intersections. The set of equivalence relations is not closed under set union, but we can still add a whole lot of equivalence relations to our knowledge base. Let there be two elementary classes from possibly different relations:

$$[x]_P \text{ and } [y]_R.$$

Then, $\chi([x]_P \cup [y]_R)$ induces an equivalence relation of index 2. If we iterate this process, we can construct equivalence relations for *any union* of basic categories of $\bar{\bar{\mathbf{R}}}$.

Example 6.12 For example,

$$
\begin{aligned}
[\blacksquare]_{shape} & \cup [\blacksquare]_{colour} = \{\blacksquare, {\color{gray}\blacksquare}, \square, \blacktriangle, \bullet\} \\
[\blacksquare]_{shape} & \cup [\bigcirc]_{colour} = \{\blacksquare, {\color{gray}\blacksquare}, \square, \triangle, \bigcirc\} \\
[\blacksquare]_{shape} & \cup [\bigcirc]_{shape} = \{\blacksquare, {\color{gray}\blacksquare}, \square, \bullet, {\color{gray}\bullet}, \bigcirc\}.
\end{aligned}
$$

By using intersections to derive basic classes from elementary ones and unions to form groups of basic categories we can define and describe a huge set of subsets of s. This set is the set of concepts we can express – and it corresponds to what we have called *hypothesis space*.

Data, information, and knowledge

Information helps us to discriminate objects from each other. Knowledge, on the other hand, allows us to operate on elementary categories to describe concepts by conjunctions (intersection) and disjunctions (union) of basic properties:

- *Data* is a set of representations of observations.
- *Information* is what we need to define a structure on the data.
- *Knowledge* is the toolbox we have to define such a structure.

So data are instances of concepts, information is what tells us whether an object belongs to a concept, and knowledge is what allows us to define a concept. The more knowledge, the more ways to describe the same concept.

6.2.1 Rough approximations

We use these relations to define a set or concept $c \subseteq s$:

Definition 6.13 — Definability. Definability

A concept (i.e., a set) c is called **R**-*definable* if there exists a set $\dot{c} \subseteq s$ such that c equals the union set of all R-equivalence classes of all objects in $\dot{c}$:

$$c \text{ is } \mathbf{R}\text{-definable} :\Longleftrightarrow \exists \dot{c} \subseteq s : c = \bigcup_{x \in \dot{c}} [x]_{\bar{\bar{\mathbf{R}}}}.$$

Otherwise, c is called **R**-*undefinable*. The dot notation $\dot{c}$ is an allusion to the pointwise definition of sets. ●

The set $\dot{c}$ is called a set of *representatives*, and, of course, every element of an equivalence class is a representative of its class. Let there be a classification $\mathfrak{c} = s/R$. Then a set $\dot{c}$ is a set of representatives for $\mathfrak{c}$ (or, equivalently, for R) if

$$\bigcup_{x \in \dot{c}} [x]_R = s \text{ and } \forall x, y \in \dot{c} : x \neq y \Longrightarrow [x]_R \neq [y]_R.$$

This allows us to *reduce* the amount of data required to store the information from our underlying information system in two different ways:

1. Reduction by knowledge:
   We already discovered that $\forall R \in \mathbf{R} : \bar{\bar{\mathbf{R}}} \preceq R$. Accordingly, the information in $\mathfrak{I}$ can be reconstructed by $\bar{\bar{\mathbf{R}}}$. We can extend $\mathfrak{I}$ to $\mathfrak{K}$ by adding all possible concept descriptions using all possible subsets of relations in **R**.

2. Reduction by representatives:
   Using the *knowledge* of $\mathfrak{K}$, a concept can be *represented* by "examples" that stand for equivalence classes. The concept can be reconstructed by joining the equivalence classes.

Example 6.14 (On the complexity of knowledge) Let us assume there is a base set s with m elements in it. There are $2^{|s|}$ subsets of s. We want to describe one out of 2^m classes by using a set of equivalence relations. Usually, we are given such a set of, say, n different relations $\mathbf{R} = \{R_i : i \in \mathbf{n}\}$. But how many possible equivalence relations are there on a base set of size m? The number of equivalence relations is the m-th Bell number, which in our case is

$$B(m) = \sum_{k \in \mathbf{m}} \binom{m}{k} B(k).$$

The Bell numbers increase at a truly exorbitant rate; for considerable small sets s of size $m = 20$ one can already define 5,832,742,205,057 different equivalence relations.

Let us examine the set of basic categories we can use to define a concept $c \subseteq s$ using a set $\mathbf{R}$ of relations. The number of basic categories equals the index of $\overline{\overline{\mathbf{R}}}$. If we assume c to be definable at all, there must exist a union of basic classes (or, equivalently, a union of intersections of elementary classes) that equals c. This expression does not need not to be unique; even for fixed c and $\mathbf{R}$ there can be many different ways to define c. The number of possible hypotheses that can be built by union sets of basic categories is $2^{|s/\overline{\overline{\mathbf{R}}}|}$, that is, 2 to the power of the index of $\overline{\overline{\mathbf{R}}}$. Of course some of the union sets will be the same, but that does not affect the fact that there are so many different ways to *compute* them. Let us call the set of all these union sets Φ. To describe c in terms of some $\varphi = c_1 \cup c_2 \cup \cdots \cup c_k \in \Phi$ (and recall that c may be definable by a huge number of such unions) we can pick a representative for every basic category c_i in any of these descriptions. This means in turn that there are $\prod_{i \in \mathbf{k}} |c_i|$ different sets of representatives that we can use to describe φ.

These few numbers should demonstrate the infeasability of an uninformed brute force method to discover knowledge. But they also demonstrate the vast amount of complexity hidden in knowledge – or, vice versa, they also demonstrate that with relatively little additional knowledge one can cover information of immensely additional complexity.

But what if our knowledge is not sufficient to describe x *exactly*? If x is only *nearly* R-definable, we speak of *approximate* definitions.

Definition 6.15 — Lower/upper approximations. Lower/upper approximations
Let there be a concept $c \subseteq s$ and an equivalence relation R. We define the *lower* and *upper R-approximations* of c as

$$[\![R]\!]c := \{x : x \in s \wedge [x]_R \subseteq c\} \quad (6.6)$$
$$\langle\!|R|\!\rangle c := \{x : x \in s \wedge [x]_R \cap c \neq \emptyset\}. \quad (6.7)$$

The *R-boundary* of a concept c is the set defined by the difference of the upper and the lower approximations:

$$\dot{\langle\!|R|\!\rangle} c := \langle\!|R|\!\rangle c - [\![R]\!]c. \quad (6.8)$$

The narrower this region, the closer our approximation to c. For a given set c, the *(R-)rough (c-)set* is defined as the tuple $\langle [\![R]\!]c, \langle\!|R|\!\rangle c\rangle$. To reduce notational effort, we write $[\![\mathbf{R}]\!]c := [\![\overset{\mathbf{R}}{=}]\!]c$ and $\langle\!|\mathbf{R}|\!\rangle c := \langle\!|\overset{\mathbf{R}}{=}|\!\rangle c$.

●

The term "rough set" was first coined by Pawlak (1984). We can define a *rough characteristic function* $\chi_R : \wp(s) \to \{\mathbf{0}, {}^1\!/_2, \mathbf{1}\}$ as

$$\chi_R(c)(x) := \begin{cases} \mathbf{1}, & \text{if } x \in [\![R]\!]c \\ {}^1\!/_2, & \text{if } x \in \dot{\langle\!|R|\!\rangle} c \\ \mathbf{0}, & \text{if } x \notin \langle\!|R|\!\rangle c. \end{cases} \quad (6.9)$$

Lower and upper approximations

A set or a concept c usually has crisp boundaries: an object belongs to it or not.

But if there are two indiscernible objects $x \overset{\mathbf{R}}{=} y$, and one of them (say, x) is element of c, is then $y \in c$, too?

- Yes it is,
  ... if *all* elements of $[x]_{\mathbf{R}}$ are in c, that is, if $[x]_R \subseteq c$.
- Perhaps it is,
  ... if *some* elements of $[x]_{\mathbf{R}}$ are in c, that is, if $[x]_{\mathbf{R}} \cap c \neq \emptyset$.

An equivalent definition of lower and upper approximations is

$$[\![R]\!]c := \bigcup\{c' \in s/R : c' \subseteq c\} \quad (6.10)$$
$$\langle\!|R|\!\rangle c := \bigcup\{c' \in s/R : c' \cap c \neq \emptyset\}. \quad (6.11)$$

Quite obviously, it holds that

$$[\![R]\!]c \subseteq c \subseteq \langle\!|R|\!\rangle c. \quad (6.12)$$

The lower approximation of a set is the union of all basic categories that are fully included in c. This means that if a basic category $[x]_R$ is a subset of c, then x and all objects that are indiscernible from x are instances of c. So whenever an object falls into the category $[x]_R$, then *it must be*

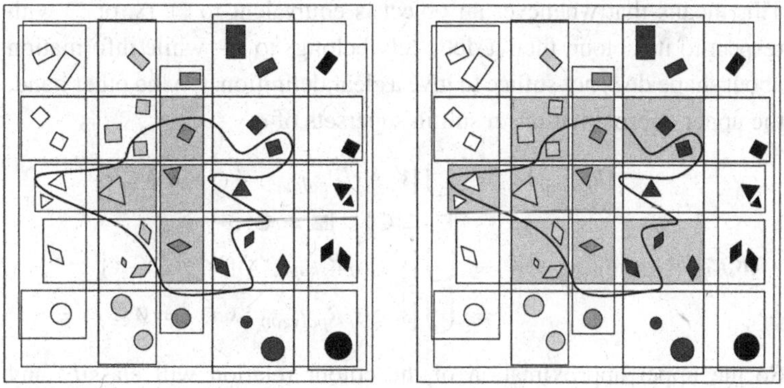

Fig. 6.4 Lower and upper approximations of a concept

an element of c.[3] The upper approximation of a concept c is the set of all objects that belong to classes that intersect with c. So if some $x \in c$, then all objects y that cannot be distinguished from x belong to the upper approximation as well. The reason is that we know that x is an instance of c. Then one might induce that all other objects that are indiscernible from x *may* also belong to c. Because we are talking equivalence relations here, objects can be equivalent or not – but there is nothing in between. This might make the idea behind upper approximations a bit harder to grasp. It might be easier to understand when weakening the notion of equivalence to similarity.[4] If x belongs to c and y is *similar* to x, then y could be an element of c, too. Figure 6.4 shows the lower and upper approximations of a concept c in our running example domain.

Example 6.16 Again, consider $\mathfrak{K}$ as in Example 6.9. Let the (unknown) concept be defined in terms of the following objects:

$$c \;:=\; \{\blacktriangle, \square, \triangle, \bigcirc\}.$$

Then,

$$\begin{aligned}
[\![R_{colour}]\!]c &= \bigcup\{s' \in s/R_{colour} : s' \subseteq c\} = \{\square, \triangle, \bigcirc\} \\
[\![R_{shape}]\!]c &= \bigcup\{s' \in s/R_{shape} : s' \subseteq c\} = \emptyset \\
[\![R_{polygon}]\!]c &= \bigcup\{s' \in s/R_{polygon} : s' \subseteq c\} = \emptyset.
\end{aligned}$$

[3] This why we use the notation $[\![R]\!]$ instead of $\underline{R}$: x being an element of the lower approximation of a concept c necessarily implies that x belongs to c. In modal logic, such operators are denoted by boxes ($\square$). The dual construction, a sufficiency criterion, is represented by diamonds ($\diamond$), which is why we shall use $\langle\!|R|\!\rangle$ for upper approximations.

[4] Which, formally, can be achieved by dropping the requirement of transitivity.

This means that whenever an object is equivalent to □, △, or ○ with respect to its colour, then it definitely belongs to $\overline{c}$ – while information about shape does not suffice to give a clear definition. On the other hand, the upper approximations result in supersets of c:

$$\begin{aligned}
\llparenthesis R_{colour} \rrparenthesis c &= \bigcup \{s' \in s/R_{colour} : s' \cap c \neq \emptyset \subseteq c\} \\
&= \{\square, \triangle, \bigcirc\} \cup \{\blacksquare, \blacktriangle, \bullet\} \\
\llparenthesis R_{shape} \rrparenthesis c = \llparenthesis R_{polygon} \rrparenthesis c &= \bigcup \{s' \in s/R_{shape} : s' \cap c \neq \emptyset \subseteq c\} \\
&= \bigcup \{s' \in s/R_{polygon} : s' \cap c \neq \emptyset \subseteq c\} = s.
\end{aligned}$$

So the upper approximation of the colour relation will classify any grey or black object as a member of c (which is wrong for ■ and ●), but the upper approximations of the remaining relations do not deliver any helpful information: whichever shape an object has, it may or may not belong to c (because c contains representatives of all possible shapes).

Now recall that $\bar{\bar{\mathbf{P}}}$ for any set of relations $\mathbf{P} \subseteq \mathbf{R}$ is a relation itself. Because $R_{shape} \subset R_{polygon}$, we know that $\bar{\bar{\mathbf{P}}} \cap \{R_{shape}\} \subseteq \bar{\bar{\mathbf{P}}} \cap \{R_{polygon}\}$. So let $\mathbf{P}_1 := \{R_{colour}, R_{shape}\}$ and $\mathbf{P}_2 := \{R_{colour}, R_{polygon}\}$. Then,

$$\begin{aligned}
[\![\mathbf{P}_1]\!] c &= \bigcup \left\{s' \in s/\bar{\bar{\mathbf{P}}}_1 : s' \subseteq c\right\} \\
&= \{\blacktriangle\} \cup \{\bigcirc, \square, \triangle\} = c
\end{aligned}$$

whereas

$$\begin{aligned}
[\![\mathbf{P}_2]\!] c &= \bigcup \left\{s' \in s/\bar{\bar{\mathbf{P}}}_s : s' \subseteq c\right\} \\
&= \{\bigcirc, \square, \triangle\} \subset c
\end{aligned}$$

and

$$\begin{aligned}
\llparenthesis \mathbf{P}_2 \rrparenthesis c &= \bigcup \left\{s' \in s/\bar{\bar{\mathbf{P}}}_s : s' \cap c \neq \emptyset\right\} \\
&= \{\blacktriangle, \blacksquare\} \cup \{\bigcirc, \square, \triangle\} \supset c.
\end{aligned}$$

Not surprisingly, finer relations contribute to more accurate approximations.

In the preceding example we already made use of a fact that, even if it seems obvious, deserves a lemma:

Inclusion of relations carries over to refinement. For any $\mathbf{P} \subseteq \mathbf{R}$ and $R, R' \in \mathbf{R}$ it holds that

$$R \subseteq R' \iff \bar{\bar{\mathbf{P}}} \cap \{R\} \preceq \bar{\bar{\mathbf{P}}} \cap \{R'\} \iff \overline{\overline{\mathbf{P} \cup \{R\}}} \subseteq \overline{\overline{\mathbf{P} \cup \{R'\}}}. \quad (6.13)$$

Exercise 6.17 (◇) Prove the "$\Longleftarrow$"-direction of the first equivalence in Equation (6.13).

We already know what it means for a concept to be definable using an equivalence relation R. Now, upper and lower approximations provide us with a tool for *rough definability*.

Rough definability

Definition 6.18 — Rough definability.
We say that

1. c is R-definable if and only if $[\![R]\!]c = \langle\!|R|\!\rangle c = c$.
2. c is rough with respect to R if and only if $[\![R]\!]c \neq \langle\!|R|\!\rangle c$. ●

Exercise 6.19 (◇) Is it true that if $[\![R]\!]c = c$, then $\langle\!|R|\!\rangle c = c$?

To complete this introductory section on the basic concepts of rough set data analysis we need to explain what it means to deliver an approximation of a *classification* rather than a single *class*. The definition is straightforward.

Rough approximations of classifications

Definition 6.20 — Rough approximations of classifications.
Let there be a classification $\mathfrak{c} = \{c_i : i \in \mathbf{k}\}$. The *(R-)rough* (𝔠*-)approximation* is defined as the set of all R-approximations of all c_i:

$$[\![R]\!]\mathfrak{c} \quad := \quad \{[\![R]\!]c_i : i \in \mathbf{k}\} \tag{6.14}$$

$$\langle\!|R|\!\rangle\mathfrak{c} \quad := \quad \{\langle\!|R|\!\rangle c_i : i \in \mathbf{k}\}\,. \tag{6.15}$$

The *(R-)rough* (𝔠*-)classification* is the set of all R-rough classes:

$$\{\langle [\![R]\!]c_i, \langle\!|R|\!\rangle c_i\rangle : i \in \mathbf{k}\}\,. \tag{6.16}$$

●

As we have seen in Example 6.16, upper and lower approximations can be defined for indiscernability relations and, therefore, for sets of relations.

> **Rough approximations**
> Concepts c can be approximated by lower and upper bounds using knowledge $\mathbf{R}$. An object is an element of the lower approximation if all its $\mathbf{R}$-equal objects are in c, too. An object is an element of the upper approximation if it has an $\mathbf{R}$-equal object that belongs to c.
> A *rough set* is a tuple consisting of the lower and upper approximations, and a *rough classification* is the set of all rough classes.

6.2.2 Degrees of roughness

We already discovered that $[\![R]\!]c \subseteq \langle\!|R|\!\rangle c$. It follows immediately that $|[\![R]\!]c| \leq |\langle\!|R|\!\rangle c|$. So there exists a natural way of comparing the *roughness* of two equivalence relations P and R with respect to a reference set c by comparing their relative sizes of the boundary regions. If

$$\frac{|[\![P]\!]c|}{|(\!|P|\!)c|} \leq \frac{|[\![R]\!]c|}{|(\!|R|\!)c|}, \tag{6.17}$$

then it appears that R is more accurate than P. This leads to a numerical measure of roughness.

Definition 6.21 — Sharpness. Sharpness

The *sharpness* or *accuracy* of the R-approximation of c is defined as

$$sharp_R(c) = \frac{|[\![R]\!]c|}{|(\!|R|\!)c|}. \tag{6.18}$$

We define $roughness_R(c) = 1 - sharp_R(c)$. ●

As already motivated by Definition 6.20, the interesting part is to make a meaningful statement concerning the quality of classifications instead of single classes. Accordingly, we define:

Definition 6.22 — Sharpness (classification). Sharpness (classification)

The *sharpness* or *accuracy* of the R-approximation of a classification $\mathfrak{c}$ is defined as

$$sharp_R(\mathfrak{c}) := \frac{\sum_{i \in \mathbf{k}} |[\![R]\!]c_i|}{\sum_{i \in \mathbf{k}} |(\!|R|\!)c_i|} \tag{6.19}$$

$$utility_R(\mathfrak{c}) := \frac{\sum_{i \in \mathbf{k}} |[\![R]\!]c_i|}{|s|}. \tag{6.20}$$

While $sharp_R(\mathfrak{c})$ describes the ratio of sure knowledge to vague knowledge, $utility_R(\mathfrak{c})$ describes the percentage of correctly R-classifiable objects in s with respect to $\mathfrak{c}$. ●

Where there are rough boundaries there is vague membership, too. Let there be a concept $c \subseteq s$ and an object $x \in s$. Then, "$\in$" is a family of equivalence relations. This becomes clear when defining membership through a characteristic function (instead of the other way round). If the characteristic function $\chi(c)$ is a feature in $\mathbf{F}$, then $\in_c$ is an equivalence relation induced by it.[5] It is clear that rough membership is always membership with respect to R-approximations. We write:

$$\begin{aligned} x \in_{[\![R]\!]} c &:\Longleftrightarrow [\![R]\!]c.x \Longleftrightarrow x \in [\![R]\!]c \\ x \in_{(\!|R|\!)} c &:\Longleftrightarrow (\!|R|\!)c.x \Longleftrightarrow x \in (\!|R|\!)c. \end{aligned} \tag{6.21}$$

In this way we can reformulate the relation between approximations pointwise:

$$[\![R]\!]c \subseteq c \subseteq (\!|R|\!)c \quad \text{if and only if} \quad [\![R]\!]c.x \Longrightarrow x \in c \Longrightarrow (\!|R|\!)c.x.$$

Example 6.23 Let us take another look at our example world in $\mathfrak{K}$ as defined in Example 6.9:

[5] Then the entire family of $\in$-relations is the set of relations induced by all $\{\chi(c) : c \in \wp(s)\}$.

$$s = \{\bullet, \blacksquare, \blacktriangle, \bigcirc, \square, \triangle, \bigcirc, \square, \triangle\}$$
$$c = \{\blacktriangle, \square, \triangle, \bigcirc\}$$

with relations $\mathbf{R} = \{R_{colour}, R_{shape}, R_{polygon}\}$. Using our results from Example 6.16, we find that

$$\begin{array}{llll} & \langle\!|R_{colour}|\!\rangle c.\blacksquare & \text{because } \blacksquare \in \langle\!|R_{colour}|\!\rangle \{\blacktriangle, \square, \triangle, \bigcirc\} & = \left\{\begin{array}{l}\bigcirc, \triangle, \square, \\ \bullet, \blacktriangle, \blacksquare\end{array}\right\} \\ \text{but} & \neg[\![R_{colour}]\!]c.\blacksquare & \text{because } \blacksquare \notin [\![R_{colour}]\!] \{\blacktriangle, \square, \triangle, \bigcirc\} & = \{\square, \triangle, \bigcirc\}. \end{array}$$

Similarly,

$$\begin{array}{llll} & \langle\!|R_{shape}|\!\rangle c.\bigcirc & \text{because } \bigcirc \in \langle\!|R_{shape}|\!\rangle \{\blacktriangle, \square, \triangle, \bigcirc\} & = s \\ \text{but} & \neg[\![R_{shape}]\!]c.\bigcirc & \text{because } \bigcirc \notin [\![R_{shape}]\!] \{\blacktriangle, \square, \triangle, \bigcirc\} & = \{\}. \end{array}$$

Similar considerations apply to rough set inclusion: the usual set notation $c' \subseteq c$ means that if some $x \in s$ is c'-ish, then it is c-ish, too: $x \in c' \Longrightarrow x \in c$. So if some x is R-roughly c'-ish, it means that x is an element of an R-approximation of c'-ish objects:

$$c' \subseteq_{[\![R]\!]} c \;:\Longleftrightarrow\; [\![R]\!]c' \subseteq [\![R]\!]c \tag{6.22}$$
$$c' \subseteq_{\langle\!|R|\!\rangle} c \;:\Longleftrightarrow\; \langle\!|R|\!\rangle c' \subseteq \langle\!|R|\!\rangle c. \tag{6.23}$$

Exercise 6.24 ($\diamondsuit$) Does this mean that every roughly c'-ish x is R-roughly c-ish, too?

Example 6.25 Let c be as in Example 6.23 and $c' = \{\square, \triangle, \bigcirc\}$. Then it holds that

$$\begin{aligned} [\![R_{colour}]\!]c' &= \{\square, \triangle, \bigcirc\} \\ &\subseteq \{\square, \triangle, \bigcirc\} \\ &= [\![R_{colour}]\!]c \end{aligned}$$

and

$$\begin{aligned} \langle\!|R_{colour}|\!\rangle c' &= \{\square, \triangle, \bigcirc\} \\ &\subseteq \{\blacksquare, \blacktriangle, \bullet, \square, \triangle, \bigcirc\} \\ &= \langle\!|R_{colour}|\!\rangle c. \end{aligned}$$

Also, $c' \subseteq c \subseteq s$ implies that

$$[\![R]\!]c' \subseteq [\![R]\!]c \subseteq Rs \text{ and } [\![R]\!]c' \supseteq [\![R]\!]c \supseteq Rs.$$

Its meaning is clear: the more objects we know, the smaller the region of uncertainty!

As usual, mutual inclusion can be used define equality:

$$c =_{[\![R]\!]} c' :\Longleftrightarrow [\![R]\!]c = [\![R]\!]c' \text{and} \quad c =_{\langle\!|R|\!\rangle} c' :\Longleftrightarrow \langle\!|R|\!\rangle c = \langle\!|R|\!\rangle c'. \tag{6.24}$$

Again, R-rough equality is a property of R rather than a property of two roughly equal objects $x, y \in s$. The interesting thing about inclusion is not *set* inclusion. Of course it is nice to know that some x is c-ish because it is c'-ish. But the really interesting thing is what it means for *different relations* to define such dependencies. Imagine that $\llbracket P \rrbracket c \subseteq \llbracket R \rrbracket c$. Then, obviously, R is able to identify *more* objects to be c-ish than P. In other words, R appears to have more information about c.

Example 6.26 Recall Example 6.25. Now we shall compare different *relations* instead of different sets. For more interesting results we choose another target concept c with

$$c := \{\square, {\color{gray}\blacksquare}, \blacksquare, \bigcirc\}\,.$$

Then

$$\begin{aligned} \llbracket R_{shape} \rrbracket c &= \llbracket R_{shape} \rrbracket \{\square, {\color{gray}\blacksquare}, \blacksquare, \bigcirc\} = \{\square, {\color{gray}\blacksquare}, \blacksquare\} \\ &\supseteq \llbracket R_{polygon} \rrbracket \{\square, {\color{gray}\blacksquare}, \blacksquare, \bigcirc\} = \{\} \\ &= \llbracket R_{polygon} \rrbracket c. \end{aligned}$$

As one can see here, the finer and *smaller* relation based on knowledge about *shape* has a *larger* lower approximation of c than the lower approximation by way of *polygon*. Intuitively the reason is that a *larger* relation (such as $R_{polygon}$) creates *fewer* equivalence classes. Because $R_{shape} \subseteq R_{polygon}$, we know that every *shape*-basic category is a subset of a *polygon*-basic category. Therefore, the *polygon*-knowledge is coarser than the *shape* knowledge. And the finer the knowledge, the smaller the steps we can make to approximate a concept. The *polygon* knowledge is not fine enough to describe basic categories that are fully included by c, but *shape* is. For upper approximations we obtain

$$\begin{aligned} \llparenthesis R_{shape} \rrparenthesis c &= \llparenthesis R_{shape} \rrparenthesis \{\square, {\color{gray}\blacksquare}, \blacksquare, \bigcirc\} = \{\square, {\color{gray}\blacksquare}, \blacksquare, \bigcirc, {\color{gray}\bullet}, \bullet\} \\ &\subseteq \llparenthesis R_{colour} \rrparenthesis \{\square, {\color{gray}\blacksquare}, \blacksquare, \bigcirc\} = \{\bigcirc, {\color{gray}\bullet}, \bullet, \square, {\color{gray}\blacksquare}, \blacksquare, \triangle, {\color{gray}\blacktriangle}, \blacktriangle\} = s \\ &= \llparenthesis R_{colour} \rrparenthesis c. \end{aligned}$$

We conclude that the finer the knowledge, the smaller the upper approximation and the larger the lower approximation.

We can also conclude:

> **Knowledge and concept approximations**
> The finer a relation, the more basic the categories. The more basic the categories, the smaller the equivalence classes. The smaller the equivalence classes, the higher their descriptive power. The higher the descriptive power, the more knowledge. The more knowledge, the smaller the boundary region.

Exercise 6.27 ($\Diamond$) Confirm all the examples. Determine $\llbracket \mathbf{P} \rrbracket c$ and $\llparenthesis \mathbf{P} \rrparenthesis c$ for several $\mathbf{P} \subseteq \mathbf{R}$ and various $c \subseteq s$.

6.3 Rough knowledge structures

The most important issue when understanding machine learning as compression is to delete redundant information. In most data collections there is redundancy – that is, there are data that do not contribute to the information content of the entire set of data. However, redundancy has a huge advantage in everyday life: Redundant data can be used to reconstruct information that would be lost given that a certain datum is missing.[6]

Example 6.28 Let us take a look at our standard example using the underlying information system $\mathfrak{I}$ with the target concept c as defined in Example 6.23:

$x \in s$	id	f_{colour}	f_{shape}	$f_{polygon}$	$t(x)$
△	1	*white*	△	1	1
○	2	*white*	○	0	1
□	3	*grey*	□	1	0
▲	4	*black*	△	1	1
■	5	*black*	□	1	0
○	6	*grey*	○	0	0
●	7	*black*	○	0	0
□	8	*white*	□	1	1
△	9	*grey*	△	1	0

Now, through the eyes of a database engineer, why do we store so-called *oid*s in the *id* column if all the objects are unique anyway? Why do we store the $f_{polygon}$ information if it contains less information than f_{shape}? And why don't we just drop all the columns and use *id* instead?

Exercise 6.29 Compare the utility of all the features:

- ◊ Determine $\text{entropy}_t(f, s)$ for all $f \in \{id, f_{colour}, f_{shape}, f_{polygon}\}$!
- ◊ Determine $\text{entropy}_t(f, s)$ for $f := f_{colour} \times f_{shape}$!
- ◊ Determine $utility_{\mathbf{P}_i}(\mathfrak{c})$ for: $\mathbf{P}_1 = \{R_{colour}\}, \mathbf{P}_2 = \{R_{shape}\}, \mathbf{P}_3 = \{R_{polygon}\}, \mathbf{P}_4 = \mathbf{P}_1 \cup \mathbf{P}_2$ and $\mathbf{P}_5 = \mathbf{P}_1 \cup \mathbf{P}_3$

Let us now reconsider the knowledge base $\mathfrak{K}$. We concluded that knowledge (and the ability to discriminate different things from each other) can be considered to be an equivalence relation $\bar{\bar{\mathbf{R}}}$. Some concepts are definable and others are only roughly definable – and in some cases our knowledge is maximal in the sense that we can discriminate every single object from every other single object:

$$s/\bar{\bar{\mathbf{R}}} = \{\{x\} : x \in s\}.$$

[6] Can you reconstruct a text from an ASCII file where one byte is missing? Can you do the same for the same text in zipped form?

In any case, there may be many different ways to define some $\mathbf{P} \subseteq \mathbf{R}$, all of which create the same quotient set. But as soon as $\mathbf{P}$ is a proper subset of $\mathbf{R}$ and the quotient sets are the same, then it does not hurt to drop some information from $\mathbf{R}$.

Relations that do not add to the knowledge are *dispensable*, and, in fact, they are even *redundant*. So if $\bar{\bar{\mathbf{R}}}$ does not change when removing R from $\mathbf{R}$, then R does *not contribute* any elementary class that is not already describable in terms of intersections of basic categories from $\mathbf{R} - \{R\}$. It is, in other words, *redundant* knowledge.

Definition 6.30 — Dispensability.

Dispensability

We call $R \in \mathbf{R}$ *dispensable* in $\mathbf{R}$ if

$$\bar{\bar{\mathbf{R}}} = \overline{\overline{\mathbf{R} - \{R\}}}; \tag{6.25}$$

otherwise, R is *indispensable*. $\mathbf{R}$ is called *irreducible* if R is indispensable in $\mathbf{R}$ for all $R \in \mathbf{R}$; otherwise, R is called *reducible* or *redundant*.

Irreducibility of $\mathbf{R}$ means that there is no $R \in \mathbf{R}$ which we can remove from $\mathbf{R}$ without changing $\bar{\bar{\mathbf{R}}}$ (i.e., losing "crispness"). Redundant sets of knowledge are reducible by deleting dispensable relations.

Example 6.31 In our example world, $\mathbf{P} = \{R_{shape}, R_{colour}\} \subset \mathbf{R}$ is irreducible, because both R_{shape} and R_{colour} are indispensable:

$$\begin{aligned}
s/\bar{\bar{\mathbf{P}}} &= \{\{\bigcirc\}, \{\triangle\}, \{\square\}, \{{\color{gray}\bullet}\}, \{{\color{gray}\blacktriangle}\}, \{{\color{gray}\blacksquare}\}, \{\bullet\}, \{\blacktriangle\}, \{\blacksquare\}\} \\
s/R_{shape} &= \{\{\bigcirc, {\color{gray}\bullet}, \bullet\}, \{\square, {\color{gray}\blacksquare}, \blacksquare\}, \{\blacktriangle, \triangle, {\color{gray}\blacktriangle}\}\} \\
s/R_{colour} &= \{\{\bigcirc, \triangle, \square\}, \{{\color{gray}\bullet}, {\color{gray}\blacktriangle}, {\color{gray}\blacksquare}\}, \{\bullet, \blacktriangle, \blacksquare\}\}.
\end{aligned}$$

Because $s/\bar{\bar{\mathbf{P}}} \neq s/R_{shape}$ and $s/\bar{\bar{\mathbf{P}}} \neq s/R_{colour}$, both relations are indispensable in $\mathbf{P}$. Hence, $\mathbf{P}$ is irreducible. In contrast to this, $\mathbf{R}$ is redundant:

$$\begin{aligned}
s/\bar{\bar{\mathbf{R}}} &= \{\{\bigcirc\}, \{\triangle\}, \{\square\}, \{{\color{gray}\bullet}\}, \{{\color{gray}\blacktriangle}\}, \{{\color{gray}\blacksquare}\}, \{\bullet\}, \{\blacktriangle\}, \{\blacksquare\}\} \\
&= s/\bar{\bar{\mathbf{P}}}.
\end{aligned}$$

Exercise 6.32 (◊) For the example above, let $c = \{\blacktriangle, \triangle, \blacksquare\}$. Determine $(\!|R_{colour}|\!)c$, $(\!|R_{shape}|\!)c$, $[\![R_{colour}]\!]c$, and $[\![R_{shape}]\!]c$.

There are relations that seem to be dispensable because they do not contribute to our ability to discriminate things (i.e., our knowledge). Thus it seems a good idea to *reduce* a knowledge base by discarding all dispensable relations. Accordingly, what remains after deleting redundant knowledge is a *reduct*.

Reduct

Definition 6.33 — Reduct.
We call $\mathbf{P} \subseteq \mathbf{R}$ a *reduct* of a set of relations $\mathbf{R}$ if $\mathbf{P}$ is irreducible and carries the same indiscernability knowledge as $\mathbf{R}$. We write

$$\mathbf{P} \in \mathrm{Red}(\mathbf{R}) :\Longleftrightarrow \begin{cases} \mathbf{P} \text{ is irreducible} \\ \bar{\bar{\mathbf{P}}} = \bar{\bar{\mathbf{R}}}. \end{cases} \tag{6.26}$$

In general, reducts are *not unique*. ●

Because the uniqueness property does not hold in general, there may exist several reducts for a given family $\mathbf{R}$ of equivalence relations.

Example 6.34 Let us first take a look at our standard example $\mathfrak{K}$: for $\mathbf{R} = \{R_{shape}, R_{colour}, R_{polygon}\}$, $\mathbf{P} = \{R_{shape}, R_{colour}\} \in \mathrm{Red}(\mathbf{R})$. However, it is the only reduct: $\mathrm{Red}(\mathbf{R}) = \{\mathbf{P}\}$. For the information system $\mathfrak{I}$ and the induced knowledge base $\mathfrak{K}'$, we have $\mathbf{R}' = \mathbf{R} \cup \{\mathit{1}\}$. Then $\mathbf{R}'$ has two reducts:

$$\mathrm{Red}(\mathbf{R}') = \{\{R_{colour}, R_{shape}\}, \{\mathit{1}\}\}. \tag{6.27}$$

●

The number of reducts $|\mathrm{Red}(\mathbf{R})|$ can be interpreted as a degree of redundancy of $\mathbf{R}$.

Exercise 6.35

◇ Prove Equation (6.27) in Example 6.34.
◇ Show that $\mathbf{R}$ and $\{R_{colour}, R_{shape}, \mathit{1}\}$ are not reducts of $\mathbf{R}$.
◇ Prove that if $|\mathrm{Red}(\mathbf{R})| > 1$, then $\bigcup \mathrm{Red}(\mathbf{R}) \notin \mathrm{Red}(\mathbf{R})$.
◆ Show that for $\mathrm{Red}(\mathbf{R}) = \{\mathbf{P}_i : i \in \mathbf{n}\}$ and $\forall i, j \in \mathbf{n} : \mathbf{P}_i = \mathbf{P}_j \longrightarrow i = j$, their union $\mathbf{Q} := \{R : \exists i \in \mathbf{n} : R \in \mathbf{P}_i\} = \bigcup \mathrm{Red}(\mathbf{R})$ is not a reduct: $\mathbf{Q} \notin \mathrm{Red}(\mathbf{R})$.

So if there are several reducts for $\mathbf{R}$, say, $\mathbf{P}$ and $\mathbf{Q}$, the knowledge in $\mathbf{R}$ can be expressed by different subsets of knowledge. As we have seen in Example 6.14, there can be too many such subsets as to be able to efficiently choose one that best fits our needs. Usually we would expect the knowledge in our knowledge base to consist of three different kinds of knowledge regarding their "importance":

- Some kind of "basic" knowledge without which we are hopelessly lost.
- Some kind of "detail" knowledge that, when present, suffices to speak about the world up to a desired level of detail.
- Additional, abundant knowledge that increases our eloquence to speak about the world but which actually does not contribute to the level of detail (and, hence, is redundant).

To decide whether a relation belongs to one or another set of knowledge depends on what we want to be able to express and which other parts of knowledge we already have. This is why there are reducts and why they are not unique.

Arguing from the point of view of conceptual knowledge modelling, we would assume there is some fundamental knowledge that all semantically equivalent formulations of the knowledge should share. If there is such *core* knowledge, it should be contained in all reducts. There seem to be relations that are simply absolutely indispensable and they occur in every reduct – even though they may not provide sufficient knowledge on their own.

Definition 6.36 — Core. Core
The set of relations in $\mathbf{R}$ that occur in *every* reduct $\mathbf{P} \in \text{Red}(\mathbf{R})$ is called the *core* of $\mathbf{R}$:

$$\text{Cor}(\mathbf{R}) := \{R \in \mathbf{R} : \mathbf{P} \in \text{Red}(\mathbf{R}) \longrightarrow R \in \mathbf{P}\} \tag{6.28}$$
$$= \bigcap_{\mathbf{P} \in \text{Red}(\mathbf{R})} \mathbf{P} = \bigcap \text{Red}(\mathbf{R}). \tag{6.29}$$

If the core is not empty, then there exist relations that are indispensible in any attempt to describe a concept. If the core is empty, it is so because there do not exist any reducts, or because there are several disjoint sets of relations one of which must appear in any reduct (see Example 6.34).

●

We conclude that, for any $\mathbf{Q} \in \text{Red}(\mathbf{R})$, it holds that $\text{Cor}(\mathbf{R}) \subseteq \mathbf{Q} \subseteq \mathbf{R}$, and if $\mathbf{Q}$ is irreducible, then any $\mathbf{P} \subseteq \mathbf{Q}$ is irreducible, too.

Rough knowledge structures

Rough knowledge is what one has if one is able to roughly describe new concepts in terms of old ones. The roughness of the description depends on the knowledge.

Knowledge discovery means to *reduce* data by discarding redundancy. Some parts of the knowledge are dispensable in general, and others are not because they are required in any reduct. A small part of knowledge may be essential and absolutely irreducible.

Example 6.37 Consider the set s of differently coloured geometric shapes and the set of relations as in example 6.34. We examine subsets $\mathbf{P}_i \subseteq \mathbf{R} \cup \{I\}$:

i	$\mathbf{P}_i$	$s/\bar{\bar{\mathbf{P}}}_i$
1	$\mathbf{R}$	{{○}, {△}, {□}, {◎}, {◬}, {▣}, {●}, {▲}, {■}}
2	$\{I\}$	{{○}, {△}, {□}, {◎}, {◬}, {▣}, {●}, {▲}, {■}}
3	$\{R_{colour}, R_{shape}\}$	{{○}, {△}, {□}, {◎}, {◬}, {▣}, {●}, {▲}, {■}}
4	$\{R_{colour}, R_{polygon}\}$	{{○}, {△, □}, {◎}, {◬, ▣}, {●}, {▲, ■}}
5	$\{R_{colour}\}$	{{○, △, □}, {◎, ◬, ▣}, {●, ▲, ■}}

$\mathbf{P}_2$ and $\mathbf{P}_3$ are reducts of $\mathbf{R}$; $\mathbf{P}_4$ and $\mathbf{P}_5$ are not. The core is the intersection of reducts: $\text{Cor}(\mathbf{R}) = \bigcap \text{Red}(\mathbf{R}) = \{\}$. ●

Reducts and cores are powerful concepts, but what we need is a method to compare the expressiveness of the relations with respect to (i.e., *relative* to) a given classification. Because we agreed that classes of a classification are disjoint, a classification is just another partition, which in turn can be considered to be the result of building the quotient of another equivalence relation.[7] Therefore, relative expressiveness is something that we can measure for any pair of (sets of) equivalence relations.

6.4 Relative knowledge

A special kind of structured knowledge

It depends on the concept which parts of knowledge are redundant and which parts are required or essential. Usually we are given such a concept c or a classification $\mathfrak{c}$. Much more interesting are the following two questions:

- If there are several approximations of a concept by several different reducts, which one shall we choose?
- Given two sets of relations, how can we describe their potential to describe the knowledge in their respective counterpart?

Do different parts of knowledge somehow *depend* on each other?

For a given information system or knowledge base all we did so far was to fish for subsets of knowledge satisfying conditions of necessity or sufficiency. This process was the first step away from a pointwise characterisation of data towards a relational one. Knowledge is indispensable if it is required to tell different objects from each other – or if it cannot be reduced without increasing coarseness.

We shall now examine the *relationship* between two different sets of knowledge with respect to their expressive power: is one part of knowledge sufficient to describe another part of knowledge?

Example 6.38 Let there be a concept $c \subseteq s$. Then we can assume there is an equivalence relation R_c (of index 2) induced by the characteristic function $\chi(c)$. It creates a classification $\mathfrak{c} = \{c, \overline{c}\} := s/R_c$. Now imagine a set $\mathbf{P} \subseteq \mathbf{R}$. In machine learning $\chi(c)$ is called the target function t, which we want to approximate. Lower and upper approximations come in quite handy at this point.

To pick the best fitting hypothesis from hypothesis space, we need to find a set $\mathbf{P}$ such that we can construct c from $s/\overline{\overline{\mathbf{P}}}$ as accurately as possible.

[7] And, of course, by any other *set* $\mathbf{S}$ of equivalence relations and the quotient $s/\overline{\overline{\mathbf{S}}}$.

Given $s/\bar{\bar{\mathbf{P}}}$, the reconstruction of $\mathfrak{c}$ means to find two (disjoint) union sets of $\bar{\bar{\mathbf{P}}}$-basic categories such that

$$s/\bar{\bar{\mathbf{P}}} = \{c'_0, c'_1, \ldots, c'_{n-1}\},$$

where

$$c \approx \bigcup_{i \in \mathbf{k_1}} c'_i \quad \text{and} \quad \overline{c} \approx \bigcup_{i \in \mathbf{k_0}} c'_j$$

for $\mathbf{k_1} \cup \mathbf{k_0} = \mathbf{n}$. Because we do not require strict but only approximate equality, $\mathbf{k_1}$ and $\mathbf{k_0}$ need not be disjoint.

Another method of defining $\mathfrak{c}$ is the enumeration of class representatives (see Definition 6.13). Then, $\mathfrak{c}$ is described by two sets $\dot{c}_1$ and $\dot{c}_0$ such that

$$c \approx \bigcup_{x \in \dot{c}_1} [x]_{\bar{\bar{\mathbf{P}}}} \quad \text{and} \quad \overline{c} \approx \bigcup_{x \in \dot{c}_0} [x]_{\bar{\bar{\mathbf{P}}}}.$$

Again, it is not neccessarily the case that $\dot{c}_1 \cap \dot{c}_0 = \emptyset$. Therefore it can be that, for some $c \in \dot{c}_1 \cap \dot{c}_0$, we cannot decide whether $x \in c$ or $x \in \overline{c}$. In such a case, $\mathbf{P}$ provides only rough knowledge: $(\!|\mathbf{P}|\!)c.x$ and $(\!|\mathbf{P}|\!)\overline{c}.x$. To constructively define the region in c (and thus the subdomain of R_c) for which $\mathbf{P}$ delivers correct predictions, we should first focus on the set for which $\mathbf{P}$ suffices to deliver correct predictions:

Definition 6.39 — Relative positive knowledge. Relative positive knowledge
Let there be two equivalence relations P and Q. The *P-positive region for Q (on s)* is the union set of all P-elementary classes that belong to Q-classes:

$$[\![P \trianglelefteq Q]\!]s := \bigcup_{q \in s/Q} [\![P]\!]q = \bigcup_{\mathfrak{q}} [\![P]\!]q_i \tag{6.30}$$

$$= [\![P]\!]q_0 \cup [\![P]\!]q_1 \cup \cdots \cup [\![P]\!]q_{k-1}, \tag{6.31}$$

where s/Q is a partition or a classification of objects in s with respect to knowledge Q: $\mathfrak{q} = \{q_0, q_1, \ldots, q_{k-1}\} = s/Q$. The P-positive region is the set of objects for which by P we can positively confirm their membership to Q-classes. ●

An equivalent pointwise definition of the relative positive region is

$$[\![P \trianglelefteq Q]\!]s := \{x \in U : [x]_P \subseteq [x]_Q\}. \tag{6.32}$$

Exercise 6.40 (◊) Prove Equation (6.32).

If rough set theory is new for you (or if you are already familiar with rough set theory and the additional symbol $\trianglelefteq$ appears a bit odd to you), then try to read it out loud as the word *for*:

Relative positive knowledge

Technically speaking, the P-positive region for Q, $[\![P \trianglelefteq Q]\!]s$, is the (disjoint) union set of all P-lower approximations of all $c \in s/Q$.

Its meaning is that $[\![P \trianglelefteq Q]\!]s$ is the set of all objects where *P-knowledge suffices for modelling Q-knowledge.*

Let us take a closer look at this. We always considered approximations with respect to a given or otherwise somehow predefined concept c or a set $\mathfrak{c}$ of such classes. By comparing P with Q we examine P-approximations with respect to "dynamically defined" classifications $\mathfrak{q} = \{q_0, q_1, q_2, \ldots, q_{k-1}\} = s/Q$ as defined by Q.

Exercise 6.41 (◇) In most textbooks on rough sets, $[\![P \trianglelefteq Q]\!]s$ is denoted $Pos_P(Q)$. Let there be an arbitrary classification $\mathfrak{c}$ of s. Show that

$$Pos_P(Q) = \bigcup_{c \in \mathfrak{c}} [\![P \trianglelefteq Q]\!]c$$

to prove that our definition allows a more detailed and *relative* usage of the term "P-positive region of Q."

Exercise 6.42 (◆) Prove the following equation:

$$[\![p \trianglelefteq Q]\!]s \quad = \quad \bigcup_{i \in \mathbf{k}} \left\{ x \in U : [\![p]\!]q_i.x \longrightarrow [x]_p \subseteq [x]_Q \right\}$$

The last equation of the preceding exercise appears to be trivial: if something is an element of a lower set approximation, then it is an element of this set. But it is *not* that easy. q_i is defined in terms of Q, whereas $[\![P]\!]q_i$ is defined in terms of P (or, to be precise, "in terms of P in terms of Q"). Figure 6.5 displays two examples. At this point, it becomes clear why we introduced the dotted membership notation. The equation

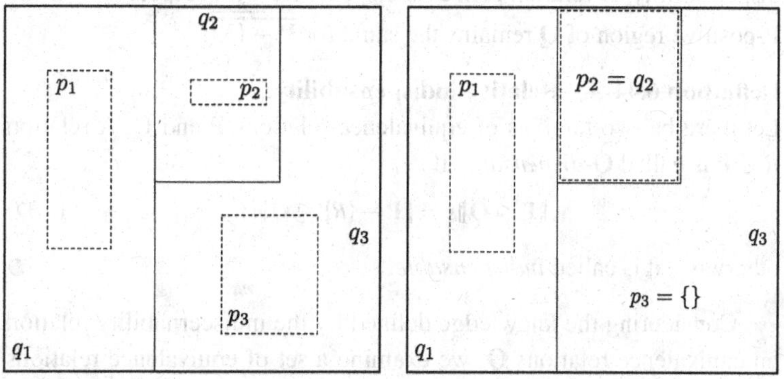

Fig. 6.5 The P-positive region of Q, $[\![P \trianglelefteq Q]\!]s$

$$[\![P]\!]c.x \longrightarrow [\![Q]\!]c.x$$

reads: "If x is c-ish according to our knowledge P, then it is c-ish according to Q, too." If this implication is true for some x, x is an element of the P-positive region of Q and so are all objects $y \in s$ that are P-equivalent:

$$[\![P \trianglelefteq Q]\!]c.x \iff [\![P]\!]c.x \longrightarrow [\![Q]\!]c.x. \tag{6.33}$$

Of course, we can lift the above definitions from simple sets s to classifications $\mathfrak{c}$:

$$[\![P \trianglelefteq Q]\!]\mathfrak{c} := \bigcup_{c \in \mathfrak{c}} [\![P \trianglelefteq Q]\!]c. \tag{6.34}$$

But what if P is an indiscernability relation built from a set $\mathbf{P}$ of relations? And, similarly, what if $Q = \bar{\bar{\mathbf{Q}}}$? Can we lift our definition to sets of relations as well? – Yes! Again, we generalise our idea to sets of equivalence relations by using their respective indiscernability relations:

$$[\![\mathbf{P} \trianglelefteq \mathbf{Q}]\!]s := [\![\bar{\bar{\mathbf{P}}} \trianglelefteq \bar{\bar{\mathbf{Q}}}]\!]s. \tag{6.35}$$

Then again, $[\![\mathbf{P} \trianglelefteq \mathbf{Q}]\!]s$ is the set of objects where $\mathbf{P}$ can be used for describing $\mathbf{Q}$-knowledge. The direction of $\trianglelefteq$ is motivated by the following equivalent definition:

$$[\![\mathbf{P} \trianglelefteq \mathbf{Q}]\!]s := \left\{x \in s : \exists q \in s/\bar{\bar{\mathbf{Q}}} : [x]_{\bar{\bar{\mathbf{P}}}} \subseteq q\right\}. \tag{6.36}$$

In the literature, and, of course, in Pawlak (1984), $\trianglelefteq$ is written as $\Rightarrow$, which indiates the logic behind inclusion and also reflects the pointwise notation in Equation (6.33).

Exercise 6.43 (◊) Prove the equivalence of Equation (6.36) and Equation (6.35).

Now we can try to lift the definition of dispensability to relative dispensability. A relation R in $\mathbf{P}$ is dispensable with respect to $\mathbf{Q}$ if the $\bar{\bar{\mathbf{P}}}$-positive region of $\bar{\bar{\mathbf{Q}}}$ remains the same for $\overline{\overline{\mathbf{P} - \{R\}}}$:

Definition 6.44 — Relative indispensability. Relative indispensability

Let there be two families of equivalence relations $\mathbf{P}$ and $\mathbf{Q}$. A relation $R \in \mathbf{P}$ is called $\mathbf{Q}$-*dispensable* if

$$[\![\mathbf{P} \trianglelefteq \mathbf{Q}]\!]s = [\![\mathbf{P} - \{R\} \trianglelefteq \mathbf{Q}]\!]s; \tag{6.37}$$

otherwise, it is called *indispensable*. ●

Considering the knowledge defined by the indiscernability relation on equivalence relations $\mathbf{Q}$, we examine a set of equivalence relations $\mathbf{P}$. If the set of objects that can be correctly $\bar{\bar{\mathbf{Q}}}$-classified by $\bar{\bar{\mathbf{P}}}$ remains the same if we discard R from $\mathbf{P}$, then R is redundant in our attempt to

Q-classify objects using knowledge **P**. Therefore, relative dispensability gives rise to relative irreducibility. If all the relations are indispensable in a set **P** with respect to a set **Q**, **P** cannot be reduced any further without losing information. Speaking in terms of objects in our universe, reducing **P** implies a loss of knowledge with respect to **Q** if $\llbracket \mathbf{S} \trianglelefteq \mathbf{Q} \rrbracket s \subset \llbracket \mathbf{P} \trianglelefteq \mathbf{Q} \rrbracket s$ for any $\mathbf{S} \subset \mathbf{P}$.

Relative implication

Definition 6.45 — Relative implication.
Let there be three sets of relations, **P**, **Q** and **R**. **P** is called **Q**-*irreducible* if and only if every $P \in \mathbf{P}$ is **Q**-indispensable:

$$\forall P \in \mathbf{P} : \llbracket \mathbf{P} \trianglelefteq \mathbf{Q} \rrbracket s \supset \llbracket (\mathbf{P} - \{P\}) \trianglelefteq \mathbf{Q} \rrbracket s. \tag{6.38}$$

P **Q**-*implies* (subsumes) **R** if the **R**-positive region for **Q** is included in the **P**-positive region for **Q**:

$$\llbracket \mathbf{R} \trianglelefteq \mathbf{Q} \rrbracket s \subseteq \llbracket \mathbf{P} \trianglelefteq \mathbf{Q} \rrbracket s. \tag{6.39}$$

We then write $\mathbf{P} \overset{\mathbf{Q}}{\supset} \mathbf{R}$. ●

An example is shown in Figure 6.6. We can distinguish three cases:

1. For all the objects ●, it holds that $\llbracket \mathbf{R} \rrbracket q_i.$● *and* $\llbracket \mathbf{P} \rrbracket q_i.$●.
2. For all ◍, we have $\llbracket \mathbf{P} \rrbracket q_i.$◍ but *not* $\llbracket \mathbf{R} \rrbracket q_i.$◍.
3. For ○ it holds that *neither* $\llbracket \mathbf{P} \rrbracket q_i.$○ *nor* $\llbracket \mathbf{R} \rrbracket q_i.$○.

Obviously, it cannot be the case that $\llbracket \mathbf{R} \rrbracket q_i.x$ but $\neg \llbracket \mathbf{P} \rrbracket q_i.x$, because all lower **R**-approximations are subsets of the **P**-lower approximations. So we have all possible combinations of memberships and they exactly model the implication relation:

$$\llbracket \mathbf{R} \rrbracket q_i.x \Longrightarrow \llbracket \mathbf{P} \rrbracket q_i.x. \tag{6.40}$$

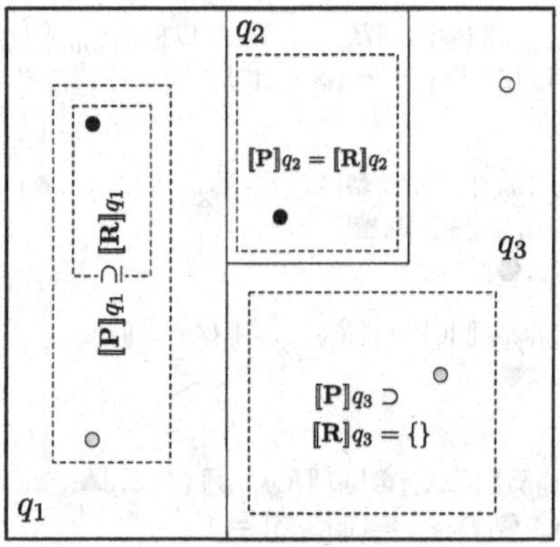

Fig. 6.6 Relative implication in rough sets

The inverted subset relation may look a bit confusing at first glimpse. But the reason for it is simple: the positive region of **R** is smaller than (i.e., included in) the positive region of **P**. This means that **P** can explain *more* than **R** or that **R** is *weaker* than **P**. Therefore, **P** *subsumes* **R**.

Note that relative implication is not defined in terms of a subset relation between **P** and **R** but rather on their respective positive regions with respect to **Q**. Therefore, and this is why it is called *implication*, $\supset$ is a property of the knowledge encoded in sets of relations where the amount of knowledge is measured extensionally by the sets of objects that can be classified correctly.

In many books on rough sets, there is no *relative implication*, only *dependency*. It is written $\Rightarrow$ and defined as

$$\mathbf{P} \Rightarrow \mathbf{R} :\iff \mathbf{P} \overset{\mathbf{Q}}{\supset} \mathbf{R},$$

and, to make the confusion complete, spoken as "**R** depends on **P**". So we speak of "implication" and use the symbol $\supset$, whereas other books use the implication symbol $\Rightarrow$ and call it "dependency".

Because $\mathbf{P} \preceq \mathbf{P} - \{R\}$, it holds that $[\![\mathbf{P} - \{R\} \trianglelefteq \mathbf{Q}]\!]s$ is a proper subset of $[\![\mathbf{P} \trianglelefteq \mathbf{Q}]\!]s$ if and only if **P** is **Q**-independent.

Exercise 6.46

◇ Prove the last statement.
◇ Prove that $\mathbf{P} \Rightarrow \mathbf{R} \iff \mathbf{P} \overset{\top}{\supset} \mathbf{R}$.
◇ Prove or disprove that $[\![\mathbf{P} \trianglelefteq \mathbf{Q}]\!]s = [\![\mathbf{R} \trianglelefteq \mathbf{Q}]\!]s \iff \mathbf{P} \equiv \mathbf{R}$.

Example 6.47 Let us again consider the knowledge base from Example 6.28. Then, for $c = \{\bigcirc, \triangle, \blacksquare\} \subseteq s$, we find

$$\begin{aligned}
[\![R_{colour} \trianglelefteq R_{shape}]\!] \quad s &= \textstyle\bigcup_{q \in s/R_{shape}} [\![R_{colour}]\!] q \\
&= [\![R_{colour}]\!] \{\bigcirc, ◯, \bullet\} \cup [\![R_{colour}]\!] \{\triangle, △, \blacktriangle\} \cup \\
&\quad [\![R_{colour}]\!] \{\square, □, \blacksquare\} = \{\} \cup \{\} \cup \{\} = \\
&= \emptyset
\end{aligned}$$

$$\begin{aligned}
[\![R_{colour} \trianglelefteq R_{shape}]\!] \quad c &= [\![R_{colour}]\!] \{\bullet\} \cup [\![R_{colour}]\!] \{\triangle\} \cup [\![R_{colour}]\!] \{□\} \\
&= \{\bullet\} \cup \{\triangle\} \cup \{□\} = \{\bullet, \triangle, □\} \\
&= c
\end{aligned}$$

$$\begin{aligned}
[\![R_{polygon} \trianglelefteq R_{shape}]\!] \quad s &= [\![R_{polygon}]\!] \{\bigcirc, ◯, \bullet\} \cup [\![R_{polygon}]\!] \{\triangle, △, \blacktriangle\} \cup \\
&\quad [\![R_{polygon}]\!] \{\square, □, \blacksquare\} \\
&= \{\bigcirc, ◯, \bullet\}
\end{aligned}$$

$$\begin{aligned}
[\![R_{polygon} \trianglelefteq R_{shape}]\!] \quad c &= [\![R_{polygon}]\!] \{\bigcirc\} \cup [\![R_{polygon}]\!] \{\triangle\} \cup [\![R_{polygon}]\!] \{\blacksquare\} \\
&= \{\bigcirc, \triangle, \blacksquare\} \\
&= c
\end{aligned}$$

$$\begin{aligned}
[\![R_{shape} \trianglelefteq R_{polygon}]\!] \quad s &= [\![R_{shape}]\!] \{\bigcirc, ◯, \bullet\} \cup [\![R_{shape}]\!] \{\triangle, △, \blacktriangle, \square, □, \blacksquare\} \\
&= \{\bigcirc, ◯, \bullet, \triangle, △, \blacktriangle, \square, □, \blacksquare\} = s
\end{aligned}$$

$$\begin{aligned} [\![R_{shape} \trianglelefteq R_{polygon}]\!] \quad c &= [\![R_{shape}]\!]\{\bigcirc\} \cup [\![R_{shape}]\!]\{\triangle, \blacksquare\} \\ &= \{\bigcirc, \triangle, \blacksquare\} \\ &= c. \end{aligned}$$

Example 6.48 Let us take a closer look at dependent sets of knowledge:

$$\begin{aligned} [\![\{R_{shape}, R_{colour}\} \trianglelefteq \mathit{1}]\!]s &= s \\ &\supset \\ \{\bigcirc, \bigcirc, \bullet\} &= [\![\{R_{polygon}, R_{colour}\} \trianglelefteq \mathit{1}]\!]s. \end{aligned}$$

This shows that $\{R_{shape}, R_{colour}\}$ $\mathit{1}$–implies $\{R_{polygon}, R_{colour}\}$:

$$\{R_{shape}, R_{colour}\} \overset{\mathit{1}}{\supset} \{R_{polygon}, R_{colour}\}.$$

And, again, dependency and indispensability give rise to the definition of reducts:

Example 6.49 In our running example, it holds that

$$[\![\mathbf{R} \trianglelefteq \mathit{1}]\!]s = [\![\mathbf{R} - \{R_{polygon}\} \trianglelefteq \mathit{1}]\!]s. \tag{6.41}$$

This means that $R_{polygon}$ is $\mathit{1}$-dispensable and, because $\mathit{1} \preceq R$ for all $R \in \mathbf{R}$, $R_{polygon}$ is dispensable. Equivalently, there exists a reduct of $\mathbf{R}$ without $R_{polygon}$ in it.

Accordingly, we define:

Relative reducts and relative cores

Definition 6.50 — Relative reducts and relative cores. Let there be three sets of equivalence relations $\mathbf{P}, \mathbf{Q}, \mathbf{R}$ and $\mathbf{P} \subseteq \mathbf{R}$. $\mathbf{P}$ is called a $\mathbf{Q}$-*relative reduct* of $\mathbf{R}$ if and only if:

1. $[\![\mathbf{P} \trianglelefteq \mathbf{Q}]\!]s = [\![\mathbf{R} \trianglelefteq \mathbf{Q}]\!]s$.
2. $\mathbf{P}$ is $\mathbf{Q}$-irreducible.

The set of all $\mathbf{Q}$-reducts of $\mathbf{R}$ is denoted $\text{Red}(\mathbf{R} \trianglelefteq \mathbf{Q})$. Then,

$$\text{Cor}(\mathbf{R} \trianglelefteq \mathbf{Q}) \quad := \quad \bigcap \text{Red}(\mathbf{R} \trianglelefteq \mathbf{Q}) \tag{6.42}$$

is called the $\mathbf{Q}$-*relative core of* $\mathbf{R}$. ●

The above definition can be broken down as follows. A $\mathbf{Q}$-relative reduct is a subset $\mathbf{P}$ of $\mathbf{R}$ such that the expressiveness of $\mathbf{R}$ with respect to $\mathbf{Q}$ does not suffer from the loss of relations missing in $\mathbf{P}$.

First, it is said that $[\![\mathbf{P} \trianglelefteq \mathbf{Q}]\!]s = [\![\mathbf{R} \trianglelefteq \mathbf{Q}]\!]s$. That is quite simple: $\mathbf{P}$ has the same positive region for $\mathbf{Q}$ as $\mathbf{R}$ has. They are, pointwise, equivalent with respect to $\mathbf{Q}$: an object of s belongs to the $\mathbf{R}$-positive region of $\mathbf{Q}$ if and only if it belongs to the $\mathbf{P}$-positive region of $\mathbf{Q}$. Speaking in terms of extensional set definitions, it does not matter at all whether we choose $\mathbf{R}$ or $\mathbf{P}$: both have the same expressve power, and even if they do not suffice to describe all the $\mathbf{Q}$-knowledge, they can correctly describe exactly the same subset of objects in s.

Second, **Q**-irreducibility of **P** means that we cannot drop any relation $P \in \mathbf{P} \subseteq \mathbf{R}$ without losing information relative to **Q**-knowledge: **P** is **Q**-independent if every $P \in \mathbf{P}$ is **Q**-indispensable. It means that for all $P \in \mathbf{P}$,

$$[\![\mathbf{P} \trianglelefteq \mathbf{Q}]\!]s \neq [\![\mathbf{P} - \{P\} \trianglelefteq \mathbf{Q}]\!]s.$$

In other words, **P** cannot be reduced any further and it is a smallest subset of **R** that is still capable of describing **Q** to the same extent as **R**.

Exercise 6.51 (◊) Show that $\text{Red}(\mathbf{R} \trianglelefteq \mathbf{R}) = \text{Red}(\mathbf{R})$.

It should have become clear that rough set theory is concerned with *relations* and their expressive power on *actual* data rather than sets of objects with terminologic information. We can define a relation's dispensability or utility with respect to a given classification, and we can define reducts and cores with respect to given classification information. In other words, our toolbox of rough set operators is now complete and we can describe what we need to *learn* new concepts in a supervised learning setting.

Given a target classification $\mathfrak{c}$ defined by an unknown target function $t : s \to \mathbf{k}$ and its induced equivalence relation R_t, we want to extract knowledge in terms of cores and reducts relative to this classification from a dependent knowledge base. But there is still an open issue here: what does it mean for $\mathfrak{K}$ that t is unknown? It means that the intensional *definition* of t is not known. All we have is that, for some $s \subseteq U$, we know a family of characteristic functions

$$\chi : \wp(s) \to (s \to \mathbf{2})$$

that, for every $x \in s$, determines whether $x \in c \in \wp(s)$; that is, $\chi(c)(x) = \mathbf{1} \iff x \in c$. These functions provide us with the *labels* in our sample that we can use for a learning task. Accordingly, we would pick a sample $\mathbf{s}$ from $\mathfrak{K}$ of the form

$$\mathbf{s} \;=\; \{\langle x, \langle \chi(c_0)(x), \ldots, \chi(c_{k-1})(x)\rangle\rangle : x \in s' \subseteq s\}. \qquad (6.43)$$

If $k = 2$, then $\mathfrak{c} = \{c_0, c_1\} = \{c, \overline{c}\}$ and $\chi(c)(x) = 1 \iff \chi(\overline{c})(x) = 0$. Therefore, binary learning problems result in much simpler sample structures:

$$\mathbf{s} = \{\langle x, \chi(c)(x)\rangle : x \in s' \subseteq s\}.$$

Similary, samples for k-ary classifications can be represented by samples of tuples $\langle x, i\rangle$ if $\chi(c_i)(x) = 1$. For nominal learning problems, there is no difference between a multi-valued domain of the target function and an according sparse vector of 0's with only one 1. Things are a bit different for ordinal target values, because the ordering on $\text{cod}(t)$ has to be preserved in a binary vector representation.

Learning by rough sets
Knowledge discovery by rough sets means finding the smallest subsets of relations that are capable of describing the presented data and which can be used to (roughly) describe whether *any* object belongs to a certain class.

We are now able to compare sets of relations to other sets of relations with respect to their expressive power concerning a new/unknown concept based on observed data:

- The more knowledge we have, the finer ("crisper") is our view on the domain.
- We can build specific (basic) concept descriptions from elementary concepts by intersections and complex concepts by unions of basic concepts.
- We can identify dispensable relations, reducts, and cores.
- We have a set of arithmetic measures we can use to estimate quantitatively.

With a few more arithmetic measures of sharpness and utility, we can

1. Identify redundant relations
2. Discover unknown concepts
3. Find minimal, sufficiently accurate approximations of known concepts.

And this is what we need to learn by finding knowledge that has been lost in too much information.

6.5 Knowledge discovery

Given a knowledge base $\mathfrak{K}$ with $\mathbf{R} = \{R_{f_i} : i \in \mathbf{n}\} \cup \{R_t\}$, we call t a *decision attribute* that describes a new (unknown) concept $c = \{x \in s : t(x) = \mathbf{1}\}$. Whenever t is binary, it is the characteristic function of the target concept c; for nominal t, s/R_t is a target classification $\mathrm{c} = \{\{x \in s : t(x) = i\} : i \in \mathbf{k}\}$. The information system $\mathfrak{I}\,\langle s, \mathbf{F}, V_{\mathbf{F}}\rangle$ then has a special feature t called the *decision attribute*, and, accordingly, the table representing $\mathfrak{I}$ together with t is called a *decision table*:

s	0	1	$\cdots$	$n-1$	t
x_0	$f_0(x_0)$	$f_1(x_0)$	$\cdots$	$f_{n-1}(x_0)$	$\mathbf{1}$
x_1	$f_0(x_1)$	$f_1(x_1)$	$\cdots$	$f_{n-1}(x_1)$	$\mathbf{0}$
$\vdots$	$\vdots$	$\vdots$		$\vdots$	$\vdots$

By using our newly acquired relational language of (rough) concepts, we can reformulate what it means to be concerned with *new* knowledge about *unknown* concepts c.

We call c a *new* or *unknown* concept if there is no relation $R_f \in \mathbf{R}$ for which f is a characteristic function of c (or, at least, approximately equal). Still, c is (roughly) *learnable* by $\mathfrak{K}$ if c can be (roughly) described by $\bar{\bar{\mathbf{R}}}$. Then, the characteristic function of this (rough) set in terms of unions of basic classes is, in fact, new *terminologic knowledge*. The mere (rough) pointwise approximation of a concept c does not make any new knowledge. To *learn c* means to find a *description* of t in terms of knowledge **R**. And this brings us back to approximations of c.

At the same time, learning means to be able to *compress* data. We already do so by giving intensional definitions of sets of objects. But compression and especially *generalisation* cannot take place without *dropping* knowledge. Lossless compression means to drop redundant knowledge only: it means to find *reducts*. Generalising also asks for dropping knowledge that at first glimpse weakens the *sharpness* of a concept description. To avoid overgeneralisation we should discard only those parts of knowledge whose *utility* appears rather weak.

Knowledge discovery by rough sets

Knowledge discovery means to define a *new* relation R_h for which $s/R_h \approx s/R_t$. R_h is defined in terms of $\bar{\bar{\mathbf{P}}}$-elementary classes, where $\mathbf{P} \subseteq \mathbf{R}$ is as small as possible and $[\![R_h \trianglelefteq R_t]\!]s$ is as big as possible.

Actually, knowledge discovery means to discover *dependencies* of knowledge in relation to (newly) observed data. Therefore, we need to ask the following questions:

- Reasoning about knowledge:
  1. Are there *redundant* relations?
  2. Are there *similar* relations?
  3. Are there redundant or similar *complex* concepts?
  4. Is there *(in)dispensable* knowledge around?
- Reasoning about new observations:
  1. Can the new concept be described by existing relations?
  2. Can it be approximated?
  3. If so, to which extent and accuracy?

So now we analyse our knowledge and decide which elements we shall keep and which we shall discard so as to yield a minimal set of relations that induces an optimal approximation of the target partition. An exhaustive search in hypothesis space is not feasible. But we are lucky. Our framework allows us to define a few measures that help to heuristically guide our search for promising hypotheses. There are basically two issues in relational knowledge discovery that correspond to unsupervised and supervised learning.

Identifying potentially interesting sets of objects. If there are sets of objects that cannot be distinguished by $\bar{\bar{\mathbf{R}}}$ (i.e., all the blocks in $s/\bar{\bar{\mathbf{R}}}$), then each of these sets may represent an unknown concept – simply because of the fact that we are unable to describe them. This case, however, is rather rare; usually we collect and store data models so as to be able to explicate the information therein. This implies a (possibly strong) bias because strict modelling prevents learning beyond what our preconception expects. It requires an expert to understand whether $s/\bar{\bar{\mathbf{R}}}$ represents a reasonable breakdown of the structure of our domain. Finding such sets is, theoretically, simple: all we have to do is compute $s/\bar{\bar{\mathbf{R}}}$. For the expert who is expected to interpret our findings, this may not be helpful at all. Most likely he will ask for a simpler representation of the domain structure. Then we face the problem of (efficiently) finding reducts. Because there may be many such reducts, the next problem is to choose the one that is most explanatory to the expert.

Circumscribing a new property in terms of present knowledge. Let there be some knowledge, say $\mathbf{Q}$. Imagine we can use $\mathbf{Q}$ to describe a certain classification $\mathfrak{c}$. This means that some $\mathfrak{c}$ is (roughly) definable by $\mathbf{Q}$. What does it mean to *learn*, then? It means to acquire some *new* knowledge to describe $\mathbf{Q}$. Because $\mathbf{Q} \subseteq \mathbf{R}$, a new "chunk" of knowledge $\mathbf{P} \subseteq \mathbf{R}$ can be considered to be a hypothesis describing $\mathbf{Q}$ if it is able to describe $\mathfrak{c}$ suffciently well. In this case, $\mathbf{Q}$ provides a teacher signal t, and we are *searching* for a set $\mathbf{P} \in \wp(\mathbf{R})$ to approximate $\mathbf{Q}$. There are several methods to determine whether $\mathbf{P}$ is a good candidate to describe $\mathbf{Q}$. An ideal hypothesis $\mathbf{P}$ should satisfy the following requirements:

1. $\mathbf{P}$ should be *small*; ideally, it should be smaller than $\mathbf{Q}$ and much smaller than $\mathbf{R}$.
2. $\mathbf{P}$ should be *novel*. If $\mathbf{P}$ is more or less the same as $\mathbf{Q}$, then there seems to be no reason to consider $\mathbf{P}$ as *newly discovered* knowledge. A first idea towards modelling novelty is that $\mathbf{P}$ should not share significantly more than $\mathrm{Cor}(\mathbf{R} \trianglelefteq \mathbf{Q})$ relations with $\mathbf{Q}$.
3. $\mathbf{P}$ should not be much less accurate than $\mathbf{Q}$; that is, $\mathbf{Q}$ should (at least to a certain degree) depend on $\mathbf{P}$.
4. Finally, $\mathbf{P}$ should be more general than $\mathbf{Q}$.

The generality of knowledge chunks can be determined with respect to different parts of our universe. Let $\mathbf{R}$ be the set of all relations we can use to describe our domain. Then, all expressions over elements of $\mathbf{R}$ form the *representation space*. A target concept (or classification) $\mathfrak{c}$ is given by an (unknown) function t. It is represented by a (partially defined) decision attribute. Now, let there be two hypotheses $\mathbf{P}$ and $\mathbf{Q}$ to describe $\mathfrak{c}$. Both **P** and **Q** can be assumed to be (proper) subsets of **R**. To be able to compare both hypotheses we need to estimate their respective accuracies. For this we have a measure as defined in Definition 6.22.

In terms of *searching* a subsumption lattice of hypotheses, we need a corresponding order relation modelling generality. We can compare two sets **P** and **Q** of knowledge according to their generality by comparing their respective positive regions for a "reference" set. So **P** is more general than **Q** if

$$[\![\mathbf{Q} \unlhd \mathbf{R}]\!]s' \approx [\![\mathbf{P} \unlhd \mathbf{R}]\!]s' \quad \text{and} \quad [\![\mathbf{Q} \unlhd \mathbf{R}]\!]s \subseteq [\![\mathbf{P} \unlhd \mathbf{R}]\!]s \tag{6.44}$$

for $s' \subseteq s$. It means that knowledge **P** is able to positively correctly classify more objects of the domain than **Q**.

Exercise 6.52 (◊) The last definition of generality is not to be confused with coverage. Explain.

Again, the question is where to start searching, how to proceed, and when to stop.

> **Searching for the best hypothesis**
> Rough set data analysis allows us to identify potentially interesting sets of objects. This is what we refer to as *unsupervised learning*.
> Rough set data analysis also allows us to acquire new knowledge by searching for new sets of knowledge that can describe a classification defined by a decision attribute. This is what is called *supervised learning*.

6.5.1 Utility

Utility is a measure that says something about the *degree* of usefulness. It describes *how much* a relation (or a set of relations) contributes to the ability of describing knowledge. Definition 6.22 gave us a means to estimate a relation's usefulness with respect to a class or classification.

To quantitatively describe the usefulness of a set of relations, we could simply determine the relative size of the positive region:

Definition 6.53 — Relative utility. Relative utility
We define the *(relative) utility of* **P** *(on s) for describing knowledge* **Q** to be

$$utility_s(\mathbf{P} \unlhd \mathbf{Q}) \quad := \quad \frac{|[\![\mathbf{P} \unlhd \mathbf{Q}]\!]s|}{|s|}. \tag{6.45}$$

The quotient describes the relative number of objects that by **P** can be correctly classified with respect to the classification $\mathfrak{c} = s/\bar{\bar{\mathbf{Q}}}$. ●

In prose, the utility of a set of relations is the quotient of the number of correctly classified objects using this set of relations and the number of all objects under consideration, $|s|$. When designing an algorithm to determine reducts, the algorithm will proceed stepwise; that is, to decide in every single step which relation to drop or to add, we would compute the utility of a singleton set $\mathbf{P} = \{P\}$ for $\mathbf{Q}$:

$$utility_s(\mathbf{P} \trianglelefteq \mathbf{Q}) \quad = \quad \frac{|\bigcup_{c_i \in s/\bar{\bar{\mathbf{Q}}}} [\![P]\!] c_i|}{|s|} = \frac{1}{|s|} \sum_{i=0}^{\mathbf{k}} |[\![P]\!] c_i|, \qquad (6.46)$$

where $k = |s/\bar{\bar{\mathbf{Q}}}|$. The equality holds because of the pairwise disjointness of the equivalence classes.

Usually, utility is a measure with respect to a target classification. But because a target classification is just a set quotient like any other quotient, we can use utility to describe the dependencies between any *arbitrary* sets of equivalence relations. And, of course, we can extend the definition of utility to classifications rather than just sets:

$$utility_{s/\bar{\bar{\mathbf{R}}}}(\mathbf{P} \trianglelefteq \mathbf{Q}) \quad := \quad \frac{1}{|s|} \sum_{c_i \in s/\bar{\bar{\mathbf{R}}}} |[\![\mathbf{P} \trianglelefteq \mathbf{Q}]\!] c_i|. \qquad (6.47)$$

It is clear that if $utility_s(\mathbf{P} \trianglelefteq \mathbf{Q}) = 1$, $\mathbf{P}$ is good enough for describing $\mathbf{Q}$ on the entire domain. In this case it must hold that $[\![\mathbf{P} \trianglelefteq \mathbf{Q}]\!]s = s$ and therefore $\mathbf{P} \preceq \mathbf{Q}$. We can also conclude that $\mathbf{P}$ implies $\mathbf{Q}$: $\mathbf{P} \supset \mathbf{Q}$. If, on the other hand, $utility_s(\mathbf{P} \trianglelefteq \mathbf{Q}) = 0$, then the numerator must be 0. This can happen only if $[\![\mathbf{P} \trianglelefteq \mathbf{Q}]\!]s$ is empty, and that means that *all* lower $\mathbf{P}$-approximations of $\mathbf{Q}$-classes are empty: $\forall c \in s/\bar{\bar{\mathbf{Q}}} : [\![\mathbf{P}]\!]c = \emptyset$. In other words, $\mathbf{P}$ cannot positively describe anything that $\mathbf{Q}$ is concerned with.

The interesting case is when $0 < utility_s(\mathbf{P} \trianglelefteq \mathbf{Q}) < 1$. Then, the larger the value, the larger the positive region. The smaller it is, the less $\mathbf{P}$ seems to be appropriate for describing $\mathbf{Q}$. Another equivalent formulation is that the average sharpness of $\mathbf{P}$-approximations of $\mathbf{Q}$-classes increases as the utility of $\mathbf{P}$ for $\mathbf{Q}$ increases (and vice versa).[8] Finally, it means that $\mathbf{P}$ implies $\mathbf{Q}$ not entirely, but at least up to a certain degree.

In this way, we are able to order sets of relations with respect to the degree of their ability to mutually describe each other. Then, we want to find a smallest set $\mathbf{P}$ of equivalence relations with maximum utility to describe each other set – thus we would reduce redundant knowledge. If such a set would also prove to have a high utility for describing $\mathfrak{c}$, we would have found a beautiful, non-redundant and concise description of our target classification.

[8] If, $R :\in \mathbf{P}$ and $\mathfrak{c} := s/\mathbf{Q}$, then we can see that $utility_s(\mathbf{P} \trianglelefteq \mathbf{Q})$ is the same as $utility_R(\mathfrak{c})$ (see Definition 6.22).

Definition 6.54 — Partial implication. Partial implication
Let there be knowledge base $\mathfrak{K} = \langle s, \mathbf{R} \rangle$ and $\mathbf{P}, \mathbf{Q} \subseteq \mathbf{R}$. We say that $\mathbf{P}$ *implies* $\mathbf{Q}$ to a degree k if and only if

$$k = utility_s(\mathbf{P} \trianglelefteq \mathbf{Q}) = \frac{|[\![\mathbf{P} \trianglelefteq \mathbf{Q}]\!]s|}{|s|}. \tag{6.48}$$

We then write $\mathbf{P} \overset{k}{\supset} \mathbf{Q}$. ●

Recall that every set $\mathbf{P}$ or $\mathbf{Q}$ consists of relations or attributes. Therefore, utility or partial dependance means the "utility of a set of attributes". If we reconsider the earlier definitions of lower and upper approximations, it becomes clear that the utility of a set of attributes is not determined uniformly by all attributes, but that some attributes may contribute more than others. In this way we can deduce a measure of individual attribute significance from the definition of a set's utility or dependence.

6.5.2 Attribute significance

Some attributes seem to have greater descriptive powers than others. All machine learning methods try to find the most significant ones first so as to quickly converge to a solution. Decision trees utilise an information measure, and support vector machines generate separating planes. In rough set theory, we want to find a smallest set of attributes that we accordingly may assume to be more significant than redundant attributes.

Just as a reminder, let us reconsider the way information gain methods tackle this problem.

Example 6.55 Consider again the following information system:

s	f_0	f_1	f_2	f_3	f_t
0	1	•	♡	c	0
1	0	•	♠	b	/
2	2	•	♣	b	1
3	1	•	♣	c	/
4	1	•	♡	a	1
5	2	∘	♣	b	1
6	2	•	♠	b	/
7	0	•	♠	a	1

A quick analysis shows that

$$\text{entropy}_t(s) = -\frac{1}{8}\log_3\frac{1}{8} - \frac{3}{8}\log_3\frac{3}{8} - \frac{4}{8}\log_3\frac{4}{8} \approx 0.89,$$

and that for all $f_i \in \mathfrak{F}$, entropy$_t(f_i, s)$ has the following values:

$$
\begin{array}{llllll}
0: & \frac{2}{8}\,\text{entropy}(\{1,7\}) & + \frac{3}{8}\,\text{entropy}(\{0,3,4\}) & + & \frac{3}{8}\,\text{entropy}(\{2,5,6\}) \\
\approx & \frac{1}{4}\cdot 1 & + \frac{3}{8}\cdot 1 & + & \frac{3}{8}\cdot 0.58 \\
\approx & 85\% & & & \\[1em]
1: & \frac{1}{8}\,\text{entropy}(\{5\}) & + \frac{3}{8}\,\text{entropy}(\{0,2,4\}) & + & \frac{4}{8}\,\text{entropy}(\{1,3,6,7\}) \\
\approx & \frac{1}{8}\cdot 0 & + \frac{3}{8}\cdot 0.58 & + & \frac{4}{8}\cdot 0.51 \\
\approx & 47\% & & & \\[1em]
2: & \frac{2}{8}\,\text{entropy}(\{0,4\}) & + \frac{3}{8}\,\text{entropy}(\{1,6,7\}) & + & \frac{3}{8}\,\text{entropy}(\{2,3,5\}) \\
\approx & \frac{1}{4}\cdot 1 & + \frac{3}{8}\cdot 0.58 & + & \frac{3}{8}\cdot 0.58 \\
\approx & 68\% & & & \\[1em]
3: & \frac{2}{8}\,\text{entropy}(\{4,7\}) & + \frac{4}{8}\,\text{entropy}(\{1,2,5,6\}) & + & \frac{2}{8}\,\text{entropy}(\{0,3\}) \\
\approx & \frac{1}{4}\cdot 0 & + \frac{1}{2}\cdot 0.63 & + & \frac{1}{4}\cdot 0.63 \\
\approx & 47\%. & & &
\end{array}
$$

As one can see, both features f_1 and f_3 provide maximum information gain. ●

How do we extract the most significant (useful) attributes without any assumptions or heuristic guidelines? Let $\mathfrak{c} = s/\mathbf{T}$ and imagine $\mathbf{Q}$ is our current subset of attributes that we want to reduce to find a reduct. To determine a minimal set of attributes $\mathbf{P} \subseteq \mathbf{Q}$, $\mathbf{R} = \mathbf{Q} - \mathbf{P}$ with maximum utility, we need to

1. Drop attributes R such that $\mathbf{P} = \mathbf{Q} - \{R\}$, where the loss of R causes the least *utility loss* on $\mathfrak{c} = s/\mathbf{T}$
2. Keep attributes $R \in \mathbf{P}$ that would cause the most *utility loss* with respect to $\mathfrak{c} = s/\mathbf{T}$.

This is simply the idea behind top-down and bottom-up computations of reducts *relative to* $\mathbf{T}$. First, note that

$$
\begin{aligned}
\mathit{utility}_s(\mathbf{P} \trianglelefteq \mathbf{T}) &\leq \mathit{utility}_s(\mathbf{Q} \trianglelefteq \mathbf{T}) && (6.49)\\
\mathit{utility}_s((\mathbf{Q} - \mathbf{P}) \trianglelefteq \mathbf{T}) &\leq \mathit{utility}_s(\mathbf{Q} \trianglelefteq \mathbf{T}). && (6.50)
\end{aligned}
$$

Then, based on relative utility, we define an attribute's *significance* similar to *information gain* (see Equation (5.8)):

Attribute significance

Definition 6.56 — Attribute significance.
The *significance* of a set of attributes is the *loss of utility* caused by its removal:

$$
\mathit{significance}_s(\mathbf{P} \trianglelefteq \mathbf{T}) = \mathit{utility}_s(\mathbf{Q} \trianglelefteq \mathbf{T}) - \mathit{utility}_s(\mathbf{Q} - \mathbf{P} \trianglelefteq \mathbf{T}) \quad (6.51)
$$

is called the *(Q-relative) relative significance* of $\mathbf{P}$ for $\mathbf{T}$. ●

Exercise 6.57 (◊) Let $\mathbf{S} = \mathbf{Q} - \mathbf{P}$. Then,

$$
\mathit{significance}_s(\mathbf{P} \trianglelefteq \mathbf{T}) + \mathit{significance}_s(\mathbf{S} \trianglelefteq \mathbf{T}) = \mathit{significance}_s(\mathbf{Q} \trianglelefteq \mathbf{T})
$$

is in general *not* true. Prove!

Knowledge discovery by rough set analysis

The idea behind knowledge discovery by rough sets then means to:

- Reduce **Q** to **P** by deleting **S** such that

$$significance_s(\mathbf{S} \trianglelefteq \mathbf{T}) = utility_s(\mathbf{Q} \trianglelefteq \mathbf{T}) - utility_s(\mathbf{P} \trianglelefteq \mathbf{T})$$

  is *minimised*
- Build **P** by adding relations **S** to **Q** until

$$significance_s(\mathbf{P} \trianglelefteq \mathbf{T}) = utility_s(\mathbf{Q} \trianglelefteq \mathbf{T}) - utility_s(\mathbf{S} \trianglelefteq \mathbf{T})$$

  is *maximised*.

Putting rough set theory into an application means to implement a search algorithm. We have to provide efficient tools to compute **P** as a hypothesis to describe a target **T** when we start off with a given set $\emptyset \subseteq \mathbf{Q} \subseteq \mathbf{R}$. Han et al. (2003) present a method for an efficient search for reducts in databases that is based on a bottom-up search method. It makes use of the fact that database management systems offer optimised algorithms by which cores can be computed quite efficiently; see also Vaithyanathan and Lin (2008). The amount of data to be checked for further search is decreased by using class representatives instead of all of the class members. Li and Cercone (2005) also present a similar approach, but instead of making use of the efficiency of database systems, the search for cores and reducts is performed by using an evolutionary algorithm wrapped around the ROSETTA system (Øhrn et al. 1998; Øhrn (1999)). Finding cores by genetic algorithms alone has been presented in Wróblewski (1995).

The fact that rough set theory focuses on *concepts* rather than on classes is reflected in its popularity in formal concept analysis: for example, Yao and Chen (2006), Düntsch et al. (2002), and Xu et al. (2008). The logic behind rough sets, its algebraic properties, and relation to other logics or soft computing approaches has been studied extensively (Düntsch 1988, 1997; Orlowska 1993; Parsons et al. 1994; Yao 2003).

6.6 Conclusion

What is rough set theory good for, you might ask? What does it offer that entropy-based heuristically guided decision tree induction does not have? Well, the answer is

Less!

It definitively lacks one important property, and this is *the value of a feature for an object.* If, in a decision tree, N_f is the least node subsuming two objects x and y, then we know that N_f has at least two different successor nodes N_x and N_y subsuming x and y, respectively. We also know that $\varphi(N_x)$ and $\varphi(N_y)$ differ in only one literal in the precondition. This difference is exactly in the value of feature f: $f(x) = v_x \neq v_y = f(y)$.

In rough set theory, all we know is that $f(x) \neq f(y)$ because $x \neq_{R_f} y$. We lost knowledge about the actual values v_x and v_y. But does it hurt? Not at all. First, we can reconstruct v_x by asking $\mathfrak{I}$ about $f(z)$ for an arbitrary $z \in [x]_{R_f}$. We need to save the value for one element of this class only and know that all equivalent objects share the same value. Second, not only do we not really lose information – we even compress our knowledge further: The information that from some decision node on downwards $f(z) = v_x$ holds for all subsumed objects is stored in *every* subsumed node. Sure, we can create a more efficient data structure, but when we try some kind of rule-based post-pruning, we need all the literals in every node again.

So there is not really a big loss here. According to our understanding of knowledge as the ability to discriminate different things from each other, we have not lost anything.

Another argument could be that, of course, we lost the *structure* of a decision tree. Is that true? You guessed it: no (as far as we are concerned with *definable* classifications). Let us take a closer look at the front of a decision tree d we induce to describe t. Of course, it represents a classification, say $\mathfrak{d} = s/D$, with every leaf node being an equivalence class. Then (presupposing t is definable), it holds that

$$\forall c_i \subseteq s : c_i \in \mathfrak{d} \Longrightarrow c_i \in s/R_t.$$

Let $\mathbf{D} \subseteq \mathbf{R}$ be the set of all the equivalence relations induced by all the features used in any of the decision nodes. It surprisingly holds that

$$\mathbf{D} \preceq D$$

because features cannot appear more than just once in a tree. So unless the least subsuming node of two leaf nodes is the root node, their rule representations contain *different* literals. The difference becomes clear when comparing Figures 4.4 and 6.2. The first one illustrates that on every level of the tree only equivalence classes are further partitioned, while $\overline{\overline{\mathbf{R}}}$ partitions the entire set s. It is, so to say, a flat tree and $\overline{\overline{\mathbf{D}}}$ is the equivalence relation that is used as the decision attribute in the root node. We can then simply enumerate all the classes and for each class we find a representative for which we find all the values required for all the features in $\mathbf{D}$ that define this class. Then, if

$$\mathbf{D} \preceq R_t,$$

D is a very good hypothesis for t. And it is not so bad if

$$\mathbf{D} \overset{\gamma}{\supset} R_t$$

for large γ.

Decision trees not only express which features are important to make a certain decision. They also express a relative dependence of features: if a feature g appears in a decision node below N_f, then we know that g is somehow required by f to approximate t. If it does *not* appear in a subtree below N_f, then it is not significant or is already included in the indiscernibility relation defined by all the features in literals in $\varphi(N_f)$.

It follows that

utility corresponds to *information* and
significance corresponds to *information gain*.

The only difference is that decision trees presuppose the validity of the assumed entropy measure, while rough set data analysis simply takes an unbiased look at the data.

Chapter 7
Inductive logic learning

Commonsense expert knowledge usually consists of *rules*. At least, rules are used to communicate expert knowledge. Such rules are represented using a suitable formal system, that is, some kind of a (terminological) logic. Herein, the terminology and factual knowledge can be seen as a knowledge base; that is, it is what we can feed into a system that we want to induce more general and previously unknown laws from our observations. This is what inductive logic learning is concerned with.

Every object x of our universe is perceived as a *pattern*. Assuming that we have an information system $\mathfrak{I} = \langle U, \mathbf{F}, V_{\mathbf{F}} \rangle$ describing all elements of our domain, then x is nothing more than a vector:

$$\rho(x) = \vec{x} = \langle f_0(x), f_1(x), \ldots, f_{n-1}(x) \rangle .$$

With a suitable representation function ρ, similar objects should be represented by similar vectors. Similarity is not so much a property of vectors but rather a property of a corresponding distance measure of which there are many. We know that assuming any of these measures in representation space means introducing some bias because any method that is based on such a measure implies a corresponding "natural" similarity of objects in the real world.

This problem is not the only reason why one would like to consider another possible way of knowledge discovery, preferably one that avoids this kind of bias. Usually there is more to a complex domain than just patterns. There are dependencies. If, for example, the pattern ■ is "similar" to the pattern □ and if the pattern ● is "similar" to the pattern ●, then we often find that ▲ is "similar" to △. As one can see, objects are similar to each other if they have the same shape. What happened here? First, there is a *rule*: *if* there is something like this and something like that, *then* there is something like so. Second, this rule actually implements "similarity": two things are of the same breed if they have the same shape. We did not presuppose too much and are rewarded with a concept and its procedural definition.

Many people prefer rules to patterns, especially when it comes to describing concepts. If we want to discover new concepts, the trick is to find new rules that describe our data. There are special kinds of rules that together form a *logic program*.

Then, knowledge discovery means rule discovery and discovering rules means to *invent logic programs*.

7.1 From information systems to logic programs

Let there be an information system $\mathfrak{I} = \langle s, \mathbf{F}, V_{\mathbf{F}} \rangle$. Every feature f_i in $\mathbf{F}$ is defined as a function:

$$f_i : s \to V_{\mathbf{i}}.$$

For $\mathfrak{I}$ we also define an information function, $I : s \times \mathbf{n} \to V_{\mathbf{n}}$, with $I(x,i) = f_i(x)$. But why do database managers speak of "tables" and "relations"?

7.1.1 Functions and relations

Functions are special cases of relations such that $f : s \rightharpoondown V_f$ is total and one-to-one. Therefore, every feature f is a heterogeneous binary relation. In the last chapter we took a closer look at a more generalised interpretation of f:

$$R : s \rightharpoondown s, \text{ where } xRy \Longleftrightarrow f(x) = f(y).$$

Therefore, an information system $\mathfrak{I}$ provides us with two sets of relations of different kinds:

- The set $\mathbf{F}$ contains heterogeneous binary relations that relate objects of our domain to some property.
- The set $\mathbf{R}$ contains equivalence relations on s relating pairs of objects of our domain that share the same properties.

R defines a classification $\mathfrak{c} = s/R$, and we know there is a set $\dot{c} \subset s$ of representatives such that the union of all R-equivalence classes of elements of $\dot{c}$ forms the partition $\mathfrak{c}$. Therefore,

$$\forall x \in \dot{c}, y \in s : y \in [x]_R \Longrightarrow f(y) = f(x).$$

Reformulating $f : s \rightarrow V_f$ as the relation $F : s \rightharpoondown V_f$, this becomes

$$\forall x \in \dot{c}, y \in s : xRy \Longrightarrow yFf(x).$$

And, finally, speaking in terms of relation algebra, it holds that

$$R^{\smile}F = F \text{ and, by symmetry of equivalence relations, } RF = F. \qquad (7.1)$$

In databases, all the features $f \in \mathbf{F}$ are called the "columns" of a table, and all $x \in s$ form the rows $\rho(x) = \vec{x} = \langle f_i(x) \rangle_{i \in \mathbf{n}}$.

Exercise 7.1 (◇) The entire table is often referred to as a (single) relation. Why? Read the definition of *heterogeneous (binary) relations.* Be sure to know about the difference between *relation algebra* and *relational algebra.*

A relation is the algebraic counterpart to what in first order logic (FOL) is called a *predicate*.

7.1.2 Semantics of first order logic

We assume the reader to be familiar with first order logic, but to elucidate its connection to relational knowledge representation and discovery, let us briefly recall the most important pieces from its semantics.

The syntax of FOL is defined by the construction of terms (Ter_Σ) and formulae (Fml_Σ) over a *signature* of function symbols, predicate symbols, connectives, quantifiers, and variable symbols. Their *meaning* is a mapping from Fml_Σ into a structure $\mathfrak{A}$ called a Σ-algebra:

Σ-algebra

Definition 7.2 — Σ-algebra.
Let Σ be a signature. We define a structure $\mathfrak{A}$, called a *Σ-algebra*, as follows:

1. A is the base set of $\mathfrak{A}$.
2. For $n > 0$ and a function symbol $f : s^n \rightarrow s \in \Sigma$, there is a function $f_A : A^n \rightarrow A$ in $\mathfrak{A}$.
3. For $n > 0$ and a predicate symbol $p : s^n \in \Sigma$, there is a relation $p_A \subseteq A^n$ in $\mathfrak{A}$.
4. For $n = 0$ and a constant symbol $c :\rightarrow s \in \Sigma$, there is $c_A \in A$ in $\mathfrak{A}$.
5. For $n = 0$ and an atom $p :\in \Sigma$, there is a *truth value* in $\mathbf{2} = \{\mathbf{0}, \mathbf{1}\}$ in $\mathfrak{A}$.

A Σ-algebra is a structure that provides some "meaning" to the syntactical elements of Ter_Σ and Fml_Σ. ●

The set Var_Σ is the set of *variable symbols*. Starting off with Var_Σ and 0-ary function symbols, we can define Ter_Σ inductively: every constant and every variable is a term. Given n terms and an n-ary function symbol we can build an n-ary term from it (and we can do so recursively to build increasingly complex terms). Formulae (Fml_Σ) are defined similarly, where atomic formulae consist of 0-ary predicate symbols, n-ary predicates can be constructed from according predicate symbols and n terms as their arguments, and complex formulae can be built from predicates and logical connectives.

Now that a Σ-algebra provides a structure in which we can interpret a formula, we need to define by which object in A a constant, a variable, a term, or even a formula is actually represented.[1] Proper interpretation requires not only to map the predicate of function symbols onto relations and functions, respectively; variables need to have a value and terms have to be evaluated to find the object they denote.

Definition 7.3 — Assignment, α.

Assignment, α

An *assignment* is defined by a function $\alpha : \mathrm{Var} \to A$ mapping variable symbols onto elements of the base set of $\mathfrak{A}$. A *modified assignment*

$$\alpha' := \alpha\left[X_0 \mapsto x_0, \ldots, X_{n-1} \mapsto x_{n-1}\right]$$

is defined as

$$\alpha'(X) = \begin{cases} x_i & \text{for } X \in \{X_i : i \in \mathbf{n}\} \\ \alpha(X) & \text{otherwise.} \end{cases} \tag{7.2}$$

●

Having defined the value (i.e., the interpretation) of a variable, we can *evaluate* terms and formulae. The value of a term or a formula depends on the values of the variables occurring in them.

Definition 7.4 — Evaluation.

Evaluation

An *evaluation* is a function delivering the result of resolving a term in its Σ-algebra $\mathfrak{A}$ based on the current variable assignment α:

$$\lfloor\cdot\rfloor_\alpha^{\mathfrak{A}} \quad : \quad \mathrm{Ter} \to A. \tag{7.3}$$

For variable symbols $X \in \mathrm{Var} \subseteq \mathrm{Ter}$, we define $\lfloor X \rfloor_\alpha^{\mathfrak{A}} := \alpha(X)$. Complex terms are evaluated recursively:

$$\lfloor f(t_0, \ldots, t_{n-1}) \rfloor_\alpha^{\mathfrak{A}} \quad := \quad f_A(\lfloor t_0 \rfloor_\alpha^{\mathfrak{A}}, \ldots, \lfloor t_{n-1} \rfloor_\alpha^{\mathfrak{A}}). \tag{7.4}$$

●

In addition to this, we define a *substitution* σ. A substitution is an expression

$$\sigma \quad = \quad \left[X_0 \mapsto t_0, X_1 \mapsto t_1, \ldots, X_{n-1} \mapsto t_{n-1}\right] \tag{7.5}$$

[1] From now on, we will drop the indices and simply write Var, Ter, and Fml when the reference algebra and signature are clear from the context.

that specifies a function implementing a syntactical operation on terms and formulae. Substitutions are written post-fix; and the meaning of $\varphi\sigma$ is that for all $X \mapsto t \in \sigma$, every occurrence of X is replaced by t. So far, all we can do is compute terms or apply some term-rewriting rule – but the interesting thing is to *evaluate* formulae $\varphi \in \mathrm{Fml}$. FOL formulae, when "evaluated", should deliver a value that tells us whether a formula describes a situation that is somehow "true" or "false". Now that substitutions act on the syntax only, what does it mean? In a formula's evaluation, a substitution causes a modification of an assignment. "True" and "false" are values in $\mathfrak{A}$, but if we say that a formula is "true", we actually mean that it is *valid*:

Validity, $\models$

Definition 7.5 — Validity, $\models$.
Let $\mathfrak{A}$ be a Σ-algebra and $\varphi, \psi \in \mathrm{Fml}$. We call φ *valid in* $\mathfrak{A}$ *under* α ($\mathfrak{A} \models_\alpha \varphi$) if

$$\begin{array}{lll}
\mathfrak{A} \models_\alpha p(t_0, \ldots, t_{n-1}) & :\Longleftrightarrow & \left\langle \downarrow t_0 \downarrow_\alpha^{\mathfrak{A}}, \ldots, \downarrow t_{n-1} \downarrow_\alpha^{\mathfrak{A}} \right\rangle \in p_A \\
\mathfrak{A} \models_\alpha p & :\Longleftrightarrow & \downarrow p \downarrow_\alpha^{\mathfrak{A}} = \mathbf{1} \\
\mathfrak{A} \models_\alpha (\neg\varphi) & :\Longleftrightarrow & \mathfrak{A} \not\models_\alpha \varphi \\
\mathfrak{A} \models_\alpha (\varphi \wedge / \vee / \rightarrow \psi) & :\Longleftrightarrow & \mathfrak{A} \models_\alpha \varphi \text{ and/or/implies } \mathfrak{A} \models_\alpha \psi \\
\mathfrak{A} \models_\alpha \forall X : \varphi & :\Longleftrightarrow & \forall a \in A : \mathfrak{A} \models_{\alpha[X \mapsto a]} \varphi \\
\mathfrak{A} \models_\alpha \exists X : \varphi & :\Longleftrightarrow & \exists a \in A : \mathfrak{A} \models_{\alpha[X \mapsto a]} \varphi .
\end{array}$$

Herein, $\alpha\,[X \mapsto a]$ means that the function α at X is redefined so as to deliver the value $a \in s_A$. φ is *valid in* $\mathfrak{A}$ if $\mathfrak{A} \models_\alpha \varphi$ for all α, and φ is called *valid* if φ is valid in every $\mathfrak{A}$. ●

The substitution lemma states that

$$\mathfrak{A} \models_\alpha \varphi\,[X_i \mapsto t_i]_{i \in \mathbf{n}} \quad :\Longleftrightarrow \quad \mathfrak{A} \models_{\alpha[X_i \mapsto a_i]_{i \in \mathbf{n}}} \varphi, \tag{7.6}$$

where for all $i \in \mathbf{n}$, $a_i = \downarrow t_i \downarrow_\alpha^{\mathfrak{A}}$.

7.1.3 Deduction

Deduction or inference means to draw conclusions. So if there is an argument that we agree to be admissible somehow, we want to be able to draw corresponding conclusions in $\mathfrak{A}$. This suggests calling $\mathfrak{A}$ a *model*:

Model

Definition 7.6 — Model.
A Σ-algebra $\mathfrak{A}$ is called *a model* of a formula $\varphi \in \mathrm{Fml}$ if and only if

$$\mathfrak{A} \models \varphi \quad :\Longleftrightarrow \quad \forall \alpha \in A^{\mathrm{Var}} : \mathfrak{A} \models_\alpha \varphi \tag{7.7}$$

for all assignments α. For a set of formulae $\Phi \subseteq \mathrm{Fml}_\Sigma$, we define $\mathfrak{A} \models \Phi :\Longleftrightarrow \forall \varphi \in \Phi : \mathfrak{A} \models \varphi$. ●

The question of whether an algebra is a model depends on the interpretation of the signature and, of course, on the assignments.

Exercise 7.7 (◊) Learn about special kinds of algebras and models, the so-called *Herbrand algebras* and *Herbrand models* (e.g., Mazzola et al. 2006; Sperschneider and Antoniou 1991).

A naturally or intuitively valid inference means that from one formula (or a set of formulae) follows another. It means that if the first formula has a model, the second one should be valid in this algebra as well! This makes inference a relation between models.

Definition 7.8 — Entailment. Entailment

A set $\Phi \subseteq \mathrm{Fml}$ *entails* a formula $\varphi \in \mathrm{Fml}$ if and only if every model of Φ is a model of φ, too:

$$\Phi \approx\!\!\!\mid\; \varphi \quad :\Longleftrightarrow \quad \forall \mathfrak{A} : \mathfrak{A} \models \Phi \Longrightarrow \mathfrak{A} \models \varphi. \tag{7.8}$$

Φ entails a set Ψ of formulae if and only if it entails every formula $\psi \in \Psi$. Usually, the entailment relation is denoted $\models$; to avoid confusion with the model relation as defined in Definition 7.6, we use $\mid\!\approx$ instead. ●

The deduction rule that is most common in everyday life is *modus ponens*. It states that if from a certain premise we may draw a certain conclusion, and if that premise is a valid statement, then the conclusion also must be valid.

> **Modus ponens**
>
> Thinking implies being; or, as Descartes put it: "Cogito ergo sum". The premise is *to be thinking*, and once *you think*, you *must be*. Therefore, if you *think*, you *are*. In other words:
>
> $$\mathfrak{A} \models \varphi \wedge \mathfrak{A} \models (\varphi \longrightarrow \psi) \Longrightarrow \mathfrak{A} \models \psi.$$

Example 7.9 Let $\mathfrak{A} \models \{\varphi, (\varphi \longrightarrow \psi)\}$. Then, $\mathfrak{A}$ is necessarily a model of each element of this set of formulae:

$$\mathfrak{A} \models \varphi \text{ and } \mathfrak{A} \models (\varphi \longrightarrow \psi).$$

Therefore, we can assume that $\lfloor \varphi \rfloor_\alpha^{\mathfrak{A}} = \mathbf{1}$ and $\lfloor (\varphi \longrightarrow \psi) \rfloor_\alpha^{\mathfrak{A}} = \mathbf{1}$. By modus ponens we know that

$$\{\varphi, (\varphi \longrightarrow \psi)\} \mid\!\approx \{\psi\}.$$

Because $\lfloor \varphi \longrightarrow \psi \rfloor_\alpha^{\mathfrak{A}} = \mathbf{1}$ and $\lfloor \varphi \rfloor_\alpha^{\mathfrak{A}} = \mathbf{1}$, we know by the definition of $\longrightarrow$ that $\lfloor \psi \rfloor_\alpha^{\mathfrak{A}} = \mathbf{1}$. Therefore, every model of $\{\varphi, (\varphi \longrightarrow \psi)\}$ is also a model of $\{\psi\}$. Hence, $\mathfrak{A} \mid\!\approx \psi$. ●

Exercise 7.10 (◊) Show that $\Phi \mid\!\approx \{\psi_0, \ldots, \psi_{n-1}\} \Longleftrightarrow \Phi \mid\!\approx (\psi_0 \wedge \cdots \wedge \psi_{n-1})$.

Entailment is simple to understand but difficult to show: one has to find *all* models of Φ and then check whether each such model is a model of the formula under consideration, too. This is, for a machine, at least cumbersome if not impossible. But what is logic good for if there is no proper way to implement entailment?

There appears to be a loophole, though: suppose that $\Phi \approx\!\!\!\!\models \varphi$. Then,

$$\begin{aligned} & \forall \mathfrak{A} : \mathfrak{A} \models \Phi \implies \mathfrak{A} \models \varphi \\ \text{iff } & \forall \mathfrak{A} : \mathfrak{A} \not\models \varphi \implies \mathfrak{A} \not\models \Phi \\ \text{iff } & \forall \mathfrak{A} : \mathfrak{A} \models (\neg\varphi) \implies \mathfrak{A} \not\models \Phi \\ \text{iff } & \forall \mathfrak{A} : \mathfrak{A} \models \Phi \implies \mathfrak{A} \not\models (\neg\varphi). \end{aligned} \tag{7.9}$$

In FOL there exist *two* truth values, **0** and **1**. So if $\Phi \approx\!\!\!\!\models \varphi$, it cannot be the case that $\Phi \approx\!\!\!\!\models (\neg\varphi)$, too. And this means that

$$\Phi \approx\!\!\!\!\models \varphi \text{ if and only if } \Phi \cup \{(\neg\varphi)\} \text{ has no model,} \tag{7.10}$$

or

$$\forall \mathfrak{A} : ((\mathfrak{A} \models \Phi \implies \mathfrak{A} \models \varphi) \text{ if and only if } \mathfrak{A} \not\models (\neg\varphi)). \tag{7.11}$$

This is a bit tedious to write down, so we define a special symbol $\square$ for FOL formulae that do not possess *any* model:

$$\forall \mathfrak{A} : \mathfrak{A} \not\models \square. \tag{7.12}$$

Together with Equation (7.10) this gives

$$\Phi \approx\!\!\!\!\models \varphi \iff \Phi \cup \{(\neg\varphi)\} \approx\!\!\!\!\models \square. \tag{7.13}$$

However, there are still some universal quantifiers hidden in this definition. Checking the validity or entailment of formula sets requires us to examine *all* interpretations. The semantics of FOL was defined in a way that allows one to compute a term's value in an algebra, but, by the substitution lemma, we can lift (or rather push down) the problem to the underlying formal system whose syntax is given by a grammar. By the substitution lemma we can choose where to carry out variable assignments – on a syntactic level or on a semantic level. The idea is to find a similar technique to make proving entailment easier – by shifting the problem back onto the syntactic level.

There are many such methods, and they are called *calculi*. They all consist of different sets of term-rewriting rules. For illustration, we give one example.

Example 7.11 For all sets Φ of well-formed FOL formulae we define the following rule: if a string $v \in \Phi$ and if there is a string $(v \rightarrow w) \in \Phi$, then w is also a string in Φ. Such a rule usually is written as

$$\frac{v \quad (v \rightarrow w)}{w}.$$

Carrying out this simple term-rewriting rule we do what semantically corresponds to the modus ponens. ●

The good news is that there are some calculi that are sound and complete, like Hilbert's calculus HK, sequent calculi like LK, and resolution (RES). Whenever one can derive φ from Φ, then Φ entails φ, and whenever Φ entails φ, then φ can be derived from Φ. The bad news is that these calculi cannot be implemented to perform efficiently in all cases (the interested reader might want to learn more about Kurt Gödel's completeness theorem). But the worst news is that for every "interesting" logic language set of formulae Φ is in general *undecidable* (c.f. the famous works of Alonzo Church and Alan Turing). Nearly all problems are "interesting", especially in the case of knowledge discovery. You will not be satisfied if you do not learn anything interesting while reading this book, for example, will you?

The question is whether we can define a subset of predicate logic that still allows us to formulate the most "interesting" problems and for which there exists a satisfying calculus. Well, there is. In analogy to Equation (7.13) it allows us to prove things this way:

$$\Phi \approx\models \varphi \iff \Phi \cup \{(\neg\varphi)\} \vdash \square. \tag{7.14}$$

Sets of FOL formulae can be syntactically transformed into sets of formulae all of which have the same form. Examples are *disjunctive* and *conjunctive normal form* where the latter one is the most important to us. The derivation calculus to which we alluded in the previous chapter is called *resolution* and it is based on the idea of proofs by *refutation* as defined in Equation (7.14).

Definition 7.12 — FOL resolution. FOL resolution

Let there be two formulae φ and ψ that both consist of a disjunction of positive or negative atomic formulae (called *literals*). For a disjunction of literals $\bigvee_{i \in I} \lambda_i$ we simply write $\{\lambda_0, \ldots, \lambda_{I-1}\}$.

Let $\lambda_\varphi \in \varphi$ and $(\neg\lambda_\psi) \in \psi$ and a unifying substitution σ such that $\lambda_\varphi\sigma = \lambda_\psi\sigma$. We then define the *resolution rule* RES as

$$\frac{\{\kappa_0, \ldots, \lambda_\varphi, \kappa_{k-1}\} \quad \{\nu_0, \ldots, (\neg\lambda_\psi), \nu_{n-1}\}}{\{\kappa_0, \ldots, \kappa_{n-1}, \nu_0, \ldots, \nu_{m-1}\}\,\sigma}\,\mathsf{RES}. \tag{7.15}$$

For two *parent clauses* φ and ψ we denote the conclusion after applying RES the *resolvent* and write $\varphi \sqcap^{\sigma}_{\mathsf{RES}} \psi = \chi$. A derivation in the resolution calculus is written $\{\varphi, \psi\} \vdash_{\mathsf{RES}} \chi$. ●

We conclude:

Resolution

The resolution principle is based on the modus ponens rule. The structure of a resolution proof is based on refutation:

$$\Phi \vdash \varphi \implies \Phi \approx \varphi \text{ but } \Phi \approx \varphi \not\Rightarrow \Phi \vdash \varphi$$
$$\text{whereas } \Phi \approx \varphi \iff \Phi \cup \{(\neg\varphi)\} \vdash \Box.$$

We end this section with a nice observation. Let there be a function *depth* that delivers the depth of a term as

$$depth(t) = \begin{cases} 0, & t \in \text{Var} \cup \text{Ter}^0 \\ \max\{depth(t_i) : i \in \mathbf{n}\} + 1, & t = f(t_0, \ldots, t_{n-1}), \end{cases}$$

where Ter^0 is the set of constants. The depth of a literal is the maximum depth of all the terms in the literal, and the depth of a clause is the maximum depth of all the literals in it. Because resolving a literal requires the application of a substitution, the depth of the remaining literals in the resolvent cannot be smaller than those in the parent clauses.

7.2 Horn logic

7.2.1 Logic programs

Still, full FOL leaves us with many possible collections of positive and negative atomic formulae that create a problem of choice in efficient resolution proofs. Therefore, we restrict FOL to the following subset.

Horn logic

Definition 7.13 — Horn logic.
Horn logic HOL is the subset of FOL containing a set $\Phi' \in \text{Fml}_{\text{HOL}}$ for every set $\Phi \subseteq \text{Fml}_{\text{FOL}}$ such that

1. $\forall \mathfrak{A} : \mathfrak{A} \models \Phi \iff \mathfrak{A} \models \Phi'$,
2. $\forall \varphi \in \Phi' : \varphi = ((\psi_0 \wedge \psi_1 \wedge \cdots \psi_{n-1}) \longrightarrow \psi_n)$,

where all ψ_i, $i \in \mathbf{n} \cup \{\mathbf{n}\}$ are *atomic formulae*. By a simple transformation, every formula φ has the form

$$(\neg\psi_0) \vee (\neg\psi_1) \vee \cdots \vee (\neg\psi_{n-1}) \vee \psi_n.$$

It is written as

$$\varphi = \{\neg\psi_0, \neg\psi_1, \ldots, \neg\psi_{n-1}, \psi\},$$

and it is called a *clause* and each element of it is called a *literal*. By restricting the length of the conclusion of the rule to one atomic formula, every such clause has *at most one positive literal*. Such clauses are called *Horn clauses* (Horn 1951). ●

According to Definition 7.13, there are three different types of Horn formulae: let λ_i be positive literals. Then,

1. *Facts* are unary clauses that consist of exactly one positive literal. A fact is written as[2]
$$\{\lambda_0\} = \{p(t_0, \ldots, t_{n-1})\} = p(t_0, \ldots, t_{n-1}). \tag{7.16}$$
2. A *rule* consists of exactly one positive literal and at least one negative literal. Rules are written as
$$\begin{aligned} & (\neg\lambda_0) \vee (\neg\lambda_1) \vee \cdots \vee (\neg\lambda_{m-1}) \vee \lambda_m \\ = & \{\neg\lambda_0, \neg\lambda_1, \ldots, \neg\lambda_{m-1}, p(t_0, \ldots, t_{n-1})\} \\ = & p(t_0, \ldots, t_{n-1}) \text{:- } \lambda_0, \ldots, \lambda_{m-1}. \end{aligned} \tag{7.17}$$
3. A *goal* consists of negative literals only:
$$\{(\neg\lambda_0), \ldots, (\neg\lambda_{m-1})\} = \text{?- } \lambda_0, \ldots, \lambda_{m-1}. \tag{7.18}$$
4. The *empty clause*, $\square$, has no literal:
$$\{\} = \square = \texttt{fail}. \tag{7.19}$$

The huge benefit now is that SLD resolution is sound and complete with respect to Horn logic and, especially, that there is a simple and (more or less) efficient algorithm to carry out proofs. Let φ be a conjunction of positive literals $\lambda_0 \wedge \cdots \wedge \lambda_{n-1}$ and let Π be a set of Horn clauses. Then,

$$\Pi \vdash_{SLD} \varphi \quad :\Longleftrightarrow \quad \Pi \cup \{\neg\lambda_0, \ldots, \neg\lambda_{n-1}\} \vdash_{RES} \square \tag{7.20}$$
$$\Longleftrightarrow \quad \Pi \approx \varphi. \tag{7.21}$$

This is a more than fair compensation for losing some expressiveness.

Logic programs

A *literal* is a positive or a negative atomic formula. A set of literals is called a *clause*. A *Horn clause* is a clause with at most one positive literal. A set of Horn clauses is a *predicate definition*. A set of predicate definitions is called a *logic program*.

The huge advantage in efficiency gain can be illustrated as follows. A proof starts off with a set of negative literals. For each negative literal (from left to right), there must be either a fact so the literal can be resolved or a rule. If there is such a fact, the literal disappears, and we can carry on to resolve the next literal of the goal clause (if there is no next literal, we have derived the empty clause and the refutation proof was successful). If there is no matching fact but only a rule, then the current negative literal is resolved and replaced by the negative literals from the rule it has been resolved with. Then we have a new sequence of negative literals (with a possibly different assignment because we

[2] The dot "." belongs to the syntax definition of a fact.

had to apply a unifying substitution) replacing the former goal literal. We then try reducing the new goal clause to the empty clause by trying again to delete all the remaining literals by facts or rules. Using a special method called *unification* for finding unifying substitutions, a resolution proof becomes a linear sequence of single literal resolutions. This special version of resolution is known as SLD resolution (Kowalski 1973; Kowalski and Kuehner 1977). A nice first-hand story of the first steps of logic programming is Kowalski (1988). SLD resolution can be implemented by a stack machine (Aït-Kaci 1999; Warren 1983),[3] which in turn builds the basis of the programming language Prolog.

7.2.2 Induction of logic programs

The method by which a machine acquires a logic program to describe a set of facts (or HOL formulae) is called *inductive logic programming*. By the nature of HOL, this learning paradigm focuses on *rule induction*. In terms of knowledge representation and discovery it means that the sample can be formulated as a set of *facts* and the background knowledge can be formulated using a terminological framework as provided by some expert. Hypotheses are formulated with respect to the same terminology and, therefore, are easy to interpret.

Example 7.14 Here is an example of what it means for a knowledge base to "naturally" or "intuitively" represent an expert's knowledge. Let there be two people, Mr. Rhineheart and Mr. Anderson. They both work for the same company, Metacortex, a computer firm running an expert system called Oracle. While Rhineheart is a manager, Anderson is a programmer. Yet, both of them may use Oracle. Mr. Smith, who is not a Metacortex employee, may not use use the Oracle program. The question is, who, in general, may use a Metacortex program? We represent factual knowledge Π as

$$\left\{ \begin{array}{ll} \mathit{manager}(\mathit{rhinehart}). & \mathit{programmer}(\mathit{anderson}). \\ \mathit{employer}(\mathit{rhinehart}, \mathit{metacortex}). & \mathit{employer}(\mathit{anderson}, \mathit{metacortex}). \\ \mathit{runs}(\mathit{metacortex}, \mathit{oracle}). & \mathit{program}(\mathit{smith}). \end{array} \right\}.$$

Our sample $\mathbf{s}$ looks like

$$\left\{ \begin{array}{l} \langle \mathit{may\_use}(\mathit{anderson}, \mathit{oracle}), \mathbf{1} \rangle\,, \\ \langle \mathit{may\_use}(\mathit{rhineheart}, \mathit{oracle}), \mathbf{1} \rangle\,, \\ \langle \mathit{may\_use}(\mathit{smith}, \mathit{oracle}), \mathbf{0} \rangle \end{array} \right\}.$$

Obviously, a *Person may_use* a *Program* of a *Company* in which he is *employed* only if

[3] The discerning reader might insist on a correctness proof; he can find one in Börger and Rosenzweig (1994).

$$H = \left\{ \begin{array}{l} may\_use(Program, Person) :- \\ \quad runs(Company, Program), \\ \quad employer(Company, Person). \end{array} \right\}$$

This rule forms terminological knowledge or, rather, a hypothesis H that together with Π could explain **s**. Note that this rule does not only answer the above question about access rules at Metacortex but also within *all* companies.

Exercise 7.15 (◇) Prove that $\Pi \cup H \approx\!\!\models \varphi \iff \langle \varphi, \mathbf{1} \rangle \in \mathbf{s}$ with arbitrary Π and H and **s** as above.

Note that the rule is more general than the set of facts: first, it makes use of *variables* rather than atoms, and, second, some knowledge appears to be *dispensable* as it seems that it is irrelevant whether a person is a manager or a programmer – as long as he works for the right company. Logic programs live from *variables*. What may sound trivial has two crucial consequences. From the computational point of view, variables are something we would like to avoid whenever possible. But from a logic point of view, (common) variables *connect* literals. Literals that are not connected are independent (we shall explain in detail what connectedness means later). Therefore it can well be that parts of a rule that only contain irrelevant/independent variables can safely be pruned away without changing the semantics of a formula. So if we use HOL as a representation language for samples and background knowledge, it would be desirable to make the machine learn a logic program by itself. Russell (1992, 1995) supports the idea of induction as the origin of scientific axioms, and Polya (1968) worked on inductive reasoning and scientific discovery by analogy. Popper (2002), on the other hand, claims that scientific proof theory must be based on the deductive test, because induction itself is invalid. We shall see later that Popper's claim is at least weakly supported by our notion of induction. For now, it shall suffice to give a commonsense description of inductive generalisation.

Inductive generalisation
Machine learning in the context of terminological knowledge means to inductively generalise over a set of observed facts.

We now try to formulate the idea a bit more formally.

Definition 7.16 — Learning problem. Learning problem

Let Π be a satisfiable set of Σ-formulae. We call Π the (terminological) *background knowledge*. A *sample* is a set of atomic Σ-formulae φ_i together with a truth value that describes their desired satisfiability conditions:

$$\begin{aligned} \mathbf{s} &= S(m,t) \\ &= \left\{ \langle \varphi_i, t(\varphi_i) \rangle : t(\varphi_i) = \lfloor \varphi_i \rfloor_{\alpha}^{\mathfrak{A}} \in \mathbf{2} \text{ for } i \in \mathbf{m} \right\}. \end{aligned} \tag{7.23}$$

The *learning problem* is to find a $H \subseteq$ Fml for which

$$\Pi \cup H \approx \varphi \iff t(\varphi) = \mathbf{1} \tag{7.24}$$

$$\iff \lfloor \varphi \rfloor_{\alpha}^{\mathfrak{A}} = \mathbf{1} \tag{7.25}$$

holds for *any* φ (and not only for those seen in the sample). ●

Therein, $\mathfrak{A}$ is the Herbrand algebra with signature Σ defined in Π and $\lfloor \cdot \rfloor_{\alpha}^{\mathfrak{A}}$ is the Herbrand interpretation. A learning problem would not be a learning problem if Equation (7.24) was satisfied for $H = \emptyset$, that is, if $\Pi \approx \varphi_i \iff t(\varphi_i) = \mathbf{1}$ already. So we are left with the task of inducing new formulae H such that together with Π we can prove what we want to be true and disprove what we want to be wrong. We restricted ourselves to HOL, so we can reformulate: we want to find H such that

$$\Pi \cup H \approx \varphi_i \iff t(\varphi_i) = \mathbf{1}.$$

Note that there are a few things different here. First, $S(m,t)$ is missing a measure μ. The choice function implemented by S here is *deterministic* and defined by SLD resolution: the set of examples is a *sequence* of facts. Second, the union $\Pi \cup H$ suggests a *monotonic* refinement of knowledge. We know that if $\Pi \cup \{\varphi\}$ is unsatisfiable, so is $\Pi \cup H \cup \{\varphi\}$.

Exercise 7.17 (◊) Read up on the compactness theorem.

Knowledge discovery tries to *generalise* to find new knowledge; this means that the deductive closure of Π should be a subset of $\Pi \cup H$. Together they mean that knowledge discovery by logic induction is at most monotonic in the sense that it preserves falsity. This observation might help mollify Popper's objections against the induction principle.

Of course, learning is more than just generalisation. If $\Pi \approx \neg\varphi$ but $t(\varphi) = \mathbf{1}$, no monotonous refinement would occur by adding H to Π such that $\Pi \cup H \approx \varphi$ and $\Pi \cup H$ being consistent. We would rather refine Π by specialising it in a way that $\Pi' \not\approx \neg\varphi$.

7.2.3 Entailment, generality, and subsumption

Generality comes in many flavours. An equivalence relation is more general than another if the former is a superset of the latter. Most sets are considered to be more general than their subsets. In Heyting algebras, any expression $x \sqcup y$ is more general than both x and y: the maximum of two natural numbers is greater than or equal to both, the union of two sets is greater than or equal to both, and the disjunction of two propositional variables is true under three assignments whereas each single variable is true under only two of them.

Generality
One thing is *more general* than another if it is bigger in some way.

It seems natural to define a relation of generality on sets of formulae along the same line:

$$\Phi \text{ is more general than } \Psi \;:\Longleftrightarrow\; \Phi \sqcup \Psi = \Phi.$$

All we need is to find a suitable definition of $\sqcup$.

Definition 7.18 — Theory. Theory

The *theory* of a set Φ of formulae is the closure of Φ under $\approx$:

$$Th(\Phi) := \{\varphi : \Phi \models\!\!\approx \varphi\}. \tag{7.26}$$

Given a calculus C with a derivation relation $\vdash_C$, the *deductive closure of Φ under $\vdash_C$* is

$$Cl_{\vdash_C}(\Pi) = \{\varphi : \Phi \vdash_C^* \varphi\} \tag{7.27}$$

with * being the Kleene star. If $Th(\Phi) \subseteq Cl_{\vdash_C}(\Phi)$, then C is called *complete*; C is called *correct* if $Cl_{\vdash_C}(\Phi) \subseteq Th(\Phi)$. ●

Exercise 7.19 (◊) Give examples for finite and infinite theories. Think of Ter^0_Σ, A, and function symbols in Σ.

Exercise 7.20 (◊) Just for thinking: given a theory Ψ, are there different Φ_i with $Th(\Phi_i) = \Psi$? Is there a smallest one? Is there exactly one smallest?

Let us briefly consider what it means for one theory to be more general than another.

Example 7.21 We define a relation of generality as follows: Φ is more general than Ψ if $Th(\Psi) \subseteq Th(\Phi)$. By Equation (7.26),

$$Th(\Psi) \subseteq Th(\Phi) \iff \forall \varphi : \Psi \models\!\!\approx \varphi \Longrightarrow \Phi \models\!\!\approx \varphi.$$

Let us assume that $Th(\Psi) \subseteq Th(\Phi)$. Imgine some φ for which $\varphi \notin Th(\Psi)$ but $\varphi \in Th(\Phi)$. Since $\varphi \notin Th(\Psi)$, we know that $\Psi \not\models\!\!\approx \varphi$. By the rule of the excluded middle we then know that $\Psi \models\!\!\approx \neg\varphi$. Hence, $\neg\varphi \in Th(\Psi)$. And, since $Th(\Psi) \subseteq Th(\Phi)$, it follows that $\neg\varphi \in Th(\Phi)$, too. But then,

$$\Phi \models\!\!\approx \varphi \text{ and } \Phi \models\!\!\approx \neg\varphi \tag{7.28}$$

which is a rather uncomfortable situation. ●

The last example led us into some kind of a logic trap. Therefore, we will have to deal with a satisfying definition of a generality relation again later.

The property of equivalence remains unaffected:

Equivalence, $\Phi \cong \Psi$

Definition 7.22 — Equivalence, $\Phi \cong \Psi$.
Let there be two formula sets $\Phi \neq \Psi$. Φ and Ψ are called *equivalent*, written $\Phi \cong \Psi$, if their corresponding theories are the same: $Th(\Phi) = Th(\Psi)$. ●

It is nice to compare sets of formulae. But a comparison of two formula sets requires the sets to be effectively comparable in the first place. And because our goal is to find a relation of generality between two sets of formulae step by step, we have to induce sets of formulae by stepwise induction of single formulae. This requires a relation of generality between single formulae rather than sets of them.

Example 7.23 Let Π consist of the following facts:

$$\Pi = \{colour(\blacksquare, black), colour(\blacksquare, black)\}.$$

Let the sample be as

$$\mathbf{s} = \{\langle shape(\blacksquare, square), \mathbf{1}\rangle, \langle shape(\blacksquare, square), \mathbf{1}\rangle\}.$$

What do we need to deduce the examples $\mathbf{s}$ from Π? Well, all black objects are squares:

$$h_0 = colour(X, black) \longrightarrow shape(X, square).$$

This is true in the sense that $\Pi \cup \{h_0\} \models \mathbf{s}$. h_0 seems to be a good choice, because it remains valid even if we observe $\{colour(\bigcirc, white)\}$. On the other hand, the observation of a white circle allows us to reformulate h_0:

$$h_1 = \neg colour(X, white) \longrightarrow shape(X, square).$$

Obviously, there are *two* different hypotheses, both of which are compatible with our background knowledge and both of which are able to describe all our observations. But what happens if there appears

$$colour(\square, grey)\ ?$$

We observe a strange phenomenon:

$$\Pi \cup \{h_0\} \not\models shape(\square, square) \quad \text{whereas} \quad \Pi \cup \{h_1\} \models shape(\square, square).$$

By common sense it is clear that every model of h_0 is also a model of h_1 – but *not* vice versa! And this means that h_1 *entails* h_0:

$$\{h_1\} \approx\!\!\!\mid\; h_0.$$

By abuse of language we abbreviate and write $h_1 \approx\!\!\!\mid\; h_0$. ●

This leads to the following definition of generality.

Generality of formulae

Definition 7.24 — Generality of formulae.
Let φ, ψ be formulae. φ is called *more general than* ψ, if

$$\{\varphi\} \approx \psi.$$

If φ is more general than ψ we say that φ *subsumes* ψ, written $\varphi \succsim \psi$. ●

Don't be confused about the symbol $\succsim$. It does *not* mean that φ is somehow *less* than ψ but rather that φ somehow "implies" ψ.

Exercise 7.25 (◇) Prove that

$$\varphi \succsim \psi \quad \Longleftrightarrow \quad \left\{\langle \mathfrak{A}, \alpha\rangle : \downarrow\varphi\downarrow^{\mathfrak{A}}_{\alpha} = \mathbf{1}\right\} \subseteq \left\{\langle \mathfrak{A}, \alpha\rangle : \downarrow\psi\downarrow^{\mathfrak{A}}_{\alpha} = \mathbf{1}\right\}. \quad (7.29)$$

Generality is a concept that can be defined in many different ways. Even though there is no such thing as a distribution in FOL, let us just try a little *Gedankenexperiment*.

Example 7.26 Suppose there is a set Π of n Horn formulae and a distribution μ on Π. We define a μ-relative generality of a Horn formula set Φ as

$$gen^{\Pi}_{\mu}(\Phi) = \mu(\{\psi \in \Pi : \Phi \approx \psi\}).$$

Then, we call a set Φ of Horn formulae more general than a set Ψ of Horn formulae if its generality is greater than the generality of Ψ:

$$\Phi \succsim^{\Pi}_{\mu} \Psi :\Longleftrightarrow gen^{\Pi}_{\mu}(\Phi) \geq gen^{\Pi}_{\mu}(\Psi).$$

●

Let us examine whether the definition of $\succsim$ in terms of gen^{Π}_{μ} is a suitable approximation of $\approx$. In terms of semantic implication, Φ is more general than Φ' if $\Phi' \approx \Phi$. Suppose that for $\Phi = \{\varphi_i : i \in \mathbf{n}\}$ it holds that $\Phi' \approx \varphi_i$. It follows immediately that $\Phi' \approx \varphi_0 \wedge \cdots \wedge \varphi_{n-1}$ and, hence, $\Phi' \approx \Phi$. Now let there be a set of witnesses (or test cases) $\Psi = \{\psi_i : i \in \mathbf{k}\}$. We examine the set of test cases that are covered by Φ:

$$\Omega' = \{\psi \in \Psi : \Phi' \approx \psi\} = \Psi - \{\psi \in \Psi : \Phi' \approx \neg\psi\}.$$

Then, of course, $\Phi' \approx \Omega' \subseteq \Psi$. The same holds for Φ: $\Phi \approx \Omega \subseteq \Psi$. But because $\Phi' \approx \Phi$, every $\psi \in \Omega'$ must also be an element of Ω. Hence,

$$\mu(\Omega') \leq \mu(\Omega).$$

This means that $gen^{\Psi}_{\mu}(\Phi) \geq gen^{\Psi}_{\mu}(\Phi')$ and, therefore, $\Phi \succsim \Phi'$. So whenever $\Phi' \approx \Phi$, it follows that $\Phi \succsim \Phi'$.

But what about the reverse direction? Can we conclude from $\Phi \succsim \Phi'$ to $\Phi' \approx \Phi$, too? Suppose that $gen^{\Psi}_{\mu}(\Phi) \geq gen^{\Psi}_{\mu}(\Phi')$ for two consistent sets Φ and Φ'. For reasons of simplicity but without loss of generality we can construct the following contradiction. First, $\mu(\Omega) = \mu(\Omega')$ satisfies the inequality above. Also, let $\Psi = \{\psi, \neg\psi\}$

and $\mu(\Omega) = \mu(\{\psi\}) = \mu(\{\neg\psi\}) = \mu(\Omega')$.[4] If $\Phi' \approx\!\!\!\models \Phi$ is true, we know that

$$\begin{array}{lll} \Phi' \approx\!\!\!\models \Phi \approx\!\!\!\models \Omega & = \{\psi\} & \text{and, by definition,} \\ \Phi \approx\!\!\!\models \Omega' & = \{\neg\psi\}, & \end{array}$$

which obviously leads to a contradiction.

We conclude that whenever $\Phi' \approx\!\!\!\models \Phi$, then $\Phi \models\!\!\!\lessapprox \Phi'$. But if $gen_\mu^\Psi(\Phi) \geq gen_\mu^\Psi(\Phi')$, then it is *not* necessarily the case that $\Phi' \approx\!\!\!\models \Phi$.

What could be the motivation behind defining such a strange measure of generality? As you know, proving $\Phi \approx\!\!\!\models \varphi$ is not trivial. But in the example above, Ψ is finite and all the formulae we are concerned with are Horn formulae. The measure μ can be considered as a value describing a formula's *importance* – be it whatever you like. It just means that if $\mu(\{\psi_0\}) \geq \mu(\{\psi_1\})$, then it is more important to be able to show ψ_0 than it is to show ψ_1. To determine $gen_\mu^\Psi(\Phi)$, try to prove one ψ_i after another. For every successful proof $\Phi \vdash \psi_i$ we add $\mu(\{\psi\}_i)$ to the generality of Φ. We can also determine $gen_\mu^\Psi(\Phi')$ for arbitrary Φ' – and even $gen_\mu^\Psi(\Phi)$ or $gen_\mu^\Phi(\Psi)$.[5] In this way we can relate two sets of formulae according to their relative generality with respect to a reference set of formulae. Hence, gen_μ^Π is a heuristic measure that may help to efficiently find a theory that is able to describe the most important cases of our reference set. Most of the time we are happy if algorithms are correct in *most* of the cases, so it may well suffice for some application purposes.[6]

We conclude that it is a very good idea to look out for a cheap version of $\models\!\!\!\lessapprox$, some relation that we can confirm, in the best case, by syntactical means only and from which we can more or less reliably infer whether one formula entails another. Our initial interpretation was that the more general a formula set is, the more possible interpretations it has. But when approximating the entailment ($\approx\!\!\!\models$)-based subsumption relation ($\models\!\!\!\lessapprox$) by generality (gen_μ^Ψ) we find that it is complete but not correct. To be on the safe side, we would prefer it to be correct rather than complete. Luckily for us, there is such a definition of the subsumption relation.

Subsumption, $t \models\!\!\!\lessdot t'$

Definition 7.27 — Subsumption, $t \models\!\!\!\lessdot t'$.
Let $t, t' \in$ Ter and let λ, λ' be literals from Fml. A term t θ-*subsumes* a term t' if and only if there is a substitution θ such that $t\theta$ becomes t (the same applies to literals):

[4] Note that Ψ is a simple set of test cases; nothing is being said about consistency.

[5] If you feel like experiencing déjà vu, take a look at Equation (6.38).

[6] As always, there remains to explain where μ comes from. But this is an issue that we will come back to in the next chapter.

$$t \mathrel{\ltimes} t' :\Longleftrightarrow \exists\theta : t\theta = t' \quad \text{and} \quad \lambda \mathrel{\ltimes} \lambda' :\Longleftrightarrow \exists\theta : \lambda\theta = \lambda'. \tag{7.30}$$

A term or literal v is called a generalisation over a set of terms or literals w_i if and only if, for every w_i, v subsumes w_i. We then write $v \mathrel{\ltimes} \{w_0, \dots, w_{n-1}\} :\Longleftrightarrow \forall i \in \mathbf{n} : v \mathrel{\ltimes} w_i$. ●

Exercise 7.28 (◊) Prove that for literals λ, λ' it always holds that $\lambda \mathrel{\ltimes} \lambda'$ if and only if $\lambda \mathrel{|\!\approx} \lambda'$!

θ-subsumption appears to be a very nice property that can be evaluated very efficiently by simple term unification. But this is true for simple terms or literals only. We are not able to decide whether for two *non-unary clauses* one subsumes the other yet. Let there be two Horn clauses of equal length:

$$\begin{aligned} \varphi = \kappa_0 \quad &\text{:-} \quad \kappa_1, \dots, \kappa_{n-1} \\ \psi = \lambda_0 \quad &\text{:-} \quad \lambda_1, \dots, \lambda_{n-1}. \end{aligned}$$

Then it seems reasonable to argue that $\varphi \mathrel{\ltimes} \psi$ if there is a unifier such that $\varphi\theta = \psi$, or, in detail, if

$$\forall i \in \mathbf{n} : \kappa_i\theta = \lambda_i.$$

The nice thing is that Horn clauses have at most one positive literal each. This makes two clauses of different lengths still look a bit similar:

$$\begin{aligned} \varphi = \kappa_0 \quad &\text{:-} \quad \kappa_1, \dots, \kappa_{m-1} \\ \psi = \lambda_0 \quad &\text{:-} \quad \lambda_1, \dots, \lambda_{n-1}. \end{aligned}$$

Assume that $m < n$. Let us examine two different cases. First we assume that

$$\forall i \in \mathbf{m} : \lambda_i\theta = \kappa_i. \tag{7.31}$$

That is a good start, but ψ cannot be more general than φ for another reason: to conclude that $\kappa_0 = \lambda_0\theta$, a resolution proof along ψ requires $\lambda_m\theta \wedge \cdots \wedge \lambda_{n-1}\theta$ to be true, too. Hence ψ has stronger restrictions on $\lambda_0\theta$ than φ has on κ_0, which makes the set of models of ψ a subset of the set of models of φ.

Second, we assume the reverse case:

$$\forall i \in \mathbf{m} : \kappa_i\theta = \lambda_i. \tag{7.32}$$

Up to m, it is again the case that φ subsumes ψ literal-wise. Additionally, once $\psi\theta$ is satisfiable, φ is satisfiable, too. This is a much better way to define a generality relation between two *formulae* than by equality as in Equation (7.30).

Definition 7.29 — Subsumption, $\varphi \mathrel{\ltimes} \psi$.

Subsumption, $\varphi \mathrel{\ltimes} \psi$

Let $\varphi, \psi \in \mathrm{Fml}_{\mathrm{HOL}}$. φ *θ-subsumes* ψ if, for a subset of ψ, each of its literals is subsumed by a literal in φ:

$$\varphi \models\!\!\!\mid_\theta \psi \quad :\Longleftrightarrow \quad \varphi\theta \subseteq \psi. \tag{7.33}$$

Note that $\varphi \models_\theta \psi$ implies that $\varphi \models_\approx \psi$, but not vice versa. ●

Exercise 7.30 (◇) Show that $\varphi \models_\approx \psi \not\Longrightarrow \varphi \models_\theta \psi$.

Recall our hierarchical representation of the domain of geometric shapes in Section 4.4.

Example 7.31 We model a part of this concept hierarchy as a small logic program Π:

$$\begin{aligned}
shape(X, tetragon) \quad &:- \quad shape(X, square).\\
shape(X, tetragon) \quad &:- \quad shape(X, rhombus).\\
shape(X, angled) \quad &:- \quad shape(X, tetragon).\\
shape(X, angled) \quad &:- \quad shape(X, triangle).
\end{aligned}$$

Suppose we also have knowledge about the forms and colour, of ●, ■, ◇, ◆, △, and ▲. Then we observe the following sample:

$$\mathbf{s} \;=\; \{\langle \bullet, \mathbf{0}\rangle, \langle \blacksquare, \mathbf{1}\rangle, \langle \diamond, \mathbf{0}\rangle, \langle \blacklozenge, \mathbf{1}\rangle, \langle \triangle, \mathbf{0}\rangle, \langle \blacktriangle, \mathbf{1}\rangle\},$$

which provides us with information about instances of a concept *black_polygon*. Let us compare three possible hypotheses:

$$\begin{aligned}
h_0 \; &:= \; black_polygon(X) :- \; colour(X, black), shape(X, tetragon).\\
h_1 \; &:= \; black_polygon(X) :- \; colour(X, black), shape(X, angled).\\
h_2 \; &:= \; black_polygon(X) :- \; shape(X, tetragon).\\
h_3 \; &:= \; black_polygon(X) :- \; colour(X, black).
\end{aligned}$$

Then,

$$\begin{array}{lccc}
 & h_2 \models_\theta h_0, & h_2 \not\models_\theta h_1, & h_1 \not\models_\theta h_0\\
\text{whereas} & h_2 \models_\approx h_0, & h_2 \models_\approx h_1, & h_1 \models_\approx h_0.
\end{array}$$ ●

It is nice to know that θ-subsumption is sufficient for entailment. But we did not take into account the entirety of our background knowledge and the provided sample. Let us take a closer look at h_3.

For all positively labelled examples in **s**, we can prove they are black polygons:

$$\forall x : \langle x, \mathbf{1}\rangle \in \mathbf{s} \Longrightarrow \Pi \cup \{h_3\} \models_\approx black\_polygon(X).$$

So the coverage of h_3 is perfect – but it is not correct:

$$\Pi \cup \{h_3\} \vdash black\_polygon(\bullet),$$

but $t(\bullet) = \mathbf{0}$. On the other hand, h_0 is too specific:

$$\forall x : \Pi \cup \{h_0\} \models_\approx black\_polygon(X) \Longrightarrow \langle x, \mathbf{1}\rangle \in \mathbf{s},$$

but $\Pi \cup \{h_0\} \not\models_\approx black\_polygon(\blacktriangle)$ and $t(\blacktriangle) = \mathbf{1}$. And, finally, h_2 is neither correct nor complete:

$$\Pi \cup \{h_2\} \vdash \mathit{back\_polygon}(\Diamond) \quad \text{but} \quad t(\Diamond) = \mathbf{0} \text{ and}$$
$$\Pi \cup \{h_2\} \nvdash \mathit{back\_polygon}(\blacktriangle) \quad \text{but} \quad t(\blacktriangle) = \mathbf{1}.$$

In the last example we considered the satisfaction sets of hypotheses to find a description of their generality. We already know this idea: in Example 7.26 we defined the generality of a formula based on the importance of all formulae that can be deduced. With a slight adjustment we obtain a measure based on the size of the satisfaction set of h_i:

$$gen_{\mu}^{\Pi \trianglelefteq \mathbf{s}}(\{h_i\}) := \mu^n(\{\varphi : \Pi \cup \{h_i\} \approx\!\!\!\!\!\!\models \varphi \iff \langle \varphi, \mathbf{1} \rangle \in \mathbf{s}\}).$$

If we assume $\mu(\{\varphi\}) = \frac{1}{|\mathbf{s}|}$,[7] then

$$gen_{\mu}^{\Pi \trianglelefteq \mathbf{s}}(\{h_0\}) = \frac{5}{6},\ gen_{\mu}^{\Pi \trianglelefteq \mathbf{s}}(\{h_1\}) = \frac{6}{6},\ \text{and } gen_{\mu}^{\Pi \trianglelefteq \mathbf{s}}(\{h_2\}) = \frac{2}{6}.$$

Interestingly, *gen* appears to model an error measure rather than model a measure of generality. This is due to the fact that in the calculation above we did not simply count the number of derivable formulae but rather the number of *correctly* derivable formulae where correctness is expressed *relative to* **s**. We define:

Definition 7.32 — Generality of formulae, $\varphi \succsim_{\Gamma} \psi$.
Let φ, ψ be formulae, Π a logic program, and Γ a set of formulae. φ is called *more general than ψ relative to* Γ, written $\varphi \succsim_{\Gamma} \psi$, if

$$\forall \chi \in \Gamma : \Pi \cup \{\psi\} \approx\!\!\!\!\!\!\models \chi \implies \Pi \cup \{\varphi\} \approx\!\!\!\!\!\!\models \chi.$$

Whenever a "test case" χ is provable by ψ, it can also be proved by φ. If φ is more general than ψ relative to Γ, we also say that φ Γ-*subsumes* ψ, written $(\varphi \trianglelefteq \Gamma) \succsim (\psi \trianglelefteq \Gamma)$. ●

Generality of formulae, $\varphi \succsim_{\Gamma} \psi$

Now we have a set of different working definitions of generality, all of which help to form a partially ordered set of hypotheses.

Exercise 7.33 ($\Diamond$) Show that $\succsim$ as in Definition 7.24 and $\trianglelefteq$ are partial order relations on the set of Horn clauses.

A partial order relation can also be defined equationally. Usually one defines $x \sqsubseteq y :\iff x \sqcup y = y$ in relation algebra. What would be the according meet and/or join operators in a lattice with any of our partial order relations? This question is not of academic interest only. Example 7.31 is a demonstration of what it means to *overgeneralise* or *overspecialise*. The safest thing (and we shall see that even this is not always safe enough) is to make the refinement steps as small as possible. When we are looking for a formula subsuming a set of formulae, it

[7] Assuming μ to be i.i.d. means simply to count the number of covered instances.

would be wise to try the *most specific generalisation* first; and if we want to specialise from a set of formulae, it seems a good idea to start off with the *most general specialisation*. Because we are mostly concerned with generalisation and because θ-subsumption worked quite well (and it is easy to compute), we define the *least general (θ) generalisation* as follows.

Least general generalisation

Definition 7.34 — Least general generalisation.
Let φ, ψ, χ, ξ be terms, literals, or FOL formulae. We say that φ is a *least general generalisation (lgg)* of χ and ξ if every other generalisation ψ of χ and ξ is a generalisation of φ, too:

$$\varphi = \chi \curlyvee \xi \quad :\Longleftrightarrow \quad \varphi \mathrel{|\!\!\preccurlyeq} \{\chi, \xi\} \wedge \forall \psi : \psi \mathrel{|\!\!\preccurlyeq} \{\chi, \xi\} \Longrightarrow \psi \mathrel{|\!\!\preccurlyeq} \varphi. \tag{7.34}$$

For $\xi_0 \curlyvee \cdots \curlyvee \xi_{n-1}$ we write $\bigcurlyvee \{\xi_0, \ldots, \xi_{n-1}\}$. If $\mathrel{|\!\!\preccurlyeq}$ is defined by $\mathrel{|\!\!\lhd}$, we write $\triangledown$ for $\curlyvee$. The least general generalisation and θ-subsumption was introduced by Plotkin (1969, 1971). ●

Note that the least general generalisation is nothing more than a least upper bound. Hence the definition also carries over to *arbitrary subsumption relations*! For our purposes it suffices to consider two alternative versions:

1. Using θ-subsumption $\mathrel{|\!\!\lhd}$ as an order relation, the least general generalisation is denoted by $\triangledown$.
2. We use the notation $\mathrel{|\!\!\preccurlyeq}$ as an order relation with the join operator $\curlyvee$ to describe the subsumption with respect to *entailment* ($\mathrel{|\!\!\approx}$).

The syntactic least generalisation $\triangledown$ can be considered as the dual operation of the most general unifier μ on the set of terms or literals.

Exercise 7.35 (◇) Prove that, for φ, ψ in $\mathrm{Ter}_{\mathrm{FOL}}$ or literals, $\varphi \mathrel{|\!\!\lhd} \psi \Longleftrightarrow \{\varphi, \psi\}\mu = \psi$.

Least general generalisation

Looking for new knowledge that can describe things we were not able to describe before, we need to refine our theory by generalising our hypotheses of the target concept.

Generality is a relation that is easy to describe but not to determine. The trick is to find a feasible definition of generality that is sufficiently close to what our intended measure of generality is. Because knowledge discovery is a stepwise search process, it is very important to define operators that allow for small steps to avoid overgeneralisation.

7.3 Heuristic rule induction

Suppose there is a set of facts that we want to describe. If all these facts share a common term structure, it may be possible to find a factual representation for a hypotheses by computing the least general generalisation. But as we have seen in Example 7.31 already, we usually look for rules rather than for facts: Something is x-ish *if* it is y-ish and z-ish, or if it is not an a but a b. Actually, we do not look for a *single* rule h but rather for a *set* of rules H (see Definition 7.16).

Therefore, to discover new (rule-based) knowledge, we start off with a set of facts **s** and some background knowledge Π and an (empty) set H. We then (repeatedly) refine H until $\Pi \cup H$ describes the target sufficiently well.

7.3.1 Refinement operators on H

Let us consider clauses first. In simplified notation, a rule clause looks like:

$$\begin{aligned} pred(\vec{t}_0) \quad :- \quad & pred_1(\vec{t}_1), \\ & \ldots \\ & pred_{k-1}(\vec{t}_{k-1}), pred_k(\vec{t}_k), pred_{k+1}(\vec{t}_{k+1}), \\ & \ldots \\ & pred_{n-1}(\vec{t}_{n-1}), \end{aligned}$$

where $\vec{t}_i$ are *sequences* of terms; that is, the length $\ell(\vec{t}_i)$ is the arity of the i-th predicate symbol $pred_i$. Let us assume that $\vec{X}_i$ is the set of (free) variables in $\vec{t}_i$. As we know from the definition of θ-subsumption, substituting variables from $\bigcup \vec{X}_i$ with new terms makes this rule more specific. Concerning the occurrence of literals, we observe that

- Dropping a literal $pred_k$ from the rule body makes the rule *more general.*
- Adding a literal $pred_n$ to the rule body makes the rule *more specific.*

Whereas literals form clauses, clauses build logic programs. Similarly, we can

- *Generalise* H by *adding* a rule, thus increasing the set of inferrable formulae
- *Specialise* H by *deleting* rules and reducing $Cl_{\mathrm{RES}}(\Pi \cup H)$.

This motivates a very simple algorithm for refining of logic programs.

First extract two sets $E^{\mathbf{0}}$ and $E^{\mathbf{1}}$ from **s**:

$$E^x \quad := \quad \{\varphi \, : \, \langle \varphi, x \rangle \in \mathbf{s}^x\}. \tag{7.35}$$

$E^{\mathbf{1}}$ is called the set of *positive examples* and $E^{\mathbf{0}}$ is the set of *negative examples.* In the second step, determine all those formulae $\varphi \in E^{\mathbf{1}}$ that cannot be deduced and all formulae $\psi \in E^{\mathbf{0}}$ that are provable:

Fig. 7.1 Refining H

```
H := ∅;
WHILE (P ∪ N ≠ ∅) DO
{
    φ := choose(P)
    H := generalise(H, φ)
    P := P − {φ}
    ψ := choose(ψ, N)
    H := specialise(H, ψ)
    N := N − {ψ}
};
```

$$P := \left\{\varphi \in E^{\mathbf{1}} : \Pi \cup H \nvdash_{\mathsf{SLD}} \varphi\right\} \qquad N := \left\{\psi \in E^{\mathbf{0}} : \Pi \cup H \vdash_{\mathsf{SLD}} \psi\right\}.$$

Then, P and N are the sets of formulae that are "misclassified" by our program. Therefore, in the third step, *refine H* by generalising until all positive examples are covered and specialise it until negative examples are no longer covered. For an initially empty H, the procedure as shown in Figure 7.1 can be applied. Not surprisingly, the crucial part is hidden in the implementation of the choice function *choose* and the refinement operations *generalise* and *specialise*. We start off with generating rules without body literals, that is, facts that, by finding a "suitable" generalisation, should cover as many elements of $E^{\mathbf{1}}$ as possible. Then we add literals to the rule bodies so as to minimise the set N of mistakenly subsumed negative examples. FOIL is an information gain guided heuristical version of this algorithm.

7.3.2 Heuristic refinement

Quinlan (1991; Quinlan and Cameron-Jones 1993; Quinlan and Cameron 1995) presents an algorithm for induction of FOL formulae, called First Order Induction of Logic Programs (FOIL). It adds the idea of information gain (see Sections 5.2 and 5.3) to the algorithm in Figure 7.1. The resulting algorithm is shown in Figure 7.2. Again there remain a few open questions: what does it mean to be a "best predictor"? How does *FoilGn* work? Where do the variables $\vec{X}$ come from?

The best predictor is a literal with maximum support on $E^{\mathbf{1}}$, where support is the relative number of examples subsumed by this literal:

$$support(\varphi, \Phi) := \frac{|\{\psi \in \Phi : \varphi \mathrel{|\!\triangleleft} \psi\}|}{|\Phi|}. \tag{7.36}$$

Supposing that all elements in $E^{\mathbf{1}}$ share a common predicate symbol, the case is pretty clear.

Fig. 7.2 FOIL

01 $H := \emptyset$
02 `WHILE` $E^1 \neq \emptyset$ `DO`
03 { $h := p(\vec{X})$ `:- .`
04   `WHILE` $(E^0 \neq \emptyset)$ `DO`
05   { $\lambda := \arg\max_\lambda FoilGn(\lambda, h)$
06         $h := h \cup \{\lambda\}$
07         $E^0 := \{\varphi \in E^0 : h \vdash \varphi\}$
08   }
09     $H := H \cup \{h\}$
10     $E^1 := E^1 - \{\varphi \in E^1 : H \vdash \varphi\}$
11 }
12 `RETURN` H

In line 3, $p(\vec{X})$ with $p : s^n \in \Sigma$ and $n = \ell(\vec{X})$ is the "best predictor" for t. In line 5, λ is a literal chosen from Σ that is added as a body literal to h in line 6.

The next two questions address the process of literal adding. Let us first briefly discuss the origin of variables in newly introduced body literals. Consider a clause like

$$\begin{aligned} pred(\vec{t}_0) \quad \text{:-} \quad & pred_1(\vec{t}_0), \\ & \ldots \\ & pred_{k-1}(\vec{t}_{k-1}), \underline{\qquad}, pred_{k+1}(\vec{t}_{k+1}), \\ & \ldots \\ & pred_{n-1}(\vec{t}_{n-1}). \end{aligned}$$

Note that the k-th literal is missing – it is the one we are about to add. Which variables can we assume to be of interest in defining the k-th body literal? There are different kinds of variables: if X does not occur anywhere else in the clause, then it is a free, singleton variable. Singleton variables do not impose any restrictions on the satisfaction set of the clause.[8] As a consequence, such variables are rather useless.[9] Then there are variables that appear in the head or in the body or in both. Variables that appear in the rule head obviously play an important role in the definition of the semantics of the predicate. Variables occurring in a literal together with a variable from the head seem to be important, too, a bit less, maybe – but still "connected" to the head variables. We can iterate this process to define a measure of variable linkage. FOIL does not take into account considerations like these, but we will rediscover them when we talk about inverted entailment. Finally, the *sequence* of literals

[8] Which is why, when consulting a clause with a singleton variable in it, a Prolog interpreter throws a warning message. In most cases this is due to a spelling mistake. If it isn't, then it is recommended to use so-called *anonymous* variables "_" instead.

[9] There is an important exception to which we shall come back later.

has a large impact on the procedural semantics of a logic program: it does not make sense to try to prove a literal with a free variable if this variable is bound to a value in following literals.[10] This gives rise to the following strategy for finding useful variable bindings: when we add

$$pred_k(X_0, X_1, \dots, X_{k-1})$$

we know that *pred* must be a known predicate name with arity n_k and at least one X_j must occur somewhere in $\vec{t}_i$, $i \in \mathbf{k}$.[11] We can also bind a variable to another variable using unification. Then $pred(X_j, t)$ actually becomes $X_j = t$, where all variables in t must occur in $\vec{t}_i$, $i \in \mathbf{k}$.

Example 7.36 Consider again Example 7.31. To make things easier, we add to our representation ρ the unary predicates by a simple representation shift:

$$\tau : colour(X, C) \mapsto C(X) \text{ and } \tau : shape(X, S) \mapsto S(X).$$

Then,

white(◇).	*white*(△).		
black(●).	*black*(■).	*black*(◆).	*black*(▲).
triangle(△).	*triangle*(▲).		
tetragon(◆).	*tetragon*(◇).	*tetragon*(■).	
circle(●).			

Again, we want to learn *black_polygon* using the sample **s** from Example 7.31. The first hypothesis according to line 3 in the algorithm (Figure 7.2) is then

$$h = black\_polygon(X) :- .$$

It has a maximum support of 1. On the other hand, it is way too general because it can be satisfied by σ = [$X \mapsto$ ■], [$X \mapsto$ △], or [$X \mapsto$ ◇]. Therefore, we need to specialise h. The signature provides five different candidates with two different variables each and the old predicates:

$black(X)$,	$white(X)$,	$triangle(X)$,	$tetragon(X)$,	$circle(X)$,
$black(Y)$,	$white(Y)$,	$triangle(Y)$,	$tetragon(Y)$,	$circle(Y)$,
$shape(X, Y)$,	$shape(Y, X)$,	$shape(X, Z)$,	$shape(Z, X)$,	$shape(Z, Y)$,
$colour(X, Y)$,	$colour(Y, X)$,	$colour(X, Z)$,	$colour(Z, X)$,	$colour(Z, Y)$.

As one can see, the second row is entirely useless – why should we introduce a free variable Y that is not connected to the clause head? For similar reasons, $shape(Z, Y)$ and $colour(Z, Y)$ are out of the question. It seems a good idea to penalise the introduction of new variables, which makes the unary predicate symbols the prime candidates.

[10] Prolog would produce the error message "Arguments not sufficiently instantiated".
[11] In FOIL it is assumed that new literals are *appended* to the body; i.e. $k = n$.

We now have to choose between five different predicates modelling two different features. A well-known heuristical method is to choose the literal that brings about the largest information gain. Therefore, we need to adjust the definitions of entropy (see Definition 5.7) and information (see Definition 5.12) to our special needs here. The sets we examine here are sets of formulae. They can be ground facts as in sets of examples or entire clauses as in hypotheses that we are about to refine. Our interest lies in the proportion of things that we want to deduce and those we don't (or rather which we want to prove false). The FOIL algorithm works its way through the set of positive and negative examples by iteratively adding to H and in each step deleting the positive examples that are covered and the negative examples that are excluded (see lines 7 and 10 in Figure 7.2). Therefore, the entropy of $\mathbf{s}$ is simply the entropy of the set of examples with respect to their target classification:

$$\text{entropy}_t(\mathbf{s}) \quad := \quad \sum_{x \in \mathbf{2}} \frac{|E^x|}{m} \log_2 \frac{|E^x|}{m}, \tag{7.37}$$

where $m = |\mathbf{s}|$. Using this entropy measure we can determine the information of a single literal:

$$\begin{aligned} &\text{entropy}_t(p(\vec{X}), \mathbf{s}) \\ &= \sum_{x \in \mathbf{2}} \frac{|\{\varphi \in E^x : p(\vec{X}) \vdash_{\mathrm{SLD}} \varphi\}|}{|E^x|} \text{entropy}_t(\{\varphi \in E^x : p(\vec{X}) \vdash_{\mathrm{SLD}} \varphi\}). \end{aligned} \tag{7.38}$$

Example 7.37 Let us now determine the information gain for adding the different literals to our (initially empty) hypothesis H with *black_polygon* being our target predicate. First, $\text{entropy}_t(\mathbf{s}) = 1$. Then, we arrange s such that we can easily compute the entropies:

X	*white(X)*	*triangle(X)*	*tetragon(X)*	*circle(X)*	$t(X)$
◇	1	0	1	0	0
△	1	1	0	0	0
●	0	0	0	1	0
■	0	0	1	0	1
◆	0	0	1	0	1
▲	0	1	0	0	1

We compare

$$\begin{aligned} &\text{entropy}_t(\textit{white}, \{◇, △, ●, ■, ◆, ▲\}) \\ &= -\frac{|\{◇, △\}|}{6}\text{entropy}_t(\{◇, △\}) - \frac{|\{●, ■, ◆, ▲\}|}{6}\text{entropy}_t(\{●, ■, ◆, ▲\}) \\ &= -\frac{1}{3} \cdot 0 - \frac{2}{3} \cdot \left(-\frac{1}{4}\log_2\frac{1}{4} - \frac{3}{4}\log_2\frac{3}{4}\right) \approx \frac{2}{3} \cdot 0.81 = 0.54 \end{aligned}$$

and

$$
\begin{aligned}
& \text{entropy}_t(\textit{tetragon}, \{\Diamond, \triangle, \bullet, \blacksquare, \blacklozenge, \blacktriangle\}) \\
= \; & -\frac{1}{2}\text{entropy}_t(\{\Diamond, \blacksquare, \blacklozenge\}) - \frac{1}{2}\text{entropy}_t(\{\triangle, \bullet, \blacktriangle\}) \\
= \; & -\frac{1}{2}\left(-\frac{1}{3}\log_2\frac{1}{3} - \frac{2}{3}\log_2\frac{2}{3} - \frac{1}{3}\log_2\frac{1}{3} - \frac{2}{3}\log_2\frac{2}{3}\right) \\
= \; & -\frac{1}{3}\log_2\frac{1}{3} - \frac{2}{3}\log_2\frac{2}{3} \approx 0.92.
\end{aligned}
$$

Exercise 7.38

◇ Determine the entropies of *black* and *triangle*.

◆ Determine $\textit{utility}_s(\{P\} \trianglelefteq \{t\})$ for $P \in \{\textit{white}, \textit{triangle}, \textit{circle}, \textit{tetragon}\}$.

◆ Determine $\textit{significance}_s(\{P\} \trianglelefteq \{t\})$ for $P \in \{\textit{white}, \textit{triangle}, \textit{circle}, \textit{tetragon}\}$.

◆ Determine

$$
\begin{aligned}
& \text{Red}(\{\textit{white}, \textit{black}, \textit{triangle}, \textit{tetragon}, \textit{circle}\} \trianglelefteq \{\textit{black\_polygon}\}) \\
\text{and} \quad & \text{Cor}(\{\textit{white}, \textit{black}, \textit{triangle}, \textit{tetragon}, \textit{circle}\} \trianglelefteq \{\textit{black\_polygon}\}).
\end{aligned}
$$

In the examples above we implicitly count the number of possible assignments of a variable to a ground term. The quality of a literal $p(\vec{X})$ depends on the number of possible instantiations of $\vec{X}$ such that it subsumes a positive or negative example. This is a question of subsumption rather than of entailment. Accordingly, we want to choose $p(\vec{X})$ to maximise the set $\{\varphi \in E^1 : p(\vec{X}) \mathrel{|\!\!<} \varphi\}$ and minimise the set $\{\varphi \in E^0 : p(\vec{X}) \mathrel{|\!\!<} \varphi\}$. The reason is clear: suppose we want to learn a binary predicate, for example, *has_more_edges*. Then, on our domain of six different objects, there are $6^2 = 36$ different bindings that we would have to check.

Example 7.39 The predicate *has_more_edges* has the following meaning: `has_more_edges` : $s^2 \in \Sigma$ and $\rfloor$ `has_more_edges` $(X, Y) \lfloor_\alpha^{\mathfrak{A}} = \mathbf{1} :\Longleftrightarrow \alpha(X) R \alpha(Y)$, where the relation R is defined as

R	$\Diamond$	$\triangle$	$\bullet$	$\blacksquare$	$\blacklozenge$	$\blacktriangle$
$\Diamond$	1	1	1	1	1	1
$\triangle$	0	1	1	0	0	1
$\bullet$	0	0	1	0	0	0
$\blacksquare$	1	1	1	1	1	1
$\blacklozenge$	1	1	1	1	1	1
$\blacktriangle$	0	1	1	0	0	1.

(7.39)

This simple table leads to a very interesting observation: if we fix α at the point Y to $\bullet$, that is, $\alpha := \alpha[Y \mapsto \bullet]$, then `has_more_edges`$(X, Y)$ is true for any other instantiation of X; but if we choose $\alpha := \alpha[X \mapsto \bullet]$, then `has_more_edges`$(X, Y)$ is satisfiable only if $Y = \bullet$.

The consequence is that a literal can be assigned a measure defined by the number of possible instantiations that are compatible with **s**. So whereas in Equation (7.38) the information content of $p(\vec{X})$ was measured by the number of entailed examples, we avoid $\approx$ (or $\vdash$) by counting the number of instantiations of $\vec{X}$ that are compatible with **s**. For this reason, we examine the *Herbrand universe* – that is, roughly speaking, the set of all ground terms that we can build over our signature Σ and which we can substitute for variables in formulae. It is the base set A of a Herbrand interpretation $\mathfrak{A}$.[12] Luckily, we do not have any function symbols here, so we cannot construct terms larger than atomic complexity – that makes the base set A of $\mathfrak{A}$ a finite set of instances for variables. In our example, it means that

$$\downarrow x \downarrow_{\alpha}^{\mathfrak{A}} = x \text{ for all } x \in \{\lozenge, \triangle, \bullet, \blacksquare, \blacklozenge, \blacktriangle\} = A.$$

Accordingly, we define a variant of FOIL-Gain to describe the utility of adding a literal $\lambda = p(\vec{X})$ to a clause h as follows.

Definition 7.40 — FOIL-gain, $\text{gain}_t^{\text{FOIL}}(\lambda, h)$. FOIL-gain, $\text{gain}_t^{\text{FOIL}}(\lambda, h)$
The estimated gain of adding literal λ to a clause h is measured by the entropy loss on the set of h-compatible assignments with respect to **s**:

$$\text{gain}_t^{\text{FOIL}}(\lambda, h) = c_\lambda \cdot \left(\log_2 \frac{p_\lambda}{p_\lambda + n_\lambda} - \log_2 \frac{p_h}{a_h} \right). \tag{7.40}$$

Herein, $-\log_2(p_h/a_h)$ describes information of h with

$$p_h := \left| \left\{ \alpha \in A^{\text{Var}} : \downarrow h \downarrow_{\alpha}^{\mathfrak{A}} = \mathbf{1} \right\} \right|$$

and $a_h = |A^{\text{Var}}|$. The expected information after adding λ is described by

$$\begin{aligned} p_\lambda &:= \left| \left\{ \alpha \in A^{\text{Var}} : \downarrow h \cup \{\lambda\} \downarrow_{\alpha}^{\mathfrak{A}} = \mathbf{1} \right\} \right| \\ n_\lambda &:= \left| \left\{ \alpha \in A^{\text{Var}} : \downarrow h \downarrow_{\alpha}^{\mathfrak{A}} = \mathbf{0} \wedge \downarrow h \cup \lambda \downarrow_{\alpha}^{\mathfrak{A}} = \mathbf{0} \right\} \right|. \end{aligned}$$

Finally, the term is weighted by a factor

$$c_\lambda := \left| \left\{ \alpha \in A^{\text{Var}} : \downarrow h \downarrow_{\alpha}^{\mathfrak{A}} = \mathbf{1} \wedge \downarrow h \cup \lambda \downarrow_{\alpha}^{\mathfrak{A}} = \mathbf{0} \right\} \right|,$$

which describes the "selectivity" of λ. ●

Example 7.41 Let the initial hypothesis be the most general description of our target predicate:

$$H = \{h\} = \{\textit{has\_more\_edges}(X, Y) :- .\}.$$

[12] A closer look at Herbrand models is beyond the scope of this chapter; the interested reader is encouraged to read Huth and Ryan (2004) and Mazzola et al. (2006).

The question is, which literal λ should we add to the rule body of h? We can choose from all predicates in Σ and equality:

$$\Sigma = \{white : s, triangle : s, tetragon : s, circle : s, =: s \times s\}.$$

Because the set of variables we have to consider is $\{X, Y\}$, there are $6 \cdot 6 = 36$ different assignments α corresponding to 36 different substitutions σ. For each of these substitutions we check the validity of the literals with respect to **s**. For $h = has\_more\_edges(X, Y) :- .$, the matrix in Equation (7.39) shows the number of correct instantiations. There are 25 **1**-entries, which means that there are 25 different possible substitutions that agree with **s**. Accordingly, the entropy of h alone can be described by $-\log_2(25/36) \approx 0.53$. For all other predicate symbols, the instantiation of Y is irrelevant. Using formula (7.40) we obtain

λ	p_λ	n_λ	c_λ	$\text{gain}_t^{\text{FOIL}}(\lambda, h)$
$white(X)$	9	3	15	1.11
$triangle(X)$	6	6	19	−2.84
$tetragon(X)$	18	0	7	9.47
$circle(X)$	1	5	24	−49.41

(7.41)

As a result, the biggest gain is delivered by the literal *tetragon*. This is quite reasonable because every tetragon has four edges and there is no object with more than four edges. The result then becomes

$$H = \{has\_more\_edges(X, Y) :- tetragon(X).\}.$$

Still we are not perfect:

$$\Pi \cup H \not\vdash_{\text{SLD}} has\_more\_edges(\triangle, \bullet) \text{ but } \triangle R \bullet.$$

Exercise 7.42 (♦) Complete the example. First, examine whether $H = h \cup \{\lambda\}$ requires an additional body literal. Then continue with the outer loop of the algorithm in Figure 7.2, add a new clause head $has\_more\_edges(\vec{X})$, and continue with adding body literals.

Comparing the outcome of a FOIL learning process to a decision tree induction process as described in Section 5.3 is not straightforward. Here we deal with *relations* between pairs of variables – namely, whether X has more edges than Y. Every unary predicate corresponds to a single feature, but explaining a relation between two variables requires information about both variable instantiations. As a consequence, we need to create a table with 36 rows, where for every feature we need two columns to represent all possible bindings of two variables. The target feature t then is defined by

$$t(\langle X, Y \rangle) = \alpha(X) R \alpha(Y),$$

which corresponds to all the entries in Equation (7.41). So the information system that we would have to feed into a decision tree induction procedure would be

			white		*triangle*		*tetragon*		*circle*		*has_more_edges*
	X	Y	X	Y	X	Y	X	Y	X	Y	(X, Y)
1	◇	◇	1	1	0	0	1	1	0	0	1
2	◇	△	1	1	0	1	1	0	0	0	1
3	◇	●	1	0	0	0	1	0	0	1	1
⋮											⋮
18	●	▲	0	0	0	1	0	0	1	0	0
⋮											⋮
36	▲	▲	0	0	1	1	0	0	0	0	1

The resulting tree is shown in Figure 7.3.

Exercise 7.43

◇ Which leaf node has a non-zero error rate? Which assignments are wrongly classified as satisfying instantiations?

◆ Verify the decision tree in Figure 7.3 and compare it to your results from Exercise 7.42.

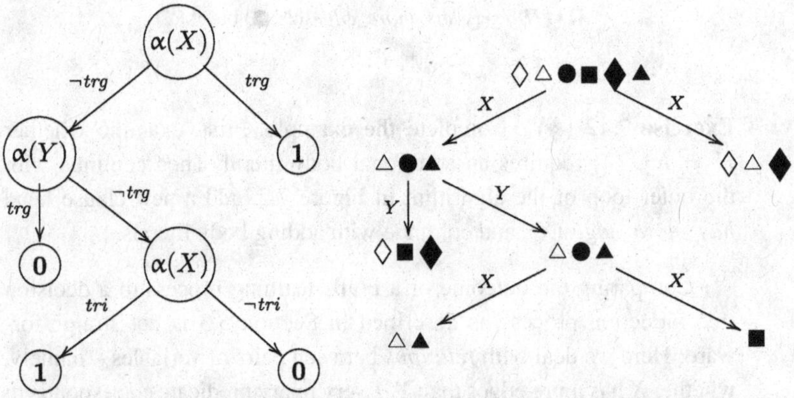

The edge labels *trg* and *tri* and their negations denote whether the variable assignments of the corresponding root node belong to the satisfaction sets for the predicates *triangle* and *tetragon*, respectively. The edge labels in the tree on the right-hand side are the variables that are examined for *R*. Note that the equivalence classes induced therein always consist of elements where all the elements of one successor node have less edges than all the elements of the other one (from left to right).

Fig. 7.3 A decision tree for Example 7.41

7.4 Inducing Horn theories from data

The general idea behind the induction of logic programs is the discovery of relational knowledge. Just as we discovered rough set data analysis to be an abstract version of decision tree induction without a heuristic information gain measure as in decision tree induction, we now examine an unbiased method for inducing Horn theories from sets of examples. In Section 7.2.3 we defined several order relations that mimic a *more-general-than* relation. Based on these order relations we were able to define refinement operators, $\curlyvee$ and $\triangledown$ (see Definition 7.34). By generalising sets of terms by $\triangledown$ we have already gained a lot – it just requires another little representation shift.

Example 7.44 Instead of representing an object's properties by several predicates, we introduce a data structure. Whereas in Example 7.36 the signature contained several additional unary predicate symbols, we now add a function symbol $r : \mathbf{2}^4 \to A$. The purpose is that each argument of the term represents a unary predicate from the last signature definition. For example,

$$\rho(\blacksquare) = r(\mathbf{0}, \mathbf{0}, \mathbf{1}, \mathbf{0}, \mathbf{1}).$$

The entire set of objects together with their target functions then becomes

$$\begin{array}{llllll}
black_polygon(& r(\mathbf{1}, & \mathbf{0}, & \mathbf{1}, & \mathbf{0}), & \mathbf{0}) \\
black_polygon(& r(\mathbf{1}, & \mathbf{1}, & \mathbf{0}, & \mathbf{0}), & \mathbf{0}) \\
black_polygon(& r(\mathbf{0}, & \mathbf{0}, & \mathbf{0}, & \mathbf{1}), & \mathbf{0}) \\
black_polygon(& r(\mathbf{0}, & \mathbf{0}, & \mathbf{1}, & \mathbf{0}), & \mathbf{1}) \\
black_polygon(& r(\mathbf{0}, & \mathbf{0}, & \mathbf{1}, & \mathbf{0}), & \mathbf{1}) \\
black_polygon(& r(\mathbf{0}, & \mathbf{1}, & \mathbf{0}, & \mathbf{0}), & \mathbf{1}).
\end{array}$$

Then, E^1 is the set of all objects whose last argument is $\mathbf{1}$ and thus indicates that the structure in the first argument represents an instance of the target concept.

By this trick we transformed a set of formulae with different predicate symbols into a set of literals with identical predicate symbols. At the same time, the information about the properties of an object is shifted from the assignments of variables to instantiations of a term with function symbol r. This allows us to reason about variable instantiations by comparing ground term structures.

At this point it becomes clear why we insisted on examining the idea behind representation in such detail. It is very important to understand the huge difference that such a small representation change makes in inference – and, even more, in inductive reasoning.

Representation shifts revisited

Representing properties of objects by predicates requires a relation for each predicate. The actual proposition about a concrete object then is stored as a variable assignment. Reasoning about relations between objects is then a task to be carried out on possible variable assignments.

By shifting the meaning of predicates into term structures, the concrete objects become ground terms. Ground terms can be compared syntactically without bothering about variable instantiations.

7.4.1 Syntactic generalisation revisited

Now that we have transformed our knowledge into a set of unifiable literals with identical term structures, we can

- Specialise our knowledge:
  Suppose there are two unifiable clauses φ and ψ containing non-ground terms. Then there exists a μ such that $\chi = \varphi\mu = \psi\mu$. Furthermore, we know that $\varphi \approx\!\!\!\!\!\! \models \chi$ and $\psi \approx\!\!\!\!\!\! \models \chi$.
- Generalise our knowledge:
  Given two (ground) clauses χ and ξ, there exists a least general generalisation $\varphi = \chi \nabla \xi$ and we know that $\varphi \approx\!\!\!\!\!\! \models \chi$ and $\varphi \approx\!\!\!\!\!\! \models \xi$.

Exercise 7.45 (◇) Prove that, given

$$\Pi = \{black\_polygon(X) :- black(X), tetragon(X)., black(\blacksquare)., tetragon(\blacksquare).\},$$

it holds that $\lfloor black\_polygon(\blacksquare) \rfloor_{\alpha}^{\mathfrak{A}} = \mathbf{1}$.

Let us examine two positive instances of our target concept, *black_polygon*:

$$\chi = \{black\_polygon(r(\mathbf{0},\mathbf{0},\mathbf{1},\mathbf{0}),\mathbf{1})\}$$
$$\xi = \{black\_polygon(r(\mathbf{0},\mathbf{1},\mathbf{0},\mathbf{0}),\mathbf{1})\}.$$

Then,

$$\varphi = \chi \nabla \xi = \{black\_polygon(r(\mathbf{0},X,Y,\mathbf{0}),\mathbf{1})\}.$$

Next, let us examine the set of formulae ψ for which $\Pi \cup \{\varphi\} \approx\!\!\!\!\!\! \models \psi$: There are 2^2 different assignments instantiating each of the two variables X and Y with one of the truth values from $\mathbf{2}$:

α				
X	Y	$r : \mathbf{2}^4$	$x \in A$	t
0	**0**	$r(\mathbf{0},\mathbf{0},\mathbf{0},\mathbf{0})$	?	**1**
0	**1**	$r(\mathbf{0},\mathbf{0},\mathbf{1},\mathbf{0})$	{■, ◆}	**1**
1	**0**	$r(\mathbf{0},\mathbf{1},\mathbf{0},\mathbf{0})$	{▲}	**1**
1	**1**	$r(\mathbf{0},\mathbf{1},\mathbf{1},\mathbf{0})$	?	**1**

We note two interesting things. First, there are two assignments that do not map to a corresponding constant in A, because an object cannot have two shapes at once or none at all. Second, there is one evaluation of the term that can be mapped onto propositions about *two different objects*. It means that $\downarrow \mathit{black\_polygon}(X), \mathbf{1} \downharpoonleft_{\alpha}^{\mathfrak{A}}$ is $\mathbf{1}$ for all $x \in U$ for which $\rho(x) = r(\mathbf{0}, Y, Z, \mathbf{0})$, where $\alpha(X) = \neg\alpha(Y)$. And this happens to be the set {■, ◆, ▲}, which – hooray! – is the set of all black polygons.

Exercise 7.46 (◆) This maybe is a bit too much work for an exercise, but you should try it nevertheless. Find a representation ρ that is suitable for modelling *has_more_edges*. Then, transform the knowledge according to ρ and examine the hypotheses generated by applying ∇ to various (wisely chosen) subsets of $E^{\mathbf{1}}$.

After all, resolution is just ordinary calculus. If we simply try and "mirror" specialising operators to yield generalising operators, why shouldn't we try and invert the resolution rule itself? Because the resolution rule crucially depends on unification and, thus, on substitutions, we need to think about *inverse substitutions*. There is a small problem associated with reverse applications of substitutions:

Example 7.47 Let $\psi = p(X, a)$ and $\sigma = [X \mapsto a]$. Then

$$\psi\sigma = p(a, a).$$

If we now "revert" σ to $\sigma^{\smile} = [a \mapsto X]$, we suddenly have

$$\varphi = p(X, X)$$

and $\varphi \mid\!\!\triangleleft\, \psi$ (note that $\psi \not\approx p(b, b)$, but $\varphi \not\approx p(b, b)$). In other words, $\psi\sigma\sigma^{\smile} \neq \psi$. ●

Exercise 7.48 (◇) Prove that $\psi\sigma\sigma^{\smile} \mid\!\!\triangleleft\, \psi$ but $\psi \not\mid\!\!\triangleleft\, \psi\sigma\sigma^{\smile}$.

To avoid this problem, one needs a more technical definition of inverse substitutions involving positions of subterms.

Subterm positions

Definition 7.49 — Subterm positions.
Let $t \in \mathrm{Ter}$ be a term with function symbol $f : s^n \to s \in \Sigma$ and $t_i, i \in \mathbf{n}$ its arguments. Then, $t\,\langle i \rangle$ is t's i-th argument. By recursion, $t\,\langle i \rangle\,\langle j \rangle$ is the j-th argument of the i-th argument of t.

We abbreviate the composition of several position indices by simply concatenating them: $t\,\langle i_0, \ldots, i_{k-1} \rangle := t\,\langle i_0 \rangle \cdots \langle i_{k-1} \rangle$. ●

Let $\sigma = [X_i \mapsto t_i : i \in \mathbf{n}]$. We then determine the positions of all X_i in t, where each X_i may occur several times, and rewrite σ as

$$\sigma = \left[(X_i, \vec{p}_i) \mapsto t_i : X_i \text{ occurs at } p_i \text{ in } t\right]. \tag{7.42}$$

This allows us to define a position-aware inversion of substitutions:

Definition 7.50 — Inverse substitution, σ^{-1}. Let $t \in$ Ter and $(X_i, \vec{p}_i)$ with $X_i \in$ Var, $i \in \mathbf{n}$ variables occurring in t at positions $\vec{p}_i$. Let σ be a substitution acting on t. Then, $\sigma^{\smile}$ is called an *inverse substitution* if

Inverse substitution, σ^{-1}

$$t\sigma\sigma^{\smile} = t,$$

where for every $t \mapsto (X, \vec{p})$ in σ^{-1} there exists $(X, \vec{p}) \mapsto t$ in σ. ●

Exercise 7.51 (◊) For Example 7.47, define σ^{-1}. Show that any σ^{-1} is a subset of $\sigma^{\smile}$. First argue using the number of occurrences of variables; then give a second proof by comparing the relational properties of σ^{-1} and $\sigma^{\smile}$.

Exercise 7.52 Let $\Phi = \{\varphi_i : i \in \mathbf{3}\}$ with

$$\begin{aligned}\varphi_0 &= pred(X, f(Y)) \\ \varphi_1 &= pred(g(X), f(g(X))) \\ \varphi_2 &= pred(a, Z).\end{aligned}$$

◊ Determine all pairwise unifiers for all pairs of formulae in Φ.

◊ Determine all unifiers for Φ.

◊ Determine $\chi_{ij} = \varphi_i \triangledown \varphi_j$, for all $i, j \in \mathbf{3}$ and $\triangledown\Phi$.

◊ For each lgg χ_{ij} and every formula φ in Φ, determine σ^{-1} such that $\varphi\sigma^{-1} = \chi_{ij}$.

If you are familiar with the Prolog programming language, you might have learned that clauses are nothing more than just special terms. Given a Horn clause

$$\lambda \leftarrow \lambda_0, \ldots, \lambda_{n-1} = pred(\vec{X}) :\text{-}\ pred_0(\vec{X}_0), \ldots, pred_{n-1}(\vec{X}_{n-1}),$$

the internal representation is a binary term with function symbol : - , with the first argument being the rule head and the second argument the *list* of body literals:

$$:\text{-}\ (pred(\vec{X}), [pred_0(\vec{X}_0), \ldots, pred_{n-1}(\vec{X}_{n-1})]).$$

There remains one problem: how can we unify two lists of different lengths? Again, the internal representation of Prolog helps a lot. Lists are nothing more than recursive terms where the function symbol represents concatenation:

$$\begin{aligned} & :\text{-}\ (pred(\vec{X}), [pred_0(\vec{X}_0), \ldots, pred_{n-1}(\vec{X}_{n-1})]) \\ = \ & :\text{-}\ (pred(\vec{X}), [pred_0(\vec{X}_0)|[pred_1(\vec{X}_1)|[\cdots|[pred_{n-1}(\vec{X}_{n-1})|[\,]]\cdots]]]) \\ = \ & \leftarrow (\lambda, dot(\lambda_0, dot(\lambda_1, dot(\cdots dot(\lambda_{n-1}, nil)\cdots)))) \end{aligned}$$

with a special constant *nil*. Now let there be two clauses $\varphi = \{\kappa, \kappa_0, \ldots, \kappa_{n-1}\}$ and $\psi = \{\lambda, \lambda_0, \ldots, \lambda_{m-1}\}$. Assuming that $m = n$,

φ and ψ are unifiable if κ, κ_i and λ, λ_i are unifiable. Because the order of literals in a clause has no impact on its declarative semantics, we can reorder them to allow a match. If $m > n$, we simply unify the matching subterms and then add the remaining literals of ψ by applying the unifier to them.

If there are two clauses χ and ξ and their lgg $\varphi = \chi \triangledown \xi$, it is quite likely that the deductive closure becomes incompatible with Π.

Example 7.53 Again, we need another representation ρ for our example domain. This time, we add predicate symbols *colour* : s^2 and *shape* : s^2 to our signature, similar to the representation we chose in Example 7.31. Then, Π becomes

colour(●, *black*).	*colour*(■, *black*).	*colour*(◇, *white*).
colour(◆, *black*).	*colour*(△, *white*).	*colour*(▲, *black*).
shape(●, *circle*).	*shape*(■, *square*).	*shape*(◇, *diamond*).
shape(◆, *diamond*).	*shape*(△, *triangle*).	*shape*(▲, *triangle*).

If we now encounter two ground clauses, say

$$\begin{aligned} \chi &= \mathit{black\_polygon}(\blacksquare) :- \mathit{colour}(\blacksquare, \mathit{black}), \mathit{shape}(\blacksquare, \mathit{square}). \\ \xi &= \mathit{black\_polygon}(\blacklozenge) :- \mathit{colour}(\blacklozenge, \mathit{black}), \mathit{shape}(\blacklozenge, \mathit{diamond}).,\end{aligned}$$

the least general generalisation becomes

$$\varphi = \chi \triangledown \xi \quad = \quad \mathit{black\_polygon}(X) :- \mathit{colour}(X, \mathit{black}), \mathit{shape}(X, Y).$$

and via $\sigma = [X \mapsto \bullet, Y \mapsto \mathit{circle}]$ we can conclude $\Pi \cup \{\varphi\} \not\approx \mathit{black\_polygon}(\bullet)$.

This is a strong argument for *including factual background knowledge* into the process of inducing generalisations. It means that we look for some $\varphi = \chi \triangledown \xi$ for which $\Pi \cup \{\varphi\} \not\approx E^{\mathbf{0}}$. In other words, we are looking for a generalisation *relative* to E.

Relative least generalisation

Definition 7.54 — Relative least generalisation.
Let Φ be a set of ground facts and κ, λ be two literals. Then,

$$\kappa \triangledown_{\Phi} \lambda \quad := \quad (\{\kappa\} \cup \neg\Phi) \triangledown (\{\lambda\} \cup \neg\Phi). \tag{7.43}$$

The *least general generalisation relative to* Φ is defined in terms of ordinary lgg, where each literal is expanded to a full clause with Φ as the rule body and the original literal as the rule head. ●

The problem with $\triangledown_{\Phi}$ is that it is defined for literals rather than clauses. The definition only covers unary clauses – and single literals are simple terms with their outmost term constructor symbol being a predicate symbol rather than a function symbol.

But the definition works even on clauses with non-empty bodies. Because clauses are sets of literals with no ordering in them, we can rearrange them by, for example, lexicographic ordering without changing their semantics.[13] Then, the fact that two clauses χ and ξ have a least general generalisation means that χ and ξ have a common subset of literals. Let χ and ξ be such clauses with exactly one positive literal $\kappa \in \chi$ and $\lambda \in \xi$. If the positive literals in $\kappa \in \chi$ and $\lambda \in \xi$ have a generalisation, then the relative least general generalisation has exactly one positive literal. The remaining literals can be generalised pairwise:

$$(\kappa \triangledown \lambda) :- (\chi_0 \triangledown \xi_0), (\chi_1 \triangledown \xi_1), \ldots, (\chi_k \triangledown \xi_k), \varphi_0, \ldots, \varphi_m,$$

where χ_i and ξ_i are pairs of literals from χ and ξ, respectively, and the remaing literals φ_i are the ground facts. If χ and ψ are unary clauses (as in the definition above), or if they do not have any predicate symbols in their body literals in common, then the expression from above implodes to the case of unary clauses:

$$(\kappa \triangledown \lambda) :- \varphi_0, \ldots, \varphi_m.$$

Note that there is a huge bias in this definition: we assumed the two clauses to be of equal length or at least of having a common prefix in the lexicographic ordering of all the body literals. We then generalised pairwise and dropped the literals that do not have "partners" for generalisation. But why should we only generalise $\chi_i \triangledown \xi_i$ and not $\chi_i \triangledown \xi_j$ for $j \neq i$? Obviously, generalising rules is not that trivial.

Example 7.55 Let us try and compute $\chi \triangledown_\Pi \xi$ with χ = *black_polygon*(■), ξ = *black_polygon*(◆), and Π as in the previous example. Then, $\chi \triangledown_\Pi \xi$ is

black_polygon(■) :-
colour(●, *black*), *colour*(■, *black*), *colour*(◇, *white*),
colour(◆, *black*), *colour*(△, *white*), *colour*(▲, *black*),
shape(●, *circle*), *shape*(■, *square*), *shape*(◇, *diamond*),
shape(◆, *diamond*), *shape*(△, *triangle*), *shape*(▲, *triangle*).

$\triangledown$

black_polygon(◆) :-
colour(●, *black*), *colour*(■, *black*), *colour*(◇, *white*),
colour(◆, *black*), *colour*(△, *white*), *colour*(▲, *black*),
shape(●, *circle*), *shape*(■, *square*), *shape*(◇, *diamond*),
shape(◆, *diamond*), *shape*(△, *triangle*), *shape*(▲, *triangle*).

The inverse substitution required to find the lgg of the two clauses above is $\sigma^{-1} = [$■ $\mapsto X$, ◆ $\mapsto X]$:

13 "Semantics" here means declarative semantics, not procedural.

$$
\begin{array}{l}
\mathit{black\_polygon}(X) :- \\
\quad \mathit{colour}(\bullet, \mathit{black}), \quad \mathit{colour}(X, \mathit{black}), \quad \mathit{colour}(\Diamond, \mathit{white}), \\
\quad \mathit{colour}(X, \mathit{black}), \quad \mathit{colour}(\triangle, \mathit{white}), \quad \mathit{colour}(\blacktriangle, \mathit{black}), \\
\quad \mathit{shape}(\bullet, \mathit{circle}), \quad \mathit{shape}(X, \mathit{square}), \quad \mathit{shape}(\Diamond, \mathit{diamond}), \\
\quad \mathit{shape}(X, \mathit{diamond}), \quad \mathit{shape}(\triangle, \mathit{triangle}), \quad \mathit{shape}(\blacktriangle, \mathit{triangle}).
\end{array}
$$

Because X is the only variable occurring in the clause head and the rule body, and because all literals that do not contain X are valid ground literals anyway (because they come from Π), we can simplify the clause to

$$
\begin{array}{l}
\mathit{black\_polygon}(X) :- \\
\quad \cancel{\mathit{colour}(\bullet, \mathit{black})}, \quad \mathit{colour}(X, \mathit{black}), \quad \cancel{\mathit{colour}(\Diamond, \mathit{white})}, \\
\quad \mathit{colour}(X, \mathit{black}), \quad \cancel{\mathit{colour}(\triangle, \mathit{white})}, \quad \cancel{\mathit{colour}(\blacktriangle, \mathit{black})}, \\
\quad \cancel{\mathit{shape}(\bullet, \mathit{circle})}, \quad \mathit{shape}(X, \mathit{square}), \quad \cancel{\mathit{shape}(\Diamond, \mathit{diamond})}, \\
\quad \mathit{shape}(X, \mathit{diamond}), \quad \cancel{\mathit{shape}(\triangle, \mathit{triangle})}, \quad \cancel{\mathit{shape}(\blacktriangle, \mathit{triangle})}.
\end{array}
$$

This can be reduced further to

$$
\begin{array}{l}
\mathit{black\_polygon}(X) :- \\
\quad \mathit{colour}(X, \mathit{black}), \quad \mathit{shape}(X, \mathit{square}), \quad \mathit{shape}(X, \mathit{diamond}).
\end{array}
\tag{7.44}
$$

Finally, let us recall Definition 7.29. We already found a more general rule as far as variable instantiations are concerned by applying a least general inverse substitution. But we can generalise *further* by dropping body literals. Because φ has three body literals, there are $2^3 = 8$ possible candidates for rule bodies. As one can imagine,

$$
\begin{array}{lcl}
h_1 & = & \mathit{black\_polygon}(X) :- \mathit{colour}(X, \mathit{black}), \mathit{shape}(X, \mathit{square}). \\
h_1 & = & \mathit{black\_polygon}(X) :- \mathit{colour}(X, \mathit{black}), \mathit{shape}(X, \mathit{diamond}).
\end{array}
$$

are the most promising ones – and they can be found efficiently by calculating the support of the different rules (see Equation (7.40)) or the gain of involved literals (Definition 7.40).

Exercise 7.56 (◇) Find all eight possible candidates and compute their support, accuracy, and coverage. It is clear that if a literal occurs in all candidates (here, *colour*(X, *black*)), it is indispensable. Compute the gain expected when adding either of the remaining literals.

Exercise 7.57 (◆) The goal is to induce a rule for *has_more_edges*. Π consists of the knowledge from the preceding examples. Add to Π a set E of ground facts stating that triangles have more edges than circles, that black squares have more edges than triangles, and that white tetragons have more edges then everything (Note: E is a set of ground facts – i.e., a set of literals with predicate symbol *has_more_edges* and two arguments that are *objects*!). Then, choose the representation of Π wisely and apply the relative least generalisation procedure to induce a rule describing the target.

Least general generalisation appears quite powerful, and relative least generalisations are even more powerful. But one big disadvantage of using ∇_Π is the possibly huge amount of body literals, which gives rise to the need for a bias. Furthermore, with such unrestricted definite clauses as Π, ∇_Π is not necessarily finite (think of variables, function symbols, and term construction!). But even if it is finite, extensional background knowledge may become intractable: the worst-case number of literals in a relative least generalisation is $(|\Pi| + 1)^{|E|}$.

For the true knowledge discoverer, all the methods discussed so far lack an important skill: the hypothesis always consists of one single clause or of a set of clauses all of which share a common clause head. Even more disappointing is that the algorithms described cannot really induce *new knowledge*. New knowledge means to be able to discriminate different things that we were not able to tell from each other before. But the *meaning* of the difference is more than just knowing that two things are different. Knowledge also means to be able to describe *why* this is the case – and new qualities usually are described by *new terms* or *new predicates*. A really knowing system should be able to say: "■ has more edges than ○, because ■ is a *polygon* and ○ is an *ellipse* – and *polygons have at least three edges* whereas *ellipses have no edges*".

Acquiring knowledgeable new knowledge requires the ability to *invent* new predicates (i.e., predicates). Here we go.

7.4.2 Inverting resolution

Wouldn't it be nice if, whenever we encounter a sequence or set of similar, ground facts, we could (after a while) generalise? Well, we can! Given $\Phi := \{p(a).,p(b).,p(c).,p(d)\}$, a simple application of lgg results in $\curlyvee\Phi = p(X)$, and, by definition, $p(X) \mid\!\lhd \Phi$, which implies $p(X) \mid\!\approx \Phi$.

Sometimes the facts we observe cannot be generalised that easily. Given $\Phi := \{p(0), p(s(s(0))), p(s(s(s(0)))), \ldots\}$, a simple application of lgg results in $\curlyvee\Phi = p(X)$. But, actually, p only describes the set of *even* numbers,

$$\Phi = \left\{p(s^i(0)) : i \in \mathbb{N} \wedge i \bmod 2 = 0\right\}.$$

The simple lgg would deliver a hypothesis $p(X)$ that is wrong in infinitely many cases. What we would like to have is richer term syntax so we are able to induce $p(s^{2n}(0))$.

Closely related to this problem – but only solvable if we were not restricted to single clauses with body literals from Π – is the question of what an even number actually *is*. Wouldn't it be great to understand that $p(0)$ and $p(s(s(X))) \leftarrow p(X)$? Similarly, if we observe

$$\Phi = \{lt(0,X), lt(s(0),s(s(0))), lt(s(s(0)),s(s(s(0)))), lt(s(0),s(s(s(0))))\},$$

a mere generalisation would not work out well: it is *not* true that every X is less than any Y.

Finally, and this is where we stopped at in the last section, consider the following case:

$$\begin{array}{ll} min(0,[0,s(s(s(0))),s(s(0))]). & min(0,[s(s(s(0))),0,s(s(0))]). \\ min(s(0),[s(s(0))),s(0),s(0)]). & min(s(s(0)),[s(s(0))]). \end{array}$$

What does it take to understand that, first,

$$min(X,[X])$$

and then that

$$min(X,[Z|Y]) \leftarrow foo(X,Z), min(X,Y)\ ?$$

Where does *foo* come frome, and what is its meaning? From an analysis of the four examples above, we can deduce that *foo* can be defined as follows:

$$\begin{array}{lll} foo(0,s(s(0))), & foo(s(s(0)),s(s(s(0)))), & foo(0,s(s(s(0)))), \\ foo(s(0),s(0)), & foo(s(s(0)),s(s(0))). & \end{array}$$

Now comes what is *really* intelligent knowledge discovery. From the five ground terms above, we can induce many true properties of the partial order relation $\leq$:

$$\begin{array}{ll} foo(0,X). & \forall x \in \mathbb{N}_0 : 0 \leq x \\ foo(X,X). & \forall x \in \mathbb{N}_0 : x \leq x \\ foo(s(X),s(Y)) :\text{-}\ foo(X,Y). & \forall x,y \in \mathbb{N}_0 : x \leq y \Longrightarrow x+1 \leq y+1 \\ foo(X,s(Y)) :\text{-}\ foo(X,Y). & \forall x,y \in \mathbb{N}_0 : x \leq y \Longrightarrow x \leq y+1 \\ foo(X,Y) :\text{-}\ foo(s(X),Y). & \forall x \in \mathbb{N}, y \in \mathbb{N}_0 : x \leq y \Longrightarrow x-1 \leq y. \end{array}$$

Exercise 7.58 (♦) What does it take to induce the transitivity rule $foo(X,Z) :\text{-}\ foo(X,Y), foo(Y,Z).$?

In the course of trying to learn *min* we came across a property describing a relation between two objects. Because we did not have any clue about the actual meaning of this relation, we simply chose *foo* as a name for it. In a next step we tried to understand what *foo* actually meant and invented the beautiful little recursive predicate definition above. Its meaning is fundamental for the definition of the minimum of a set of numbers: we invented a definition of the *less-than* relation! In this way we have discovered a new predicate and learned its definition in the same step.

We will now present three refinement operators that one can apply to derive new, more general clauses from old ones that hopefully represent suitable hypotheses for the target concept.

Truncation

Recall that resolution itself is a proof calculus that is used for inference or deduction. Even though our proofs are kinds of reverse arguments by showing a contradiction to the negation of the goal, resolution remains a *forward* calculus (hence we write "$\vdash$" rather than "$\dashv$"). It is clear that

$$:\text{-}\ \mathit{black\_polygon}(\blacksquare). \quad \text{and} \quad \mathit{black\_polygon}(X) :\text{-}\ \mathit{shape}(X, \mathit{square}).$$

resolves to

$$:\text{-}\ \mathit{shape}(\blacksquare, \mathit{square})$$

with $\sigma = [X \mapsto \blacksquare]$. But what if we knew there were two *positive ground literals* (we restrict ourselves to literals here) such that the facts they represent are true? Let there be two such ground literals λ and κ. Suppose that $\Pi \mid\!\approx \{\lambda, \kappa\}$. Then we know that negating λ and κ allows for a derivation of the empty clause, or, semantically speaking, that

$$\Pi \cup \{\neg\kappa, \neg\lambda\} \mid\!\approx \{\}.$$

So if this is the case, there must have been clauses that were resolved with $\neg\kappa$ and $\neg\lambda$; otherwise we would not have been able to deduce the empty clause.

Now let us try a little twist in the argument: supposing that $E = \{\kappa, \lambda\}$ but $\Pi \not\mid\!\approx E$, the task ahead is to find H such that $\Pi \cup H \mid\!\approx E$. So wouldn't it be a great idea to give it a try and *guess* a rule that might allow for resolving $\neg\kappa$ (and, in a second step, λ too)? The head of the rule we guess is clear: it is a literal that unifies with κ. The definition of the rule body is not that clear because there may be many literal candidates around in Π. The simplest way is to take $\neg\lambda$ as a body literal, because we know that λ should follow from $\Pi \cup H$, too. As a resolution diagram, this looks like

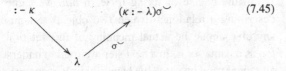

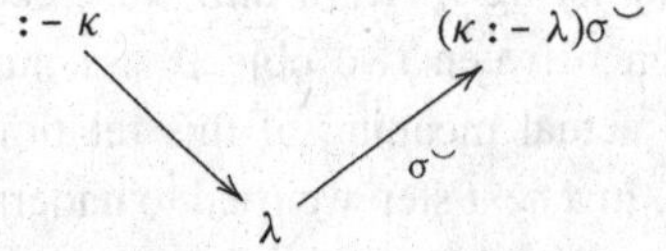

(7.45)

Definition 7.59 — Truncation. Truncation
Let there be two ground literals κ and λ. The *truncation operator* induces a rule $\kappa :\text{-}\ \lambda$ such that $\neg\kappa \sqcap^{\sigma}_{\mathsf{RES}} \kappa :\text{-}\ \lambda$ resolves to $\lambda = \lambda\sigma$. ●

Example 7.60 As a simple example, imagine two new predicate symbols *bigger* and *smallereq* with meaning as intended by their names. Their corresponding order relations are irreflexive (strict, >) and reflexive (≤). Supposing that we encounter the following two ground facts

$$\kappa \;=\; smallereq(\lozenge, \blacklozenge)$$
$$\lambda \;=\; bigger(\blacklozenge, \lozenge),$$

we construct the following resolution scheme:

$$: - \; smallereq(\lozenge, \blacklozenge) \qquad (smallereq(\lozenge, \blacklozenge) : - bigger(\blacklozenge, \lozenge))^{\sigma^{\smile}}$$

$$: - \; bigger(\blacklozenge, \lozenge)$$

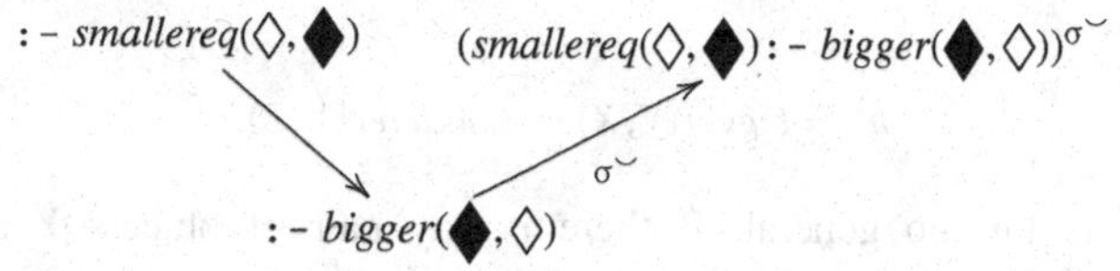

Next we need to find $\sigma^{\smile}$ such that in

$$smallereq(\lozenge, \blacklozenge) : - bigger(\blacklozenge, \lozenge)$$

terms are replaced with variables in a way such that after unifying the more general rule head with κ the resolution rule delivers λ. As one can see immediately a possible inverse substitution is

$$\sigma^{\smile} = [\lozenge \mapsto X, \blacklozenge \to Y].$$

Then the resulting rule is

$$h \;=\; smallereq(X, Y) : - bigger(Y, X).$$

This example, even though very simple, already demonstrates one crucial problem: the semantics of the invented rule depends on the choice of κ and λ. If, in the example above, we had

$$\kappa \;=\; bigger(\blacklozenge, \lozenge)$$
$$\lambda \;=\; smallereq(\lozenge, \blacklozenge),$$

the outcome would have been

$$h' = bigger(X, Y) : - smallereq(Y, X). \tag{7.46}$$

Rule h appears quite reasonable, but h' is not valid in $\mathfrak{A}$, because

$$\bullet \leq \bullet \text{ but } \bullet \not> \bullet.$$

So if there are n candidate literals onto which we could apply the truncation operator, there are n^2 (or, to be more precise, $n \cdot (n - 1)$) possible pairings. Furthermore, there is a huge set of inverse substitutions that we could apply:

Example 7.61 This time, let

$$\kappa = smallereq(\blacksquare, \triangle)$$
$$\lambda = bigger(\blacklozenge, \lozenge).$$

Apart from the fact that there are two possible arrangements for κ and λ in the resolution scheme, how could we determine a *meaningful* hypothesis by way of $\sigma^{\smile}$? Even the least general generalisation via

$$\sigma^{\smile} = [\blacksquare \mapsto V, \triangle \mapsto X, \blacklozenge \mapsto Y, \lozenge \mapsto Z]$$

leads to

$$h'' = bigger(V,X) :- smallereq(Y,Z),$$

which is far too general. If there is any pair of objects Y and Z where Y is strictly bigger than Z, then everything (V) is smaller than or equal to anything else (X). Again, this statement is *not* valid in $\mathfrak{A}$ for the same reason why h' is not valid (apply $\theta = [V \mapsto \bullet, X \mapsto \bullet, Y \mapsto \bullet, Z \mapsto \bullet]$).

Truncation comes with several problems. It requires two "suitable" ground literals, it requires a lucky hand at deciding which one shall be taken as resolvent, and it requires a "wise" choice of $\sigma^{\smile}$ – and still it is very likely to bluntly overgeneralise. Yet, it is very useful because it can generate relatively quickly a huge set of hypotheses that can be tested quite efficiently as well. Given a set $H = \{h_i : i \in \mathbf{n}\}$ of hypotheses generated by truncation, we can determine the support $support(h_i, E^{\mathbf{1}})$ of each of its members. Most support values will be close to 1 because of the proneness of truncation towards overgeneralisation. As a consequence, other error measures or measures of accuracy (see Section 3.4) should be considered. General hypotheses are not useless, though. In Section 7.3 we learned that the FOIL algorithm deliberately generates rules with empty bodies to specialise them in its inner refinement loop.

> **Truncation**
> Truncation is a very simple generalisation operator that takes two ground literals and delivers a guess for a rule that allows one to derive one of these literals from the other. It seems to be a not very wise yet useful operator, and it can be fine-tuned towards efficacy and efficiency using heuristic measures.

Exercise 7.62 Let

$$\Phi = \left\{ \begin{array}{l} has\_more\_edges(\blacksquare, \bullet), \\ shape(\blacksquare, square), \\ circle(\bullet) \end{array} \right\}.$$

◇ Try several combinations for truncation. Try several inverse substitutions.

◇ For several hypotheses of differing generality, determine their support, error, and accuracy with respect to $s = \{\lozenge, \triangle, \bullet, \blacksquare, \blacklozenge, \blacktriangle\}$.

◇ For several hypotheses, apply the inner loop of the FOIL algorithm to specialise them.

We close this section on truncation with a special case. Every successful resolution proof ends in an empty clause. If we agree to resolve exactly one literal per resolution step (as we do in SLD resolution), we know that one parent clause must be a negative literal and the other one a positive singleton, that is, a fact. If there are *several* facts sharing the same predicate in $\Pi \cup E$, then there are *several* possibilities to derive the empty clause. Let there be two such unary clauses, not necessarily unifiable but sharing the same predicate symbols $p(\vec{t}_a)$ and $p(\vec{t}_b)$. Negating them and assuming both of them appear in the last step of a resolution proof, this requires the existence of a fact $p(\vec{t})$, where $\vec{t}_a$ and $\vec{t}$ are unifiable and $\vec{t}_b$ and $\vec{t}$ are unifiable by most general unifiers μ and ν:[14]

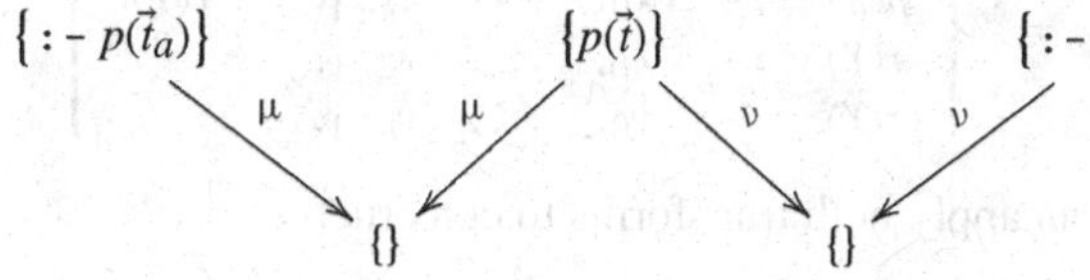

Because μ is a most general unifier, we can construct a *generalisation* $p(\vec{t}_0)$ of $p(\vec{t})$: $p(\vec{t}_0)\sigma = p(\vec{t})$.[15] Because $\vec{t}\mu = \vec{t}_a\mu$ and $\vec{t}_0\sigma = \vec{t}$, it follows that $\vec{t}_0\sigma\mu = \vec{t}\mu$. Hence, $p(\vec{t}_0) \mid\!\lhd\, p(\vec{t}_a)$ (and the same for $\vec{t}_b$ with ν):

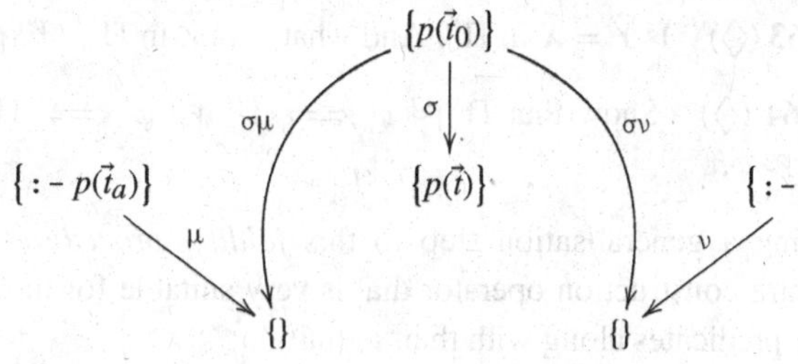

This special case simply states that given two (ground) facts, any generalisation of them can be considered a candidate for a hypothesis.

Intra-construction

To understand the next refinement operator, *intra-construction*, we first need to discuss a special method for transforming logic programs

14 Note that this is just a proposition about the *existence* of $p(\vec{t})$. It does not say anything about the actual value of $\vec{t}$, nor does it require $\vec{t}$ to to be different from $\vec{t}_a$ or $\vec{t}_b$.

15 If $\vec{t}$ consists of only variables, then $\sigma = \emptyset$ and $\vec{t}_0 = \vec{t}$.

that preserves their declarative semantics. Consider the following logic program Π that consists of two Horn clauses:

$$\Pi = \left\{ \begin{array}{lllllllll} p(\vec{X}) & :- & \kappa_0, & \ldots, & \kappa_{k-1}, & \lambda_0, & \ldots, & \lambda_{l-1}. \\ p(\vec{X}) & :- & \kappa_0, & \ldots, & \kappa_{k-1}, & \nu_0, & \ldots, & \nu_{n-1}. \end{array} \right\}.$$

We observe that both clauses contain the same k literals κ_i, $i \in \mathbf{k}$. Obviously, κ_i expresses a property that is significant to both rules defining p. So why don't we move them outside and define a new "piece of meaning" that is shared by both clauses? We rewrite Π:

$$\Pi' = \left\{ \begin{array}{llllll} p(\vec{X}) & :- & q(\vec{Y}), & \lambda_0, & \ldots, & \lambda_{l-1}. \\ p(\vec{X}) & :- & q(\vec{Y}), & \nu_0, & \ldots, & \nu_{n-1}. \\ q(\vec{Y}) & :- & \kappa_0, & \ldots, & \kappa_{k-1}. & \end{array} \right\}.$$

Then, Π and Π' are equivalent. Similarly, we can move λ_i and ν_j outside so as to make the definition of p look more homogeneous. Accordingly, Π can be also transformed into Π'':

$$\Pi'' = \left\{ \begin{array}{llllll} p(\vec{X}) & :- & \kappa_0, & \ldots, & \kappa_{k-1}, & r(\vec{Y}). \\ p(\vec{X}) & :- & \kappa_0, & \ldots, & \kappa_{k-1}, & r(\vec{Y}). \\ r(\vec{Y}) & :- & \lambda_0, & \ldots, & \lambda_{l-1}. & \\ r(\vec{Y}) & :- & \nu_0, & \ldots, & \nu_{n-1}. & \end{array} \right\}$$

Finally, we can apply both transforms to construct

$$\Pi''' = \left\{ \begin{array}{lllll} p(\vec{X}) & :- & q(\vec{Y}), & r(\vec{Z}). & \\ q(\vec{Y}) & :- & \kappa_0, & \ldots, & \kappa_{k-1}. \\ r(\vec{Z}) & :- & \lambda_0, & \ldots, & \lambda_{l-1}. \\ r(\vec{Z}) & :- & \nu_0, & \ldots, & \nu_{n-1}. \end{array} \right\}$$

Exercise 7.63 (◇) Is $\vec{Y} = \vec{X}$ in Π'? And what is in $\vec{Z}$ in Π'''? Explain.

Exercise 7.64 (◈) Show that $\Pi \approx\!\!\!\models \varphi \iff \Pi' \approx\!\!\!\models \varphi \iff \Pi'' \approx\!\!\!\models \varphi \iff \Pi''' \approx\!\!\!\models \varphi$.

By adding a generalisation step to this *folding procedure*[16] we define the intra-construction operator that is very suitable for inducing entirely new predicates along with their definition:

Definition 7.65 — Intra-construction. Intra-construction

Given two clauses with a common set of unifiable literals, *intra-construction* derives a new clause with a new body literal defined by common sets of literals in two separate clauses:

$$\frac{p(\vec{X}) :- \kappa_k, \lambda_l. \qquad p(\vec{Y}) :- \kappa_k, \nu_n.}{(q(\vec{Y}) :- \lambda_l.)\sigma_\lambda^{\smile} \qquad (p(\vec{X}) :- \kappa_k, q(\vec{Y}).)\sigma_\kappa^{\smile} \qquad (q(\vec{Y}) :- \nu_n.)\sigma_\nu^{\smile}}$$

16 The reverse procedure is called *fanning*. Both are quite common in logic programming to speed up and (re-)structure programs. In contrast to our considerations, the *procedural* semantics of Prolog then plays a major role.

with $k \in \mathbf{k}, l \in \mathbf{l}, n \in \mathbf{n}$ such that

$$(p(\vec{X}):-\kappa_k,\lambda_l.)\sigma_\kappa^{\smile} \cup \sigma_\lambda^{\smile} \quad \models \quad p(\vec{X}):-\kappa_k,\lambda_l. \tag{7.47}$$

$$(p(\vec{X}):-\kappa_k,\nu_n.)\sigma_\kappa^{\smile} \cup \sigma_\nu^{\smile} \quad \models \quad p(\vec{X}):-\kappa_k,\nu_n. \tag{7.48}$$

Note that the body literals of the newly defined rules also subsume their respective instantiations in the parent clauses. ●

Intra-construction has generalisation steps built in two places. First, the remaining rule body κ_k is generalised to $\kappa_k\sigma_\kappa^{\smile}$, and, second, the respective rule bodies are generalisations of the original body literals by application of (suitable) $\sigma_\lambda^{\smile}$ and $\sigma_\nu^{\smile}$. A third generalisation step that can be added with just a little more effort is motivated by the definition of θ-subsumption: as we have already discovered, literal dropping is one method of generalising Horn clauses. Intra-construction now allows for several options on where to drop literals. Dropping a literal $\kappa_i\sigma_\kappa^{\smile}$ from $p(\vec{X}):-\kappa_k, q(\vec{Y})$ is more general than dropping κ_i from both original rule bodies – and it is, of course, even more general than dropping some κ_i in only one of the clauses. Dropping a literal $\lambda_i\sigma_\lambda^{\smile}$ from $(q(\vec{Y}):-\lambda_l.)\sigma_\lambda^{\smile}$ is not very different than dropping it from $p(\vec{X}):-\kappa_k,\lambda_l$ (except for the fact that, of course, $\lambda_i\sigma_\lambda^{\smile} \models \lambda_i$). By dropping literals from the definitions of q we can generalise pretty selectively. Finally, we can try and apply more inverse substitutions and simultaneously drop literals λ_i and ν_j until the rule bodies are equal:

$$\frac{p(\vec{X}):-\kappa_0,\ldots,\kappa_{k-1},\lambda_0\ldots,\lambda_{l-1}. \qquad p(\vec{X}):-\kappa_0,\ldots,\kappa_{k-1},\nu_0\ldots,\nu_{n-1}.}{(p(\vec{X}):-q(\vec{Y}),r(\vec{Z}).)\sigma_\kappa^{\smile} \qquad (q(\vec{Y}):-Q.)\sigma_\lambda^{\smile} \qquad (r(\vec{Y}):-R.)\sigma_\nu^{\smile}} \tag{7.49}$$

where $Q \subseteq \left\{\kappa_i\sigma_i^{\smile} : i \in \mathbf{k}\right\}$ and $R \subseteq \left\{\chi \ : \ \exists i,j,\sigma : \chi\sigma = \lambda_i = \nu_j\right\}$.

Example 7.66 Consider the program Π that consists of the following two clauses:

$$\textit{black\_polygon}(\blacksquare) \quad :- \quad \textit{black}(\blacksquare), \textit{square}(\blacksquare). \tag{7.50}$$

$$\textit{black\_polygon}(\blacktriangle) \quad :- \quad \textit{black}(\blacktriangle), \textit{has\_more\_edges}(\blacktriangle, \bullet). \tag{7.51}$$

First, the generalised clause head is

$$\textit{black\_polygon}(X) = \textit{black\_polygon}(\blacksquare) \triangledown \textit{black\_polygon}(\blacktriangle) \tag{7.52}$$

with $\sigma^{\smile} = [\blacksquare \mapsto X, \blacktriangle \mapsto X]$. Both clauses share a common body literal *black*. We introduce a new predicate symbol p of the same arity as the number of common arguments and receive

$$\left\{\begin{array}{lll} p(\blacksquare) & :- & \textit{black}(\blacksquare)., \\ p(\blacktriangle) & :- & \textit{black}(\blacktriangle). \end{array}\right\}\sigma^{\smile} \quad = \quad \{p(X):-\textit{black}(X).\} \tag{7.53}$$

The next step is to move the two non-unifying literals outside. We define

$$\left\{\begin{array}{l} q(\blacksquare):-\ square(\blacksquare).,\\ q(\blacktriangle):-\ has\_more\_edges(\blacktriangle,\bullet). \end{array}\right\}\sigma^{\smile}$$

$$= \left\{\begin{array}{l} q(X):-\ square(X).,\\ q(X):-\ has\_more\_edges(X,\bullet). \end{array}\right\} \tag{7.54}$$

All in all, the resulting logic program H looks as follows:

$$\begin{array}{lll} black\_polygon(X) & :- & p(X), q(X).\\ p(X) & :- & black(X).\\ q(X) & :- & square(X).\\ q(X) & :- & has\_more\_edges(X,\bullet). \end{array} \tag{7.55}$$

At the very end we now have a set of Horn clauses that actually look like a proper semantic definition of what it means for an object to be a black polygon.

Exercise 7.67

- ◊ Determine the support, accuracy, and coverage of the body literals of the new rules defining $q(X)$.
- ◊ Prove that $\{q(X):-\ square(X)\} \approx\!\!\!\!\mid \{q(X):-\ has\_more\_edges(X,\bullet)\}$.
- ◊ Can you find a program $H' \subset H$ for which $H' \approx\!\!\!\!\mid \varphi \iff H \approx\!\!\!\!\mid \varphi$?
- ♦ Define a procedure that mechanises the process to find such subsets.

You might have realised that you were betrayed at a very small but crucially important point in the argumentation of intra-construction. Recall Equation 7.54: given the new predicate symbol q, we silently agreed that it shall be unary – even though in the second definition of *black_polygon* the second body literal is a *binary* predicate *has_more_edges*. A little bit of abstraction exemplifies the problem: let there be two clauses again,

$$\begin{array}{lllllllll} \varphi = & (\ p(\vec{X}) & :- & \kappa_0, & \ldots, & \kappa_{k-1}, & \lambda_0, & \ldots, & \lambda_{l-1}.\ )\sigma_\varphi\\ \psi = & (\ p(\vec{X}) & :- & \kappa_0, & \ldots, & \kappa_{k-1}, & \nu_0, & \ldots, & \nu_{n-1}.\ )\sigma_\psi. \end{array} \tag{7.56}$$

Note that σ_φ acts on the *entire* clause φ just as σ_ψ acts on the entire ψ. The consequence is that $\vec{X}\sigma_\varphi = \vec{t}_\varphi \neq \vec{t}_\psi = \vec{X}\sigma_\psi$. This does not hurt at all because we want to construct a new rule head that is a generalisation of φ and ψ anyway. Similarly, we can find generalisations of $\kappa_i\sigma_\lambda$ and $\kappa_i\sigma_\nu$. Now something very interesting may happen.

Example 7.68 Imagine $\chi = p(A,B,C):-\ q(X,C), r(A,C)$, which θ-subsumes both of the following two clauses:

$$\begin{array}{llllllll} \varphi = & (& p(A,B,C) & :- & q(X,C), & r(A,C), & u(c), & v(c,B).\ )\sigma_\varphi\\ = & & p(a,f(B),C) & :- & q(c,C), & r(a,C), & u(c), & v(c,f(b)).\\ \psi = & (& p(A,B,C) & :- & q(B,C), & r(A,C), & a(V,C,B). &)\sigma_\psi\\ = & & p(A,f(b),C) & :- & q(f(b),C), & r(A,C), & a(a,C,f(b)). & \end{array} \tag{7.57}$$

with $\sigma_\varphi = [A \mapsto a, B \mapsto f(b), X \mapsto c]$ and $\sigma_\psi = [B \mapsto f(b), V \mapsto a]$. For φ, we observe that the set of common variables in the clause head and in the q- and r-literals is a proper subset of the clause head of χ – whereas all variables occurring in χ also occur in ψ.

So if in the example above we were to generalise from the rule heads and the matching κ-literals in φ, there would be no evidence that the second argument of the rule head has any meaning at all. Fortunately, the second argument of the rule head is *linked to* to the first argument of the q-literal in ψ, which, by inverse construction of χ via $\varphi \nabla \psi$, forces a binding between those two places.

The second – much more important – problem occurs when we try to fold out the remaining body literals. We want to introduce a new predicate definition with a new predicate symbol s. Then, obviously,

$$s(\vec{X}) \quad :- \quad u(c), v(c, f(b)).\breve{\sigma_\varphi} \tag{7.58}$$

$$s(\vec{X}) \quad :- \quad a(a, C, f(b)).\breve{\sigma_\psi}. \tag{7.59}$$

The first one allows for several inverse substitutions:

- $\breve{\sigma_\varphi} = [c \mapsto X]$ suggests a generalisation to $s(B) :- u(B), V(B)$.
- A slightly more general approach already results in two alternative rule heads: assuming that C is *free* in φ, we could simply drop it from the clause head and write $s(B) :- a(X), b(X, B)$.[17] On the other hand, the then common appearance of X in

  $$u(X), v(X, f(b)) \text{ and } p(A, B, C) :- q(X, C)$$

  suggests that the semantics of s depends on q – and the semantics of p depends on the value of X. Therefore, it would be safer to induce

  $$s(B, X) :- u(X), v(X, B).$$

- $\breve{\sigma_\varphi} = [\,]$ leaves the rule body untouched – yet we have two options to construct the clause head: both

  $$s(c, B) :- u(c), v(c, B) \text{ and } s(B) :- u(c), v(c, B)$$

  seem to be reasonable generalisations.

Similarly, ψ offers many options for generalisations. We do not go into too much detail, because the idea should be clear by now. But one should be aware *how insanely many options* there are to construct a new predicate and its definition:

[17] Or, even more general, just $s(B) :- u(X), v(Y, B)$.

- First, the empty inverse substitution leads to the same arity dilemma as the empty inverse substitution on φ. We could infer three different unary clause heads (if we assume the ordering to be irrelevant), three different binary clause heads, and one tertiary clause head, which sums up to seven alternatives for the empty inverse substitution only.
- For all of these options mentioned previously, we can now find a whole set of inverse substitutions acting on all the subsets of terms occurring in any place in $a(a, C, f(b))$. The subterms are $\{a, C, b, f(b)\}$ such that we can construct 16 (2^4) different substitution schemata; and for each we can choose from any combination of variables!

Exercise 7.69 (♦) From a purely semantic point of view, the safest thing would be to carry all the variables with us all the time. This means that any rule head $p(\vec{X})$ can be expanded to $p(\vec{X}, \vec{V})$, where $\vec{V}$ contains *all* variables occurring in all the literals of the clause. Redefine the intra-construction operator such that all variables are kept at all times. Then, define a (heuristic) procedure to determine minimal sets of "relevant" variables to cut down the predicate arities after the intra-construction procedure.

It should have become clear by now that refinement via intra-construction is as well defined as truncation is. But it is also as computationally expensive as truncation (actually, a lot more). If we restrict ourselves to clauses with *exactly one* body literal, we can at least give a simple description of an intra-construction procedure. Figure 7.4 presents such a pseudo-code program. Even though the restriction to single-body literals is so strict that the most important parts of the expressiveness of HOL are lost, it still illustrates our desperate need for good heuristic measures to guide the search for promising hypotheses.

Intra-construction

Intra-construction is a refinement operator that allows one to invent new predicates. The principle is based on two ideas. First, fold out common literals of several instances of a rule and then generalise the resulting rule; second, invent new predicates for all disjoint sets of body literals and generalise them.

The big problem with inventing new predicates is that, because we do not know what they mean, we don't know which variables they really depend on. We also don't know which generalisation from a huge number of options we should apply. And, finally, we don't even know how to call it and give it a proper name for the new predicate.

Exercise 7.70 (♦) Give a rough estimate of the number of different programs that can be induced from $\{p(\vec{X}_i) :- \lambda_i. : i \in \mathbf{n}\}$ by the algorithm shown in Figure 7.4.

01 $\Pi = \{p(\vec{X}_i) :\text{-}\ \lambda_i. : i \in \mathbf{n}\}$
02 $\lambda := \lambda_0;$
03 $\texttt{FOR}\ i := 1\ \texttt{TO}\ n$
04 $\quad \lambda := \lambda \triangledown \lambda_i$
05 $\texttt{NEXT}$
06 $\kappa := q(V_0, \ldots, V_{k-1})$ where $\{V_j : j \in \mathbf{k}\} \subseteq \ulcorner(\bigcup_{i \in \mathbf{n}} \{\sigma_i : \lambda\sigma_i = \lambda_i\})$
07 $\texttt{RETURN}\ \{p(\vec{X}_i) :\text{-}\ \kappa.\} \cup \{\kappa\sigma_i : i \in \mathbf{m}\}$ for some $\mathbf{m} \subseteq \mathbf{n}$

Note three nondeterministic operations here: in line 6, a "suitable" subset of variables has to be chosen. In the same line, σ_i are not uniquely defined; all that is required is that $\lambda \mathrel{|\!\!\lhd} \lambda_i$. Finally, the new body literal κ is defined by m new unary clauses that are chosen from n different variable assignments.

Fig. 7.4 Intra-construction for binary clauses

Absorption

There is one very important type of clause that we already spoke of but which we are not able to induce yet. These are clauses with multiple occurrences of literals – especially those where the rule head predicate symbol also appears in the rule body. It is the class of *recursive* predicates.

Recursion is a simple concept – but trying to induce recursive predicates is not that easy. Just recall the problems we had with finding suitable inverse substitutions. On the one hand we need not care about the set of body literals to choose and, therefore, the solution to the problem of which arguments are connected to each other comes for free. The real problem we are concerned with is recursion on *recursive types* of terms. But logic programs have no such thing as *types*. It is impossible for us to infer the structure of a generalisation of a term from its "sort": if $t_0 = 3$ and $t_1 = 2.0$, what is $t_0 \triangledown t_1$ – is it some $X \in \mathbb{N}$ or $X \in \mathbb{R}$? If $t_0 = [\,]$ and $t_1 = [a, b]$, is $t_0 \triangledown t_1$ just a free variable X that can be instantiated with whatever we like? Or is it a *list*? Or is it a list with at most two elements? And if $t_1 = [X]$, do we want to allow some $t \mathrel{|\!\!\lhd} \{t_0, t_1\}$, where t can also take a recursive list type like $[[], [[]], [[], [[]]]]$?

To make things easier at the beginning, consider the following two propositional Horn clauses:

$$A :\text{-}\ \vec{B}. \quad \text{and} \quad C :\text{-}\ A, \vec{D}. \tag{7.60}$$

There is not much we can do in SLD resolution, but note that in the left clause A is the rule head (hence a positive literal) and in the right clause it is a negative literal. So in full resolution we could infer

$$C :\text{-}\ \vec{B}, \vec{D}. \tag{7.61}$$

Let us now reverse this resolution step. Imagine $A :\text{-}\ \vec{B}$ and $C :\text{-}\ \vec{B}, \vec{D}$ were known. Then,

$$A :- \vec{B} \qquad\qquad C :- A, \vec{D}$$

$$C :- \vec{B}, \vec{D},$$

where the directions of the arrows indicate our inductive process. There is not much of recursion in here – but before we come to it, let us lift our idea of *absorption* to FOL. Because variables are enough of a hassle and we agreed that E consists only of single literals, we simplify our inverse resolution scheme to a version with only a unary parent clause:

$$p(\vec{X}_0). \qquad\qquad q(\vec{Y}_1) :- \lambda_0, \ldots, \lambda_{k-1}, p(\vec{X}_1), \lambda_{k+1}, \ldots, \lambda_{n-1}.$$

$$\xrightarrow{\ \sigma\ } \qquad\qquad \xrightarrow{\ \theta^{\smile}\ }$$

$$(q(\vec{Y}_0) :- (\lambda_0, \ldots, \lambda_{n-1}))\theta\sigma, \tag{7.62}$$

where σ unifies $p(\vec{X}_0)$ and $p(\vec{X}_1)$ and θ is a specialisation of λ_i.

Definition 7.71 — Absorption. Absorption

The absorption operator takes a unary clause and a definite clause and returns a generalisation of the clause that is obtained by adding the literal of the unary clause to the rule body:

$$\frac{\{\kappa\}\,\sigma \qquad (\{\nu\} \cup \{\neg\lambda_i : i \in \mathbf{n}\})\theta}{\{\nu\} \cup \{\neg\lambda_i : i \in \mathbf{n}\} \cup \{\neg\kappa\}}. \tag{7.63}$$

We rewrite and change the instantiating assignments σ and θ into inverse substitutions:

$$\frac{\kappa. \qquad \nu :- \lambda_0, \ldots, \lambda_{n-1}.}{(\nu :- \lambda_0, \ldots, \lambda_{k-1}, (\kappa\sigma^{\smile}), \lambda_{k+1}, \ldots, \lambda_{n-1}.)\theta^{\smile}}. \tag{7.64}$$

There remain two open questions: where is recursion and how do we define the inverse substitutions? The first question is easy to answer. Absorption can be used to learn recursive predicates by choosing κ and $\nu :- \lambda_0, \ldots, \lambda_{n-1}$ such that both κ and ν are literals sharing a common predicate symbol. From the resolution scheme and the absorption rule, we then know that

$$\kappa \models \nu \text{ because } \nu = \kappa\sigma\theta. \tag{7.65}$$

The question about how to compute suitable inverse substitutions cannot be answered that easily. Therefore, we give an example illustrating the induction process of a recursive predicate with manual, "wise" choices of $\sigma^{\smile}$ and $\theta^{\smile}$.

Example 7.72 This time we cannot give a decent example in our domain of geometric objects because it is difficult to find a proper instance for a recursive predicate there. Therefore, please recall the example from the beginning of this section where we invented the *less-than* relation in the course of learning the *minimum* predicate. Imagine now that

$$\begin{aligned} \kappa &= lt(X, s(X)) \\ \nu &= lt(Y, s(s(Y))). \end{aligned}$$

Furthermore, let us assume that $n = 0$; that is, there are no further λ_i-body literals involved. Then, the recursive rule we are about to invent has the form

$$(\nu :- (\kappa\sigma^{\smile}))\theta^{\smile}.$$

This becomes

$$lt(X, s(X)) \searrow lt(Y, s(s(Y))). \nearrow (lt(Y, s(s(Y))) :- (lt(X, s(X)))\sigma^{\smile})\theta^{\smile}$$

By inspiration we choose $\sigma^{\smile} = [s(X) \mapsto Z]$. Hence,

$$lt(X, s(X)) \searrow lt(Y, s(s(Y))). \nearrow (lt(Y, s(s(Y))) :- lt(X, Z))\theta^{\smile}$$

Then, a second miracle happens and we feel like choosing $\theta^{\smile} = [s(Y) \mapsto Z, Y \mapsto X]$:

$$lt(X, s(X)) \searrow lt(Y, s(s(Y))). \nearrow lt(X, s(Z)) :- lt(X, Z)$$

The result is a new, logically correct arithmetic rule: whenever X is less than Z, X is less than $Z + 1$, too.

Exercise 7.73 (◇) Let there be $\kappa = lt(0, X)$ and $\nu = lt(0, s(Y))$. Find $\sigma^{\smile}$ and $\theta^{\smile}$ such that you can induce $lt(s(X), s(Y)) :- lt(X, Y)$. Why is this a wonderful result?

To gain a short impression of the algorithmic formulation of absorption and all the problems connected to it, take a look at Figure 7.5. For our purposes it is not important to really understand the algorithm outlined in Figure 7.5. The interested reader can find a more

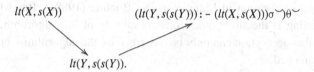

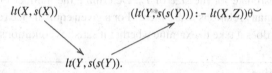

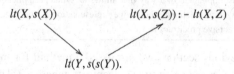

LET $\varphi := \{\kappa\}$, $\psi := \nu \cup \{\neg\lambda_i : i \in \mathbf{n}\}$
$T_p := \{\langle t,p\rangle : t$ is a term at position p in $\varphi \cup \psi\}$
Choose $T_p' \subseteq T_p$
Find an equivalence relation $\equiv$ on $T_p' \times T_p'$ where:
  $R \equiv S$ if and only if
  a) $s \mathrel{|\!\lhd} r$ for all $\langle s,p\rangle \in S$ and $\langle r,p\rangle \in R$
  b) for all $\langle s,p\rangle \in S$, s occurs in φ
  c) for all $\langle r,q\rangle \in R$, r occurs in ψ
Compute σ such that $S\sigma = R$ for all $R \equiv S$
$\theta_i^{\smile} = \left[\langle r, \langle p_1,\ldots,p_n,q_1,\ldots,q_m\rangle\rangle \mapsto V :\ \text{for all}\ \ r \in T_p'/\equiv\right]$, where:
  all V are different variables which do not occur within $\varphi \cup \psi$
RETURN $(\nu \cup \{\neg\lambda_i : i \in \mathbf{n}\} \cup \kappa\sigma)\theta^{\smile}$

Fig. 7.5 An informal description of the absorption procedure

detailed elaboration in Muggleton and Buntine (1988a). But what *is* interesting is the sheer monstrous complexity of this algorithm. It is clear that absorption can only be described by this algorithm – but not implemented.

Exercise 7.74 (◇) Take a closer look at the algorithm in Figure 7.5. Give an estimate for the size of T_p. Determine the number of possible T_p'. How many relations $\equiv$ are there? For a given equivalence relation $\equiv$, how long does it take to examine whether it satisfies conditions a–c (◆)?

Absorption

The absorption operator comes with bad news and good news: it is very powerful when it comes to learning recursive predicates. The bad news is that it is virtually infeasible and very hard to implement in a way that allows an efficient application. The good news is that, as far as relational knowledge representation is concerned, there is no need to learn recursive predicates at all.

In the previous sections we discussed a method for inducing logic programs that was based on two concepts of generality. The first one is that of θ-subsumption. Given a formula φ, one can simply try and create some $\sigma^{\smile}$ and return $\varphi\sigma^{\smile}$ as a hypothesis. A slightly more intelligent method included literal dropping. Including another set of formulae Φ into this process, we discovered ∇_Φ as a generalisation procedure relative to a given set of knowledge. The second concept that we modified to create a new method for inducing new Horn formulae was resolution. We discovered three different special cases for which we described one operator each.

But unification and deduction are derivation processes. Our hope is that reversal of derivation leads to something like induction. In both cases, there is no semantics involved. Yet the presented "induction calculi" are, procedurally, infeasible. So, to implement a working system, we need strong biases. There are several possible solutions. First, we can restrict the language – for example, by allowing only a certain maximum number of variables or literals in each clause. We can also try and introduce types or sorts into our language. But, most importantly, a good search procedure is required – based on a suitable guiding heuristics.

In the next chapter we will discover a few more, and we will rediscover several ideas to greater detail.

7.4.3 Semantic biases

Inverting resolution means defining a calculus with a rule set that implements a new derivation relation $\dashv$. We were looking for some H such that, for a given Π, we can explain E, which means that $\Pi \cup H \approx E$. Because semantics was too expensive, we reduced $\approx$ to $\vdash$ and developed refinement operators like ∇_Φ, intra-construction, and so on, such that $\mathit{refine}(\Pi \cup H) \vdash \varphi \Longrightarrow \mathit{refine}(\Pi \cup H) \approx \varphi$. In this section, we will discover a few more techniques for defining biases.

Restricting model size

The great thing about *ground* models is that there are no longer any variables. Recall the notion of a *Herbrand interpretation* (footnote 12). With at least one non-constant function symbol in Σ, the Herbrand base is (due to recursion) infinite. This is, theoretically, a very bad starting basis for an efficient search for H. However, by the *compactness theorem* and the work of Löwenheim and Skolem (Hodges 1993), we know that it suffices to find an unsatisfiable subset to show that $\Pi \cup H$ is unsatisfiable. The procedure of a refutation proof by resolution makes use of exactly this property. It is based on the efficient construction of an unsatisfiable subset (by adding the negation of the goal) and, by the law of the excluded middle, conclude that if the negation leads to failure, the non-negated goal must have been true.

Exercise 7.75 (◊) Look up the *compactness theorem* and the *Löwenheim–Skolem theorem.*

We now define a method for constructing *finite* models that are admittedly not complete because they are defined by finite application of the resolution rule:

h-easy ground models

Definition 7.76 — *h*-easy ground models.
Let Φ be a set of of HOL formulae. We define

$$Th^h_\vdash(\Phi) \quad := \quad \left\{\varphi \in \mathrm{Fml}_{\mathrm{HOL}} : \Phi \vdash^i_{\mathrm{SLD}} \varphi \wedge i \leq h\right\}, \tag{7.66}$$

where $\vdash^{i}_{\mathsf{SLD}}$ denotes an SLD resolution proof of length i.[18] ●

So instead of searching a potentially infinite hypothesis space, we restrict ourselves to a finite one. Additionally, this restriction is defined in terms of the minimum length of derivations required to infer a formula.

Restricting the set of possible assignments

In the last section we mentioned the concept of *connectedness*. We discovered that a variable occurring in a clause body has – due to the nature of SLD resolution – a certain impact on the semantics of a predicate. More specifically, a variable occurring in a clause is predetermined in the number of possible bindings by the number of variables, their assignments, and their common appearance. This requires the notion of *variable depth* in a clause: let there be a clause

$$\lambda_0 :- \lambda_1, \ldots, \lambda_{n-1}.$$

Then, all the variables occurring in the clause head λ_0 have depth 0. If some variable X occurs in L_i for the first time, then its depth is the maximum depth of all variables occurring in the literals L_j plus one (where $i \in \mathbf{n}$ and $j \in \mathbf{i}$):

$$\text{depth}(X) \quad := \quad \min\{\text{depth}(Y) : X, Y \text{ occur in } \lambda_j, j \in \mathbf{i}\} + 1. \qquad (7.67)$$

We now formulate a very important property of variables: it is their *degree (of freedom)*:

Example 7.77 On our base set s = {◇,△,●,■,◆,▲}, we examine the number of (type compatible) variable assignments for the predicates *bigger*, *colour*, *shape*, and *has_more_edges*:

Predicate	# possible α	# satisfying σ
bigger	$6 \cdot 6 = 36$	$2 \cdot 4 = 8$
colour	$6 \cdot 2 = 12$	$4 + 2 = 6$
shape	$6 \cdot 3 = 18$	$1 + 1 + 2 + 2 = 6$
has_more_edges	$6 \cdot 6 = 36$	$5 + 4 + 3 = 12$

Imagine now that we would like to model a predicate that describes whether printing one object *needs_more_ink* (*nmi*) than another. Then,

nmi(◆, X) is true for all X, because ◆ requires most ink of all objects.

nmi(○, X) requires that X = △, because △ is the object that requires least ink.

nmi(X, ●) requires $X \in$ {■, ◆, ▲}.

[18] This definition is a simplification of the more abstract idea of h-easiness: h is a recursive, computable function, such that for each φ_i that is valid in our model we need at most $h(i)$ derivation steps to deduce φ_i from Φ. Here, define h to be a constant value.

Obviously, every black object requires more ink than all the white objects, and for most black objects it holds that the more edges it has, the more ink it requires (the exception is that ◆ needs more ink even though it does not have more edges than ■).

We define:

Free assignment degree of a variable

Definition 7.78 — Free assignment degree of a variable. Let there be a clause $\lambda_0 :- \lambda_1, \ldots, \lambda_{n-1}$ and the i-th literal

$$\lambda_i = p_i(X_0, \ldots, X_k).$$

The *free assignment degree* of X_j in λ_i (written degfree(X_j, λ_i)) is the number of variables in $\{X_j, \ldots, X_k\}$ that also appear in $\{X_0, \ldots, X_{j-1}\}$ or in any other literal λ_k, $k \in \mathbf{i}$. ●

As a rule of thumb, degfree(X_j, λ_i) increases with growing i and j, which is due to the top-down and left-to-right resolving strategy of SLD resolution.

Example 7.79 Let

$$nmi_0(X_0, Y_1) :- colour_1(X_0, C_1), colour_2(Y_0, C_1), hme_3(X_0, Y_1).$$

where the indexing is just to identify the occurrence of a variable in a different literal. It states that for two objects of the same colour, the one with more edges requires more ink. The depths of all the variables are

	X_0	Y_0	X_1	C_1	Y_2	C_2	X_3	Y_3
depth(X) =	0	0	0	1	0	1	0	0

The values of degfree(X_j, λ_i) are

	λ_i			
degfree$(\cdot)$	0	1	2	3
$j = 0$	0	1	1	2
$j = 1$	0	0	1	1

Supposing that $\alpha(X_0) = ▲$, there are six possible substitutions for Y_0 of which only three are valid ($\alpha(Y_0) \in \{◇, △, ●\}$). The value of C is not restricted yet. So for all three variables X, Y, C in the clause we have $1 \cdot 6 \cdot 2 = 12$ different assignments to choose from. Because $X_1 = X_0$, there is only one possible value for C_1, namely, `black`, ruling out the factor 2 from the number of possible instantiations such that we are left with only six alternatives. In literal 2, the fact that $C_2 = C_1 =$ `black` reduces the number of possible instantiations for Y_2 to only four because there are only four black objects in s. In literal 3, all our variables are instantiated. We conclude that there can be at most four different values for Y (rather than six). ●

A literal λ is called *determinate* if each new variable in it has exactly *one possible* binding given the bindings of the other variables. We can lift this property to clauses and predicates and say that a clause is determinate if all of its literals are determinate and a predicate is determinate if all of its clauses are determinate.

Definition 7.80 — *ij*-determinacy. *ij*-determinacy

A literal λ is called *i-determinate* if it is determinate and if

$$\max\{\text{depth}(X) : X \text{ occurs in } \lambda\} \leq i,$$

that is, the maximum depth of its variables is bounded by i.

A clause $\lambda_0 :- \lambda_1, \ldots, \lambda_{n-1}$ is called *ij*-determinate if and only if

1. i is the maximum depth at which a determinate variable occurs.
2. j is the maximum degree of any variable occurring in $\lambda_1, \ldots, \lambda_{n-1}$. ●

An example of the application of the biases discussed so far is the learning system GOLEM (Muggleton and Feng 1990, 1992). It takes two sets of ground facts, E^0 and E^1, as samples and Π as background knowledge. Π is also assumed to be ground; if it is not, it is represented by an *h*-easy version of it. The result is that Π consists of ground facts only (or can be transferred into one). On this set of formulae, ∇_Π is applied on pairs of examples to infer hypotheses for the target predicate. Variable introduction is biased by setting a threshold for i and j: we may not generalise to new variables or simply introduce new variables if they would exceed the *ij*-determinacy. With these heuristics, GOLEM performs more or less the same learning loop as FOIL does:

1. To learn a single rule, randomly pick $\varphi, \psi \in E^1$ and compute $\nabla_\Pi(\varphi, \psi)$ until coverage on E^1 cannot be increased any more and no $e \in E^0$ is covered.
2. Remove redundant literals.
3. To learn sets of rules, remove the examples that are covered by a rule and continue until all examples are covered (none are left).

The directedness of SLD resolution suggests a directedness of determinacy. In fact, the definition of determinacy is motivated by SLD resolution.

Restricting declarative semantics by procedural semantics

If you are familiar with the Prolog programming language, you might have seen *predicate specifications*. The expression

$$p(+X, +Y, -Z)$$

means that when trying to resolve a (negative) literal $p(X', Y', Z')$, X' and Y' need to be *ground* terms, whereas Z' will be substituted after all body literals of the clause have been resolved.

Example 7.81 Consider our predicate *black* in Example 7.36. It takes one single argument and succeeds if the provided argument represents a black object:

$$?\text{-}black(\bullet) \sqcap_{\mathsf{RES}} black(\bullet) = \{\}.$$

In this case, we receive a definite answer, `Yes.`, for $\mu = \{\}$. But what if we ask $?\text{-}black(X)$? Then, we have several options to resolve the goal using several substitutions that in Prolog are discovered by backtracking:

$$\mu_0 = [X \mapsto \bullet],\ \mu_1 = [X \mapsto \blacksquare],\ \mu_2 = [X \mapsto \blacklozenge],\ \mu_3 = [X \mapsto \blacktriangle].$$

This is useful for collecting the set of all things we know to be black. In our case, we want to use the predicate `black` to *check* whether a *certain instance* is black. The convention then is to declare the predicate *black* as a predicate whose argument needs to be ground when trying to resolve it. It is specified by writing $black(+X)$.

The previous example was very simple because the predicate took only one argument. Now consider Example 7.53 and Equation 7.44 of the subsequent example. We induced a predicate consisting of two clauses:

$$\begin{aligned} h_0 &= black\_polygon(X) :\text{-}\ colour(X, black), shape(X, square). \\ h_1 &= black\_polygon(X) :\text{-}\ colour(X, black), shape(X, diamond). \end{aligned}$$

which were defined to check whether a certain object X is a black polygon. An experienced Prolog programmer would never define a predicate like this. If he was asked to implement a predicate `white_polygon`, he would have to copy the clauses and replace all occurrences of the ground term `black` with `white`. Instead, he would write:

$$\begin{aligned} coloured\_polygon(X, C) \quad :\text{-} \quad & colour(X, C), \\ & member(X, [square, diamond]). \end{aligned} \tag{7.68}$$

Exercise 7.82

◊ Specify the predicate *coloured_polygon* and all predicates appearing in the body of the clause. For *member*, consult a Prolog manual or, for example, Bratko (1986).

◊ Compute the free assignment degree of all the variable occurrences in the predicate definition of Equation (7.68). Then determine the smallest i and j such that the predicate is ij-determinate.

If we want to specify a predicate that delivers a definite answer substitution, things are a bit different.

Example 7.83 To retrieve objects from our knowledge base that satisfy certain goals, we implement a predicate $is\_there\_a(+C, +S, -X)$ as follows:

$$is\_there\_a(C, S, X) \quad :- \quad shape(X, S), \tag{7.69}$$

$$colour(X, C). \tag{7.70}$$

By SLD resolution and an initial assignment $\alpha(C) = black$ and $\alpha(S) = circle$, we resolve $?\text{-}shape(X, circle)$ against the fact $colour(\bullet, circle)$ by applying $\mu_0 = [X \mapsto \bullet]$. The substitution lemma then implies the assignment $\alpha(X)$ changes to $\alpha\,[X \mapsto \bullet]$ such that $\alpha(X) = \bullet$. Hence $?\text{-}colour(X, black)$ becomes $?\text{-}colour(\bullet, black)$, which, by $\mu_1 = []$, resolves with the fact $colour(\bullet, black)$ to the empty clause. Now we know that

$$\forall \alpha \in s^{\mathrm{Var}} : \alpha(X) = \bullet \Longrightarrow \Pi \models_\alpha is\_there\_a(black, circle, X). \tag{7.71}$$

This means the goal is true for a substitution $\sigma = \{X \mapsto \bullet\}$ and we can answer, "`Yes`, there is an X such that X is a black circle—namely $X = \bullet$!"

Exercise 7.84

◇ In the last example we showed that $\Pi \vdash_{\mathrm{SLD}} is\_there\_a(black, circle, \bullet)$. Why is Equation (7.71) true, too?

◇ What happens for $?\text{-}is\_there\_a(white, triangle, X)$?

◇ Let there be an alternative definition of the predicate *is_there_a*:

$$is\_there\_a(C, S, X) \quad :- \quad colour(X, C),$$
$$shape(X, S).$$

Compute the free assignment degree of all the variable occurrences. Then, determine the smallest i and j such that the predicate is ij-determinate!

◇ What happens for $?\text{-}is\_there\_a(white, triangle, X)$?
What happens for $?\text{-}is\_there\_a(black, tetragon, X)$?

From the definitions of biases we discussed so far and the observations we made by examining SLD proofs, we conclude that it is a good idea to restrict the search space for hypotheses by predetermining the predicate specifications. If we are concerned with learning from examples rather than with rule invention, we also know the predicate name and arity for which we want to learn a definition. Specifications of predicates are also known as *modes*. Modes like

> The target has a head literal, the arguments of which shall satisfy the I/O behaviour determined by $p(+X, +Y, -Z)$.

can be found in PROGOL or *m*FOIL.

Finally, a very simple method for reducing search space is simply by limiting the language available to formulate a hypothesis. One could, for example, restrict the search for hypotheses to "3-literal Horn clauses matching the template $p(\_,\_,X) :- Q(X,Y), p(\_,X,Y)$". Such limitations, also known as *predicate schemes*, were used in MOBAL (Morik et al. 1993).[19]

7.4.4 Inverted entailment

All our efforts so far concentrated on the fact that $\approx\!\!\models$ is too expensive to be checked for every single guess of what might be an appropriate hypothesis. As a consequence we focused on finding syntactical refinement operators that at least come close to inverting entailment.

Example 7.85 Computing (relative) least generalisations with respect to θ-subsumption are not least general with respect to implication. Imagine that

$$\begin{aligned} \chi &:= p(f(f(0))) :- p(0). \\ \xi &:= p(f(1)) :- p(1). \end{aligned}$$

The least general generalisation with respect to θ-subsumption is

$$\varphi = \chi \triangledown \xi = p(f(x)) :- p(y).$$

But the least general generalisation with respect to logic implication (i.e., entailment) is

$$\psi = \chi \curlyvee \xi = p(f(x)) :- p(x).$$

where $\psi = \chi\sigma^{\smile} = \xi\sigma^{\smile}$ with

$$\sigma^{\smile} = [f(0) \mapsto x, f(1) \mapsto x, 0 \mapsto x, 1 \mapsto y].$$

It is clear that

$$\varphi = p(f(x)) :- p(y) \approx\!\!\models p(f(x)) :- p(x) = \psi,$$

and it is also clear that φ is way too general!

Our example is a *recursive* predicate definition. This clause contains the same literal twice: the positive version makes the rule head, and the negative one is an element of the rule body. So when trying to resolve p, we have to resolve p again – just with another argument. Therefore, clauses that define recursive predicates are also known as *self-resolving* clauses. From this point of view one can see that φ in the preceding

[19] Note that schemes like these explicitly include depth, degree, determinacy, and specification biases. Note also that Q is a placeholder for a predicate name; it is, so to say, a second order variable.

example is rather useless: proving a certain instance of p by proving *any* instance of it leads into a vicious circle.

Exercise 7.86 (◇) Define a criterion by which one can easily determine whether an arbitrary self-resolving clause may be useful or certainly is not useful at all. Think of biases!

There is, however, one important observation that we have not taken into account so far. Gottlob (1987) states that:

Definition 7.87 — Gottlob's lemma. Gottlob's lemma

Let there be two clauses φ and ψ as follows:

$$\begin{aligned}\varphi &= \{\kappa_0, \ldots, \kappa_{k-1}, \neg\kappa_k, \ldots, \neg\kappa_{m-1}\}\\ \psi &= \{\lambda_0, \ldots, \lambda_{l-1}, \neg\lambda_l, \ldots, \neg\lambda_{n-1}\},\end{aligned}$$

where, for

$$\begin{aligned}\varphi^{\mathbf{1}} = \{\kappa_0, \ldots, \kappa_{k-1}\} \quad &\text{and} \quad \psi^{\mathbf{1}} = \{\lambda_0, \ldots, \lambda_{l-1}\}\\ \varphi^{\mathbf{0}} = \{\neg\kappa_k, \ldots, \neg\kappa_m\} \quad &\text{and} \quad \psi^{\mathbf{0}} = \{\neg\lambda_0, \ldots, \neg\lambda_n\},\end{aligned}$$

$\varphi^{\mathbf{1}}, \psi^{\mathbf{1}}$ contain only positive literals and $\varphi^{\mathbf{0}}, \psi^{\mathbf{0}}$ contain only negative literals. Then,

$$\models \varphi \longrightarrow \psi \quad \Longrightarrow \quad \varphi^{\mathbf{1}} \models\!\!\!\!\mid \psi^{\mathbf{1}} \wedge \varphi^{\mathbf{0}} \models\!\!\!\!\mid \psi^{\mathbf{0}}. \tag{7.72}$$

So when one clause implies another, its subsets of positive and negative literals subsume the corresponding subsets of the other. ●

By the deduction theorem, Equation (7.72) can be transformed into

$$\varphi \approx\!\!\!\!\mid \psi \quad \Longrightarrow \quad \varphi^{\mathbf{1}} \models\!\!\!\!\mid \psi^{\mathbf{1}} \wedge \varphi^{\mathbf{0}} \models\!\!\!\!\mid \psi^{\mathbf{0}}. \tag{7.73}$$

The hypothesis H we are to infer shall at least entail all the positive examples of our target concept:

$$\Pi \cup H \approx\!\!\!\!\mid E^{\mathbf{1}},$$

where, as you will remember, $E^{\mathbf{1}}$ is a set of *(ground) facts* $\{\{\lambda_0\}, \ldots, \{\lambda_{n-1}\}\}$. Then we can rewrite the formula as

$$\Pi \cup H \approx\!\!\!\!\mid \{\{\lambda_0\}, \ldots, \{\lambda_{n-1}\}\}.$$

Now, we try a little trick and require H to *consist of facts only*, too. Then we can write

$$\Pi \cup \{\{\kappa_0\}, \ldots, \{\kappa_{m-1}\}\} \approx\!\!\!\!\mid \{\{\lambda_0\}, \ldots, \{\lambda_{n-1}\}\}.$$

This means that there is a substitution such that $\Pi \cup \{\{\kappa_0\}, \ldots, \{\kappa_{m-1}\}\} \cup \{\{\neg\lambda_0\}, \ldots, \{\neg\lambda_{n-1}\}\}$ is not satisfiable. Furthermore, by Equation (7.72), the set of positive literals κ_i subsumes the set of positive λ_j, and the same holds for the negative literal subsets. If we now *add the negation* of E^1 to Π, we can infer a set of formulae (or, more specifically, a conjunction of literals), which we *do not want to be implied* by the hypothesis H we are looking for. Negation on clauses with free variables in them requires skolemisation to avoid existential quantifiers. Let there be a clause

$$\begin{aligned}\varphi &= \kappa_0, \ldots, \kappa_{k-1} :- \lambda_0, \ldots, \lambda_{l-1}. \\ &= \{\kappa_0, \ldots, \kappa_{k-1}, \neg\lambda_0, \ldots, \neg\lambda_{l-1}\}\end{aligned}$$

such that $\varphi^{\mathbf{0}} = \{\lambda_j : j \in \mathbf{l}\}$ and $\varphi^{\mathbf{1}} = \{\kappa_j : i \in \mathbf{k}\}$. Then, its *complement* is the *set* of all *unary clauses* where each clause is the skolemised negation of a literal in φ:

$$\overline{\varphi} := \{\{\kappa_0\}, \ldots, \{\kappa_{k-1}\}, \{\lambda_0\}, \ldots, \{\lambda_{l-1}\}\}\, \sigma_{sk}. \tag{7.74}$$

Note that this is not a single clause as was φ but an entire clausal theory consisting of a *conjunction* of unary, ground clauses.[20] Using complementation we define:

Bottom literal set, *BotLit*

Definition 7.88 — Bottom literal set, *BotLit*.
Let Π be a set of clauses and φ a clause. The set

$$\mathrm{BotLit}(\Pi, \varphi) := \{\lambda : \Pi \cup \overline{\varphi} \approx \neg\lambda \text{ and } \lambda \text{ is a ground literal}\} \tag{7.75}$$

is called the *bottom set of φ for Π*. ●

Roughly speaking, it is the set of all facts that are rejected when adding the negation of φ to our background knowledge. Now comes the trick: if we assume φ to be *true* – especially, if $\varphi \in E^1$, then a *subset* of the corresponding bottom literal set is a clause that can be considered a good hypothesis for φ!

Inverse entailment

Definition 7.89 — Inverse entailment.
Let Π be a set of clauses. Let there be a set of ground facts E^1, the positive examples. Let $\varphi = \{\kappa\}$ be a clause (in this case, a fact) from E^1. Let

$$\mathrm{BotLit}(\Pi, \varphi) = \{\lambda : \Pi \cup \{\{\neg\kappa\}\} \approx \neg\lambda \text{ and } \lambda \text{ is a ground literal}\}.$$

Then, by inverse entailment, we consider H with

$$H \models B\sigma_{sk} \text{ for some } B \subseteq \mathrm{BotLit}(\Pi, \varphi),$$

a *hypothesis* derived by *inverse entailment* from φ with respect to Π. ●

[20] More generally, the complement of any formula is its negation with all variables replaced by Skolem constants.

There are a few problems here: first, the bottom literal set is not necessarily finite. Luckily, the definition of inverse entailment includes a nice workaround as we only need to consider subsets. Therefore, we can confine our search to finite sets. The second problem is that there are still *too many* of them. Finally, there is a gap between the generality of definitions and the illustrating examples: the definitions work for *arbitrary clauses* whereas until now we have only discussed ground facts as formulae. What we are looking for is located just in the gap between – definite clauses. But first let us consider a small example.

Example 7.90 Let

$$\Pi = \left\{ \begin{array}{l} polygon(X):-\ edges(X,4)., \\ black\_tetragon(X):-\ black(X), polygon(X), square(X). \end{array} \right\}$$

$$\varphi = black\_tetragon(X):-\ edges(X,4), black(X).$$

Then, complementation leads to

$$\overline{\varphi} = \{:-\ black\_tetragon(\blacksquare)., edges(\blacksquare,4)., black(\blacksquare).\}.$$

As a result,

$$\mathrm{BotLit}(\Pi,\varphi) = \{square(\blacksquare), \neg black(\blacksquare), \neg edges(\blacksquare,4), \neg polygon(\blacksquare)\}.$$

By inverse entailment we can build *several* clauses ψ for which $\psi \models \varphi$:

$$\begin{aligned} \psi_0 &= square(\blacksquare):-\ black(\blacksquare), edges(\blacksquare,4), polygon(\blacksquare). \\ \psi_1 &= square(X):-\ black(X), edges(X,4), polygon(X). \\ \psi_2 &= square(X):-\ edges(X,4), polygon(X). \\ \psi_3 &= square(X):-\ black(X), polygon(X). \end{aligned}$$

Exercise 7.91

◊ Is there a clause ψ' for which neither $\Pi \cup \{\psi'\} \approx square(\square)$ nor $\Pi \cup \{\psi'\} \approx square(\blacksquare)$? Why?

◊ Evaluate ψ_i, $i \in \mathbf{4}$, with respect to the base set $\{\lozenge, \bullet, \triangle, \bigcirc, \blacksquare, \blacklozenge, \square, \blacktriangle\}$.

The method of inverse entailment was first presented in Muggleton (1995). Along with its theory, Muggleton presented an implementation in which the construction of saturants and the subsequent search for clauses subsuming them are guided by a heuristic measure of compression (rather than an entropy-based measure) and strong biases on the form of the clauses that are to be considered. These biases are defined in terms of so-called *mode-declarations*, which are similar to the biases we discovered in Section 7.4.3.

A beautifully concise summary of the most important ideas behind "semantic" induction is Yamamoto (1997). It refers to the most influential articles on which inverted entailment is based as well as the two most completive contributions, Rouveirol (1992) and Nienhuys-Cheng and Wolf (1996). Lloyd (2003) also gives a very compressed yet broad introduction to logic learning focusing on both inductive logic learning and the logic behind decision tree induction.

7.5 Summary

Inductive logic programming was at its peak in the mid-1990s, which is why many standard references are 15 years old by now. One of the first textbooks on inductive logic programming is Lavrac and Dzeroski (1993). A bit more detailed information can be found in Nienhuys-Cheng and de Wolf (1997). A very readable and concise summary is an extended article by Muggleton and de Raedt published in Muggleton and Raedt (1994). A recent textbook covering most important aspects of inductive logic programming is Raedt (2008). Kersting and Raedt (2000), Raedt and Kersting (2004), and Kersting (2008) focus on extensions of the inductive logic programming aproach by probabilistic methods.

Inductive logic programming is about finding logic programs that describe unknown target concepts. A program clause is a definite clause; clauses with at least one negative literal are rule clauses. The rule head represents a relation between its arguments – an n-ary predicate symbol is interpreted as an n-ary relation. The entire predicate is defined by a *disjunction* of clauses and every clause by a *conjunction* of literals. These literals again refer to other predicates, usually to predicates that are predefined in Π. Therefore, the predicate definition

$$\varphi = black\_polygon(X) \quad :- \quad black(X), tetragon(X). \qquad (7.76)$$

$$\psi = black\_polygon(X) \quad :- \quad black(X), triangle(X). \qquad (7.77)$$

is about the same as

$$x \in black\_polygon \subseteq s \quad :\Leftarrow \quad x \in (black \cap tetragon) \cup (black \cap triangle).$$

If we agree that anything we cannot prove is false, then our hypothesis becomes

$$black\_polygon \quad := \quad (black \cap tetragon) \cup (black \cap triangle).$$

So if objects, say ■, ▲, and ◆, are all black and either a tetragon or a triangle, they are indiscernible by our knowledge about black polygons. In other words, it does not matter at all whether the property of being black or being a tetragon is expressed in terms of features in a corresponding information system, by predicates or by relations.

Whenever two objects are elements of the satisfaction set of a predicate, they are indiscernible with respect to the relation by which this predicate is interpreted. For $\mathbf{R} = \{Colour, Tetragon\}$ and the program above, it holds that

$$\{\blacksquare, \blacklozenge\} = [\![\mathbf{R}]\!]\{\blacksquare, \blacklozenge\} \iff \blacksquare\bar{\bar{\mathbf{R}}}\blacklozenge$$
$$\iff \Pi \cup \{\varphi, \psi\} \not\approx \left\{ \begin{array}{l} black\_polygon(\blacksquare), \\ black\_polygon(\blacklozenge) \end{array} \right\}.$$

If there are two concepts with instances

$$\{\blacktriangle, \blacklozenge, \bullet\} \subseteq c_0$$
$$\{\triangle, \blacklozenge, \bullet\} \subseteq c_1,$$

then, with $\mathbf{R} = \{Colour, Size, Shape\}$,

$$[\![\mathbf{R}]\!]c_0 = c_0 = (\!|\mathbf{R}|\!)c_0 \quad \text{and} \quad [\![\mathbf{R}]\!]c_1 = c_1 = (\!|\mathbf{R}|\!)c_1.$$

Similarly, with just a simple representation shift involved herein,

$$c\_0(X) \;:\text{-}\; colour(X, black), size(X, Y), shape(X, Z).$$
$$c\_1(X) \;:\text{-}\; colour(X, Y), size(X, small), shape(X, Z).$$

As one can see, the above predicate definitions are highly redundant – and, equivalently, there exist reducts of $\mathbf{R}$. For $\mathbf{P} = \{Colour\}$ and $\mathbf{Q} = \{Size\}$,

$$[\![\mathbf{P}]\!]c_0 = c_0 = (\!|\mathbf{P}|\!)c_0 \quad \text{and} \quad [\![\mathbf{Q}]\!]c_1 = c_1 = (\!|\mathbf{Q}|\!)c_1.$$

The same holds for the logic program: the free variables do not contribute at all to the restriction of the satisfaction set for the predicates. Hence,

$$c\_0(X) \;:\text{-}\; colour(X, black).$$
$$c\_1(X) \;:\text{-}\; size(X, small).$$

Finally, let us consider rule induction. We observe

$$\blacklozenge, \blacksquare, \blacktriangle, \bullet \in black \;=\; s - \{\lozenge, \triangle\} = s - white$$
$$\blacksquare, \blacktriangle, \bullet, \lozenge \in large \;=\; s - \{\blacklozenge, \triangle\} = s - small$$

and

$$\blacksquare, \lozenge, \blacklozenge \in tetragon,\; triangle = \{\triangle\},\; circle = \{\bullet\}.$$

Then, for $c = \{\blacklozenge, \blacksquare, \blacktriangle\}$, we find a reduct $\mathbf{R} = \{Colour, Shape\}$ such that $[\![\mathbf{R}]\!]c = c = (\!|\mathbf{R}|\!)$. For the corresponding facts

white(◇). *white*(△).
black(●). *black*(■). *black*(◆). *black*(▲).
triangle(△). *triangle*(▲).
tetragon(◆). *tetragon*(◇). *tetragon*(■).
circle(●).

the induced rules are

$$c(X) \quad :- \quad black(X), tetragon(X).$$
$$c(X) \quad :- \quad black(X), triangle(X).$$

In this chapter we have discovered three ways of finding relational descriptions of new concepts by inducing logic programs that define corresponding satisfaction sets.

We also discovered similarities to the rough set approach and the differences in the biases utilised in decision tree induction, rough set data analysis, and inductive logic programming.

Chapter 8
Learning and ensemble learning

We discussed several paradigms of how to extract relational knowledge from sets of data. All of them were based on an intuitive understanding of what it means to learn a new concept. In this chapter we will try to find a more abstract definition of *learnability*.

The second topic of this chapter is motivated by two questions. Why should we learn one complex classifier instead of several simple ones? And why should we learn from all observations instead of from only the difficult ones?

8.1 Learnability

It is worth taking a second look at whether some question can be answered from a set of information before one tries to extract the knowledge required to derive such an answer from all the data. There is no use in trying to answer a question to which we have no answer; it is hard to try solving an ill-posed problem, and it is not a wise idea to formulate an answer in a language that is not sufficiently expressive to grasp what we want to say.

Let us recall the first definition of a learning algorithm (Definition 3.38): presupposing that a concept c actually *is learnable* (whatever that means), a learning algorithm is a procedure that from a set of examples induces a function that computes an approximation of c:

$$\texttt{Alg}(S_\mu(m, t)) = h \approx t.$$

Reverting this definition we can try to formulate a definition of *learnability*:

Learnability

Definition 8.1 — Learnability.
A problem $c \subseteq U$ is *(correct) learnable* if there is an algorithm `Alg` that, given a sample $S_\mu(m,t)$, delivers a function h such that $h = \chi(c)$.[1]
●

This definition is quite rigid, and there exist weaker versions:

1. First we consider only finite universes U. It is much easier to examine only a subset of objects and it is simpler to find a hypothesis explaining fewer examples.
2. A problem is *approximately correct* learnable if $h \approx \chi(c)$. Then, one needs to explain what "approximately" or "$\approx$" means (see footnote 1). It requires an *error measure*, of which there are two basic types: in Section 3.4.1 we defined *pointwise* error measures and measures based on sets of such errors; in Section 3.4.2 we introduced error measures that evaluate hypotheses as a whole.
3. Finally, a problem is *probably approximately correct (PAC)* learnable if, with a certain confidence, we can guarantee an approximately correct hypothesis.

8.1.1 Probably approximately correct learning

The idea of PAC learning was coined by Leslie Valiant (1984), who, in 2010, was awarded the ACM Turing award for his work.

PAC learnability

Definition 8.2 — PAC learnability.
A problem in $\mathfrak{U}$ is *PAC learnable* if there exists a *probably approximately correct (PAC)* learning algorithm `Alg`. `Alg` is PAC if there exists a lower bound for the number of required examples such that for all samples of equal or greater length, with a probability of at most δ, t can *not* be approximately correctly learned with an error of less than ε.

Let $0 < \varepsilon, \delta < 1$. Let `Alg` be a learning algorithm for $\mathfrak{U}$ with U being the base set of $\mathfrak{U}$. Let $t = \chi(c)$, $c \subseteq U$, and μ a (probability) distribution on U. `Alg` is PAC if

$$\exists m_0 : m \geq m_0 \Longrightarrow \mu^m \left\{ \mathbf{s} :\in S_\mu(m,t) : \mathrm{error}_U^\mu(\mathtt{Alg}(\mathbf{s}), t) < \varepsilon \right\} > 1 - \delta. \quad (8.1)$$

Therein, m_0 is a value that must be computable by a function of ε and δ. The ":∈" is there to denote that $S_\mu(m,t)$ is not a function but nondeterministically delivers $\mathbf{s}$. ●

[1] In terms of computational theory, c is a language in $\wp(s)$ and for every x in s there is a decision problem whether $x \in c$. Using this formulation it is clear that the problem is trivial for finite c and becomes interesting for infinite c. Even more interesting are undecidable c.

> **PAC learnability**
> A problem is *probably approximately correct learnable* if there is an algorithm for which only by defining a minimum confidence and maximum error can we guarantee that for any sample which contains at least a fixed minimum number of examples, this algorithm with a certain probability delivers a hypothesis that is sufficiently accurate – with an arbitrary and unknown distribution on our universe.

Example 8.3 Let $U = \mathbb{N}$ and $c_{\text{odd}} = \{1, 3, 5, \ldots\}$ be the set of odd numbers. Then, $h(x) = 1 :\Longleftrightarrow x \mod 2 = 0$ is a hypothesis for which $h = \chi(c_{\text{odd}})$. It is a correct hypothesis.

Example 8.4 Let U be the set of objects with shape □, ○, ◇, or △ and a colour that is *white*, *light*, *dark*, or *black*. Let c_{wwbb} be the set of sequences of two white objects followed by two black objects (i.e., all sequences have length 4^n):

$$c_{\text{wwbb}} = \left\{ (w_0 w_1 b_0 b_1)^n : \begin{array}{c} i \in \mathbf{2} \wedge w_i, b_i \in U \wedge \\ \textit{colour}(w_i) = \textit{white} \wedge \textit{colour}(b_i) = \textit{black} \end{array} \right\}.$$

We define a distance function on the set of colour values $\text{dist}_{\text{colour}} : \text{cod}(\textit{colour}) \times \text{cod}(\textit{colour}) \to \left\{0, \frac{1}{4}, \frac{1}{2}, \frac{3}{4}, 1\right\}$ as

$\text{dist}_{\text{colour}}$	□	▨	▩	■
□	0	$\frac{1}{4}$	$\frac{3}{4}$	1
▨	$\frac{1}{4}$	0	$\frac{1}{4}$	$\frac{3}{4}$
▩	$\frac{3}{4}$	$\frac{1}{4}$	0	$\frac{1}{4}$
■	1	$\frac{3}{4}$	$\frac{1}{4}$	0

Suppose the hypothesis generated by some `Alg` is the characteristic function of the set

$$c_{\text{wldb}} = \left\{ (x_{\text{white}} x_{\text{light}} x_{\text{dark}} x_{\text{black}})^n : x_i \in U \wedge \textit{colour}(x_i) = i \right\}.$$

Based on the definition of $\text{dist}_{\text{colour}}$, we define a distance measure on U^{4n} as

$$\text{dist}(x_0 x_1 x_2 x_3, y_0 y_1 y_2 y_3) := \frac{1}{4} \sum_{i \in \mathbf{4}} \text{dist}_{\text{colour}}(x_i, y_i)$$

$$\text{dist}(x_0 x_1 x_2 x_3 v, y_0 y_1 y_2 y_3 w) := \frac{\text{dist}(x_0 x_1 x_2 x_3, y_0 y_1 y_2 y_3) + \text{dist}(v, w)}{2}$$

for $v, w \in U^{4n}$. We compare an element $x \in c_{\text{wwbb}}$ and $y \in c_{\text{wldb}}$:

$x =$	◇	□	●	▲	△	◇	■	…
$y =$	○	▨	◉	◆	◇	▨	◈	…
$\text{dist}_{\text{colour}} =$	0	$\frac{1}{4}$	$\frac{1}{4}$	0	0	$\frac{1}{4}$	$\frac{1}{4}$	…
$\text{dist} =$		$\frac{1}{8}$					$\frac{1}{8}$	…

which demonstrates that the entire distance for any sequence of length n of symbols from c_{wwbb} to any sequence of length n of symbols from

Fig. 8.1 Learning discs

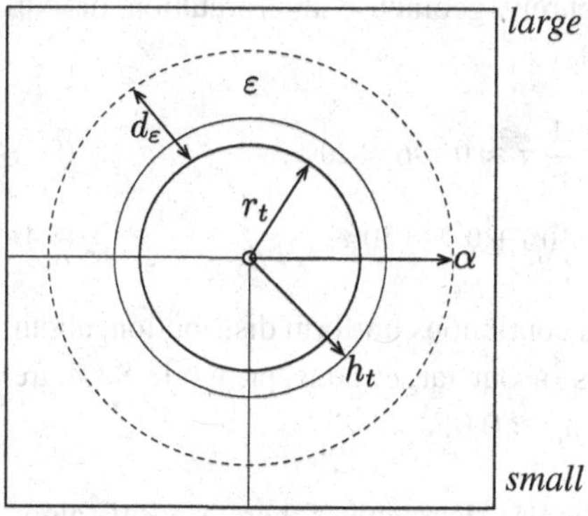

c_{wldb} is 0.125. Therefore, $h = \chi(c_{\text{wldb}})$ is ε-correct w.r.t. c_{wwbb} if $\varepsilon > 0.125$.

Now let us consider the following problem: let $U = [0, 1]^2 \subset \mathbb{R}\times\mathbb{R}$, where for an instance $x = \langle c_x, s_x \rangle$ the colour of x is described by c_x and the size of x by s_x. Note that we have left the universe with objects of only finitely many colours and sizes – the representation space is infinite! The target concept t is the set of objects that belong to the disc with centre $\left\langle \frac{1}{2}, \frac{1}{2} \right\rangle$ and radius $r_t = \frac{1}{4}$. In other words,

$$t(x) = 1 :\Longleftrightarrow x \in \left\{ x \in U : \sqrt{\left(c_x - \frac{1}{2}\right)^2 + \left(s_x - \frac{1}{2}\right)^2} \leq r_t \right\} = c. \quad (8.2)$$

For an illustration of this problem, see Figure 8.1. To compare two objects, we define

$$\text{dist}(x, y) = \sqrt{(c_x - c_y)^2 + (s_x - s_y)^2} \text{ and } \|x\| = \text{dist}\left(x, \left\langle \frac{1}{2}, \frac{1}{2} \right\rangle\right).$$

Then we allow a certain degree of uncertainty, which may result in wrong classification results. We add an "ε-region of tolerance" to the target concept, which means that we may accept slightly larger values than r_t as a hypothesis for c:[2]

$$c_\varepsilon := \{x \in U : \|x\| \leq r_t + \varepsilon\}.$$

The ε-tolerance-area c_{err} is a "rim" around the target concept with a width of ε.

[2] One might argue that an error should be symmetric; i.e., the error region is $[r_t - \frac{\varepsilon}{2}, r_t + \frac{\varepsilon}{2}]$. We focus on "larger" instead of "smaller or larger" only, because the algorithm we shall use can only overestimate the value of r_t. So even if this might be a bit confusing at this point, we make this assumption to keep the example calculation simpler for the remainder of the section.

Example 8.5 Let us try a purely geometric interpretation of our example: for $r_t = \frac{1}{4}$ and $\varepsilon = 0.1$,

$$A(c) \quad = \quad \frac{1}{16}\pi \approx 0.196 \approx 20\% \tag{8.3}$$

$$A(c_{\text{err}}) \quad = \quad A(c) + 0.1 \approx 30\%. \tag{8.4}$$

This means that, presupposing a continuous uniform distribution, about 20% of all objects are elements of our target concept, while 80% are not. From this we can calculate $d_\varepsilon \approx 0.06$.

A disc (or rather its radius) is PAC learnable if there is a PAC algorithm for it. Since the disc is defined by a certain radius r_t around $\left\langle \frac{1}{2}, \frac{1}{2} \right\rangle$, the learning algorithm has to find with a certain probability a value $r_h \leq r_t + d_\varepsilon$. An algorithm to approximate r_c by r_h is quite simple; see Figure 8.2 (left). Start with an empty hypothesis (that is, $r_h = 0$) and for every positive example x, redefine r_h to $\|x\|$ if $\|x\| > r_h$. Alternatively, we can start off with a most general hypothesis and successively restrict it (Figure 8.2, right): let $r_h > \frac{1}{2}$ and for each *negative* example that is closer to $\left\langle \frac{1}{2}, \frac{1}{2} \right\rangle$ than r_h, decrease r_h to the newly observed radius until we have processed all examples. From now on we will refer to the specialisation algorithm (see footnote 2). After m iterations, with at least one negative example in $\mathbf{s}$, it holds that

$$\frac{1}{2} \geq r_h \geq r_c.$$

The error set $\text{errset}_U(h, t)$ is the rim with width $r_h - r_c$ around the disc with radius r_c. More precisely,

$$\text{errset}_U(h, t) \quad = \quad \left\{ x \in U : r_h \geq \sqrt{\left(\frac{1}{2} - c_x\right)^2 + \left(\frac{1}{2} - s_x\right)^2} > r_t \right\}$$

$$= \quad \{ x \in U : r_t < \|x\| \leq r_h \}.$$

Learning by generalisation:

```
01   r_h := 0
02   s := S_μ(m, t)
03   FOREACH (⟨x, t(x)⟩ ∈ s) DO
04   {   IF t(x) = 1 THEN
05          r_h := max({r_h, ||x||})
06   }
07   RETURN (r_h)
```

Learning by specialisation:

```
01   r_h := 1
02   s := S_μ(m, t)
03   FOREACH (⟨x, t(x)⟩ ∈ s) DO
04   {   IF t(x) = 0 THEN
05          r_h := min({r_h, ||x||})
06   }
07   RETURN (r_h)
```

Fig. 8.2 Learning a disc

where $t(x) = 1 :\Longleftrightarrow \|x\| \leq r_c$.

But what about the actual *error* of h with respect to t? And what about the reliability of these algorithms? We examine the specialisation algorithm as shown on the right side of Figure 8.2 for the disc learning in Figure 8.1. To guarantee that h's error is not larger than some ε, we look for a *worst* hypothesis that just satisfies the error restriction. This worst case is

$$\alpha = \max\{r : \mu(F_r) - \mu(A(c)) \leq \varepsilon\}, \tag{8.5}$$

where F_r is the disc with radius r. In other words, α is the largest possible radius for a disc such that its (entire) area has an error of at most ε. This adds an entry to our diagram above, which, after slight transforms, looks as follows:

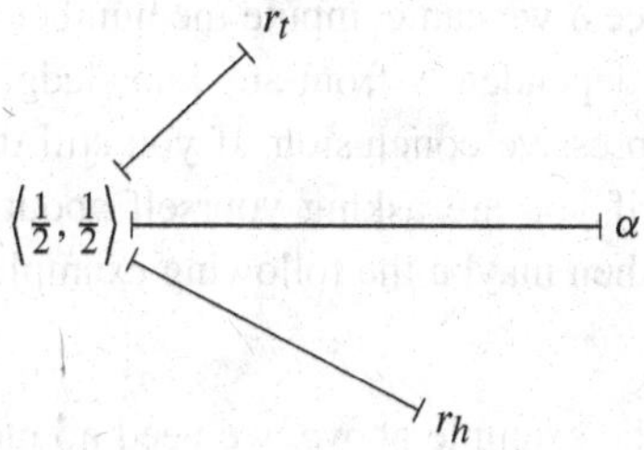

Now it is time to think about errors. Due to our definition of α, it holds that

$$\mu(\{x \in U : r_t < \|x\| \leq \alpha\}) \leq \varepsilon. \tag{8.6}$$

Because $r_h \leq \alpha$, it is also true that

$$\mu(\{x \in U : r_t < \|x\| \leq r_h\}) \leq \varepsilon. \tag{8.7}$$

It is also true that the "outer space" completes to probability 1:

$$\mu(\{x \in U : 0 < \|x\| \leq \alpha\}) + \mu(\{x \in U : \alpha < \|x\| \leq 1\}) = 1. \tag{8.8}$$

For the true error of r_h we conclude that

$$\begin{aligned} \text{error}_U^{\mu}(r_h, t) &= \mu(\{x \in U : r_t < \|x\| \leq r_h\}) \qquad (8.9) \\ &\leq \mu(\{x \in U : r_t < \|x\| \leq \alpha\}) \\ &\leq \varepsilon. \end{aligned}$$

Great! Obviously it is possible to learn a hypothesis that is at least ε-good. But what is the probability of being able to find it? To find a hypothesis we need to *see* an example that is better than α! The probability of *not seeing* such an example is the probability that none of the m examples in the rim is at most $(1 - \varepsilon)^m$. Therefore, with probability of at least $1 - (1 - \varepsilon)^m$ there *is* at least one such required example in the sample:

$$\mu^m(\{\mathbf{s} :\in S_\mu(m,t) : \text{error}_h^{\mu}(r_,)r_tU \leq \varepsilon\}) \geq 1 - (1 - \varepsilon)^m. \tag{8.10}$$

This means that the probability of picking a "good" example depends only on ε and, of course, on m. So what does it mean for the value δ of confidence? If we substitute $(1-\varepsilon)^m$ from Equation (8.10) for δ in Equation (8.1), then we find that

$$\delta > (1-\varepsilon)^m.$$

So we need to find a formula for computing a value for $m_0 \leq m$, which is the minimum value for which the above inequality becomes true. The choice $m_0 = \lceil \frac{1}{\varepsilon} \ln \frac{1}{\delta} \rceil$ satisfies all our requirements – and that means that the problem we wanted to learn is probably approximately correct learnable. We have described an algorithm (see Figure 8.2) and we have shown that by a mere definition of a maximally tolerated error of ε and a confidence δ we can compute the number of required examples – absolutely independently from any knowledge about μ! This is, in fact, a really impressive conclusion. If you still do not share a certain excitement or if you are asking yourself about the benefit of all these calculations, then maybe the following example will eradicate all doubts.

Example 8.6 In the example above, we need no more than 23 examples to approximate a disc with an arbitrary underlying distribution such that in 90% of all future predictions the error is at most 10%.

Exercise 8.7

- Prove the statement from the preceding example.
- What is the value of δ if we restrict m_0 to 18 and keep $\varepsilon = 0.1$?
- How many examples does it take if we are satisfied with a hypothesis that is better than random (that means that ε is just slightly larger than $\frac{1}{2}$) in 99% of all runs?

For the latter two questions you might want to write a little program that calculates a "table" of the dependencies between ε, δ, and m_0!

What we have shown so far is that we can find an estimate of the complexity for learning two-dimensional continuous problems. The reason for this was our running example and the idea behind finding a classifier that works sufficiently well with a minimal number of features, relations, or predicates – in short, with a minimum number of dimensions. The funny thing is that we reduced the two-dimensional problem of learning a disc to the one-dimensional problem of learning an *interval* on the real numbers, or, to be more precise, a ray. A more illustrative version of the proof presented here (including the details on how to find a term describing m_0) can be found in a manual of computational theory by Anthony and Biggs (1997).

8.1.2 Learnability and learning algorithms

For our running example domain, we showed that we can learn *any* concept that can be visualised by a disc in the plane where the plane itself is defined by a pair of features from **F**. Actually, we worked on a much harder problem than the ones given in all the previous examples because, until then, our world was *discrete*: objects had a certain colour like black, dark, or white, and they had a distinct shape like square, circle, or triangle. Even the size of an object was discrete: they were small or large. In the universe $\mathfrak{U}$ we created in this chapter, objects can have *any* shade of grey from white to black and *any* size from a minimum size 0 to a maximum size 1. This means that $\mathfrak{U}$ is infinite; it is even uncountably infinite. Yet we can find an iterative algorithm that comes to a halt after a finite number of steps and output a hypothesis satisfying a preset quality bias. This is, even modestly speaking, a wonderful result – for now.

Because the representation spaces that we have been concerned with so far are discrete, *most* of the learning problems we examined so far are PAC! This is simply due to the fact that for every *finite* hypothesis or representation space, there is a very simple algorithm that is PAC. It is so simple that it does not deserve a figure and a pseudo-code formulation, but it is so important that it deserves a knowledge box.

Finite problems are PAC learnable

Every learning problem with a finite representation space is PAC learnable:

If the set U is finite, then just enumerate all of its elements and sort them into two sets: one set representing the target concept and one set representing its complement. Then, for $\delta = 1$ and $\varepsilon = 0$, one can choose $m_0 = |U|$. This is neither elegant nor efficient – but it works.

Every learning problem with a finite hypothesis space and a representable hypothesis is PAC learnable:

In this case, we just enumerate all hypotheses and iterate them until we find one that satisfies our needs! If we want to learn a hypothesis with zero error, it requires our representation to be fine enough to describe the target concept. If it is not, we can at least find a best hypothesis after running through all the possible hypotheses.

But usually U is *infinite*. This is why we restricted the domain for learning to a finite subset at the very beginning of our journey (see Figure 3.1). In real life, any information system that we take as a base for our learning problem is "finite": first, there is only a finite amount of data s. Second, there is only a finite set of features **F**; and third, for each feature $f \in \mathbf{F}$, $\mathrm{cod}(f) = V_f$ is finite, too. The domain it represents, however, usually is *not* finite. Because of the inductive assumption (see Section 3.3) we can live with a finite subset of the domain. The restriction to only a finite set of features corresponds to a restriction of our language of hypotheses. And, finally, even continuous functions are usually quantised and are, for a defined interval, finite.

Clustering and learnability

If you take a look at Figure 8.1 again, the similarity of all approaches discussed so far becomes obvious: learning a k-NN classifier means identifying clusters.

Note that the description of the problem domain we gave in Section 4.2 lifted our representation from a discrete information system to $\mathbb{R}^n$ with a Euclidean distance measure in Equation (4.1). Note also that the k-NN hypothesis itself as defined Equation (4.2) is just the same as in Equation (8.2)!

Decision trees

In Chapter 5 we discovered an approach to an information gain-based heuristics search procedure for hierarchical clustering. The algorithms presented therein are based on discrete features, too. However, there exist extensions that are capable of working with real-valued features. They simply perform an internal quantisation by identifying relevant intervals. There are many algorithms for quantisation – ranging from a simple equal frequency binning to, again, entropy-based methods. But, basically, quantisation again is *clustering*, too.

Rough sets and learnability

In rough set theory the notion of upper and lower boundaries provides us with a beautiful vocabulary to circumscribe what in PAC learning we have called the ε-region. The definition of equivalence relations and all concepts required in rough set theory are *not* limited to finite sets, even though all examples were defined on finite domains. The equivalence class of natural numbers is a proper subset of the rational numbers that in turn is a proper subset of real numbers – and they all are at least denumerable infinite.

Exercise 8.8 (◊) Define a relation $Q \subseteq \mathbb{R} \times \mathbb{R}$ such that $[\![Q]\!]\mathbb{Q} = \mathbb{N}$ and $\langle\!|Q|\!\rangle\mathbb{Q} = \mathbb{R}$!

We also noted that $(\!|R|\!)c = \langle\!|R|\!\rangle c - [\![R]\!]c$ is the region of uncertainty around c and it is a straightforward idea to define

$$\mathrm{errset}_U(\mathbf{R}, t) := \{x \in (\!|\mathbf{R}|\!)c : x \notin \{x \in U : t(x) = \mathbf{1}\}\}.$$

But what about the distance of an object from the actual boundary of the concept? In the rough set approach there are only nominal class values, no ordinals. And if there is no (given) order, there is no (canonical) distance. But there is a *natural order*. Keeping in mind one of the baselines of this book, discernability is what makes knowledge. Accordingly, two objects are the more similar, the more knowledge it requires to distinguish between them. Therefore, *the minimal number of relations* $|\mathbf{P}|$ we need to add to $\mathbf{R}$ such that

$$x \in c \Longrightarrow x \in [\![\mathbf{P} \cup \mathbf{R}]\!]c$$

can be taken as one indicator of similarity. A measure based on this idea is very well suited for any bottom-up rough set classifier learning algorithm where (starting with an empty set or a known core) we add relations to specialise the hypothesis until it is "good" enough (which, in turn, can be estimated using any of the error measures described in Section 3.4).

Learnability and inductive logic programming

One of the most interesting topics in learning logic programs is the induction of recursive predicates. From the point of view of a logician, recursive predicates are self-resolving clauses. The unification involved in this process results in the construction of possibly infinite term structures. This problem can be solved only by examining Herbrand models or by strong syntactical biases. The introduction of these biases, whether it be the restriction to ground facts, to programs Π with only unit clauses in them, *ij*-determinacy, or any similar method, helps to draw a beautiful line between learning problems. Only a few inductive logic programming problems *are* PAC learnable; and they all require very strict assumptions in the form of the biases discussed in the chapter on inductive logic programming. In general, PAC learnability is known to be a very pessimistic concept: if there is a simple learning problem, it is PAC in most cases; if it is interesting, it is not PAC. Whenever we can formulate a hypothesis for which we cannot determine whether $h(x) = \mathbf{1}$ or $h(x) = \mathbf{0}$ in polynomial time for some $x \in U$, then *any* problem in representation space is not PAC learnable. As an example, consider the following little logic program that we assume some learning algorithm has generated to describe our hypothesis:

```
h(0, X, Y) :- Y is X + 1.
h(X, 0, Y) :- Z is X - 1, h(Z, 1, Y).
h(X, Y, Z) :-
    U is X - 1,
    V is Y - 1,
    h(X, V, W),
    h(U, W, Z).
```

Exercise 8.9 (◊) Check the validity of the hypothesis for the following triplets: $\langle 1, 1, 3\rangle$, $\langle 2, 2, 9\rangle$, $\langle 3, 3, 81\rangle$, and $\langle 4, 4, 6561\rangle$.

The argument of non-PACness is based on an important article that we shall rediscover in Section 8.3. Let us summarise:

A problem is learnable...
If there is an algorithm that can effectively (and efficiently) deliver a hypothesis solving the problem with a certain confidence and a certain maximum error.

But how do we learn in everyday life? If one problem is too big, we try to *divide and conquer*. That is, we try to break down the big problem into many small ones, each of which is simple to learn. Another method is to repeatedly learn the problem where in each iteration we focus on what we do not know yet.

8.2 Decomposing the learning problem

Imagine you want to learn a large set of facts for an exam. One method is to write down every single fact on a file card and then flip through the pile over and over again until you know them all. Usually, your collection will not cover all the topics, but it is a representative sample of all the questions that might occur in an exam.

This gives rise to several problems. Sometimes, you have too few examples cards to infer a model that is good enough (in terms of passing the exam). There are three different reasons. If you don't have enough cards, your hypothesis might be too general, it could be overfit, or it is simply bad because you picked the wrong set of cards. Sometimes, you have too many cards. This results in the problem of computational and representational complexity. With too many aspects or too many examples you are not able to find a hypothesis until examination day which sufficiently well describes what you need to know to pass. And, finally, it could be that your learning method is not appropriate for the problem, which means that *any* hypothesis is rather weak. But wouldn't it be a good idea to use *many* weak learners resulting in *many* weak hypotheses that (for example, by voting) then solve a new problem as a team? Yes! It is a good idea.

It is easier to learn a less complex problem than a very complicated one, and it is easier to learn from a smaller set of facts and within a smaller set of hypotheses. We examined the process of sampling in detail in Section 3.3. But it was not before Definition 3.70 that we began to think about a probably positive side-effect of the non-determinacy of $S_\mu(m,t)$. The first idea that comes to mind is called *subsampling*. It means to learn on subsets and then combine the classifiers for all the subsets to receive a classifier on the entire set. The problem is to find a method of combining all the classifiers $h_i = \texttt{Alg}(\mathbf{s}_i)$ with $\mathbf{s}_i \subset \mathbf{s} = S_\mu(m,t)$ to one single hypothesis h. There exist many methods for choosing $\mathbf{s}_i \subset \mathbf{s}$, and, as you can imagine, they all have different impacts on the final result. Either way, we use the term "subsampling" for any kind of systematic *downsampling* as, for example, k-th selection sampling. The second idea is *re-sampling*. It means that we learn a set of classifiers from *different samples* $\mathbf{s}_i = S_\mu(m, t)$. It means a repeated non-deterministic execution of $S_\mu(m, t)$, also resulting in a set of samples $\mathbf{s}_i$.[3]

Exercise 8.10 (◇) Give a short example for each of the three methods mentioned above and explain the differences.

8.2.1 Bagging

Bagging means to find a set of experts, form a single committee, and then present the problem to the committee rather than an individual expert.

> **Bagging**
> Bagging is a metalearning approach, where the same learning algorithm is presented a number of different samples each of which results in an individual predictor. The hypothesis is defined by an aggregation of all predictors.
> The idea behind bagging is to make learning simpler on subsets of the problem and to yield a better result by the "knowledge of majority".

If we have a sample $\mathbf{s}$ from which it is hard to learn a good hypothesis, then we generate a set of subsamples $\mathbf{s}_i$, learn hypotheses h_i (representing experts) from them, and then combine all the hypotheses to one (being the committee) that shall describe the whole sample. "Bagging" is an acronym formed from *bootstrapping* that refers to an initial process of forming a set of samples that is used for the subsequent process. After learning comes *aggregating*, which means that we have to combine all the hypotheses.

Aggregation of hypotheses, h_{agg}

Definition 8.11 — Aggregation of hypotheses, h_{agg}.
Let there be set of k samples $\mathbf{s}_i$, $i \in \mathbf{k}$. If cod(t) is numerical, the *aggregated* hypothesis is the *average* over all $h_i = \mathtt{Alg}(\mathbf{s}_i)$:

$$h_{agg}(x) = \frac{1}{k}\sum_{i=1}^{k} h_i(x) = \frac{1}{k}\sum_{i=1}^{k} \mathtt{Alg}(\mathbf{s}_i)(x). \tag{8.11}$$

[3] We have used the terms "subsampling" and "re-sampling" very informally. Sampling itself is a broad research field with strong links to the theory of information. In this diction we would state that downsampling comes along with a loss of bandwidth and, thus, information. One idea is to deliberately lose only those parts that cause confusion in learning and keep those from which we gain knowledge. In image recognition, edges are made explicit by increasing contrast – which means to throw away all nuances.

If t is nominal, that is, $\mathrm{cod}(t) = \{1, 2, \ldots, j\}$, the *aggregated* hypothesis is

$$h_{agg}(x) = \mathrm{mcv}_{\pi(2)}(\{\langle i, h_i(x)\rangle : i \in \mathbf{k}), \tag{8.12}$$

that is, delivers the answer j on which most h_i agree.[4] ●

With a given set of k (different) samples $\mathbf{s}_i$ the case is simple – basically, we are done with bagging. The problem is that usually we are supplied only *once* with a *fixed* sample $\mathbf{s} = S_\mu(m, t)$. To apply bagging on one single sample, we have to find a method by which we can *generate* a set $\{\mathbf{s}_i : i \in \mathbf{k}\}$. A simple method is to independently choose *subsets* of $\mathbf{s}$.

By our inductive hypothesis, ϕ on $\mathbf{s}$ approximates μ on U. Therefore it also should be preserved under the average of repeatedly *randomly* drawing subsets.

Definition 8.12 — Bootstrap approximation.
Given some sample $\mathbf{s}$ of length m, we define k data sets $\mathbf{s}_i, i \in \mathbf{k}$, each of length $m_i \leq m$. Every sample $\mathbf{s}_i$ contains m_i examples, all of which are drawn at random and with replacement. Note that if an example is drawn several times for $\mathbf{s}_i$, it appears only once in $\mathbf{s}_i$. ●

Bootstrap approximation

As a result of this procedure we now have a set of k different subsamples $\mathbf{s}_i$ from which we hope to form k different hypotheses h_i as well and from which we can define an aggregated hypothesis. This method makes use of two very important properties in our learning scenario:

1. Because $\mathbf{s}_i$ are drawn at random (i.e., presupposing a uniform distribution on $\mathbf{s}$) and because $\mathbf{s}$ is drawn with respect to μ, the average probability of an object x to occur in a sample $\mathbf{s}_i$ is $\phi(\{x\})$ (see Definition 3.33).
2. All $\mathbf{s}_i$ are nearly always pairwise different (this is an immediate conjecture of the previous observation).

Throughout the book we made another implicit assumption: for different samples, the same algorithm will produce different hypotheses as well (see Section 3.6 and Theorem 3.69).

This gives rise to a very important question: What does it take for a learning algorithm to deliver different hypotheses for different examples? And, even more important: Is the difference between different examples proportional to the difference between the resulting hypotheses?

[4] The most common value function mcv was defined in Equation (4.3). We need to collect all the results together with the number i of the predictor such that multiple occurrences in the set are preserved. The function $\pi(2)$ is simply the projection on the second element of the tuples.

Example 8.13 Imagine we observe sequences of objects from our running example – and the target function is a predictor for the colour value of any object in U. Again, a small representation shift on our underlying information system helps a lot:

colour	□	□	■	■	■
$\rho : U \rightarrow$ *Colour*	*white*	*light*	*grey*	*dark*	*black*
$\rho' : U \rightarrow [0, 1]$	0	$\frac{1}{4}$	$\frac{1}{2}$	$\frac{3}{4}$	1

Let $t : U^n \rightarrow [0, 1]$ with

$$t(\langle x_0, x_1, \ldots, x_{n-1}\rangle) = \frac{1}{n} \sum_{i \in \mathbf{n}} colour(x),$$

where n is an odd number. So t is simply the arithmetic mean of the greyscale values. Note that this value is a rational number from the interval $[0, 1]$, whereas all the values x_i are from the set $\left\{0, \frac{1}{4}, \frac{1}{2}, \frac{3}{4}, 1\right\}$. Let us now imagine that our hypothesis space contains only four hypotheses:

$$\begin{aligned} h(x)_0 &= 0 \\ h(x)_1 &= \mathrm{mcv}_{colour}(\{\langle i, colour(x_i)\rangle : i \in \mathbf{n}\}) \\ h(x)_2 &= \mu_{1/2}(\{\langle i, colour(x_i)\rangle : i \in \mathbf{n}\}) \\ h(x)_3 &= 1, \end{aligned}$$

which means that our learning algorithm can choose from only four predictors: the first one always predicts white, the second one the most common value, the third one the median, and the fourth one always predicts black. It is clear by intuition that for a *small* change in the supplied training sample the resulting hypotheses will not differ *too much*. Only with a very small sample size or large differences in the distribution of the target values between two samples $\mathbf{s}$ and $\mathbf{s}'$ could it happen that $\mathtt{Alg}(\mathbf{s}) = h_0$ and $\mathtt{Alg}(\mathbf{s}') = h_3$.

Exercise 8.14 (♦) This exercise requires the reader to be familier with statistics (but then it should be easy). Can you give an estimate for the expected (maximum) error of hypotheses h_0, h_1, h_2, and h_3? For the interested reader we suggest reading up on Chebychev's theorem in measure theory.

Example 8.15 Multi-layer perceptrons are universal function approximators that for a small change in their input produce only a small change in the output. However, only a small change in the presented sample can result in drastically different hypotheses (sometimes even by only rearranging the example sequences); see Breiman (1996).

The property of "local robustness" against changes in the presented samples is known as *stability*:

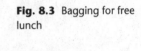

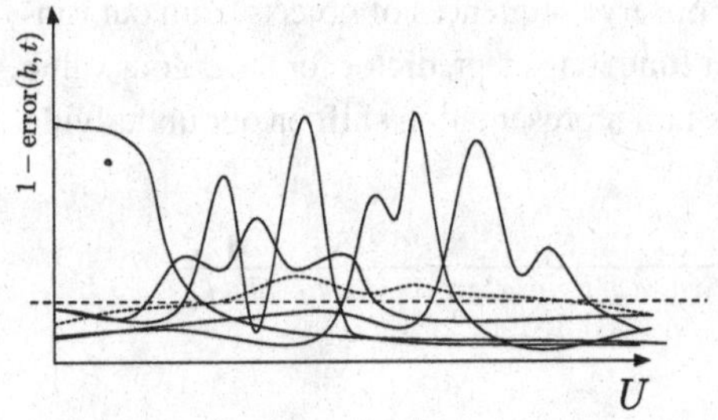

Fig. 8.3 Bagging for free lunch

Stability of learning algorithms

Definition 8.16 — Stability of learning algorithms.
An algorithm `Alg` is called *stable* if for a "small" change from **s** to **s**′,

$$\texttt{Alg}(\mathbf{s}) = h \approx h' = \texttt{Alg}(\mathbf{s}'). \tag{8.13}$$

`Alg` is called *unstable* if a small change in **s** results in a large change of the predictive behaviour of h. ●

Because t remains constant, two hypotheses h and h' delivered by an *unstable* algorithm have different errors on one common test set. In allusion to the no-free-lunch theorem, the situation can be illustrated as in Figure 8.3. An unstable base learner will produce many hypotheses that specialise on different parts of the universe. And, in sum, there are "specialists" for nearly every subset of the domain, which in a process of aggregation together with a majority of all other hypotheses will more likely come to a correct prediction. We now circumstantiate the intuitive understanding of bagging with a (slightly simplified) version of the argument in Breiman (1994).

Assume there is a sample $\mathbf{s} = S_\mu(m, t)$ (drawn with respect to and representing μ). Let cod(t) be numerical. By Definition 3.44, we choose the quadratic error measure for numerical values as in Equation (3.26). Then, the aggregated hypothesis h_{agg} is an *average* predictor for μ learned on a sample with distribution ν:

$$h_{agg}(x) = E_\nu(h(x)), \tag{8.14}$$

where E_ν denotes the expected (target) value for x based on the distribution on **s**. Bagging increases the quality of learning if it reduces the expected error of the hypothesis. Therefore, let us take a look at errors:

$$\text{error}_s(h, t) \quad = \quad E_\nu(E_\mu(\text{dist}(t(x), h(x))))$$

and the error of h_{agg} is

$$\text{error}_s(h_{agg}, t) \quad = \quad E_\mu(\text{dist}(t(x), E_\nu(h(x))).$$

With some knowledge of statistics, this leads to the following inequality:

$$\text{error}_s(h_{agg}, t) \leq \text{error}_s(h, t) \tag{8.15}$$

The less equal the both sides are, the lower is h_{agg}'s mean squared error in relation to that of h. And this explains why bagging works for unstable learners only. Let $\mathbf{s}_i$, $i \in \mathbf{k}$, be a sequence of similar, but different samples:

- If **A** is stable, all h_i will be similar to h_{agg} and both sides of the inequality are nearly *equal*.
- If **A** is unstable, we have an increasing chance of *different* h_i. The more of them that differ to an increasing extent, the more the right side increases over the left.

The more μ differs from the distribution ν on the sample, the more likely $\mathbf{s}_i$ will differ from $\mathbf{s}$. Accordingly, the improvement by bagging depends on the stability/instability turnover point of `Alg` – and this point depends on μ, the size m of $\mathbf{s}$, the difference between μ and ν, and, finally, `Alg` itself. If, however, some $h = \texttt{Alg}(\mathbf{s})$ is nearly optimal, then no bagging will improve the results.

Bagging

Bagging is a very simple method that allows one to improve learning results by aggregating several partial hypotheses. It works for unstable algorithms.

8.3 Improving by focusing on errors

Consider again the scenario of learning from a set of file cards. It is a good idea to learn subsets as we have seen in the previous section. But nobody does. What we do instead is some kind of *boosting*:

Boosting

Boosting means to iterate the learning process where in each iteration we put more emphasis on the objects that we were not able to describe properly in the previous iteration.

The idea behind ensemble learning – whether bagging or boosting – is that in general it is much more complicated to learn in one shot rather than by divide-and-conquer. When trying to learn several subproblems in parallel, there is the risk of putting effort in learning the same thing twice because one learner does not know what the other does. This is an argument for an iterated learning approach. The second argument is that one usually focuses on what still has to be done rather than what we have already accomplished. Such a general principle can be applied to *all* learning problems and *all* learning algorithms (called *base learners*) in a boosting approach. Let us reformulate the knowledge box from above with a small touch of formal terminology.

Definition 8.17 — Boosting algorithm. Boosting algorithm

A *boosting algorithm* repeatedly calls a (weak) *base learner* that produces a locally accurate but globally bad hypothesis with a *different* sample each time. The result is a sequence of hypotheses where all the errors we made in a step i have an increased probability of being picked as a learning example in step $i+1$:

If $x \in \text{errset}_s(h_i, t)$, then

$$\phi\left(\left\{\mathbf{s}_i : \begin{array}{c}\langle x, t(x)\rangle \in \mathbf{s}_i \wedge \\ \mathbf{s}_i :\in S(m,t)^i\end{array}\right\}\right) \leq \phi\left(\left\{\mathbf{s}_{i+1} : \begin{array}{c}\langle x, t(x)\rangle \in \mathbf{s}_{i+1} \wedge \\ \mathbf{s}_{i+1} :\in S(m,t)^{i+1}\end{array}\right\}\right), \quad (8.16)$$

where $S(m,t)^k$ denotes the set of all samples that are drawn by $S_\mu(m,t)$ in the k-th iteration. This means that examples that we cannot classify correctly will be dealt with in the next step with increasing probability. ●

Note that ϕ is a distribution over a set of samples as elementary events whereas μ is a distribution over U. As we know, it is μ that determines the behaviour of $S_\mu(m,t)$, and the expression in Equation (8.16) actually states that μ has to change from step i to $i+1$ because it is the "importance" of some x that influences the behaviour of the learning algorithm or the choice of samples submitted to this algorithm.

But even if we know *how* to change μ, we couldn't – because we don't know what to change. At this point the idea of subsampling comes in handy. We assume that we have *one* single fixed sample $\mathbf{s} = S_\mu(m,t)$. Then we work with a distribution ϕ on this sample rather than with μ on U.

None of the algorithms we have discussed so far made use of any additional information such as a distribution of the sample. However, there are many such algorithms; just imagine an explicit weight value that, for example, locally distorts a distance measure in a k-means clustering algorithm. Then, centroids would not just wander to the plain centre of gravity in the scenario as shown in Figure 4.2, but they would be drawn more into the direction of the "heavy weights".

If the base learner does *not* make use of the probability distribution over $\mathbf{s}$, then we can simply simulate this by subsampling with $\mathbf{s}_i$ drawn from $\mathbf{s}$ with respect to the changing distribution. We still have to decide what the initial probability distribution ϕ_0 shall look like. The simplest way is to assume an independent identical distribution.[5] Based on this choice, we can now examine a first version of a boosting algorithm as introduced by Schapire (1990). First, we need to redefine $\text{cod}(t) := \{-1, 1\}$ for arithmetic reasons. Then we assume there is a base learning

[5] Even though this *appears* to be an unbiased choice, it is not. There is no qualitative difference between the assumption of i.i.d. and a binomial distribution or any other.

Fig. 8.4 AdaBoost.BO (Schapire 1990, 2002)

```
i := 0; s := S_μ(m, t); φ_0 := i.i.d.
WHILE (i < k) DO
{   choose α_i ∈ ℝ;
    h_i := Alg(φ_i, s);
    ∀ ⟨x, t(x)⟩ ∈ s : φ_{i+1}({x}) := (1/ν_i) φ_i({x})^{−α_i h_i(x) t(x)};
    i := i + 1;
}
return(h_agg := sgn Σ_{i∈k} α_i h_i(x))
```

algorithm Alg that is better than random. Such a learning algorithm is called a *weak learner*. We define

$$\forall e \in \mathbf{s} : \phi_0(\{e\}) := \frac{1}{m}. \tag{8.17}$$

Then we iterate Alg k times and after the i-th iteration define ϕ_{i+1} by increasing $\phi_i(\{\langle x, t(x)\rangle\})$ if $x \in \text{errset}_s(h_i, t)$ and then normalise using a factor $\frac{1}{\nu_i}$ to ensure that ϕ_{i+1} is a proper probability distribution again. The new probability value of such an object is defined in terms of its old probability, an adaptation value, and the difference of h_i and t measured in terms of their product (remember that we defined $\text{cod}(t) = \{-1, 1\}$). Then Alg is called again – either on the same sample with the new distribution or on a new sample that is drawn with respect to the new distribution. The process ends after k rounds and the result is the average of all hypotheses: -1 if the weighted sum of all hypotheses' answers is negative and 1 otherwise. The pseudo-code of this algorithm (called *AdaBoost.BO*) is shown in Figure 8.4.

Example 8.18 Imagine the following artificial case, which is just to illustrate the boosting mechanism (we neglect α_i and simply produce a new i.i.d. ϕ_{i+1} on the previously wrongly classified examples): $s = \{●, △, ■, □\}$ and $t(x) = \mathbf{1} :\Longleftrightarrow$ *colour*$(x) =$ *black*. Let $\phi_0(\{x\}) = \frac{1}{m} = \frac{1}{4}$. In this case, let us assume that Alg delivers a hypothesis h_0 when presented $\mathbf{s}_0 = \{\langle x, t(x)\rangle : x \in s\}$:

s	●	△	■	□
t	1	-1	1	-1
ϕ_0	$\frac{1}{4}$	$\frac{1}{4}$	$\frac{1}{4}$	$\frac{1}{4}$
h_0	1	1	-1	1

The error set is $\text{errset}_s(h_0, t) = \{△, ■, □\}$. We have h_0, which is correct on ●, and now repeat learning on a new sample:

s	●	△	■	□
t	1	-1	1	-1
ϕ_1	0	$\frac{1}{3}$	$\frac{1}{3}$	$\frac{1}{3}$
h_1	1	-1	1	1

such that the error set of h_1 is $\{\square\}$. Therefore, in the second step,

s	●	△	■	□
t	1	−1	1	−1
ϕ_2	0	0	0	1
h_2	1	−1	−1	1

But if `Alg` still is not able to learn □, then it does not change anything anymore. Let us aggregate now:

s	●	△	■	□
t	1	−1	1	−1
$\sum h_i$	$1+1+1$	$1-1-1$	$-1+1+1$	$1+1+1$
	3	−1	1	3
h_{agg}	1	−1	1	1

This is of course an oversimplified example, because it assumes that in the $i+1$-st run `Alg` knows that it simply shall copy the answer of h_i for all objects that have a probability of 0.

At the very beginning we stated that there is no real difference between learning a binary problem and learning a nominal problem. The argument was that we can shift a representation from a nominal function $t_N : U \to \mathbf{k}$ to k binary functions $t_i : U \to \mathbf{2}$ with $t_i(x) = \mathbf{1} :\Longleftrightarrow t(x) = i$. There are two boosting algorithms that differ slightly in how they cope with nominal target value sets. The first one suffices to show the most important property of boosting:

The advantage of boosting

Let there be a weak base learning algorithm that in k turns produces an error of $\text{error}_s^{\phi_i}(h_i, t) \leq \frac{1}{2}$ on the *training sample*. Then there exists an upper bound for the error of the aggregated hypothesis that drops exponentially in the number of iterations.

The major improvement in AdaBoost.M1 is that it has a bailout option if the error of the base learner *increases* above $\frac{1}{2}$ and that the entire sample error of the hypothesis is taken into account. The error of a hypothesis h_i is the probability weighted sum of all false predictions:

$$err_i := \text{error}_s^{\phi_i}(h_i, t), \tag{8.18}$$

as defined in Equation (3.30), and a binary distance measure as in Equation (3.27). If this error is larger than $\frac{1}{2}$, the procedure terminates immediately (otherwise, it would be an ever increasing error). Then ϕ_i is changed by a factor $\frac{err_i}{1-err_i}$ on every false prediction of h_i. The rest of the algorithm is just about the same as AdaBoost.B0, except, of course, for the final hypothesis. It is simply the response for which the cumulated error is minimal. The pseudo-code is shown in Figure 8.5. To see how ϕ_i changes in AdaBoost.M1 over time, we use the following example.

Fig. 8.5 AdaBoost.M1 (Freund and Schapire 1996)

```
i := 0; s := S_μ(m, t); φ_0 := i.i.d.
WHILE (i < k) DO
{
    h_i := Alg(φ_i, s);
    err_i := φ_i(errset_s(h_t, t));
    IF err_i > 1/2 THEN k := i − 1 ; break;
    α_i := err_i/(1 − err_i)
    FORALL x ∈ s DO
    {  IF (h_i(x) ≠ t(x)) THEN
          φ_{i+1}({x}) := (α_i/ν_i) φ_i({x});
       ELSE
          φ_{i+1}({x}) := (1/ν_i) φ_i({x});
       ENDIF
    }
}
return (h_agg(x) = arg max_c {(Σ_{i∈k} ln 1/α_i) : h_i(x) = c})
```

Note that just as in AdaBoost.B0, the call of Alg with information ϕ_i can be simulated by subsampling ($h_i :=$ Alg$(S_{\phi_i}(m', t))$ on the base set s of $\mathbf{s}$).

Example 8.19 This time, we have a set of 12 objects and wrong predictions for every odd integer in the i-th iteration.

$x \in s$	$h_i(x) = t(x)$	ϕ_i	$\alpha_i \cdot \phi_i$	ϕ_{i+1}
1	0	0.055	0.128	0.088
2	1	0.100	0.100	0.069
3	0	0.025	0.058	0.040
4	1	0.200	0.200	0.277
5	0	0.025	0.058	0.040
6	1	0.155	0.155	0.107
7	0	0.085	0.198	0.137
8	1	0.020	0.020	0.014
9	0	0.030	0.070	0.048
10	1	0.150	0.150	0.103
11	0	0.125	0.291	0.201
12	1	0.025	0.025	0.017

The error of h_i is $err_i = 0.3$. Accordingly, $\alpha_i = 0.43$ and $\nu_i = 1.45$. Multiplication with ϕ_i then gives ϕ_{i+1}, as in the last column.

We end this rather theoretical excursion to ensemble learning by the boosting theorem. Suppose that $err_i \leq \frac{1}{2}$ for all $i \in \mathbf{k}$ and let $\delta_i = \frac{1}{2} - err_i$. Then,

$$\begin{aligned}\text{error}_s(h_{agg}, t) &= \frac{|\{i : h_{agg}(x_i) \neq t(x_i)\}|}{m} \\ &\leq \prod_{i \in \mathbf{k}} \sqrt{1 - 4\delta_i^2} \\ &\leq e^{\left(-2 \sum_{i \in \mathbf{k}} \delta_i^2\right)}.\end{aligned}$$

This means that in this case the error of the aggregated hypothesis can be reduced with increasing iterations; actually, the error converges exponentially in the number of iterations against zero. The downside of this really impressive result is that the error we are talking about is the error on the training sample $\mathbf{s}_{\text{train}}$. Therefore, the entire boosting approach depends on the adequacy of the chosen sample, and a maximum accuracy on this sample will nearly always lead to overfitting and much less impressive results on a test set. But, supposing the sample is chosen wisely, it holds that whenever the error on the training sample decreases, it does so on any other sample (hopefully) (Freund and Schapire 1996).

In general, it is a good idea to think of boosting as

- Repeated sub- or resampling on a set of observations with
- A given (unknown) distribution *measure* on the entities being observed
- And a *deliberate adaptive sampling bias* by an error-dependent change of the probability distribution ϕ that is taken for sampling or as additional knowledge for `Alg`.

In many cases, boosting helps a lot (for both binary and nominal problems), but it may require some changes the base learner. A simple case is where we simulate $\texttt{Alg}(\phi, \mathbf{s})$ by $\texttt{Alg}(S_\phi(m, t))$. An extension of AdaBoost.M1, called AdaBoost.M2, explicitly requires `Alg` to work with ϕ_i and to deliver a value in $[0, 1]$ as a measure of plausibility back to the boosting algorithm as it is required for more sophisticated changes in ϕ_{i+1}.

8.4 A relational view on ensemble learning

So why bagging and boosting and why all those measures, probabilities, and expectation values? Knowledge about a square means to be able to say that □ is a square and △ is not. And a ◇ is not a □ as a ○ is not a ▲. There is no probably, there is no approximately, and there is no lucky sampling in relational knowledge discovery. Right? Wrong!

8.4.1 Dividing the sample set

Bagging means learning classifiers that specialise on subsets of the sample. Why shouldn't we try and learn rough set classifiers for subsets of the universe? This time, let us take a closer look at rough set classifiers

Relational bagging

In a relational setting, bagging means that for a set of k subsamples $\mathbf{s}_i$ of size $m' \leq m$, `Alg` computes k hypotheses $\mathbf{P}_i$ approximating $c_i := s_i \cap c$ with $s_i = \{x : \langle x, t(x) \rangle \in \mathbf{s}_i\}$. The most important thing to know before asking whether a certain learning algorithm can benefit from bagging is whether the algorithm is stable. Finding a rough set classifier is an *unstable* procedure.

Exercise 8.20 (◊) Give an example.

Once we have found k hypotheses, we need to aggregate them. Assume there is a function *agg* and we want

$$\mathbf{P}_{agg} := agg(\{\mathbf{P}_i : i \in \mathbf{k}\}) \approx t.$$

Because we are dealing with rough classifiers, we have a weak and a strong interpretation of target class predictions:

$t(x)$	**0**	**1**
rough	$x \notin [\![\mathbf{P}_{agg}]\!]c$	$x \in (\!|\mathbf{P}_{agg}|\!)c$
strict	$x \notin (\!|\mathbf{P}_{agg}|\!)c$	$x \in [\![\mathbf{P}_{agg}]\!]c$

This means that if $x \in (\!|\mathbf{P}_{agg}|\!)$, the rough classifier could answer "$x \in c$", because if x is in the boundary region, it is in the upper approximation, too. Also, the classifier could answer "$x \notin c$", because the boundary region has an empty intersection with the lower approximation. For the same reason, the strict predictor cannot deliver an answer because the boundary region is exactly the region whose elements are neither outside the upper approximation nor inside the lower. In Equation (6.9) we defined the rough characteristic function with three values. Using this definition, k sets of equivalence relations model k characteristic functions on k sets $c_i \subseteq c$. Without a further analysis of the c_i we could build an aggregated classifier function by voting again:

$$\chi_{agg}(c)(x) := \mathrm{mcv}_{\pi_2} \{\langle i, \chi_i(c_i)(x) \rangle : i \in \mathbf{k}\}. \tag{8.19}$$

Another, very simple, method is

$$h_{agg}(x) := \begin{cases} \mathbf{1}, & \text{if } x \in \bigcup_{i \in \mathbf{k}} [\![\mathbf{P}_i]\!]c_i \\ \mathbf{1/2}, & \text{if } x \in \left(\bigcup_{i \in \mathbf{k}} (\!|\mathbf{P}_i|\!)c_i\right) - \left(\bigcup_{i \in \mathbf{k}} [\![\mathbf{P}_i]\!]c_i\right) \\ \mathbf{0}, & \text{else.} \end{cases} \tag{8.20}$$

Exercise 8.21 (◊) Change the definition of h_{agg} by replacing $\bigcup$ with $\bigcap$ or by using a few more set operations. Are they equivalent? What are the differences?

What does bagging mean for the relation sets? Let us assume that every c_i is definable. Then there exist reducts $\mathbf{P}_i \in \mathrm{Red}_{c_i}(\mathbf{R})$ that define c_i, but even if $\bigcup_{i \in \mathbf{k}} c_i = c$, it is *not* true that

$$\bigcup_{i=1}^{k} \mathbf{P}_i \in \mathrm{Red}_c(\mathbf{R}). \tag{8.21}$$

The problem here is that reducts are not unique: $\text{Red}_{c_i}(\mathbf{R}) = \{\mathbf{P}_i^1, \mathbf{P}_i^2, \ldots, \mathbf{P}_i^{r_i}\}$. Furthermore, the union of two (different) reducts is never a reduct. Cores are unique, but – if there are at least two disjoint reducts – they can be empty, which is not very helpful either. If we try to construct a reduct of **R** for c by some operations on the cores of $\mathbf{P}_i$, it might be the case that some cores themselves are empty, or that two of them are disjoint, which leaves the candidate for the core of **R** for c empty (even if it is not). All we can state for sure is that

$$\text{whenever } R \in \text{Cor}_{c_i}(\mathbf{R}) \text{ then } R \in \text{Cor}_c(\mathbf{R}). \tag{8.22}$$

Because the core $\text{Cor}_{c_i}(\mathbf{R})$ can be empty, we define a table $T(i,j) = |\{R \in \text{Red}_{c_j}(\mathbf{R}) : R \in \mathbf{P}_i\}|$ with $1 \leq j \leq k$ and $1 \leq i \leq |\text{Red}_{c_j}(\mathbf{R})|$. If $T(i,j) = |\text{Red}_{c_j}(\mathbf{R})|$, then R_i must be an element of $\text{Cor}_c(\mathbf{R})$. Computing this table is computationally infeasible because we would have to check all reducts for all c_i. Accordingly, there is no canonical efficient bottom-up implementation to determine a core from reducts using a bagging-like method.

If, on the other hand, we try to construct reducts from cores (i.e., top-down), we can apply a very simple method (because cores are unique). For a set s of objects, the discernability matrix $\mathbb{D}(\mathbf{P})$ contains the names of all relations by which x_i and x_j can be discriminated. If for some i,j it holds that $D(i,j) = \{R\}$, then R must be an element of $\text{Cor}_s(\mathbf{F})$, because then R is the *only* relation by which x_i and x_j can be discriminated. The runtime complexity of computing the core in this way is $\mathcal{O}(\frac{1}{2}|\mathbf{R}|m^2)$, where the worst case is $\text{Cor}_c(\mathbf{R}) = \mathbf{R}$. Using the same method in bagging with k bags of size m', we obtain $\mathcal{O}(\frac{1}{2}|\mathbf{R}|n(m')^2)$. Furthermore, the algorithm in Figure 8.6 benefits from parallel computations of smaller discernability matrices.

The complexity of finding reducts depends on the number of relations and the size of the data set. But it also depends on the number k of bags one chooses, the number m' of the size of the smaller samples, and the "validity" of the hypotheses that are generated. The converse implication of Equation (8.22),

$$R \notin \text{Cor}_{c_i}(\mathbf{R}) \Longrightarrow R \notin \text{Cor}_c(\mathbf{R}), \tag{8.23}$$

becomes true only for $m' \approx m$ and, until $m' = m$, large k.

Clusters and trees

The popularity of clustering in statistical domains and the simplicity of the bagging procedure have led to a widespread combination of the two methods; especially in data mining scenarios. There even exists a library for bagged clustering based on Leisch (1999) with

```
01   PROC relBag (F, s, k, M)
02   {   H := F; C = {}
03       FOREACH(i ∈ k)
04       {   sᵢ := randomselect(M, s);
05           Cᵢ := core(sᵢ, H);
06           H := H − Cᵢ; C := H + Cᵢ;                    % + denotes concatenation
07       };
08       H := sortby(β, H);
09       WHILE (errorₜ(C, s) ≥ ε ∨ H = {})
10       {   R := first(H); R := tail(H);
11           IF (errorₜ(C, s) > errorₜ(C ∪ {R}, s)) THEN {C := C + {R}};
12           H := R;
13       }
14       return (C);
15   }
```

Fig. 8.6 Relational bagging

an application to market segmentation (Dolnicar and Leisch 2000). Dudoit and Fridlyand (2003) describe an application in the area of bio-informatics, a discipline of increasing importance and with a strong background in statistical methods. Accordingly, the authors stress the use of bagging in reducing the variation over several runs of clustering algorithms by the averaging behaviour of bagging.

Decision tree induction is, as we have seen, basically the same as recursive partitioning with heuristic guidance. Tree induction algorithms have been used extensively in empirical evaluations of both bagging and boosting (Freund and Schapire 1996; Quinlan 1996, 2001).

Bagging for inductive logic programming

Averaging out a large variance on hypotheses is very important in statistical approaches. Another prime candidate for bagging is inductive logic programming. The first reason is that there are no probabilities in Horn logic, which makes bagging easier than boosting in a straightforward implementation. One of the biggest problems in inductive logic programming is searching. FOIL does an information gain–guided search (see Section 7.3) whereas PROGOL uses an A^*-like algorithm with heuristics described in Section 7.4.3. All these algorithms start off with a single sample – and have to carry out the search sequentially, considering, evaluating, and refining (or refusing) each hypothesis after another. By choosing several *subsets* of the sample one can try and induce a hypothesis for each of these subsets. Exactly this idea is described and implemented by Page et al. (2002) and, subsequently, in Mooney et al. (2004).

8.4.2 Focusing on errors

In a relational boosting approach we do not have a probability distribution that we could adjust to focus on learning error sets.

Instead of boosting the probability of those examples that are misclassified by a hypothesis h_i, we only remove the set of already correctly classified objects from the set of entities to be taken into consideration; that is, we restrict the search for a hypothesis to what in rough set theory is the boundary region.

Boosting rough sets

Given a hypothesis **H**, the problem is to find a relation R that is a good candidate to rule out as many elements from the boundary region as possible by adding or removing it from **H**.

This can be done only heuristically and, as such, is a source of bias. The algorithm shown in Figure 8.7 uses a function *sortby* to pick the "best" relation (determined by the heuristic function β). One possible heuristics could be information gain; there are many other, computationally even cheaper methods (e.g., choosing an R whose index has a certain property). Another, more expensive, method is to validate R against a test sample $\mathbf{s}_{\text{test}}$ and choose $\beta(R) = \text{error}_t(R, \mathbf{s}_{\text{test}})^{-1}$. To learn c from $\mathbf{F}$ we choose $R \in \mathbf{F}$ with $R = \arg\max\{\beta(R) : R \in \mathbf{F}\}$, hoping that it generates a fine-grained partition that has a minimal boundary region on the target concept. We then iterate this process on the boundary region only.

Note that – in contrast to standard boosting – we do not keep a sequence of hypotheses, but we iteratively build a reduct starting from the empty set. As such, it is a bottom-up learning algorithm.

```
PROC relBoost (H, s)
{ IF (good_enough(H)) THEN return(H);
  C := sortby(β, F − H);
  WHILE (error_t(H, s) ≥ ε)
  { C =: [C|R];
    IF(error_t(H ∪ C, s) < error_t(H, s)) THEN
    { relBoost(H ∪ C, errset_t(H ∪ C, s)); }
    ELSE
    { return(H ∪ relBoost(R, errset_t(H ∪ C, s)); }
  }
  return(⊥);
}
```

Fig. 8.7 Relational "boosting" by re-learning errors only

Boosting clusters and trees

Just as in bagging, the increasing popularity of boosting showed the highest impact on otherwise popular knowledge discovery methods (see the paragraph on clusters and trees in Section 8.4.1). A pretty recent development and evaluation of an application of boosting to clustering is described in Frossyniotis et al. (2004). Recall also that boosting is a trick to add more information to a learning problem than what it is explicitly provided with. A distribution μ, which we assume to be unknown, basically is nothing but *knowledge*. For example, for each (target) concept in $\mathfrak{U}$ we can add a dimension (i.e., feature) to the underlying information system $\mathfrak{I}$, each of which encodes the characteristic function of the concept. Then, each such feature defines a distribution itself with

$$\phi_c(\{x\}) = \begin{cases} \frac{1}{m}, & \text{if } x \in c \\ 0, & \text{else.} \end{cases}$$

As a result, the *product* space carries all the information as it inherits the product measure. The task of learning c then becomes, statistically speaking, the task of learning ϕ_c. Adding such knowledge to the learning algorithm by expanding Alg(**s**) to Alg(ϕ_c,**s**) (as in line 4 of the algorithms in Figures 8.4 and 8.5) or by subsampling with respect to ϕ_c may help to improve the quality of the resulting hypothesis. Another kind of knowledge is "local equivalence", which means that we are not able to describe an entire equivalence class but only the equivalence between selected pairs of objects. This is known as *linkage* in clustering. A relational point of view is that a linkage relation (or its dual concept, a *non-linkage*) represents subsets of equivalence relations. The search for equivalence relations, then, is the search for so-called *minimal rectangles*, which are difunctional relations (Jaoua et al. 2009). Adding reflexivity to them (which is a safe thing to do as we can assume every single object to be linked to itself) then induces an equivalence relation (see Section 2.1.7). This additional knowledge (which, again, can be expressed in terms of a distribution on the set of all pairs of objects) is used for the boosted clustering method described in Liu et al. (2007).

8.5 Summary

We have seen that PAC learning is a very pessimistic view on knowledge discovery but it reflects very well what knowledge discovery is about.

The learning dilemma

If a problem is finite, it can be solved by enumeration – which cannot really be considered to be a procedure that builds on what we would call *knowledge*.

In general, the more *interesting* a problem is, the more *complex* it is, too. One aspect of the *interestingness* of knowledge is the sheer *need* for it. And the stronger the need, the more likely it is that the knowledge is not trivial and well hidden – if it exists at all.

The morale is: What we know or what we can learn with small effort is not interesting – and anything that is interesting is hard to learn.

In the references you will quite often find the term "data mining" – and with the recent advent (or rediscovery) of relational methods "relational data mining" as well. People often explain this term by the metaphor of mining for rare diamonds in a huge pile of gravel. To us, knowledge discovery means finding answers to the following questions:

- Is there a cognoscible[6] structure in the pile of gravel?
- If so, can this structure be explained in terms of our knowledge?
- And if we then find something else, are we able to explain why we found it, and where would be a promising region to look for another piece?

None of these problems are easy. In this chapter we have described two ensemble-techniques and their applications to relational methods. Both of them are *divide-and-conquer* strategies: *Bagging* means to divide the pile into several heaps and analyse each of them on its own. *Boosting* means to start off with a simple random search in the pile that in its behaviour is constantly being refined. If our hypothesis is good enough for a certain part of the pile, we know we can search it efficiently later on and focus on finding another, refined technique that will increase the current efficiency on the remaining part of the pile.

This metaphor, in contrast to the mining metaphor, also illustrates the difference between knowledge discovery and data mining:

Mining for information and the discovery of knowledge

Instead of digging for valuable *pieces* of information in a mine of data, knowledge discovery is about finding *concepts* and *procedures* that describe whether mining will discover something at all – and, if so, where it would be best to dig first.

6 Note that one synonym for "cognoscible" is "discernible"!

Chapter 9
The logic of knowledge

If we assume knowledge to be what it takes to make rational decisions, then knowledge is not logic. It is not even logic when we assume it is representable in an information system.

Many decisions (and every answer to a question *is* a decision) are far from being discrete, deterministic, or deductively comprehensible.

Yet, the simplest question we can ask is, "Is *x* equal to *y*?" And it takes knowledge in the form of the ability to discern different things from each other to decide whether one should answer "Yes" or "No".

During the last decades, machine learning evolved from theories of reasoning in artificial intelligence to an essential component of software systems. Statistical methods outperform logic-based approaches in most application domains – and with increasing computational power it has become possible to *generate and test* classifiers. As a more sophisticated approach, *ensemble learning* implements divide-and-conquer strategies on the learning problem. With the further increase of data collections (e.g., data warehouses), the problem we are facing is not concerned with *how* we can induce a classifier that supports our model assumptions on the data but rather to understand *what* kind of information there actually *is*. In machine learning, this approach is known as *knowledge discovery*.

9.1 Knowledge representation

Because we are used to describing knowledge in the language of terminologic logic, we quite often identify knowledge representation with logic models. In Chapter 3 we saw that knowledge can be represented in many, many different ways. Each representation formalism has its own advantages and disadvantages.

We may also find several alternative representations for one and the same set of knowledge. If there are two such alternatives, they can be equivalent – or not. If they are equivalent, we can argue that there is a lossless representation shift from one representation space into the other (and back). This is not just a fun thing to do; it is also of practical relevance. It can be that the kind of knowledge that we are looking for can be found much more easily in one representation system than in another. In such a case we would first translate the source representation into the one that is easy to work with, induce a hypothesis, and then – if we wish – translate it back into the original language.

If the two systems are *not* equivalent, then a representation shift is always conjoined to some loss of information. Such a loss can be deliberate for two reasons. First, if the loss is tolerable, then we can accept a weaker hypothesis. The level of tolerance is often defined by a trade-off between the loss of accuracy and the gain of efficiency. Second, loss can be useful (if we lose the right things). Imagine again the metaphor of searching for a diamond in a heap of gravel. The heap is the source representation. We now apply a lossy transform and use a huge fan to blow all the stones onto a large conveyor belt. This transform is lossy, because the strong air stream takes away all the dust and little pieces of gravel that are too light to be a valuable diamond.

Next, we ask ourselves where all the evidence comes from that we build our hypotheses upon. One of the most important terms we deal with was first described in Section 3.3, when we were talking about *samples*. Our quest for knowledge is *biased* in many, many ways. Some biases are due to the representation (one cannot express the number $\frac{x}{y}$ in $\mathbb{N}$ unless x is a multiple of y), and others are due to the samples or the method by which the samples are taken. Again, just as with representations of different advantages and disadvantages, biases are not always negative. If we know that the number we are looking for is $\frac{x}{y}$ with $x, y \in \mathbb{N}$, then there is no need to inspect all numbers in $\mathbb{R}$; it is sufficient to inspect $\mathbb{Q}$. And whenever $x \leq y$ we also know that $0 < \frac{x}{y} \leq 1$.

Finally, we ask ourselves what it means for a hypothesis to be "good". Goodness is just another bias – because we stop our search for the best hypothesis once the one we have found is good enough. On the other hand, it is by no means guaranteed that any artificial measure of quality (of which there are so many) reflects "adequacy", "suitability", or any kind of measure to describe whether it is meaningful in real life.

All of these concepts – representation, representation shifts, information loss, biases, and all the different measures of quality – could be very well described in terms of relations only.

9.2 Learning

This section consists of descriptions of several relational or logic learning paradigms:

- Clustering, where one wants to find a meaningful partitioning of the data set.
- Decision tree induction, which is about an efficient search for hierarchical clustering.
- Rough set data analysis as an unbiased and exhaustive approach for finding minimal sets of relations that suffice to describe the target concept.
- Inductive logic programming, which can be considered an improvement of the relational approaches where the extension of concepts in a relational description corresponds to the satisfaction set of a corresponding predicate definition.

The similarities are huge as the fact that we can describe all paradigms in less than one sentence suggests.

9.2.1 Clustering

Classification means to decide into which class c_i in a given classification "$\mathfrak{c} = \{c_i : i \in \mathbf{k}\}$ some object $x \in U$ belongs. Given a set of predefined clusters (i.e., a classification), then k – NN is a simple *voting* algorithm that assigns to x the same class identifier $i \in \mathbf{n}$ as most of the k-nearest neighbours of x have. The notion of "near" presupposes a distance measure – and there are many such measures. The simplest one is a binary measure we use in the evaluation of hypotheses as well. If two objects are the same, their distance is 0; otherwise, it is 1. Reducing a multi-class learning problem ($|\mathfrak{c}| > 2$) to n binary problems is not possible using this measure because we are not able to decide which classifier should be trusted if there are several that return 1. But if we can use a Euclidean measure, then the minimum distance of an object to all the cluster centroids can be taken as an aggregated hypothesis.[1]

Learning clusters means to learn equivalence classes by defining disjoint subsets of objects representing classes. It starts by randomly choosing class representatives: the random choice of centroids c_i. Then,

[1] This shows the connectedness of a relational representation, representation transforms, a clustering approach, and the notion of using a set of hypotheses to compute an aggregated hypothesis as coined by bagging.

for every object $x \in U$, the algorithm has to decide for which i it shall be true that $x \in [c_i]$. This decision is made by asking a distance measure again (see Figure 4.2). Relationally, the task to assign some x the correct class index i means to find the right minimal rectangle to which x belongs (see Section 8.4.2).

9.2.2 Decision trees

I hesitated about including the induction of decision trees in this book. After all, there are many other machine learning approaches that were not mentioned in this book: artificial neural networks, Bayesian reasoning, support vector machines, just to name a few. Even though decision tree induction makes use of an entropy-based heuristics, it is still a relational method. The resulting tree is just a "recipe" for classifying a new and unknown object along a hierarchy of partitions. Whether such a hierarchy is expressed in terms of a tree, by a concept hierarchy as in Figure 4.3, by a recursive relational notation as in Equation (7.26), or by a set of rules as in Section 5.5.2 – it is just a matter of personal preference. The only thing that makes decision tree induction a bit different from all other relational approaches is just that it does not work without biases – but *with* biases, it is one of the most efficient.

9.2.3 Rough sets

Rough set data analysis is, finally, relational learning without any bells and whistles. What makes it so special, though, is, first, the non-numerical method of representing vague membership and, more importantly, its framework for reasoning about sets of relations rather than about relations between objects. Decision tree induction does not "think" about dependencies between relations. It simply chooses the one that has the highest expected information gain in each step. When applying a rule-based post-pruning method, there is a nice effect showing that this greedy method is in fact myopic: If it wasn't, then rule-based post-pruning could never result in a forest (see Figure 5.9). Rough set data analysis has a broader view on the hypothesis space. If there are different alternatives for adding a relation P or Q to a set of relations $\mathbf{R}$ such that both $\llparenthesis \mathbf{R} \cup \{P\} \rrparenthesis c_i \subseteq \llparenthesis \mathbf{R} \rrparenthesis$ and $\llparenthesis \mathbf{R} \cup \{Q\} \rrparenthesis c_i \subseteq \llparenthesis \mathbf{R} \rrparenthesis$, then both $\mathbf{R} \cup \{P\}$ and $\mathbf{R} \cup \{Q\}$ are candidates for promising reducts. If c_i is just one of many classes in $\mathfrak{c}$, then the power of rough set data analysis lies in the comparison of the utility of P and Q in terms of $\mathfrak{c}$. Whereas decision tree induction simply chooses between P and Q with respect to their information content on c, we can take into account $[\![\{P\} \trianglelefteq \mathbf{R}]\!]\mathfrak{c}$ and its relation to $[\![\{Q\} \trianglelefteq \mathbf{R}]\!]\mathfrak{c}$. Another very important thing about rough set theory is that has been studied in connection with multi-valued and multi-modal logics (Orlowska 1993; Yao 2003; Düntsch 1997) and formal concept analysis (Xu et al. 2008; Düntsch et al. 2007).

9.2.4 Inductive logic programming

The last learning paradigm we discussed was inductive logic programming. It is by far the most powerful of all the approaches presented. Simple inductive logic programming learning problems are PAC learnable (Džeroski et al. 1992), but it is also, in terms of computational effort, the most expensive of all methods presented here. Especially when not restricted to Horn clauses – which is required when we want to work with a proper negation and a non-restricted logic representation language – then one has to abandon all hope. Similarly, the logic of negation as failure makes it difficult to properly define when a negative example is not implied by a theory. On the other hand, it is exactly this that brings about the idea of Heyting algebras as interpretations of logic programs and connects the semantics of logic programs to rough set theories. Understanding Horn theories as approximations is not a new idea (Kautz et al. 1995), but there were only few contributions from the inductive logic programming community that are mostly due to the generally rather negative results (e.g., Nock and Jappy 1998). Every $R \in \mathbf{F}$ also defines a binary predicate $r(x, f_R(x))$.The satisfaction set of r is the set of all instantiations of x for which r holds and whose meaning equals the corresponding R-equivalence class:

$$[x]_R = \{y \in U : r(y, f_R(x))\}.$$

To derive $r(x, v)$ from a given set of clauses Π, that is, $\Pi \cup H \vdash r(x, v)$, one needs to show that there is a correct answer substitution θ such that $(\Pi \cup H \cup \{\neg r(x, v)\})\theta \vdash \Box$. An optimal hypothesis H guarantees that

$$\forall\theta : r(X, f_R(X))\theta \iff (\Pi \cup H\{\neg r(X, V)\})\theta \vdash \Box. \tag{9.1}$$

Because $\vdash$ is correct but not complete, we are able to give a lower approximation of r where $[\![H]\!]r$ describes a subset of the satisfaction set of r:

$$[\![H]\!]r \quad :\iff \quad \{y : (\Pi \cup H \cup \{\neg r(X, V)\})\theta \vdash \Box\}. \tag{9.2}$$

A *Horn reduct* Π' of Π is a set of clauses where, for each clause $\varphi \in \Pi'$, there is a clause $\psi \in \Pi$ and a substitution θ such that $\varphi \subseteq \psi\theta$ and both Π and Π' induce the same theory. Translating the original definition of a reduct, $\Pi' \in \mathrm{Red}_s(\Pi)$ holds if $\Pi' \in \mathrm{Red}_s(\Pi)$ is true and the satisfaction set of Π' equals the satisfaction set of Π on s. As an example, let us consider the case of *literal dropping* and its relationship to building reducts. Let there be two clauses,

$$t(x,1) \leftarrow p_1(x,f_1(x)) \wedge \cdots \wedge p_k(x,f_k(x)) \wedge p_{k+1}(x,f_{k+1}(x)) \text{ and}$$
$$t(x,1) \leftarrow p_1(x,f_1(x)) \wedge \cdots \wedge p_k(x,f_k(x)).$$

Obviously, the former implies the latter. If the satisfaction sets of both are the same, then the second clause is a *reduct* of the first one by dropping one literal, or, equivalently, by dropping one feature or equivalence relation. If

$$t(x,1) \leftarrow p_1(x,a) \wedge p_2(x,b)$$
$$t(x,1) \leftarrow p_1(x,a) \wedge p_2(x,c),$$

one can induce $t(x,1) \leftarrow p_1(x,a) \wedge p_2(x,y)$ or even $t(x,1) \leftarrow p_1(x,a)$.

9.3 Summary

One of the main goals of this book is to present several paradigms of knowledge discovery in a unifying framework. This may result in a state of mild confusion – some students reported to me that it all appears to be the same anyway and I should stop repeating myself. Well, at a certain level of abstraction things *are* equal. By now, you know why: just drop all clusters except for one, prune your decision tree right after the root node, choose as a hypothesis the set of relations with only the universal relation in it or define a predicate with variables in the head only and an empty body. Then, everything seems to be just about the same.

But if everything appears to be just the same, then there are no differences – and this means that there is no knowledge available to discriminate different things from each other. So what we want to do in knowledge discovery is to analyse things as they are or, rather, things as they are represented. Then, by analysis of their representations and an underlying structure of representations, we can form hypotheses that help to group different objects into different classes. The problem is to define a method by which we can induce such a hypothesis.

There are several such methods. And, of course, the different algorithms are *not* the same. But they do share common properties. This offers two very important opportunities:

- If one looks at a problem from different perspectives, one is more likely to identify general issues in solving the problem. This can help to identify mistakes or indicate weaknesses in the different representations (and models or assumptions on the data or the algorithms).
- If one method can solve a certain problem with some difficulties and another method can solve another problem with some other difficulties, too – maybe

> they can profit from each other by changing problems, or, from the point of view of a programmer, change the paradigm rather than the problem.

The more knowledge one puts into something, the less new knowledge one can get out of it. Therefore, one should let the facts speak for themselves and build models on observation – rather than looking for examples where one hopes they would satisfy one's (biased) model.

> Take a look at it and make it wrong first.
> Then, take another look at it.
> And then, make it better.

Notation

This book uses its own nomenclature. To make all the different approaches comparable, I tried to put a certain system in the notation.

Fonts. The following fonts are used in this book. With a few exceptions, their meanings are

$\mathrm{a}, \mathrm{b}, \mathrm{c}, \ldots$	entities/atoms/objects, elements of a set
$\ldots, x, y, z$	variables (and also sets)
$\ldots, X, Y, Z$	variables (in Horn logic or as random variables)
$\ldots, f, g, h, \ldots$	functions
$\ldots, P, Q, R, \ldots$	relations
$\ldots, \mathbf{F}, \ldots, \mathbf{P}, \mathbf{Q}, \mathbf{R}, \ldots$	sets of relations
$\mathfrak{A}, \mathfrak{B}, \mathfrak{C}, \ldots$	structures like algebras or representation spaces
$\mathfrak{c}, \mathfrak{d}, \mathfrak{q}, \ldots$	sets of (disjoint) classes
$\alpha, \gamma, \delta, \ldots$	variables, constants, and parameters
$\varphi, \psi, \ldots, \kappa, \lambda, \nu, \ldots$	formulae and literals
μ, ϕ	measures and (probability) distributions
σ, θ, μ	substitutions and unifiers

Special sets. We deal with a few special sets and structures that have standard names and are used throughout the entire book.

The domain of a learning problem is denoted by $\mathfrak{D}$. It is represented in a representation space $\mathfrak{U}$ called the universe. The base set of $\mathfrak{U}$ is the set U. Similarly, algebras are denoted by capital fraktura letters, e.g., $\mathfrak{A}$. Their base sets are referred to by the corresponding uppercase italic Roman letters, A.

Sets in general are denoted by a simple small s; if we want a set to denote a certain subset of U with a distinguished meaning, we call it a class c. A set of classes is called a classification $\mathfrak{c}$.

Boldface upright numbers like $\mathbf{0}, \mathbf{1}, \mathbf{2}, \ldots, \mathbf{k}$, denote sets with 0, 1, 2, and k elements. The set of the truth values $\mathbf{0}$ and $\mathbf{1}$ is written $\mathbf{2}$. As usual, $\mathbb{N}, \mathbb{N}_0, \mathbb{Q}$, and $\mathbb{R}$ denote the natural numbers, the natural numbers with 0, and the rational and real numbers.

There is one set that is very important to us: it is the set of examples and it is called a sample. It consists of pairs of objects $x \in U$ and a target value and is written **s**. Given such a sample, s refers to the set of elements x in **s**.

Special variables. The length of a sample is the cardinality of **s**. The number of examples in a sample is $m = |\mathbf{s}|$. n usually denotes the number of features $|\mathbf{F}|$. Both m and n are also used to denote upper or lower bounds for running indices or to denote exponentation as in $f : s^m \to s^n$. Running indices are, as usual, indicated by i, j, k, l and the like. The number of classes in a classification is denoted by k: $\mathfrak{c} = \{c_i : i \in \mathbf{k}\}$.

Arrows and operations on relations. To avoid confusion between sets $\mathbf{x}$ of cardinality x and vectors, we mark vectors by a superscripted small arrow: $\vec{x} = \langle x_0, x_1, \ldots, x_{n-1} \rangle$.

Speaking of arrows, $\to$ is used in function declarations whereas $\longrightarrow$ indicates an implication (note the different lengths!). To distinguish between the domain and the codomain of a relation, we declare relations using a "half" arrow: so R: $(x_0 \times \cdots \times x_{m-1}) \rightharpoondown (y_0 \times \cdots \times y_{n-1})$ means the same as $R \subseteq x_0 \times \cdots x_{m-1} \times y_0 \times \cdots y_{n-1}$. dom($R$) is the domain of R and cod(R) is its codomain. The preimage and image of s under R are written $^\ulcorner\! R s$ and $R^\urcorner s$. The complement of R is $\overline{R}$ (the same for sets: $\overline{s} = U - s$) and the inverse or converse is written as $R^\smile$. s/R is the quotient or partition of s by R; its elements are equivalence classes $[x]_R$. The identity relation is denoted by I; the universal and empty relations are denoted by $\top\!\!\top$ and $\perp\!\!\perp$ (or $\emptyset$), respectively.

Special functions. Characteristic functions are written as $\chi : \wp(U) \to (U \to \mathbf{2})$, which for a set $s \subseteq U$ gives $\chi(s) : s \to \mathbf{2}$. The representation of $\mathfrak{D}$ in $\mathfrak{U}$ is a function ρ, and representation transforms are functions τ mapping different representations onto each other. The most important function of all is t. It denotes the target function and is the function that labels all examples $x \in s$ with the sought value $i \in \mathbf{k}$ to define a classifier.

Some other functions we need are $|y|_x$, which evaluates the number of occurrences of x in y (with y a vector or a word). If x is a scalar, then $|x|$ is its absolute value; if x is a set, then $|x|$ is the cardinality of x. $\ell(\vec{x})$ is the dimension of the vector $\vec{x}$ and $\ell(x)$ is the length of a sequence (which, basically, is the same).

Other (standard) functions are written in upright Roman letters, even if they occur in math environments. Examples are $\min x$, $\mathrm{BotLit}(\varphi)$, $\mathrm{entropy}_s(f, t)$, and so on.

Arithmetics. We use the following functions and operators:

$x \cdot y$	(or xy) scalar multiplication
$x \cdot \vec{y}$	(or $x\vec{y}$) scalar multiplication
$\vec{x} \cdot \vec{y}$	(or $\vec{x}\vec{y}$) dot product
$s_0 \odot s_1$	pairwise intersection of sets of sets: $\{s'_0 \cap s'_1 : s'_0 \in s_0, s'_1 \in s_1\}$
$\circ$	concatenation
$\bullet$	Hadamard product; componentwise product of two vectors/matrices
$\times$	set/cross product

Generalised operators are $\sum$ for sums and $\prod$ for products and large versions of boolean operators such as $\bigvee$ and $\bigwedge$.

Notational oddities

To avoid double indexing we sometimes use an array-like notation to refer to arguments of vectors: $x[i]$ is the i-th component $x[i] = x_i$ of $\vec{x}$. In very rare cases, we need the projection function $\pi_i : s_0 \times \cdots \times s_{n-1} \to s_i$.

Order relations. In analogy to $\leq$ and $\subseteq$ we use to $\sqsubseteq$ to denote a generalised version of the less than or equal to relation. Special kinds of order relations are subsumption relations. We use $\models\!\!\preccurlyeq$ to denote generality. One special version is that of θ-subsumption, which we write $\models\!\!\lhd$. The model relation is $\models$; we distinguish the entailment relation by using a different symbol, $\models\!\!\approx$. A derivation is indicated by $\vdash$.

Operators. Operators are defined in the same way as the relation symbols. Accordingly, $\sqcap$ and $\sqcup$ are the generalised meet and join operations by which $\sqsubseteq$ and its converse can be defined. A resolution step is written as $\sqcap_{\mathrm{RES}}$. We also have the least general generalisation operators $\curlyvee$ and $\triangledown$, which come along with the subsumption relations $\models\!\!\preccurlyeq$ and $\models\!\!\lhd$. In Horn logic, we use typewriter fonts for logic operators `:-` and `?-`. Definitions are indicated by a prefix colon ($:=, :\Longleftrightarrow, :\in$).

References

Aït-Kaci, H. (1999). *Warren's Abstract Machine: A Tutorial Reconstruction*. MIT Press.

Anthony, M. and Biggs, N. (1997). *Computational Learning Theory*, 2nd edn. Cambridge University Press.

Ash, R. B. (1965). *Information Theory*. Dover Publications.

Barron, A., Rissanen, J., and Yu, B. (1998). The minimum description length principle in coding and modeling. *IEEE Transactions on Information Theory*, **44**(6):2743–2760.

Börger, E. and Rosenzweig, D. (1994). The WAM – definition and compiler correctness. In Beierle, C. and Plümer, L., editors, *Logic Programming: Formal Methods and Practical Applications*. North-Holland.

Bratko, I. (1986). *PROLOG for Artificial Intelligence*. Addison-Wesley.

Breiman, L. (1994). *Bagging Predictors*. Technical Report 421, University of California, Berkeley.

Breiman, L. (1996). Heuristics of instability and stabilization in model selection. *Annals of Statistics*, **24**(6).

Breiman, L., Friedman, J., Olshen, R., and Stone, C. (1984). *Classification and Regression Trees*. Wadsworth.

Cestnik, B., Kononenko, I., and Bratko, I. (1987). Assistant 86: A knowledge-elicitation tool for sophisticated users. In *Progress in Machine Learning*. Sigma, pp. 31–45.

Chaitin, G. J. (1966). On the length of programs for computing binary sequences. *JACM*, **13**:547–569.

Chaitin, G. J. (1987). *Information, Randomness and Incompleteness – Papers on Algorithmic Information Theory*. World Scientific Press.

Clark, P. and Niblett, T. (1989). The CN2 algorithm. *Machine Learning*, **3**(4):261–283.

Dolnicar, S. and Leisch, F. (2000). *Getting More Out of Binary Data: Segmenting Markets by Bagged Clustering*. Technical Report 71, Vienna University of Economics and Business Administration.

Dudoit, S. and Fridlyand, J. (2003). Bagging to improve the accuracy of a clustering procedure. *Bioinformatics*, **19**(9).

Düntsch, I. (1988). Rough sets and algebras of relations. In Orlowska, E., editor, *Incomplete Information: Rough Set Analysis*. Physica-Verlag, pp. 95–108.

Düntsch, I. (1997). A logic for rough sets. *Theoretical Computer Science*, **179**(1–2):427–436.

Düntsch, I., Gediga, G., and Orlowska, E. (2002). Relational attribute systems. *International Journal of Human-Computer Studies*, **56**(3).

Düntsch, I., Gediga, G., and Orłowska, E. (2007). Relational attribute systems II: Reasoning with relations in information structures. In *Transactions on Rough Sets VII*, volume 4400 in Lecture Notes in Computer Science. Springer, pp. 16–35.

Džeroski, S., Muggleton, S., and Russell, S. (1992). PAC-learnability of determinate logic programs. In *Proc. 5th ACM Workshop on Computational Learning Theory*. ACM Press, pp. 128–135.

Fisher, D. H. (1987). Knowledge acquisition via incremental conceptual clustering. *Machine Learning*, **2**(2):139–172.

Freund, Y. and Schapire, R. E. (1996). Experiments with a new boosting algorithm. In *Proc. 19th Intl. Conf. Machine Learning*, pp. 148–156.

Frossyniotis, D. S., Likas, A. C., and Stafylopatis, A. (2004). A clustering method based on boosting. *Pattern Recognition Letters*, **25**(6):641–654.

Goldblatt, R. (2006). *Topoi*, 2nd edn. Dover Publications.

Gottlob, G. (1987). Subsumption and implication. *Information Processing Letters*, **24**(2):109–111.

György, P. (1968). *Induction and Analogy in Mathematics*, Vol. I of *Mathematics and Plausible Reasoning*. Princeton University Press.

Han, X., Lin, T. Y., and Han, J. (2003). A new rough sets model based on database systems. *Fundamenta Informaticae*, **59**(2-3):135–152.

Hastie, T., Tibshirani, R., and Friedman, J. (2001). *The Elements of Statistical Learning*. Springer-Verlag.

Hodges, Wilfrid. (1993). *Model Theory*. Cambridge University Press.

Horn, A. (1951). On sentences which are true of direct unions of algebras. *Journal of Symbolic Logic*, **16**(1):14–21.

Hunt, E., Marin, J., and Stone, P. (1966). *Experiments in Induction*. Academic Press.

Huth, M. and Ryan, M. (2004). *Logic in Computer Science*, 2nd edn. Cambridge University Press.

Jaoua, A., Duwairi, R., Elloumi, S., and Yahia, S. B. (2009). Data mining, reasoning and incremental information retrieval through non enlargeable rectangular relation coverage. In *Relations and Kleene Algebra in Computer Science*, volume 5827 of Lecture Notes in Computer Science. Springer, pp. 199–210.

Jaynes, E. T. (2003). *Probability Theory*. Cambridge University Press.

Kautz, H., Kearns, M., and Selman, B. (1995). Horn approximations of empirical data. *Artificial Intelligence*, **74**(1).

Kearns, M. J. (1990). *The Computational Complexity of Machine Learning*. MIT Press.

Kearns, M. J. and Vazirani, U. V. (1994). *An Introduction to Computational Learning Theory*. MIT Press.

Kersting, K. (2008). *Probabilistic Inductive Logic Programming*. Springer.

Kersting, K. and Raedt, L. D. (2000). Bayesian logic programs. In Cussens, J. and Frisch, A., editors, *Proc. Work-in-Progress Track at the 10th Intl. Conf. on Inductive Logic Programming*, pp. 138–155.

Kolmogorov, A. (1965). Three approaches to the quantitative definition of information. *Prob. Inf. Trans.*, **1**:1–7.

Kowalski, R. (1973). Predicate logic as a programming language. Memo 70, University of Edinburgh, Department of Computational Logic.

Kowalski, R. (1988). The early years of logic programming. *Communications of the ACM*, **31**(1):38–43.

Kowalski, R. and Kuehner, D. (1977). Linear resolution with selection function. *Artificial Intelligence*, **2**:227–260.

Lavrac, N. and Dzeroski, S. (1993). *Inductive Logic Programming: Techniques and Applications*. Ellis Horwood.

Lebowitz, M. (1987). Experiments with incremental concept formation: Unimem. *Machine Learning*, **2**(2):103–138.

Leisch, F. (1999). *Bagged Clustering*. Technical Report 51, Vienna University of Economics and Business Administration.

Li, J. and Cercone, N. (2005). A rough set based model to rank the importance of association rules. In *Rough Sets, Fuzzy Sets, Data Mining, and Granular Computing*, volume 3642 in Lecture Notes in Computer Science. Springer.

Li, M. and Vitanyi, P. (1993). *An Introduction to Kolmogorov Complexity and Its Applications*. Springer-Verlag.

Liu, Y., Jin, R., and Jain, A. K. (2007). Boostcluster: Boosting clustering by pairwise constraints. In *13th Intl. Conf. on Knowledge Discovery and Data Mining*.

Lloyd, J. (2003). *Logic for Learning*. Springer.

MacKay, D. J. C. (2003). *Information Theory, Inference, and Learning Algorithms*. Cambridge University Press.

Maddux, R. D. (2006). *Relation Algebras*. Elsevier.

Mazzola, G. B., Milmeister, G., and Weissmann, J. (2006). *Comprehensive Mathematics for Computer Scientists*, 2nd edn vols. 1–2. Springer.

Michalski, R. S. (1969). On the quasi-minimal solution of the general covering problem. In *Proc. 5th Intl. Symposium Information Processing*.

Mingers, J. (1989). An empirical comparison of pruning methods for decision tree induction. *Machine Learning*, **4**(2):227–243.

Mooney, R. J., Melville, P., Tang, L. R., Shavlik, J., de Castro Dutra, I., Page, D., and Costa, V. S. (2004). Relational data mining with inductive logic programming for link discovery. In *Data Mining: Next Generation Challenges and Future Directions*. AAAI Press.

Morik, K., Wrobel, S., Kietz, J.-U., and Emde, W. (1993). *Knowledge Acquisition and Machine Learning – Theory, Methods, and Applications*. Academic Press.

Muggleton, S. (1995). Inverse entailment and Progol. *New Generation Computing*, **13**:245–286.

Muggleton, S. and Buntine, W. (1988a). Machine invention of first-order predicates by inverting resolution. In *Proc. 5th Intl. Conf. on Machine Learning*. Kaufmann, pp. 339–352.

Muggleton, S. and Buntine, W. (1988b). *Towards Constructive Induction in First-Order Predicate Calculus*. TIRM 88-03, The Turing Institute, Glasgow.

Muggleton, S. and Feng, C. (1990). Efficient induction of logic programs. In *Proc. 1st Conf. on Algorithmic Learning Theory*. Ohmsha, pp. 368–381.

Muggleton, S. and Feng, C. (1992). Efficient induction of logic programs. In Muggleton, S., editor, *Inductive Logic Programming*. Academic Press, pp. 281–298.

Muggleton, S. and Raedt, L. D. (1994). Inductive logic programming: Theory and methods. *Journal of Logic Programming*, **19, 20**:629–679.

Muggleton, S., King, R., and Sternberg, M. (1992). Protein secondary structure prediction using logic-based machine learning. *Protein Engineering*, **5**(7):647–657.

Muggleton, S., Srinivasan, A., King, R., and Sternberg, M. (1998). Biochemical knowledge discovery using Inductive Logic Programming. In Motoda, H., editor, *Proc. 1st Conf. on Discovery Science*. Springer-Verlag.

Müller, M. E. (2006). Why some emotional states are easier to be recognized than others: A thorough data analysis and a very accurate rough set classifier. In Müller, M. E., editor, *Proc. IEEE Intl. Conf. on Systems, Man, and Cybernetics*, 2006.

Niblett, T. and Bratko, I. (1986). *Learning Decision Rules in Noisy Domains*. TIRM 86-018, The Turing Institute, Glasgow.

Nienhuys-Cheng, S.-H. and de Wolf, R. (1997). *Foundations of Inductive Logic Programming*. Springer.

Nienhuys-Cheng, S.-H. and Wolf, R. D. (1996). Least generalizations under implication. In Muggleton, S. H., editor, *6th Intl. Workshop on Inductive Logic Programming*. Springer-Verlag.

Nock, R. and Jappy, P. (1998). Function-free Horn clauses are hard to approximate. In Page, D., editor, *Proc. 8th Intl. Workshop Inductive Logic Programming*, Berlin. Springer-Verlag.

of Ockham, W. (1323). *Summa totius logicae*.

Øhrn, A. (1999). *Discernibility and Rough Sets in Medicine: Tools and Applications*. PhD thesis, Norwegian University of Science and Technology, Department of Computer and Information Science.

Øhrn, A., Komorowski, J., Skowron, A., and Synak, P. (1998). The design and implementation of a knowledge discovery toolkit based on rough sets: The ROSETTA system. In Polkowski, L. and Skowron, A., editors, *Rough Sets in Knowledge Discovery: Methodology and Applications*, volume 18 in Studies in Fuzziness and Soft Computing. Physica, pp. 376–399.

Orlowska, E. (1993). Reasoning with incomplete information: Rough set based information logics. In *Proc. SOFTEKS Workshop on Incompleteness and Uncertainty in Information Systems*, pp. 16–33.

Page, D., Costa, V. S., and Shavlik, J. (2002). An empirical evaluation of bagging in inductive logic programming. In *Proc. 12th Intl. Conf. on Inductive Logic Programming*.

Parsons, S., Kubat, M., and Donahl, M. (1994). A rough set approach to reasoning under uncertainty. *Journal of Intelligent Manufacturing*, **5**.

Pawlak, Z. (1984). On rough sets. *Bulletin of the EATCS*, **24**:94–184.

Plotkin, G. (1969). A note on inductive generalisation. *Machine Intelligence*, **5**:153–163.

Plotkin, G. (1971). A further note on inductive generalization. In *Machine Intelligence*, Vol. 6. Edinburgh University Press.

Polya, G. (1968). *Mathematics and Plausible Reasoning*. Princeton University Press.

Popper, K. R. (2002). *The Logic of Scientific Discovery*. Routledge.

Quinlan, J. (1986a). Induction of decision trees. *Machine Learning*, **1**:81–106.

Quinlan, J. (1986b). Learning from noisy data. In Michalski, R., Carbonnel, J., and Mitchell, T., editors, *Machine Learning*, Vol. 2. Kaufmann.

Quinlan, J. (1991). Determinate literals in inductive logic programming. In *Proc. 12th Intl. Joint Conf. on Artificial Intelligence*. Morgan-Kaufmann, pp. 746–750.

Quinlan, J. R. (1992). *C4.5: Programs for Machine Learning*. Morgan Kaufmann.

Quinlan, J. R. (1996). Bagging, boosting, and C4.5. In *Proc. 13th Natl. Conf. on Artificial Intelligence*. AAAI Press, pp. 725–730.

Quinlan, J. R. (2001). Relational data mining. In Džeroski, S., editor, *Relational Learning and Boosting*. Springer.

Quinlan, J. and Cameron, R. (1995). Induction of logic programs: FOIL and related systems. *New Generation Computing*, **13**:287–312.

Quinlan, J. and Cameron-Jones, R. (1993). FOIL: A midterm report. In Brazdil, P., editor, *Proc. 6th European Conf. on Machine Learning*, volume 667 of Lecture Notes in Artificial Intelligence. Springer, pp. 3–20.

Raedt, L. D. (2008). *Logical and Relational Learning*. Springer.

Raedt, L. D. and Kersting, K. (2004). Probabilistic inductive logic programming. In Ben-David, S., Case, J., and Maruoka, A., editors, *Proc. 15th Intl. Conf. on Algorithmic Learning Theory*, volume 3244 of Lecture Notes in Computer Science. Springer-Verlag.

Rouveirol, C. (1992). Extensions of inversion of resolution applied to theory completion. In Muggleton, S., editor, *Inductive Logic Programming*. Academic Press.

Russell, B. A. W. (1992). *Theory of Knowledge: The 1913 Manuscript*. Routledge.

Russell, B. A. W. (1995). *An Inquiry into Meaning and Truth*. Routledge.

Schapire, R. E. (1990). The strength of weak learnability. *Machine Learning*, **5**:197–227.

Schapire, R. E. (2002). The boosting approach to machine learning: An overview. MSRI Workshop on Nonlinear Estimation and Classification.

Schmidt, G. (2011). *Relational Mathematics*, volume 132 of *Encyclopedia of Mathematics and its Applications*. Cambridge University Press.

Shannon, C. E. and Weaver, W. (1949). *The Mathematical Theory of Communication*. University of Illinois Press. Reprints 1963, 1998.

Solomonoff, R. (1964). A formal theory of inductive inference. *Information and Control*, **7**:376–388.

Sperschneider, V. and Antoniou, G. (1991). *Logic – A Foundation for Computer Science*. Addison-Wesley.

Vaithyanathan, K. and Lin, T. Y. (2008). High frequency rough set model based on database systems. In *Proc. Fuzzy Information Processing Society (NAFIPS)*.

Valiant, L. (1984). A theory of the learnable. *Communications of the ACM*, **27**:1134–1142.

Venables, W. N. and Ripley, B. D. (2002). *Modern Applied Statistics with S*, 4th edn. Springer.

Warren, D. H. D. (1983). An abstract PROLOG instruction set. Technical Note 309, SRI International, Menlo Park, CA.

Watterson, B. (1996). *There's Treasure Everywhere*. Andrews McMeel Publishing.

Welsh, D. (1988). *Codes and Cryptography*. Oxford University Press.

Wolpert, D. H. and Macready, W. G. (1997). No free lunch theorems for optimization. *IEEE Transactions on Evolutionary Computation*, **1**(1):67–82.

Wróblewski, J. (1995). Finding minimal reducts using genetic algorithms. In *Proc. 2nd Ann. Joint Conf. on Information Sciences*.

Xu, F., Yao, Y., and Miao, D. (2008). Rough set approximations in formal concept analysis and knowledge spaces. In *Foundations of Intelligent Systems*, volume 4994 in Lecture Notes in Computer Science. Springer, pp. 319–328.

Yamamoto, A. (1997). Which hypotheses can be found with inverse entailment? In Lavrač, N. and Džeroski, S., editors, *Proc. 7th Intl. Workshop on Inductive Logic Programming*. Springer-Verlag, pp. 296–308.

Yao, Y. Y. (2003). On generalizing rough set theory. In *Proc. 9th Intl. Conf. on Rough Sets, Fuzzy Sets, Data Mining, and Granular Computing*, volume 2639 in Lecture Notes in Artificial Intelligence. Springer.

Yao, Y. Y. and Chen, Y. (2006). Rough set approximations in formal concept analysis. In Peters, J. F. and Skowron, A., editors, *Transactions on Rough Sets V*, volume 4100 in Lecture Notes in Computer Science. Springer, pp. 285–305.

Index